Study Guide to Accompany

West's Federal Taxation

1996 Edition

COMPREHENSIVE VOLUME

Eugene Willis
University of Illinois-Urbana

William H. Hoffman
University of Houston

David M. Maloney
University of Virginia

William A. Raabe
University of Wisconsin-Milwaukee

Prepared by:

David M. Maloney
University of Virginia

William A. Raabe
University of Wisconsin-Milwaukee

West Publishing Company
Minneapolis/St. Paul   New York   Los Angeles   San Francisco

WEST'S COMMITMENT TO THE ENVIRONMENT

In 1906, West Publishing Company began recycling materials left over from the production of books. This began a tradition of efficient and responsible use of resources. Today, up to 95% of our legal books and 70% of our college texts and school texts are printed on recycled, acid-free stock. West also recycles nearly 22 million pounds of scrap paper annually—the equivalent of 181,717 trees. Since the 1960s, West has devised ways to capture and recycle waste inks, solvents, oils, and vapors created in the printing process. We also recycle plastics of all kinds, wood, glass, corrugated cardboard, and batteries, and have eliminated the use of Styrofoam book packaging. We at West are proud of the longevity and the scope of our commitment to the environment.

Production, Prepress, Printing and Binding by West Publishing Company.

 TEXT IS PRINTED ON 10% POST CONSUMER RECYCLED PAPER    PRINTED WITH SOY INK™

ISBN 0–314–06472–9

CONTENTS

PREFACE

This *Study Guide* accompanies the 1996 edition of *West's Federal Taxation: Comprehensive Volume*. The textbook is designed for a thorough one- or two-semester undergraduate or graduate course in federal taxation. Thus, because the scope of the text is quite broad, you will be required to digest a large amount of fairly complex information in a short period of time.

In recognition of the difficulty of such a task, this *Study Guide* was created. It offers you an additional review of the content of the text chapters in outline form, to allow a rapid perusal. Moreover, additional problems and exercises are contained in the *Study Guide* for review. These exercises are presented in a self-evaluation format, with the suggested solutions directly following the problem statements, so that you can receive immediate feedback as to the accuracy of your answers. These problems take a number of different formats, including true and false, fill-in-the-blank, multiple choice, and short answers. We believe that this arrangement will maximize your understanding of the text material in a reasonable period of time.

It is important that you use this *Study Guide* as an *aid* to mastering the material in the textbook, and *not* as a replacement for it. We suggest that you incorporate the *Study Guide* into your regular study routine, perhaps by reviewing the Chapter Highlights after reading the text, and then working the *Study Guide* problems before attempting those assigned in the text.

David M. Maloney
William A. Raabe
March 1995

CHAPTER 1
AN INTRODUCTION TO TAXATION

CHAPTER HIGHLIGHTS

proper analysis of the US tax system begins with an examination of historical principles that guide the development of the system, and with an investigation of the various motivations that underlie existing provisions of the tax law. This chapter also introduces the reader to important tax terminology.

I.   History of US Taxation
    A.   An income tax on individuals was used to provide financing for the Civil War. When the war ended, the tax was repealed. In 1894, a new individual income tax was enacted, but the Supreme Court held the tax to be unconstitutional. After a constitutional challenge to the taxation of income, the Sixteenth Amendment, which sanctioned both the federal individual and corporate income taxes, was ratified in 1913. The present income tax on individuals was enacted in 1913. A corporate income tax was adopted in 1909.

    B.   Revenue Acts, which rewrote completely the federal tax provisions, were enacted every year or two between 1913 and 1939. These provisions were reorganized and included, in a more permanent form, in the Internal Revenue Code of 1939. Thereafter, tax laws were changed when Congress adopted amendments to the 1939 Code; i.e., a complete rewriting of the laws was unnecessary. A revised Internal Revenue Code was adopted in 1954. The 1954 Code was the controlling body of the tax law until 1986. In 1986, Congress enacted the most comprehensive overhaul of the Internal Revenue Code in over 30 years. As a result of the massive changes contained in the new law, the federal tax code was renamed the Internal Revenue Code of 1986. Nevertheless, many of the provisions of the 1954 Code were carried over to the 1986 Code.

    C.   In an effort to close various loopholes and to reduce the budget deficit, changes in the tax law have been enacted each year since 1986.

D.   One trend that has caused considerable concern is the increased complexity of the federal income tax laws, which imposes substantial taxpayer compliance costs. Congress has added to this complexity through frequent changes in the tax laws.

E.   Income tax collections from individuals and corporations constitute about half of all federal tax receipts. The FICA (Social Security) tax now constitutes about one-third of all federal tax receipts, while corporate income tax receipts have fallen drastically since the 1940s.

II.   Tax Terminology

A.   Tax rates can be structured to yield a

1.   Proportional tax: The rate of tax remains constant over the tax base;

2.   Progressive tax: Tax rates increase as the tax base grows larger; or,

3.   Regressive tax: Tax rates decrease as the tax base grows larger.

B.   Taxes should be designed with

1.   Equality of tax treatment among taxpayers in similar circumstances;

2.   Convenience of collection, computation, and administration;

3.   Certainty in application, so that tax planning can occur; and,

4.   Economical administration, which requires only nominal collection costs by the government and involves minimal compliance costs on the part of the taxpayer.

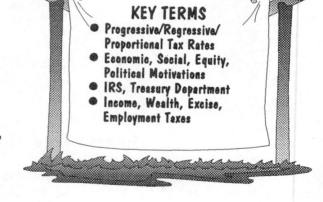

KEY TERMS
- Progressive/Regressive/ Proportional Tax Rates
- Economic, Social, Equity, Political Motivations
- IRS, Treasury Department
- Income, Wealth, Excise, Employment Taxes

C.   Types of taxes observed in recent history include

1.   *Ad valorem* taxes are taxes on wealth or capital. For instance, these taxes include the existing real property taxes and personal property taxes, presently favored by state and local governments. The real property tax features a high degree of taxpayer compliance, political manipulation of the assessment process, and assessments based on appraisals, capitalization of attendant income, and actual purchase or construction costs. However, there is inconsistent taxpayer compliance relative to personal property taxes.

2.   Transaction taxes are levied on the transfer of property among taxpayers. Examples of transaction taxes include: excise taxes, sales and use taxes; death and gift taxes; severance taxes, and the value added tax (VAT). Excise taxes are levied by federal and state governments on the exchange of specified commodities, e.g., certain "luxury" items, oil, alcohol, and tobacco. Excise taxes are effective when consumers demonstrate a price-inelastic demand for the commodity. Sales and use taxes, which are applied by state and local governments cover a multitude of transactions. Debate relative to this tax centers on the appropriate items, the sale of which will be subject to the tax. Death and gift taxes are levied by federal and state governments on lifetime or testamentary transfers of property to others. Severance taxes are imposed by some states on the extraction of natural resources. In the Common Market countries of Western Europe, the VAT has gained acceptance as a major source of revenue.

3.   Income taxes are levied chiefly by federal and state governments on the annual incremental change in the taxpayer's wealth. Specific definitions relative to includible income, and allowable deductions, vary greatly among those

governments that impose the tax. Most taxing jurisdictions attempt to ensure the collection of income taxes by requiring certain pay-as-you-go procedures.

4. Employment taxes include unemployment taxes, which finance state and federal unemployment compensation benefits, and retirement taxes, e.g., the federal FICA tax. These taxes are levied upon or collected by employers, and they provide some income security for employees. The FICA tax is paid equally by employer and employee; the FUTA tax is paid by only the employer. Debate relative to these taxes includes the proper definition of "employer" and "employee," and the desirable employment tax bases and rates.

5. Other taxes that are part of the U.S. tax system include federal custom duties and miscellaneous state and local taxes, e.g., franchise taxes, occupational taxes or license fees.

D. The responsibility for administering the federal tax laws rests with the Treasury Department.

1. The Internal Revenue Service (IRS) is part of the Treasury Department and is responsible for enforcing the tax law.

2. The IRS utilizes mathematical formulas and statistical sampling techniques to select tax returns for audit. However, due to budget constraints, only a small minority of returns are audited by the IRS.

 In a typical survey, taxpayers respond that about fifteen to twenty percent of all tax returns are audited. Actually, 1994 figures indicated that the rate was under one percent, although high-income, cash-business, and previously audited taxpayers certainly are subject to a higher rate. This looks like a good application of stratified sampling, but the IRS clearly has a public relations problem!

III. Motivations Underlying Specific Tax Provisions

A. Although the major objective of the federal tax law is to raise revenue, economic, social, equity, and political considerations play a significant role in the design of specific tax provisions.

B. Economic considerations, including a stimulation or temperance of the national economy, and encouragement or discouragement of specific activities or industries, have led to a large number of recent amendments to the Code. Examples of such economic considerations include:

1. The investment tax credit and ACRS depreciation, to encourage expenditures on long-lived productive assets, such as machinery and equipment. However, the Tax Reform Act of 1986 eliminated the investment tax credit and modified the cost recovery system, on the grounds that these provisions favored capital-intensive, rather than labor-intensive, industries, and to reduce the growing federal budget deficit.

2. Lower individual and corporate income nominal tax rates. Such measures can stimulate the general economy, by increasing disposable income.

3. Special tax treatment of technological development, including favorable treatment allowed research and development expenditures and patents, and tax credits for certain research and energy expenditures.

4. Support for farmers, thrift institutions, and small business owners. Such taxpayers can claim immediate deductions for expenditures for farm feed and fertilizers, exemption from the uniform capitalization rules for certain farmers, and the "flow-through" of the operating losses of certain small business corporations to their shareholders.

5.   Concern over the growing federal budget deficit has led to a reduction in many of the incentives that had been enacted to stimulate the economy.

C.   Social considerations also affect tax legislation. Tax-favored treatment concerning certain employer-provided life and health insurance policies, contributions to retirement plans and charitable organizations, and expenditures for child care services are a response to various social goals. On the other hand, expenditures contrary to public policy, such as bribes and fines, are discouraged by tax laws.

D.   Equity considerations with respect to the tax law attempt to maintain a sensitivity in the law toward taxpayers in various circumstances. Of course, definitions of equity often produce heated debate among interested parties. Nevertheless, the tax law offers: relief from multiple taxation through dividend income deductions; deferral of tax liability is available until the taxpayer has funds available with which to pay a tax; several provisions, such as the installment sales method, and loss carryovers, offer relief from hardships that may be created by the annual accounting period concept; and, relief from the eroding results of inflation is provided through indexation of tax brackets, standard deductions, and exemptions.

E.   Political considerations are evident in the tax law, as might be expected with respect to provisions that are forged in a legislative process. The effect of political considerations on the tax law largely are a result of special interest legislation, political expediency situations, and state and local government influences. For instance, special interest legislation has been created in response to lobbying activities by wealthy taxpayers, while various provisions attempt to ensure that those wealthy taxpayers do pay some "fair" share of tax. Examples of such provisions include the alternative minimum tax, the imputed interest rules, the passive loss rules, and the limitation on deductible investment interest expense.

F.   Tax administrators and the courts also have contributed to the system by imposing or encouraging alterations in specific provisions in the tax law. In its capacity as the protector of the national revenue, the IRS has been instrumental in securing passage of legislation designed to curtail flagrant tax avoidance practices and to ease administration of the tax laws. In addition to interpreting statutory provisions and the administrative pronouncements issued by the IRS, the federal courts have influenced tax law by formulating certain judicial concepts that serve as guides in the application of various tax provisions and by making decisions that have been of such consequence that changes in the Internal Revenue Code were enacted by Congress specifically to incorporate the decision in the Code, or to provide tax provisions that are *contrary* to the decision.

TEST FOR SELF-EVALUATION - CHAPTER 1

True or False

Indicate which of the following statements are true or false by circling the correct answer.

T   F   1.   The federal government raises a large portion of its revenue through the property tax.

T   F   2.   A value added tax resembles a national sales tax.

T   F   3.   Current tax law is based on the Internal Revenue Code of 1993.

T   F   4.   Property taxes are a form of *ad valorem* tax.

T   F   5.   Transaction taxes are most effective when consumers demonstrate a price-elastic demand for the commodity.

T   F   6.   If tax rates increase as the tax base grows larger, the tax is regressive.

T   F   7.   A severance tax is a tax on the use, consumption, or storage of tangible property.

T   F   8.   The primary purpose of some tax laws is to simplify the task of the IRS in collecting the revenue and administering the law.

T   F   9.   State governments use the sales tax as one of their primary sources of tax revenues.

T   F   10.   If tax rates decrease as the tax base grows larger, the tax is progressive.

Fill-in-the-Blanks

Complete the following statements with the appropriate word(s) or amount(s).

1.   The _____ Amendment, ratified in _____, authorized the federal income tax on individuals.

2.   _____ _____ taxes are taxes on capital or wealth.

3.   The research and development tax credit is an example of the effect of _____ considerations in the development of the tax law.

4.   The "minimum tax" on wealthy taxpayers is an example of the effect of _____ considerations in the development of the tax law.

5.   The deduction for charitable contributions is an example of the effect of _____ considerations in the development of the tax law.

6.   Adam Smith believed that a "good" tax would include provisions to assure its _____, _____, _____, and _____.

7.   With respect to employment taxes, the _____ tax is paid equally by the employer and

employee, while _____ taxes are paid by only the employer.

8.   The _____-_____-_____-_____ feature of the income tax system compels employers to withhold a specific portion of an employee's wages for taxes.

9.   _____ taxes are levied on an activity or event, or the exercise of a specific right in property or on a privilege granted.

10.   _____, _____, and _____ taxes are levied on the transfer of property and normally are determined by a percentage rate multiplied by the value involved.

11.   A(n) _____ tax is a tax on the right to receive property from a decedent.

12.   The purpose of the _____ system is to provide funds that the states can use to provide unemployment benefits.

Multiple Choice

Choose the best answer for each of the following questions.

_____ 1.   When the tax base is $10,000, the tax liability is $3,000; When the tax base is $100,000, the tax liability is $20,000. This tax has a rate structure that is:
a.   Progressive.
b.   Regressive.
c.   Proportional.
d.   Ad Valorem.

_____ 2.   When the tax base is $10,000, the tax liability is $3,000; When the tax base is $100,000, the tax liability is $35,000. This tax has a rate structure that is:
a.   Progressive.
b.   Regressive.
c.   Proportional.
d.   Ad Valorem.

_____ 3.   When the tax base is $10,000, the tax liability is $3,000; When the tax base is $100,000, the tax liability is $30,000. This tax has a rate structure that is:
a.   Progressive.
b.   Regressive.
c.   Proportional.
d.   Ad Valorem.

_____ 4.   The federal gift and estate taxes are:
a.   regressive taxes.
b.   proportional taxes.
c.   progressive taxes.
d.   the gift tax is regressive and the estate tax is progressive.

_____ 5.   The concept that recognizes the inequity of taxing a transaction when the taxpayer lacks the means with which to pay the tax is:
a.   double taxation.
b.   pay-as-you-go.
c.   revenue neutrality.
d.   wherewithal to pay.

_____ 6.   There are a number of provisions in the Internal Revenue Code that favor small
            business. They include: (More than one answer may be correct)
            a.   the corporate minimum tax.
            b.   the environmental tax.
            c.   the tax rates applicable to corporations.
            d.   the dividends-received deduction.

_____ 7.   Examples of social considerations that have affected tax legislation include:
            a.   the alternative minimum tax.
            b.   deductions for contributions to retirement plans.
            c.   the investment tax credit.
            d.   the installment sales method.

_____ 8.   The concept of equity appears in tax provisions to:
            a.   alleviate the effect of multiple taxation.
            b.   postpone the recognition of gain when the taxpayer lacks the ability or
                    wherewithal to pay the tax.
            c.   mitigate the effect of the application of the annual accounting period
                    concept.
            d.   all of the above.

_____ 9.   The last major reorganization of the Internal Revenue Code was enacted in:
            a.   1954.
            b.   1986.
            c.   1988.
            d.   1993.

_____ 10.   In addition to interpreting statutory provisions and administrative pronouncements
            issued by the IRS, the Federal courts have influenced tax law by:
            a.   formulating certain judicial concepts that serve as guides in the application
                    of various tax provisions.
            b.   changing Congressional intent as to the application of Federal tax law.
            c.   making key decisions that have led to changes in the Internal Revenue Code.
            d.   Both a and c.

_____ 11.   The federal income tax structure for individuals is:
            a.   becoming less regressive.
            b.   becoming more regressive.
            c.   becoming less progressive.
            d.   becoming more progressive.

_____ 12.   Which of the following states do not impose an income tax on individuals? More than one
            choice may be correct.
            a.   Alabama.
            b.   Georgia.
            c.   South Carolina.
            d.   Texas.
            e.   All of the above states impose an income tax.

_____ 13.   Special tax-reduction provisions supporting the owners of small businesses can be
            jusitified on the following grounds. More than one answer may be correct.
            a.   Economic expansion
            b.   Political expediency
            c.   Social justice
            d.   Equity among taxpayers

e.   All of the above

____   14.   Over time, the Internal Revenue Service has worked to
              a.   Make the federal tax system more complex.
              b.   Make the federal tax system less complex.
              c.   Keep the federal tax system at a constant level of complexity.
              d.   Both a. and b.
              e.   None of the above

SOLUTIONS TO CHAPTER 1 QUESTIONS

True or False

1.	F	Property taxes are imposed by state and local governments.
2.	T	
3.	F	Current tax law includes the Internal Revenue Code of 1986.
4.	T	
5.	F	Transaction taxes are effective when consumers demonstrate a price-inelastic demand for the commodity.
6.	F	The tax is progressive.
7.	F	The tax described is the use tax.
8.	T	
9.	T	
10.	F	The tax is regressive.

Fill-in-the-Blanks

1. 16th, 1913
2. *ad valorem*
3. economic
4. political
5. social
6. equality, convenience, certainty, economy
7. FICA, unemployment
8. pay-as-you-go
9. Excise
10. Excise, sales, severance
11. Inheritance
12. FUTA

Multiple Choice

1.	b	On a tax base of $10,000 the effective tax rate was 30% and, as the tax base increased to $100,000, the effective tax rate decreased to 20%.
2.	a	On a tax base of $10,000 the effective tax rate was 30% and, as the tax base increased to $100,000, the effective rate increased to 35%.
3.	c	On a tax base of $10,000 the effective tax rate was 30% and, as the tax base increased to $100,000, the effective tax rate remained 30%.
4.	c	
5.	d	
6.	a,b,c	The graduated tax rates and the $40,000 AMT exemption favor small businesses. The environmental tax also favors small businesses since the tax is not imposed unless a corporation's alternative minimum taxable income exceeds $2,000,000.
7.	b	
8.	d	
9.	b	
10.	d	
11.	c	In 1986 there were 15 rates ranging from 0 to 50%; the current tax structure includes rates of 0, 15, 28, 31, 36, and 39.6%.
12.	d	
13.	a,b,c	
14.	d	

CHAPTER 2

TAX DETERMINATION; PERSONAL AND DEPENDENCY EXEMPTIONS; AN OVERVIEW OF PROPERTY TRANSACTIONS

CHAPTER HIGHLIGHTS

his chapter describes the general scheme of the federal taxation of individuals, which involves the computation of an amount referred to as *taxable income*. Generally, all realized income is included in the computation, unless specifically excluded; however, deductions from income are not allowed unless they are provided in the law by Congress. Special deductions, such as the standard deduction and personal exemptions are available to individual taxpayers except in certain situations. These deductions, in essence, exempt a taxpayer's income from taxation up to specified amounts. After taxable income is determined, the tax liability is computed by reference to tax tables or tax rate schedules. Finally, tax prepayments and credits are subtracted from the gross tax liability to determine a taxpayer's net tax payable (or refund due). In addition to the discussion relating to the computation of the income tax liability, this chapter introduces the basic concepts of property transactions and their effect on the computation of taxable income.

I. Tax Formula
- A. The federal individual income tax liability is based on the concept known as *taxable income*. Taxable income is determined using the formula shown in Exhibit 2-1.
- B. Components of the Tax Formula
  1. Income (broadly conceived) includes all income, both taxable and nontaxable; however, the term is *not* equivalent to gross receipts.
  2. A number of exclusions from income have been specifically provided in the law by Congress. Congress has chosen to exclude various items from the tax base for equity, social, economic, and other reasons. Certain other items have been excluded by administrative action of the IRS.
  3. Gross income is broadly defined in the Internal Revenue Code as "except as otherwise provided . . . all income from whatever source derived." The "except as otherwise provided" refers to exclusions. Gross income includes only *realized* gains.
  4. There are two categories of deductions applicable to individual taxpayers.
     - a. Deductions *for* adjusted gross income.
     - b. Deductions *from* adjusted gross income.
  5. Expenses deductible *for* adjusted gross income include, but are not limited to the following.
     - a. Ordinary and necessary expenses incurred in a trade or business.
     - b. Reimbursed employee business expenses.
     - c. Alimony paid.

Exhibit 2-1
FORMULA FOR DETERMINING TAXABLE INCOME

> Income (broadly conceived)
> Less: Exclusions
> Equals: Gross income
> Less: Deductions *for* adjusted gross income
> Equals: Adjusted gross income
> Less: The greater of --
>   Total itemized deductions, or
>   Standard deduction
> Less: Personal and dependency exemptions
> Equals: Taxable income

    d.   Certain payments to individual retirement accounts.

    e.   Moving expenses.

    f.   Forfeited interest for premature withdrawal of time deposits.

    g.   Capital loss deductions.

    h.   Deductions attributable to rents and royalties.

6.   Adjusted gross income (AGI) is an important subtotal which serves as the basis for computing percentage limitations on certain deductions, such as medical expenses and charitable contributions.

7.   Itemized deductions, which generally are personal in nature, are deductions *from* adjusted gross income. The actual amount of itemized deductions is claimed if it exceeds the standard deduction. Otherwise, the appropriate standard deduction is claimed by a taxpayer.

8.   Certain itemized deductions that have been specified by Congress include medical expenses, certain taxes, certain interest expenses, and charitable contributions. In addition, taxpayers are allowed to itemize expenses related to the following.

    a.   The production or collection of income.

    b.   The management of property held for the production of income.

    c.   The determination, collection, or refund of any tax.

9.   The standard deduction, which is specified by Congress, is used to exempt a taxpayer's income from federal income taxes up to a certain amount. The *basic* standard deduction amounts, which are dependent on a taxpayer's filing status, are shown in Exhibit 2-2.

10.   The standard deduction amount is adjusted for inflation annually.

> Each year the tax system is adjusted to remove the effects of inflation on taxable income. This process, known as indexing, applies to the tax rate structure, the standard deduction, and other provisions in the tax code. The adjustment is based on changes in the Consumer Price Index.

11.   Certain taxpayers are not allowed to claim any standard deduction, and the standard deduction is limited for others.

12.   An *additional* standard deduction amount is allowed for a taxpayer who is either

elderly (age 65 or over) or blind.

    a.   For a single taxpayer or a taxpayer qualifying for the Head of Household status, an additional $950 (in 1995 and 1994) standard deduction is allowed ($1,900 if both elderly *and* blind).

    b.   For a married taxpayer filing jointly or separately, and for a surviving spouse, an additional $750 (in 1995 and 1994) standard deduction is allowed ($3,000 if the taxpayer *and* spouse are both elderly *and* blind).

    c.   Dependents do *not* qualify for the additional standard deduction.

Exhibit 2-2
BASIC STANDARD DEDUCTION AMOUNTS: 1994 AND 1995

Filing Status	Standard Deduction	
	1994	1995
Single	$3,800	$3,900
Married, filing jointly	$6,350	$6,550
Surviving spouse	$6,350	$6,550
Head of Household	$5,600	$5,750
Married, filing separately	$3,175	$3,275

13.   Taxpayers whose itemized deductions are less than the standard deduction amount will compute their tax using the standard deduction rather than their itemized deductions. In this situation, taxable income will be equal to adjusted gross income minus the standard deduction and personal and dependency exemptions.

14.   Taxpayers are allowed to deduct personal and dependency exemptions of $2,500 each in 1995 ($2,450 in 1994) in arriving at taxable income. An exemption normally may be claimed for the taxpayer and the taxpayer's spouse, as well as for each dependent of the taxpayer.

15.   In some situations, taxpayers may *not* use the standard deduction amount. The following individual taxpayers must itemize their deductions.

    a.   A married individual who files a separate income tax return when either spouse itemizes deductions.

    b.   A nonresident alien.

    c.   An individual making a return for a period of less than 12 months because of a change in annual accounting period.

16.   If a taxpayer may be claimed as a dependent on another taxpayer's income tax return, the basic standard deduction for 1995 is limited to the greater of the following.

    a. $650.

    b.   The dependent's *earned income* for the year, but not exceeding the basic standard deduction amount (i.e., $3,900 in 1995 assuming the dependent

is single).
17. A taxpayer (e.g., minor child) claimed as a dependent on another's (e.g., his parents') income tax return may *not* claim a personal exemption on his or her own income tax return.

II. Personal and Dependency Exemptions

A. A personal exemption of $2,500 is allowed for *each* taxpayer and for the taxpayer's spouse in 1995. The number of personal exemptions available is based on marital status as of the end of the year, except when a spouse dies during the year. A personal exemption is not allowed, however, if the taxpayer is claimed as a dependent on another taxpayer's income tax return.

B. Dependency exemptions of $2,500 are allowed for *each* eligible dependent in 1995. Five tests must be met in order for an individual to qualify as a dependent: support, relationship or member of household, gross income, joint return, and citizenship or residency.

KEY TERMS
- Adjusted Gross Income
- Standard Deduction
- Personal, Dependency Exemptions
- Recognized Gain, Loss
- Capital Gain, Loss

   1. To meet the support test, the taxpayer must provide over one-half of the support of the individual. Support includes expenditures for food, shelter, clothing, medical and dental care, and education.
   2. The relationship or member of household test requires that either of the following be true.
      a. The individual must be related to the taxpayer.
      b. The individual must be a member of the taxpayer's household for the entire taxable year of the taxpayer.
   3. The dependent's gross income must be less than the exemption amount (i.e., $2,500 in 1995). However, a parent may claim a dependency exemption for his or her child, even when the child's gross income exceeds $2,500, if the parent provided over half of the child's support and the child, at year-end, is under 19 or is a full-time student under 24. If the parent claims a dependency exemption, the dependent child may *not* claim a personal exemption on his or her own income tax return.
   4. If a dependent is married, in order to meet the joint return test, the individual may not file a joint income tax return with his or her spouse unless he or she is filing a joint income tax return in order to receive a refund of tax withheld, no tax liability would exist for either spouse on separate income tax returns, and neither spouse is required to file an income tax return.
   5. The citizenship or residency test requires that to be a dependent, an individual must be either a US citizen or resident, or a resident of Canada or Mexico for some part of the calendar year.
   6. Special rules apply in the situation involving children of divorced or separated parents, and in the situation where more than one taxpayer supports another person but where there is no one taxpayer who can meet the support test.

C. Phase-out of Exemptions
   1. Personal and dependency exemptions are phased out as adjusted gross income exceeds specified threshold amounts. The threshold amounts (which are indexed

for inflation) at which the phase-out begins are shown in Exhibit 2-3.

2. Exemptions are phased out by two percent for each $2,500 or fraction thereof by which the taxpayer's AGI exceeds the above threshold amounts. For married taxpayers filing separately, the phase-out is 2 percent for each $1,250 or fraction thereof.

III. Tax Determination
  A. Tax Table Method -- Most taxpayers who are eligible, use the Tax Table to compute their tax liability. However, the following taxpayers may not use this method.
    1. An individual who files a short period return.
    2. Individuals whose taxable income exceeds the maximum amount in the Tax Table (i.e., $100,000 for Form 1040).
    3. An estate or trust.
  B. Tax Rate Schedule Method
    1. There are five rate brackets for 1994 and 1995 (i.e., 15%, 28%, 31%, 36%, and 39.6%) for each filing status.
    2. Several terms are often used to describe tax rates.
      a. *Statutory* (or *nominal*) *rates* -- the rates in the tax rate schedules.

Exhibit 2-3
PHASE-OUT OF EXEMPTIONS: THRESHOLD AMOUNTS

	1994	1995
Single	$111,800	$114,700
Head of Household	$139,750	$143,350
Married, filing jointly	$167,700	$172,050
Surviving spouse	$167,700	$172,050
Married, filing separately	$83,850	$86,025

      b. *Marginal rate* -- the highest rate that is applied in the tax computation for a particular taxpayer.
      c. *Average rate* -- the rate that equals the tax liability divided by taxable income.
    3. An alternative tax limits the income tax rate on long-term capital gains to 28 percent.
  C. Computation of Net Taxes Payable or Refund Due -- The total tax determined by reference to the appropriate Tax Table or Tax Rate Schedule is reduced by income taxes withheld by employers on compensation paid to employees, estimated tax payments made, and various other tax credits (e.g., credit for child and dependent care expenses, foreign tax credit) to derive net taxes payable or refund due.

 An interest-free loan to the government? That's what happens if too much has been withheld from an individual's salary and the taxpayer gets a big tax refund at the end of the year. Changing the number of allowances claimed on a Form W-4 will increase the take-home pay and reduce or eliminate the year-end refund.

D.   Unearned Income of Children under Age 14 Taxed at Parents' Rate
    1.   If a child reports a positive amount of *net unearned income*, it is taxed at the parents' marginal tax rate.
    2.   A *child* for this purpose is defined as an individual who possesses the following attributes.
        a.   Has not reached the age 14 by the close of the taxable year.
        b.   Has at least one living parent.
        c.   Has net unearned income for the year.
    3.   Net unearned income is computed as provided in Exhibit 2-4.
    4.   Any amount of net unearned income is taxed at the parents' marginal tax rate. The tax is computed as though the income was included on the parent's income tax return, and allocated to the child (defined as *allocable parental tax*).

Exhibit 2-4
COMPUTATION OF "NET UNEARNED INCOME"

Unearned income
Less: $650
Less: The greater of --
*   - $650 of the basic standard deduction.*
*   -   The amount of allowable deductions directly connected with the*
*   production of the unearned income.*
Equals: Net unearned income

    5.   A parent whose child is under 14 may elect to report the child's unearned income that exceeds $1,000 on the parent's own tax income tax return if the following requirements are met.
        a.   Gross income is from interest and dividends only.
        b.   Gross income is less than $5,000.
        c.   No estimated tax has been paid in the name and Social Security number of the child.
        d.   No amount of tax has been deducted and withheld under the backup withholding rules.
        If the election is made, the child need not file an income tax return, because the child is treated as having no gross income. It is not wise in every case to make the parental election: calculations must be made both *with* the parental election and *without* the election to determine the appropriate choice.
    6.   In the case of divorced parents, the income of the custodial parent is used to determine the allocable parental tax. If a married couple files separately, the parent with the greater taxable income is the applicable parent.

For tax planning purposes, one always should know the marginal tax rate of the taxpayer, as this measures the incremental change in the tax liability due to a planning idea. With the phase-out of the exemptions and itemized deductions, as well as the potential for kiddie tax and alternative minimum tax amounts, the marginal tax rate can be very difficult to determine.

IV.   Filing Considerations
    A.   Filing Requirements
        1.   An individual must file an annual income tax return if certain minimum amounts of gross income have been received. These filing requirements generally are based on the sum of the basic standard deduction amount, the additional standard deduction amount for the elderly (but not for blindness), and the allowable personal exemptions.
        2.   A self-employed individual with net earnings from a business or profession of $400 or more must file an income tax return regardless of the amount of his or her gross income.
        3.   An individual who can be claimed as a dependent by another taxpayer must file an income tax return if any of the following applies.
            a.   Has earned income only and gross income that is more than the total allowable standard deduction.
            b.   Has unearned income only and gross income of more than $650 plus any additional standard deduction that the individual is allowed for the year.
            c.   Has both earned and unearned income and gross income of more than the larger of earned income (but limited to the applicable basic standard deduction) or $650, plus any additional standard deduction that the individual is allowed for the year.
        4.   Individual taxpayers file an income tax return on either Form 1040, Form 1040A, or Form 1040EZ, depending, in general, on the complexity of the taxpayer's financial situation. For a calendar year taxpayer, the appropriate form is due by April 15 of the following year.
    B.   Filing Status
        1.   The amount of tax on a given amount of taxable income will vary depending on the filing status of the taxpayer. A taxpayer will file as either single; married, filing jointly; married, filing separately; or head of household.
        2.   Head of household rates may be used by unmarried taxpayers who maintain a household for dependents. Further, if a married taxpayer meets the *abandoned spouse rules*, then the head of household rates may be used.
        3.   The joint return rates also apply to a surviving spouse for two years following the death of the spouse providing that the taxpayer maintains a household for a dependent child.

V.   Gains and Losses From Property Transactions -- In General
    A.   Gain or loss *may* be recognized for income tax purposes on the sale or other disposition of property to the extent of gain or loss realized. All gain is *recognized* to the extent *realized* unless a specific provision in the law provides otherwise. Realized losses may or may not be recognized, depending on the circumstances involved.
    B.   The concept of realized gain or loss can be expressed as follows.

> *Amount realized from sale or other disposition*
> *Minus: Adjusted basis of property*
> *Equals: Realized gain or loss*

1. The amount realized from the sale of property is its selling price less any costs of disposition.
2. Adjusted basis is determined as follows.

> *Cost (or other original basis) at date of acquisition*
> *Plus: Capital additions*
> *Minus: Depreciation (if appropriate) and other capital or cost recoveries*
> *Equals: Adjusted basis at date of sale or other disposition*

C. After it has been determined that gain or loss must be recognized on a sale or other disposition, then the gain or loss must be classified as to its nature (i.e., ordinary or capital).

VI. Gains and Losses From Property Transactions -- Capital Gains and Losses
   A. Special characterization is required on the sale or exchange of capital assets. While capital gains may be taxed at preferential income tax rates for individual taxpayers, capital losses may be only partially deductible in the year incurred. Any unused capital losses may be carried forward and deducted in later years.
   B. Definition of a Capital Asset
      1. The Code defines a capital asset as any property held by a taxpayer *other than* property listed in § 1221. This list includes inventory, accounts receivable, and depreciable or real property used in a business.
      2. The principal capital assets held by individuals for personal use include automobiles, personal residences, or assets held for investment, such as corporate securities and land.
   C. Computation of Net Capital Gains and Losses
      1. A holding period is short-term if an asset sold or exchanged is held for *one year or less*. Otherwise the holding period is considered long-term.
      2. Short-term gains and losses are netted against one another. Then, long-term gains and losses are netted against one another. Finally, the net short-term gains are offset against the net long-term losses or the net short-term losses are offset against the net long-term gains. If both net short-term and net long-term capital transactions are either gains or losses, then no additional netting is performed.
   D. Capital Loss Limitation
      1. Individuals may deduct (*for* adjusted gross income) net capital losses in amounts not to exceed $3,000 in any one year. Any unused amounts may be carried forward indefinitely.
      2. Corporate taxpayers may not offset net capital losses against ordinary income, only against capital gains. However, unused losses may be carried back three years and carried forward five years to offset capital gains that arise in those years.

TEST FOR SELF-EVALUATION -- CHAPTER 2

True or False

Indicate which of the following statements are true or false by circling the correct answer.

T   F   1.   Income broadly conceived (for tax purposes) only includes income that is taxable.

T   F   2.   An additional standard deduction amount is allowed if either the taxpayer or a dependent of the taxpayer is blind or over age 65.

T   F   3.   The Tax Table and the Tax Rate Schedule are basically the same and taxpayers always have a choice between the two when calculating their tax.

T   F   4.   The standard deduction amount is limited for a child who may be claimed as a dependent on his or her parents' income tax return to the greater of $650 or the dependent's earned income up to the basic standard deduction amount.

T   F   5.   Except in situations when a spouse dies during the year, the determination of marital status is made at the end of the taxable year.

T   F   6.   A self-employed individual taxpayer with net earnings from a business or profession of less than $400 would never be required to file an income tax return.

T   F   7.   A taxpayer who can be claimed as a dependent on another taxpayer's income tax return is not allowed a personal exemption.

T   F   8.   All realized gains are recognized for income tax purposes.

T   F   9.   Under the current tax calculation rules, individual taxpayers lose the benefit of the personal exemption after their adjusted gross income exceeds a certain level.

T   F   10.   Individuals may carry forward unused capital losses for an indefinite period until they are finally utilized.

T   F   11.   The dependency exemption for children of divorced parents must always be claimed by the custodial parent, regardless of the amount of support provided by the noncustodial parent.

T   F   12.   An unmarried taxpayer may claim the head of household status when a child, stepchild, or grandchild lives in the taxpayer's household for more than half of the taxable year.

T   F   13.   In order for the abandoned spouse rules to apply, an abandoned spouse must provide over half of the cost of maintaining a household and must share the household with a child (who need not be a dependent in all cases) for more than one-half of the tax year.

T   F   14.   A personal residence and an automobile owned by an individual taxpayer are both classified as capital assets.

T   F   15.   Alicia purchased a painting in 1994 for $5,000 and sold it in 1995 for $7,500.

Her gross income from the sale is $7,500.

T   F   16.   One of the most common type of expenditures that is deductible *for* adjusted gross income is medical expenses.

T   F   17.   Greta is a dependent of her parents. During 1995, she earned wages of $1,000 and received interest income of $450. Her standard deduction is $1,000.

T   F   18.   Gail is a dependent of her parents. During 1995, she received interest income of $450. Her standard deduction is $650.

T   F   19.   Corporate taxpayers that incur capital losses may never deduct those losses against ordinary income.

T   F   20.   Individual taxpayers who incur capital losses may never deduct those losses against ordinary income.

Fill-in-the-Blanks

Complete the following statements with the appropriate word(s) or amount(s).

1.   There are two categories of deductions for individual taxpayers: deductions _____ adjusted gross income and deductions _____ adjusted gross income.

2.   Assuming the abandoned spouse rules do not apply, the filing status of a married taxpayer may either be _____ or _____.

3.   The standard deduction amounts in 1995 for single taxpayers and married taxpayers filing jointly who are neither 65 years old nor blind are _____ and _____, respectively.

4.   To qualify as a dependent, the following tests must be met: _____, relationship or member of the household, _____, joint return, and citizenship or residency.

5.   To meet the support test, over _____ of the support of a dependent must be furnished by the taxpayer.

6.   A qualified surviving spouse who is 65 years of age or older and who has a dependent child must file an income tax return in 1995 if his/her gross income is _____ or more.

7.   The tax rate schedules must be used to compute an individual taxpayer's income tax liability if taxable income is more than _____.

8.   In determining the realized gain or loss from a sale, the property's _____ must be subtracted from the amount realized from the sale.

9.   Once it has been determined that the disposition of property results in recognizable gain or loss, the next step is to classify such gain or loss as _____ or _____.

10.   If an individual has net capital losses, they are deductible _____ adjusted gross income, up to a maximum of _____ per year.

11.   In 1995, the total standard deduction for a single taxpayer who is blind and 66 years old is _____.

12.   In computing taxable income, taxpayers are allowed to deduct the greater of allowable
        _____ or the _____.

13.   In order for a taxpayer to claim a relative as a dependent under a multiple support agreement,
        the taxpayer must contribute more than _____ percent of the relative's support.

14.   The *kiddie tax* does not apply once a dependent child reaches _____ years of age.

15.   In order for the *kiddie tax* to apply for 1995, the child must have unearned income in excess of
        _____.

Multiple Choice

Choose the best answer for each of the following questions.

_____   1.   Which of the following are *not* deductible as itemized deductions?
               a.   Expenses related to the production or collection of income.
               b.   Expenses related to the management of investment property.
               c.   Unreimbursed travel expenses related to employment.
               d.   Expenses related to the determination, collection, or refund of any tax.
               e.   All of the above are deductible as itemized deductions.

_____   2.   The basic standard deduction amount in 1995 for a taxpayer filing under the single
               filing status is the following amount.
               a. $2,450.
               b. $2,500.
               c. $3,800.
               d. $3,900.
               e. $5,750.

_____   3.   Mr. and Mrs. Keller file a joint income tax return for the year. Mr. Keller is 65 and
               Mrs. Keller is 64. Their eldest son, who generates no income and who is legally blind,
               single, and 29 years of age, is totally supported by the Kellers. How many exemptions
               may the Kellers claim on their income tax return?
               a.   2.
               b.   3.
               c.   4.
               d.   5.
               e.   6.

_____   4.   The McCoys, who are both age 42, are married taxpayers and have a sixteen-year-old
               daughter who attends a boarding school. The McCoys' adjusted gross income is $37,600
               and their total itemized deductions are $3,500. Assuming they file a joint income tax
               return, calculate their taxable income for 1995.
               a. $23,550.
               b. $23,900.
               c. $26,600.
               d. $31,050.
               e.   None of the above.

_____   5.   Mrs. Stooge is supported by her sons, Moe, Larry, and Curly and an old, dear friend to
               the following extent.
                          Moe   35%
                          Larry   30%

Curly   10%
Friend   25%

Assuming a multiple support agreement is filed, who may claim Mrs. Stooge as a dependent?

a.   Moe or Larry.
b.   Moe, Larry, or Curly.
c.   Moe, Larry, Curly or Friend.
d.   Moe, Larry, or Friend.
e.   Only Moe, since he contributed the most.

_____ 6. Louise qualifies to file her income tax return in 1995 using the head of household status. The amount of the basic standard deduction available is the following amount.

a. $3,800.
b. $3,900.
c. $5,600.
d. $5,750.
e.   Some other amount.

_____ 7. Doug has the following transactions during the current year: sale of his personal residence at a loss of $3,200; sale of his antique automobile at a gain of $300; and a sale of Skyview Corporation stock at a gain of $2,800. What is the amount of gain or loss to be recognized for the year by Doug?

a. $100 loss.
b. $3,100 gain.
c. $2,800 gain.
d.   No gain or loss is recognized because the assets are all personal use assets.
e.   None of the above.

_____ 8. Margaret had taxable income of $15,000 for the current year not including capital transactions. Her recognized gains and losses from sales of capital assets follow.

Short-term gains	$1,000
Short-term losses	2,000
Long-term gains	0
Long-term losses	3,000

Calculate Margaret's taxable income after consideration of the above capital transactions.

a. $11,000.
b. $12,000.
c. $13,000.
d. $14,000.
e.   None of the above.

_____ 9. Donny and Jeanna furnished over one-half of the total support of the following individuals during the current calendar year.

▸   Daughter, age 24, with gross income of $900 who is a part-time college student.

▸   Their neighbor's son, age 18, who has lived with them since March (while his parents are in France) and who has no gross income.

▸   Jeanna's brother, age 33, a full-time student with gross income of $3,600.

Donny and Jeanna file a joint income tax return for the year. How many *dependency* exemptions may they claim?

a.   5.
b.   4.
c.   3.
d.   2.
e.   1.

_____ 10.   Sally, a single, full-time college student, had over one-half of her support provided by her parents who claimed Sally as their dependent in 1995. In 1995, Sally earned $1,400 from a summer job, $53 in dividends from stock of a domestic corporation Sally inherited from her grandmother, and $1,100 in interest from a savings account funded by her parents and transferred to Sally several years ago. Sally's itemized deductions for 1995 totalled $600. What is Sally's taxable income for the year?

a.   ($447).
b. $603.
c. $103.
d. $2,553.
e.   None of the above.

_____ 11.   Juan and Connie, both age 37, have been legally separated since late 1994. Juan and Connie have five children, ages 15, 12, 9, 6, and 3. Juan's and Connie's separation agreement is silent as to which spouse may claim the dependency exemptions. Connie has always had custody of the two oldest children. During 1995, Connie has received no support from Juan. Connie, however, gave Juan a check for $3,300 in 1995 specifically for use in supporting the three children in Juan's custody. What is the maximum number of personal and dependency exemptions Connie may claim in 1995?

a.   7.
b.   6.
c.   5.
d.   4.
e.   3.

_____ 12.   During the year, the Mitchell Corporation had taxable income from operations of $28,000. In addition, the corporation sustained a short-term capital loss of $1,000 and a long-term capital loss of $1,800. By what amount will these losses reduce taxable income for the year?

a. $0.
b. $1,900.
c. $2,800.
d. $3,000.
e.   None of the above.

_____ 13.   Mr. and Mrs. Westphal, who are both over 65, file a joint income tax return which reflects the following.

Salary	$10,000
Long-term capital gain	8,000
Short-term capital loss	2,000
Rental receipts	19,000
Expenses attributed to the rental property (all are deductible)	8,000

From the above information, how much gross income do the Westphals have?
a. $19,400.

      b. $23,400.
      c. $31,400.
      d. $35,000.
      e.   None of the above.

_____ 14. Mrs. Walker's husband died on June 5 of this year. She maintains a household for herself and her unmarried son, Artie. However, Artie does not qualify as a dependent. What is Mrs. Walker's filing status?

	This Year	*Next year*
a.	Married Filing Jointly	Surviving Spouse
b.	Surviving Spouse	Head of Household
c.	Single	Single
d.	Married Filing Jointly	Head of Household
e.	Head of Household	Head of Household
f.	None of the above	

_____ 15. Bill is single and has a $47,500 salary as his sole source of income. Bill also sustains a long-term capital loss of $10,000. What is Bill's capital loss carryforward to future years?
      a. $0.
      b. $3,000.
      c. $4,000.
      d. $7,000.
      e.   None of the above.

_____ 16. Gene is a single, self-employed automatic washer and dryer repairman. From the following data, indicate if Gene needs to file an income tax return.

	This year	*Next year*
Interest Income	$ 500	$ 600
Receipts from business	10,000	12,000
Deductible business expenses	9,800	12,400

	This year	*Next year*
a.	Yes	Yes
b.	Yes	No
c.	No	Yes
d.	No	No

_____ 17. Henry Peoples, who celebrated his 65th birthday on January 1, 1996, filed a joint income tax return with his wife for 1995. Rob, their 23-year-old son, was a full-time college student until he graduated on May 21, 1995. During 1995, Rob provided 30 percent of his own support and earned $8,000 from his work as a research assistant. In addition, during 1995, Mr. and Mrs. Peoples provided all of the support for their niece Kerri, who had no income. How many personal and dependency exemptions should the Peoples claim on their 1995 joint income tax return?
      a.   2.
      b.   3.
      c.   4.
      d.   5.
      e.   None of the above.

_____ 18. Refer to the previous problem. How much should Rob claim as a personal exemption on his 1995 individual income tax return?
      a. $0.

b. $650.
c. $2,450.
d. $2,500.
e.   None of the above.

____ 19.   Don had the following items of income and expense during the year.

Salary	$28,000
Dividends	1,500
Short-term capital gain	1,000
Long-term capital loss	1,300

Additionally, Don fulfilled the pledge of $1,600 that he made to his church. What amount should Don report as his adjusted gross income for the year?
a. $28,000.
b. $29,200.
c. $29,500.
d. $30,500.
e.   None of the above.

ITEMS 20 AND 21 ARE BASED ON THE FOLLOWING DATA:

Bill, age 25, is a single, self-employed accountant. His only income is from his sole proprietorship. Bill owns the following assets used in his business.

	Adjusted Basis
Land on which his office was built	$ 5,000
Office and equipment	10,000

____ 20.   Bill must file an income tax return for 1995 if his net earnings from self-employment are at least what amount?
a. $400.
b. $2,300.
c. $2,350.
d. $3,700.
e.   Some other amount.

____ 21.   The adjusted basis of the capital assets used by Bill in his business total what amount?
a. $0.
b. $5,000.
c. $10,000.
d. $15,000.
e.   Some other amount.

____ 22.   Patti, who is independently wealthy, provided more than half the support for a cousin, nephew, and a foster parent. None of them qualified as a member of Patti's household, nor did any of these relatives have any income. Assume all other requirements for dependent status have been met. Which of these relatives could be claimed as a dependent on Patti's income tax return?
a.   None of the individuals.
b.   Nephew.
c.   Cousin.
d.   Foster Parent.

e.   Nephew and Cousin.

_____ 23.   Darron's wife died in 1992. Darron did not remarry, and continued to maintain a home
            for himself and his dependent seven year old child during 1993, 1994, and 1995,
            providing full support for himself and his child during these three years. For 1992,
            Darron properly filed a joint income tax return. Determine Darron's filing status for
            1995.
            a.   Single.
            b.   Married filing joint return.
            c.   Head of household.
            d.   Qualifying widower with dependent child.
            e.   Surviving spouse.

_____ 24.   Marilou was widowed five years ago and has lived alone at her current address since her
            husband's death. She had no income during the year but was supported in full by the
            following persons.

	Amount of Support	Percent of Total
Paul (an unrelated friend)	$3,010	43
Hortense (Marilou's sister)	3,430	49
Dave (Marilou's adopted son)	560	8
	$7,000	100

            Under a multiple support agreement, who can claim a dependency exemption for Marilou?
            a.   No one.
            b.   Paul.
            c.   Hortense.
            d.   Dave.
            e.   Hortense and Dave.

_____ 25.   Reggie (age 66) and Emmie (age 61) Wright were recently married and will file a joint
            income tax return this year. They have no dependent children but contribute over one-
            half of the support for Reggie's mother, Martha, who earned $650 from house sitting and
            received $1,800 in nontaxable social security benefits during 1995. Martha lives by
            herself in her own apartment. How many exemptions should be claimed by the Wrights for
            1995?
            a.   2.
            b.   3.
            c.   4.
            d.   5.
            e.   None of the above

_____ 26.   Ameldo, a calendar-year taxpayer, filed her 1995 income tax return on April 1, 1996,
            and included a check for the balance of tax due as shown on the return. However, Ameldo
            discovered on June 30, 1996 that she had failed to include as an itemized deduction
            $2,500 of interest expense paid on her home mortgage. In order for Ameldo to recover
            the tax that she would have saved by claiming the $2,500 deduction, by what date must
            she file an amended return?
            a.   December 31, 1998.
            b.   April 1, 1999.
            c.   April 15, 1999.
            d.   June 30, 1999.
            e.   Some other date.

_____ 27.   Marta received the following during the year.

Salary	$40,000
Gifts from parents	5,000
Royalties	1,000
Prize winnings	6,000
Child support payments	6,000
Alimony from ex-husband	10,000

What amount must Marta include in the computation of taxable income?
a. $52,000.
b. $57,000.
c. $58,000.
d. $68,000.
e.   None of the above.

____   28.   Which of the following is an itemized deduction?
a.   Alimony.
b.   Charitable contributions.
c.   Ordinary and necessary expenses incurred in a trade or business.
d.   All of the above are itemized deductions.
e.   None of the above is an itemized deduction.

____   29.   Which of the following is *not* deductible *from* adjusted gross income?
a.   Interest on a home mortgage.
b.   Charitable contributions.
c.   State and local income taxes.
d.   Certain payments to an Individual Retirement Account.
e.   All of the above are deductible *from* adjusted gross income.

____   30.   Bruce and Elizabeth, who have 3 dependent children, file a joint income tax return in 1995. They have gross income of $61,700 and itemized deductions of $3,000. Calculate their taxable income for the year.
a. $42,650.
b. $43,100.
c. $46,200.
d. $55,150.
e.   None of the above.

Code Section Recognition

Several important sections of the Internal Revenue Code are described below. Indicate, by number, the appropriate Code section.

1.   ____   Gross income is defined as "except as otherwise provided . . . all income from whatever source derived."

2.   ____   The principal section of the Code in which the definition of a capital asset is given.

3.   ____   Taxable income is defined in this Section.

Short Answer

1.   Sam and Sue are married and have 2 dependent children and a pet rabbit. Sam's and Sue's earnings from their jobs total $50,000. Their other income consists of the following.

Interest income from savings account	$1,000
Dividends	500
Municipal bond interest	600
State lottery winnings	400

They also sustain a capital loss of $2,000 on the disposition of Blue Corporation stock. Their itemized deductions during the year are $6,000. Calculate their taxable income for 1995.

2.   During the year, Leroy has the following capital transactions.

LTCG	$6,000
LTCL	2,000
STCG	2,000
STCL	4,000

How are these transactions treated?

SOLUTIONS TO CHAPTER 2 QUESTIONS

True or False

1. F   Income broadly conceived includes all income of the taxpayer, both taxable and nontaxable.
2. F   This additional standard deduction ($750 for each married taxpayer and $950 for single taxpayers) is allowed only for the taxpayer and taxpayer's spouse.
3. F   Although most taxpayers use the Tax Tables, there are certain situations when the Tax Rate Schedules *must* be used.
4. T
5. T
6. F   An income tax return would be required if certain minimum amounts of *gross income* have been received.
7. T
8. F   The tax law provides exceptions in certain situations when realized gains are not recognized.
9. T
10. T
11. F   The noncustodial parent may claim the dependency exemption if the custodial parent agrees in writing to forgo the exemption.
12. T
13. T
14. T
15. F   The gross income is computed after consideration of the $5,000 nontaxable return of capital invested in the painting.
16. F   Medical expenses are deductible *from* adjusted gross income.
17. T
18. T
19. T   Such losses may only be used to offset capital gains.
20. F   Net capital losses may offset up to $3,000 of ordinary income each year.

Fill-in-the-Blanks

1. for, from
2. married, filing jointly; married, filing separately
3. $3,900, $6,550
4. support, gross income
5. one-half
6. $9,800 ($9,800 = $6,550 + $2,500 + $750)
7. $100,000
8. adjusted basis
9. capital, ordinary
10. for, $3,000
11. $5,800 ($5,800 = $3,900 + $950 + $950)
12. itemized deductions, standard deduction
13. 10
14. 14
15. $1,300

Multiple Choice

1. e
2. d   See Table 2-1 in the text.
3. b   Mr. Keller, Mrs. Keller, and their son
4. a

Adjusted gross income	$37,600
Itemized deductions: $3,500	
(Use standard deduction)	-6,550
Personal and dependency exemptions ($2,500 X 3)	-7,500
Taxable income	$23,550

     See Example 7 in the text.

5. a   See Example 17 in the text.
6. d   See Table 2-1 in the text.
7. b $3,100 = $300 + $2,800. The loss from the sale of the personal residence is not deductible.
8. b $12,000 = $15,000 - $3,000 (net capital losses allowed--limited to $3,000 per year) See Example 37 in the text.
9. e   A *dependency* exemption may be claimed for the daughter.
10. e

AGI ($1,400 + $1,100 + $53)	$2,553
Less: Greater of basic standard deduction ($650) or earned income ($1,400) limited to $3,900	-1,400
Less: Personal exemption	-0
Taxable income	$1,153

11. e   Connie plus the two children in her custody. See Example 18 in the text.
12. a   Net capital losses are not deductible by corporations, except against capital gains.
13. d $35,000 = $10,000 + ($8,000 - $2,000) + $19,000--the rental expenses are deducted from gross income in arriving at adjusted gross income. See Example 2 in the text.
14. d   Since Artie does not qualify as a dependent, Mrs. Walker may not file using the joint return rates as a surviving spouse in the year following her husband's death; however, she does qualify for head of household status. See Example 31 in the text.
15. d   Of the $10,000 loss incurred, $3,000 is used currently and $7,000 is carried forward to future years.
16. a   In each year, Gene's gross income ($10,500 and $12,600) exceeds the sum of the standard deduction plus the personal exemption. Therefore, in each year an income tax return must be filed.
17. c   Exemptions are available for Mr. and Mrs. Peoples, Rob, and Kerri.
18. a   Because Rob is claimed as a dependent on his parents' income tax return, he may not claim a personal exemption on his own income tax return.
19. b $29,200 = $28,000 + $1,500 + $1,000 - $1,300 See Example 3 in the text.
20. a
21. a   The land, office, and equipment are assets used in a trade or business, not capital assets. See Example 34 in the text.
22. b   Of the three relatives, the nephew is the only relative that may be claimed as a dependent. The other two may not be claimed because they are not qualified members of Patti's household.
23. c   See Example 31 in the text.
24. c   Paul would not qualify to receive the exemption because he and Marilou are not related. Dave would not qualify because his support does not exceed 10 percent of the total. See Example 17 in the text.
25. b   Reggie, Emmie, and Martha
26. c
27. b $57,000 = $40,000 (salary) + $1,000 (royalties) + $6,000 (prize winnings) + $10,000 (alimony received)

28. b
29. d
30. a

Gross income		$61,700
Itemized deductions: $3,000		
(Use standard deduction)		-6,550
Personal and dependency		
exemptions ($2,500 X 5)		-12,500
Taxable income		$42,650

Code Section Recognition

1. 61
2. 1221
3. 63

Short Answer

1. Gross income:

Salary		$50,000
Interest income		1,000
Dividends		500
State lottery winnings		400
Total gross income		$51,900
Less: Deduction *for* AGI --		
Capital loss		2,000
Adjusted gross income		$49,900
Less: The greater of --		
Itemized deductions or	$6,000	
Standard deduction	6,550	6,550
Less: Personal and dependency		
exemptions ($2,500 X 4)		10,000
Taxable income		$33,350

2.   The $4,000 NLTCG is offset by the $2,000 NSTCL. A $2,000 net capital gain results.

CHAPTER 3
GROSS INCOME: CONCEPTS AND INCLUSIONS

CHAPTER HIGHLIGHTS

Gross income is a key component of the base used in calculating a taxpayer's income tax liability. The Internal Revenue Code provides an *all-inclusive* definition of gross income. However, a number of exclusions from gross income have evolved over time because of legislative, judicial, or administrative action. The method of accounting adopted by a taxpayer is important because it generally determines the period in which income is recognized. However, special rules apply in certain situations to various types of income. Finally, another important issue involves deciding who or what entity should recognize any income that is subject to tax. Nonetheless, all realized income must be recognized for income tax purposes unless a provision in the law specifically exempts the item from inclusion.

I. Gross Income -- What Is It?
   A. Definition -- Section 61 provides an *all-inclusive* definition of gross income: "gross income means all income from whatever source derived."
   B. Economic and Accounting Concepts -- An *economist's concept of income* differs from an *accountant's concept of income*. Economic income reflects consumption of goods and services during a period plus the net change in the fair market value of a taxpayer's net assets during the period. Accounting income, however, is based on the realization principle. The IRS, Congress, and the courts have rejected the economist's concept of income for tax purposes as impractical.
   C. Comparison of the Accounting and Tax Concepts of Income -- Differences exist between income tax rules and financial accounting measurement concepts because the goals of each concept differ.
   D. Form of Receipt -- Income may include any increase in wealth that is received in the form of money, property, or services.
   E. Recovery of Capital Doctrine -- *Gross receipts* (i.e., selling price) must be reduced by the amount of the capital invested (plus or minus appropriate adjustments such as capital improvements and cost recovery allowances) in determining the amount of *gross income* subject to tax.

II. Year of Inclusion
   A. Taxable Year
      1. The annual accounting period or tax year is a basic component of our tax system. Generally, an entity uses the *calendar year* to report income.

However, those taxpayers that keep adequate books and records can elect to use a *fiscal year* to report income. The fiscal year option generally is not available to partnerships, S corporations, and personal services corporations (see Chapter 5).

2.   Determining the annual accounting period is important in its impact on the taxpayer's tax liability because of the following reasons.

   a.   Congress may change the tax rate schedule.

   b.   The entity's income may fluctuate from year to year, which means that if income is shifted from one year to another, it may be taxed at a different marginal rate.

   c.   The form or status of the entity may change and a different tax rate schedule may apply.

B.   Accounting Methods

   1.   The year an item of income is reported often depends on the method of accounting a taxpayer uses.

   2.   Taxpayers generally will use either the *cash receipts and disbursements method*, the *accrual method*, or a *hybrid method* in reporting income.

   3.   The accrual method *must* be used in determining income from the sale and purchase of inventory.

   4.   The IRS may prescribe the method of accounting if a taxpayer has not adopted a method or if the taxpayer's method does not *clearly reflect income*.

   5.   Cash Receipts Method

      a.   Property or services are included in gross income in the year of actual or constructive receipt. The income need not be reduced to cash; rather, all that is necessary for income recognition is that the property or services received must have a fair market value or a cash equivalent.

      b.   A primary tax advantage of using the cash receipts method is the control that the taxpayer may have over the timing of recognition of income and expense.

   6.   Accrual Method

      a.   Gross income is recognized in the year in which it is earned, regardless of when the income is collected.

      b.   The income is earned when all events have occurred which fix the right to receive such income (the *all events test*) and its amount can be determined with reasonable accuracy.

      c.   The measure of the amount of accrual basis income is generally the amount the taxpayer has the right to receive, and not necessarily the fair market value of the receivable.

   7.   Hybrid Method -- The hybrid method is a combination of the accrual method and the cash method.

C.   Exceptions Applicable to Cash Basis Taxpayers

   1.   The *doctrine of constructive receipt* limits the ability of taxpayers to shift income arbitrarily from one year to another. If a taxpayer is entitled to receive income and it is made available to him or her, and the actual receipt is not subject to *substantial limitations* or *restrictions*, the income is considered to have been constructively received and it must be included in income.

   2.   *Original issue discount*, which is the difference between the amount due at maturity and the amount of an original loan, must be reported as

income or expense by the lender and borrower when it accrues, regardless of the taxpayer's method of accounting.

    3.   Series E and Series EE Bonds -- A taxpayer may recognize income on an annual incremental basis based on the bond's redemption value, at one of its maturity dates, or at the time the bond is redeemed.

    4.   Amounts Received under an Obligation to Repay -- When an amount has been received by a taxpayer and there is an obligation to repay the amount (e.g., loans, deposits), no income is considered realized.

D.   Exceptions Applicable to Accrual Basis Taxpayers

    1.   Prepaid income generally is included in a taxpayer's income in the year of receipt, even if it has not been earned. However, deferral opportunities exist in certain situations.

KEY TERMS
- Gross Income
- Cash, Accrual Accounting Methods
- Alimony, Child Support, Property Settlement
- Installment Method
- Below-Market Loan

    2.   Deferral of Advance Payments for Goods -- The seller can elect to defer the recognition of income in the case of receiving *advance payment for goods* until the goods are delivered if the taxpayer's method of accounting for the sale is the same for both book and tax purposes.

    3.   Deferral of Advance Payments for Services -- RevProc 71-21 permits an accrual basis taxpayer to defer recognition of income for *advance payments received for services* to be performed by the end of the year following the year of receipt. This revenue procedure, however, *does not apply* to prepaid rent or prepaid interest. For amounts received under guarantee or warranty contracts, deferral is not available unless the goods subject to such contracts are sold either with or without such contracts.

III.   Income Sources

A.   Personal Services -- The income from a taxpayer's personal services must be included in the gross income of the person who performs the services. A mere assignment of income does not shift the liability for the tax.

Because of the IRS's program of computerized matching of income reported by taxpayers and their employers, taxpayers should verify that salary and other income reported to the IRS is correct. If the W-2s and Form 1099s are incorrect, a taxpayer should have them corrected as soon as possible so the IRS's records agree with the amounts shown on the individual's tax return.

B.   Income from Property

     1.   Income from property, such as interest, dividends, or rents, must be included in the income of the *owner* of the property.

     2.   *Interest* is considered to accrue daily. Therefore, if a gift of property is made by a cash-basis donor on which interest has accrued, the donor must recognize income in the year that income is received by the donee equal to that amount which had been accrued up to the date of the gift.

     3.   When there is a sale of property on which interest has accrued, a portion of the selling price is treated as interest and taxed to the seller in the year of the sale.

     4.   *Dividends* do not accrue on a daily basis because their declaration is at the discretion of the corporation's board of directors. Dividends from property generally are taxed to the person who is the stockholder on the date of record. However, the Tax Court has held that a donor cannot shift the dividend income to a donee if a gift of property is made after the date of declaration and before the date of record.

C.   Income received by the taxpayer's agent is considered to be received by the taxpayer.

D.   Income from Partnerships, S Corporations, Trusts, and Estates

     1.   Each partner in a *partnership* must report his or her distributive share of the partnership's income and deductions for the partnership's tax year ending within or with his or her tax year, even if such amounts are not actually distributed.

     2.   A shareholder in an *S corporation* must report his or her proportionate share of the corporation's income and deductions for the corporation's tax year whether or not any distributions are actually made to the shareholder by the corporation.

     3.   The *beneficiaries of estates and trusts* generally are taxed on income that actually is distributed or required to be distributed to them. Any income not taxed to the beneficiaries is taxed to the estate or trust.

E.   Income in Community Property States

     1.   *Community property states* include Louisiana, Texas, New Mexico, Arizona, California, Washington, Idaho, Nevada and Wisconsin.

     2.   The basic difference between common law and community property law centers around the property rights of married persons.

     3.   For example, income from personal services generally is treated as having been earned 50 percent by each spouse. The treatment of income earned from property held by married couples in community property states varies by state.

IV.   Items Specifically Included in Gross Income

   A.   Alimony and Separate Maintenance Payments

     1.   Alimony payments are *taxable* to the recipient and *deductible for* adjusted gross income by the payor.

     2.   A transfer of property other than cash (e.g., appreciated property) to a former spouse pursuant to a divorce is not a taxable event. Instead, it is considered to be a division of property.

     3.   Payments made under post-1984 agreements and decrees are considered alimony if the following conditions are satisfied.

        a.   The payments are in cash.

Exhibit 3-1
EFFECT OF CERTAIN BELOW-MARKET LOANS

Type of Loan	Lender	Borrower
Gift	Interest income Gift made	Interest Expense Gift received
Compensation-related	Interest income Compensation expense	Interest expense Compensation income
Corporation to shareholder	Interest income Dividend paid	Interest expense Dividend income

       b.   The agreement does not specify that the cash payments are not alimony.

       c.   The payor and payee are not members of the same household when the payments are made.

       d.   There is no obligation to continue making the payments for any period after the death of the payee.

    4.   Special "front-loading" rules apply to post-1986 agreements to prevent property settlements from being disguised as alimony if payments in the first or second year exceed $15,000. Further, a special *alimony recapture* calculation must be made if changes in the amount of the payments exceed statutory limits. The recapture calculation would affect the net amounts considered alimony by the payor and payee.

    5.   Exceptions to the recapture rules exist in situations involving the death of the payor, if contingencies concerning property or a business exist, or if payments terminate because the payee remarries.

    6.   Amounts paid that represent child support are treated as nondeductible personal expenses rather than as alimony.

  B.   Imputed Interest on Below-Market Loans

    1.   Imputed interest rules apply to several types of below-market loans.

       a.   Gift loans.

       b.   Compensation-related loans.

       c.   Corporation-shareholder loans.

       d.   Tax avoidance loans or loans that significantly affect the borrower's or lender's federal tax liability.

    2.   The effects of the imputation to the borrower and lender differ depending on the type of loan involved. Exhibit 3-1 summarizes the effect of certain below-market loans on the lender and the borrower.

    3.   In certain situations, exceptions and limitations to the imputed interest rules apply.

       a.   Interest is not imputed on total outstanding *gift loans* of $10,000 or less between individuals, unless the loan proceeds are used to purchase *income-producing property*.

       b.   The imputed interest on loans of $100,000 or less between individuals cannot exceed the *borrower's net investment income* for the year.

  C.   Income From Annuities

    1.   The tax accounting problem associated with receiving payments under an

annuity contract is one of apportioning the amounts received between recovery of capital and income.

2. Collections received before the annuity starting date equal to or less than the post-August 13, 1982 increases in the annuity's cash value are first considered gross income, and not recovery of capital. Excess amounts received are treated as recovery of capital until the taxpayer's cost has been recovered. Any additional amounts received are included in gross income.

3. For collections received on or after the annuity starting date, an annuitant may exclude from income (as a return of capital) the proportion of each annuity payment that the investment in the contract bears to the expected return under the contract based on life expectancy tables published by the IRS.

4. The *exclusion amount* is computed as follows.

$$\frac{\text{Investment in contract}}{\text{Expected return}} \quad X \quad \text{Annuity payment}$$

This exclusion ratio applies until the annuitant has recovered his or her investment in the contract. However, once the investment is recovered, the entire amount of subsequent payments are taxable. If the annuitant dies before the investment has been recovered, the unrecovered cost is deductible in the year the payments cease (e.g., the year of death).

D. Prizes and Awards

1. The fair market value of prizes and awards generally is included in income rather than being treated as tax-free "gifts."

2. However, an award is not included in income if the following conditions are met.

     a. It is received in recognition of religious, charitable, scientific, educational, artistic, literary, or civic achievement.

     b. The recipient transfers the award to a qualified governmental unit or a nonprofit organization.

     c. The recipient has been selected without any action on his or her part to enter a contest or proceeding.

     d. There is no requirement that substantial future services be rendered as a condition to receiving the award.

3. Another exception allows for the exclusion of certain employee achievement awards of tangible personal property (e.g., a gold watch). The awards must be made in recognition of *length of service* or *safety achievement*. The ceiling on the limitation amount generally is $400; however, a ceiling of $1,600 applies for a "qualified plan award."

E. Group Term Life Insurance

1. The premiums paid by an employer for group term life insurance on an employee are excluded from the employee's income for the first $50,000 of protection if the plan does not discriminate.

2. For protection received in excess of $50,000, the covered employee must include an amount in income which is calculated based on a table in the Regulations.

3. The amount calculated as includible income is generally less than the actual cost of the protection to the employer; therefore, favorable tax treatment may result for employees even when group term life insurance coverage is in excess of $50,000.

F. Unemployment Compensation -- Section 85 provides that all unemployment

compensation benefits are includible in gross income.
G.　　Social Security Benefits
　　1.　　A portion of Social Security retirement benefits may be included in a taxpayer's gross income. The taxable amount of the benefits is determined through the application of one of two formulas that utilizes a unique measure of income -- *modified adjusted gross income (MAGI).*
　　2.　　MAGI is, generally, the sum of a taxpayer's adjusted gross income from all sources (other than Social Security receipts), the foreign earned income exclusion, and any tax-exempt interest received.

Recall that the typical taxpayer him- or herself pays one-half of the total contributions to the Social Security account. Thus, in an ideal world, no more than one-half of Social Security benefits would be taxed upon receipt, under the recovery-of-capital doctrine.

　　3.　　In the formulas, two sets of base amounts are established. This first set is as follows.
　　　　a.　　$32,000 for married taxpayers who file a joint return.
　　　　b.　　$0 for married taxpayers who do not live apart for the entire year but file separate returns.
　　　　c.　　$25,000 for all other taxpayers.
　　4.　　The second set of base amounts is as follows.
　　　　a.　　$44,000 for married taxpayers who file a joint return.
　　　　b.　　$0 for married taxpayers who do not live apart for the entire year but file separate returns.
　　　　c.　　$34,000 for all other taxpayers.
　　5.　　If MAGI plus one-half of Social Security benefits exceed the first set of base amounts, but not the second set, the taxable amount of Social Security benefits is the *lesser* of the following.
　　　　a.　　.50 (Social Security benefits).
　　　　b.　　.50 [MAGI + .50 (Social Security benefits) - (first base amount)].
　　6.　　If MAGI plus one-half of Social Security benefits exceed the second set of base amounts, the taxable amount of Social Security benefits is the *lesser* of the following.
　　　　a.　　.85 (Social Security benefits).
　　　　b.　　Sum of the following.
　　　　　　(1)　　.85 [MAGI + .50(Social Security benefits) - (second base amount)].
　　　　　　(2)　　The lesser of the following.
　　　　　　　　(a)　　The amount included through application of the first formula.
　　　　　　　　(b)　　$4,500 ($6,000 for married filing jointly).

TEST FOR SELF-EVALUATION -- CHAPTER 3

True or False

Indicate which of the following statements are true or false by circling the correct answer.

T   F   1.   The recovery of capital doctrine provides that a seller can reduce gross receipts by the adjusted basis of property sold in determining gross income.

T   F   2.   Provided a taxpayer maintains adequate books and records, a fiscal year may be selected to report income.

T   F   3.   Revenue Procedure 71-21 permits an accrual basis taxpayer to defer advanced payments for goods or services to be delivered or performed by the end of the tax year following the year of receipt.

T   F   4.   If a father "clips" interest coupons from bonds just before interest payments are due and gives the coupons to his son, the father will still have to pay taxes on the interest income.

T   F   5.   A security deposit received by a lessor (which will be returned if no damages are caused by the lessee) must be included in the lessor's income in the year of receipt.

T   F   6.   A salary check received on the evening of December 31, 1995 after banking hours is taxable in 1995.

T   F   7.   Payments properly classified as alimony should always be taken into income by the recipient and deducted by the payor.

T   F   8.   A taxpayer receiving an annuity applies the exclusion ratio only until his or her investment has been recovered.

T   F   9.   If a professional baseball player receives a brand new automobile for being the team's "outstanding fielder," he would likely be able to exclude this award from his income because it is really a gift.

T   F   10.   The actual cost to an employer for qualifying group term life insurance protection must be included in the gross income of an employee to the extent that the protection exceeds $50,000.

T   F   11.   For alimony payments under a post-1984 decree or agreement to be deductible, they must be in cash.

T   F   12.   With respect to a transfer of appreciated property to a former spouse, no gain or loss is recognized if the transfer is incident to a divorce settlement.

T   F   13.   In a transaction where a loan was extended to an employee (who is not a shareholder) by an employer at below-market rates, the employer will recognize imputed interest income and claim a compensation expense, and the employee may claim an interest deduction and report compensation income.

T   F   14.   Prizes and awards are normally excluded from income because they are really gifts.

T   F   15.   Based on the doctrine of constructive receipt, an item is not brought into income until the taxpayer has actually received cash.

T   F   16.   A contestant winning $25,000 on a television game show need not report the amount as income.

T   F   17.   Tax accounting rules are not necessarily in accordance with generally accepted accounting principles.

T   F   18.   A cash basis landlord collects a damage deposit from a tenant in 1995 and ultimately returns the amount in 1996. The amount is taxable to the landlord in 1995.

T   F   19.   The accountant's concept of income, which is based on the realization notion, has generally been accepted by the courts.

T   F   20.   The income earned by a partnership must be included in the partners' income subject to tax.

Fill-in-the-Blanks

Complete the following statements with the appropriate word(s) or amount(s).

1.   Gross income represents an increase in wealth which is recognized for tax purposes, but only after it has been _____.

2.   The _____ doctrine provides that on the sale of property, a seller can reduce the gross receipts by the adjusted basis of the property sold to determine the amount of gain or loss realized.

3.   The doctrine of _____ places certain limits on the ability of cash basis taxpayers to arbitrarily shift income from one year to another.

4.   The basic difference between _____ and _____ states centers around the property rights possessed by married persons.

5.   The nine community property states are _____, _____, _____, _____, _____, _____, _____, _____, and _____.

6.   Gross income includes income realized in any form, whether in the form of _____, _____, or _____.

7.   The imputed interest rules generally apply to various types of _____.

8.   The _____ method of accounting is required for determining purchases and sales when a taxpayer maintains an inventory.

9.   Current law excludes from an employee's income the premiums paid by an employer for the first _____ of group term life insurance protection if the plan does not discriminate.

10.   As a safeguard against a divorce related property settlement being disguised as alimony,

special rules apply to post-1986 agreements if the payments in the first two years exceed _____.

11.   Based on a divorce or separation agreement, a taxpayer may receive alimony and child support payments from the former spouse. The receipt of _____ is included in gross income, but a _____ is not.

12.   The IRS may prescribe the taxpayer's method of accounting if the method does not _____.

13.   Under the _____ rules, a cash basis taxpayer may be required to recognize interest income before the cash is received.

14.   For a single taxpayer whose MAGI plus one-half of the Social Security benefits received does not exceed $34,000, no more than _____ percent of Social Security receipts are included in gross income. If this income threshold exceeds $34,000, up to _____ percent of the Social Security benefits are included in gross income.

15.   If a taxpayer receives $6,000 in alimony and $5,000 in child support, the amount that must be included in income is _____.

Multiple Choice

Choose the best answer for each of the following questions.

_____   1.   The following is *not* a reason why determining an annual accounting period for tax purposes is important.
          a.   Congress may change the tax rate schedule.
          b.   The entity may go out of existence.
          c.   The entity's income may rise or fall between years so that placing the income in a particular year may mean that the income is taxed at different marginal rates.
          d.   The entity may undergo a change in status and a different tax rate schedule may apply (e.g., change from a sole proprietorship to a corporation).
          e.   None of the above is unimportant.

_____   2.   The following doctrine places certain limits on the ability of cash-basis taxpayers to arbitrarily shift income from one year to another in an effort to minimize taxes.
          a.   Claim of right doctrine.
          b.   Doctrine of the fruit and tree.
          c.   Recovery of capital doctrine.
          d.   Doctrine of constructive receipt.
          e.   None of the above applies.

_____   3.   A calendar-year cash-basis taxpayer deposited $5,000 in an interest-bearing passbook savings account at his bank. The sum is expected to earn approximately $500 interest per year beginning on January 1, 19X0. He anticipates a need for cash at the end of five years (December 31, 19X4) when the account will have a balance of approximately $7,500. If the taxpayer closes the account at the end of the fifth year and assuming $500 was credited to the account at the end of each year, how much income must be recognized by the taxpayer in that year?
          a. $0.

    b. $500.
    c. $2,500.
    d. $7,500.
    e.   None of the above.

_____ 4.   Nel's savings account at the local savings and loan association was credited with $600 of interest on December 31, last year. The balance prior to the inclusion of the interest income was $2,400. On February 4, of this year, she withdrew $3,000 from her account. Nel is on the cash basis. What amount must be recognized as income last year?
    a. $0.
    b. $600.
    c. $2,400.
    d. $3,000.
    e.   None of the above.

_____ 5.   Mindy and Rob are married and both are gainfully employed in Illinois. Mindy earns $28,000 as a nurse and Rob earns $34,000 as an accountant. If Mindy files a separate return, she would report how much gross income?
    a. $28,000.
    b. $31,000.
    c. $62,000.
    d.   A separate return may not be filed by Mindy.
    e.   None of the above.

_____ 6.   Assume the same facts as above, except that Mindy and Rob live in New Mexico.
    a. $28,000.
    b. $31,000.
    c. $62,000.
    d.   A separate return may not be filed by Mindy.
    e.   None of the above.

_____ 7.   Select the incorrect statement.
    a.   Appreciation in the market value of an asset would be economic income but not accounting income.
    b.   For a cash basis taxpayer, the year of payment generally determines the period in which an expense is deductible.
    c.   An accrual basis taxpayer does not always recognize the same amount of net income for book and tax purposes.
    d.   As long as a taxpayer follows generally accepted accounting principles, the Commissioner of the IRS cannot prescribe a change in accounting methods.
    e.   None of the above.

_____ 8.   The Drayer Corporation, an accrual-basis calendar-year taxpayer, sells its services under 12, 15, and 24 month contracts. The corporation services each customer every month. On October 1 of the current year, Drayer sold the following customer contracts, receiving payment as indicated.

Length of Contract	Proceeds
12 months	$9,000
15 months	7,500
24 months	4,800

The Drayer Corporation should recognize taxable income of what amount this year?

    a. $3,750.
    b. $4,350.
    c. $8,550.
    d. $21,300.
    e.   None of the above.

_____ 9. On December 1, of last year, Sandra gave her dependent son a $2,000 bond that paid 12% interest semi-annually on July 1 and January 1 (i.e., 6% twice a year). Sandra and her son are cash basis taxpayers. How much of the $120 in bond interest paid on January 1, of this year must Sandra recognize as income this year? For simplicity, assume a year has 360 days and each month has 30 days.
    a. $0.
    b. $60.
    c. $100.
    d. $120.
    e.   None of the above.

_____ 10. Eleanor purchased a ten-year annuity for $10,000 a number of years ago. She is to receive $4,000 per year for 10 years. How much should Eleanor report as income in year 1?
    a. $0.
    b. $1,000.
    c. $3,000.
    d. $4,000.
    e.   None of the above.

_____ 11. Refer to the previous question. How much gross income must Eleanor *include* in income in year 4?
    a. $0.
    b. $1,000.
    c. $3,000.
    d. $4,000.
    e.   None of the above.

_____ 12. Leon retired five years ago on December 31, from the Dart Company. Prior to his retirement, he had contributed $30,000 of after-tax earnings to an employee annuity plan. He had a life expectancy of 10 years at the time of retirement. Leon is to receive $1,000 per month for life beginning in January in the year following retirement. Leon should *include* the following amount in taxable income for the current year.
    a. $12,000.
    b. $9,000.
    c. $3,000.
    d. $0.
    e.   None of the above.

_____ 13. Which of the following is not a requirement that must be met in order for an alimony payment to be deductible for settlements reached in the current year?
    a.   Legally separated or divorced parties may not be members of the same household at the time of payment.
    b.   The payment must be made in cash.
    c.   The payment must be periodic.
    d.   The payment must not be designated as anything other than alimony (e.g., child support).
    e.   All of the above are requirements.

_____ 14. After being married for over 15 years R.J. and Sue were divorced in 1995. The following support payments have been or are scheduled to be made.

1995	$35,000
1996	20,000
1997	15,000

Based on the above, what is the amount of excess payments that must be recaptured in 1997?
a. $0.
b. $15,000.
c. $20,000.
d. $35,000.
e.   None of the above.

_____ 15. Lee is covered under a non-discriminatory, group term life insurance policy. Lee's employer pays the entire $700 cost of the $75,000 policy. Assuming that the uniform annual premium according to the Income Tax Treasury Regulations is $8 per $1,000 of coverage, what is the amount that is taxable to Lee?
a. $0.
b. $200.
c. $250.
d. $600.
e.   None of the above.

_____ 16. Assuming that in the previous problem the life insurance plan discriminated in favor of highly paid employees, what amount is taxable to Lee?
a. $0.
b. $200.
c. $250.
d. $600.
e.   None of the above.

_____ 17. Dr. Dogood practices psychology in Virginia. Her patients usually pay their office visit charges on the date of the visit or within one month. Additionally, she makes house calls for her patients suffering from acrophobia (because Dr. Dogood's office is on the 13th floor of the local high-rise professional office building). These outside visits are billed weekly, and are usually paid within two months after the patients collect from their insurance companies. Dr. Dogood is a cash basis taxpayer. Information relating to this year is as follows.

Cash received on the date of office visits	$ 40,000
Collections on accounts receivable	100,000
Accounts receivable, beginning of year	25,000
Accounts receivable, end of year	21,000

Calculate Dr. Dogood's gross income from her medical practice for this year.
a. $136,000.
b. $140,000.
c. $161,000.
d. $165,000.
e.   None of the above.

ITEMS 18 THROUGH 21 ARE BASED ON THE FOLLOWING DATA.

Carmen had the following cash receipts during 1995.

Interest on life insurance proceeds from her decedent aunt's policy left on deposit with the insurance company	$ 20
Interest on state income tax refund	22
Net rent from condominiums	18,000
Advance rent from lessees of above condominiums to be applied against rent for the last two months of the 4-year lease, ending in 1999	3,000
Dividend from a mutual insurance company on a life insurance policy	600
Dividend on corporation stock. Declared on November 15, 1994, payable on December 30, 1994, to holders of record on December 15, 1994. Dividend was received in the mail on January 1, 1995.	730
Gross amount of state lottery winnings (Carmen spent $450 on state lottery tickets, and $525 on state pari-mutuel horseracing, for which she has full documentation)	1,200

Carmen used the standard deduction on her 1995 return. Total dividends received to date on the life insurance policy do not exceed the aggregated premiums paid by Carmen.

_____ 18.   How much should Carmen include in her 1995 taxable income for interest?
     a. $0.
     b. $20.
     c. $22.
     d. $42.
     e.   None of the above.

_____ 19.   How much should Carmen include in her 1995 taxable income for rent?
     a. $21,000.
     b. $18,500.
     c. $18,125.
     d. $18,000.
     e.   None of the above.

_____ 20.   How much should she report as dividend income for 1995?
     a. $1,330.
     b. $730.
     c. $600.
     d. $0.
     e.   Some other amount.

_____ 21.   What is Carmen's total gross income for 1995?
     a. $21,772.
     b. $21,997.
     c. $22,522.
     d. $22,972.
     e.   Some other amount.

_____ 22.   Andre, an accrual basis taxpayer, leases office buildings to commercial tenants.

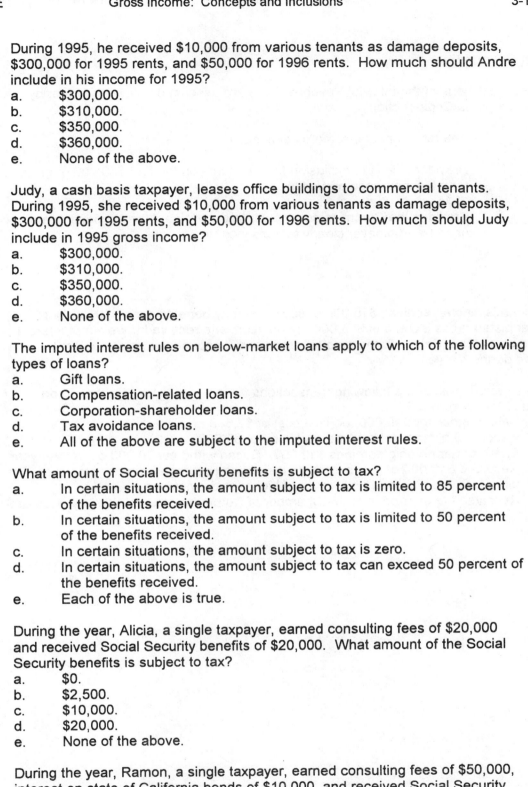

During 1995, he received $10,000 from various tenants as damage deposits, $300,000 for 1995 rents, and $50,000 for 1996 rents. How much should Andre include in his income for 1995?
- a. $300,000.
- b. $310,000.
- c. $350,000.
- d. $360,000.
- e.   None of the above.

____   23.   Judy, a cash basis taxpayer, leases office buildings to commercial tenants. During 1995, she received $10,000 from various tenants as damage deposits, $300,000 for 1995 rents, and $50,000 for 1996 rents. How much should Judy include in 1995 gross income?
- a. $300,000.
- b. $310,000.
- c. $350,000.
- d. $360,000.
- e.   None of the above.

____   24.   The imputed interest rules on below-market loans apply to which of the following types of loans?
- a.   Gift loans.
- b.   Compensation-related loans.
- c.   Corporation-shareholder loans.
- d.   Tax avoidance loans.
- e.   All of the above are subject to the imputed interest rules.

____   25.   What amount of Social Security benefits is subject to tax?
- a.   In certain situations, the amount subject to tax is limited to 85 percent of the benefits received.
- b.   In certain situations, the amount subject to tax is limited to 50 percent of the benefits received.
- c.   In certain situations, the amount subject to tax is zero.
- d.   In certain situations, the amount subject to tax can exceed 50 percent of the benefits received.
- e.   Each of the above is true.

____   26.   During the year, Alicia, a single taxpayer, earned consulting fees of $20,000 and received Social Security benefits of $20,000. What amount of the Social Security benefits is subject to tax?
- a. $0.
- b. $2,500.
- c. $10,000.
- d. $20,000.
- e.   None of the above.

____   27.   During the year, Ramon, a single taxpayer, earned consulting fees of $50,000, interest on state of California bonds of $10,000, and received Social Security benefits of $12,000. What amount of the Social Security benefits is subject to tax?
- a. $0.
- b. $10,200.
- c. $12,000.
- d. $31,700.
- e.   None of the above.

Code Section Recognition

Several important sections of the Internal Revenue Code are described below. Indicate, by number, the appropriate Code section.

1. _____   The term "gross income" is defined.

2. _____   Provides a limited exclusion for premiums on the first $50,000 of group term life insurance protection.

3. _____   Provides the Commissioner power to determine if the accounting method used by a taxpayer clearly reflects income.

Short Answer

1. Sally, who is single, receives $15,000 of social security benefits during 1995. Her other adjusted gross income is $16,000. In addition, she received tax-exempt interest income of $4,000. Calculate the amount of the social security earnings subject to taxation during the year.

2. Susan's records reflect the following transactions for the year. How are they to be treated for tax purposes?
    ▸   Sale of stock for $10,000, original cost of $7,500.
    ▸   Receipt of alimony from former husband of $8,000.
    ▸   Share of partnership earnings $12,000. Susan withdrew $8,000 during the year.
    ▸   Received $45,000 of group term life insurance coverage from her employer. The plan does not discriminate in favor of highly-paid employees.
    ▸   Received the door prize at the Chamber of Commerce annual dance valued at $1,000.

SOLUTIONS TO CHAPTER 3 QUESTIONS

True or False

1.	T	
2.	T	However, in many situations, partnerships, S corporations, and personal services corporations may not use a fiscal year.
3.	F	The Revenue Procedure only applies to services, and not to goods.
4.	T	The "fruit and tree" doctrine is applicable.
5.	F	Because the lessor has an obligation to return the money, no income is recognized.
6.	T	The amount is constructively received, and therefore taxable in 1995.
7.	T	
8.	T	
9.	F	Athletes have been unsuccessful in their attempt to exclude these awards as being in recognition of "artistic" achievement. Therefore, the award is taxable.
10.	F	The amount taken into an employee's income is based on tables in the Income Tax Regulations and does not necessarily reflect the actual cost of the coverage.
11.	T	
12.	T	
13.	T	
14.	F	Such receipts are not treated as gifts, but as gross income subject to taxation.
15.	F	There need not be an actual receipt of cash, only its constructive receipt.
16.	F	Such amounts are treated as gross income subject to taxation.
17.	T	
18.	F	
19.	T	
20.	T	

Fill-in-the-Blanks

1. realized
2. recovery of capital
3. constructive receipt
4. common law, community property
5. Louisiana, Texas, New Mexico, Arizona, California, Washington, Idaho, Nevada, and Wisconsin
6. money, property, services
7. below-market loans
8. accrual
9. $50,000
10. $15,000
11. alimony, child support payment
12. clearly reflect income
13. original issue discount
14. 50, 85
15. $6,000

Multiple Choice

1.   b
2.   d
3.   b   Income of $500 is recognized each year over a five year period.
4.   b
5.   a   Because Illinois is a common law state, Mindy must report only her salary as income on her separate return.
6.   b $31,000 = .50($28,000 + $34,000) -- Because New Mexico is a community property state this allocation is required.
7.   d   See the discussion in the text regarding the comparison of accounting and taxable income.
8.   c $8,550 = (3/12 X $9,000) + (3/15 X $7,500) + $4,800   See Example 18 in the text.
9.   c $120 X 5/6 = $100 See Example 20 in the text.
10.   c $1,000 of the $4,000 received in year 1 is a return of investment and $3,000 is reportable income. See Example 40 in the text.
11.   c   Same as 10. See Example 40 in the text.
12.   b $9,000 = $12,000 - [($30,000/$120,000 X $12,000)] See Example 40 in the text.
13.   c   This component is not required.
14.   a   There is no alimony recapture because payments did not decrease by more than $15,000 per year. See Example 27 in the text.
15.   b $200 = $8 X [($75,000 - $50,000) / $1,000] See Example 41 in the text.
16.   e   The amount included in income is the greater of the actual cost ($700) or the amount calculated in accordance with the Treasury Regulations ($600 = $8 X $75,000/$1,000). Thus, Lee must include $700 in income.
17.   b $140,000 = $40,000 + $100,000 See Example 5 in the text.
18.   d $42 = $20 + $22
19.   a $21,000 = $18,000 + $3,000
20.   b $730. The $600 "dividend" received from the mutual insurance company is considered a reduction in the cost of Carmen's life insurance coverage.
21.   d $22,972 = $42 (interest) + $21,000 (rent) + $730 (dividends) + $1,200 (lottery winnings)
22.   c $350,000 = $300,000 + $50,000. The $50,000 of prepaid rent received may not be deferred for tax purposes, even though Andre is an accrual method taxpayer. The damage deposit is not income because of the potential obligation to return the amount.
23.   c $350,000 = $300,000 + $50,000. The $50,000 of prepaid rent received may not be deferred for tax purposes. The damage deposit is not income because of the potential obligation to return the amount.
24.   e
25.   e
26.   b   The amount taxable is the *lesser* of the following:
                  .50($20,000) = $10,000 *or*
                  .50[$20,000 + .50($20,000) - $25,000] = $2,500
             See Example 42 in the text.
27.   b   The amount taxable is the *lesser* of the following:
                  .85($12,000) = $10,200 *or*
                  .85($66,000 - $34,000) + $4,500 = $31,700
             See Example 43 in the text.

Code Section Recognition

1.   61
2.   79
3.   446

Short Answer

1.   The taxable amount is $1,250, the *lesser* of the following.

■   .50($15,000) = $7,500.
■   .50[$16,000 + $4,000 + .50($15,000) - $25,000] = $1,250.

2.   The following amounts are included in Susan's income.

Sale of stock ($10,000 - $7,500)	$ 2,500
Alimony	8,000
Partnership earnings	12,000
Group term life insurance coverage	0
Door prize	1,000
Total income	$23,500

CHAPTER 4
GROSS INCOME: EXCLUSIONS

CHAPTER HIGHLIGHTS

his chapter discusses items that are specifically excluded from gross income. Even though a definition of gross income is provided in the Code, Congress has considered it necessary to indicate explicitly how certain items are to be treated, either for the sake of clarity or for the purpose of insuring some sense of equity. Congress has acted on its own initiative at times in defining gross income, but judicial and administrative influences also have played an important role in the evolution of the definition and scope of gross income.

I.   Statutory Authority -- Statutory authority for excluding certain items from gross income is provided in §§ 101 through 150 of the Internal Revenue Code. These provisions have been enacted by Congress for various purposes (e.g., to provide indirect welfare payments, to prevent double taxation, to provide incentives for socially desirable activities, to change judicially imposed decisions).

II.   Gifts and Inheritances
   A.   The recipient of a gift or an inheritance may exclude the value of such property from gross income. The recipient is, however, subject to tax on any income that is earned from holding or exchanging the property subsequent to its receipt.
   B.   A payment is not considered a gift if it represents compensation for past, present, or future services. Transfers from an employer to an employee *cannot* be excluded as a gift unless the transfer fits into one of the statutory exclusion provisions.
   C.   A *gift* has been defined by the courts as "a voluntary transfer of property by one to another without adequate consideration or compensation therefrom" which has been made "out of affection, respect, admiration, charity, or like impulses." Thus, in many cases the issue of whether a gift has been made rests on the donor's intent.

III.   Life Insurance Proceeds
   A.   Life insurance proceeds paid to a beneficiary by reason of the death of the insured generally are exempt from income taxation.

B.   The exclusion is not available if the owner of an insurance policy cancels the policy and receives an amount in excess of the policy's cost. Any such excess is income. In addition, if the beneficiary of a policy receives the insurance proceeds in payment of an amount due from the decedent, the proceeds are taxable.

C.   A further exception to the general rule applies when a life insurance contract has been *transferred for valuable consideration* to another person for ownership rights. The assignee must recognize income to the extent that insurance proceeds exceed the amount paid for the policy plus any subsequent premiums paid. However, this rule does not apply when the transfer is made to any one of the following.

    1.   A partner of the insured.
    2.   A partnership in which the insured is a partner.
    3.   A corporation in which the insured is an officer or shareholder.
    4.   A transferee whose basis in the policy is determined by reference to the transferor's basis (e.g., property transferred by gift).

D.   Interest on Life Insurance Proceeds -- Interest earned from the reinvestment of life insurance proceeds generally is subject to tax. The annuity rules are used to apportion the interest and principal elements of an insurance installment receipt. The principal element is excludible from income while the interest portion is includible in income.

IV. Employee Death Benefits

A.   When an employer makes payments to a deceased employee's surviving spouse, children, or other beneficiaries, a fundamental question must be resolved: Do the payments represent *compensation* for prior services rendered, or are they *gifts*?

B.   A statutory provision allows an automatic exclusion of the first $5,000 paid by an employer to an employee's beneficiaries *by reason of death of the employee*. The exclusion is not applicable to amounts that the employee had a nonforfeitable right to receive immediately before death, such as salary or commissions.

C.   The exclusion must be apportioned among the beneficiaries on the basis of each beneficiary's percentage of the total death benefit received.

D.   If the employer's payments exceed $5,000, the excess may be treated as a gift, and not as taxable income, if it is shown that the employer has exhibited gratuitous intent.

V. Scholarships

A.   General Information

    1.   Scholarships are payments or benefits received by a student at an educational institution that are not classified as either gifts or compensation for services. Subject to limitations, such amounts are excludible from gross income if received by degree candidates. However, if amounts received represent payment for compensation or if payments are made primarily for the benefit of the employer, then the amounts are taxable to the recipient.

    2.   The exclusion is limited to amounts required to be used for tuition, and course-required fees, books, supplies, and equipment. Amounts received for room and board are not excludible and are treated as earned income for purposes of calculating the standard deduction.

B.   Timing Issues -- If the amount eligible for exclusion is not known at the time the money is received, the transaction is held *open* until the educational expenses are paid.

C.   Disguised Compensation -- The IRS has ruled that scholarships made available by employers solely to children of key employees are taxable income to the parent-employee as disguised compensation.

VI.   Compensation for Injuries and Sickness
    A.   Damages
        1.   The tax consequences of the receipt of damages depend on the type of harm the taxpayer has experienced. For example, reimbursement for the loss of income is taxed the same as the income that is replaced, and a payment for damaged or destroyed property is treated as income if the proceeds received exceed the property's basis.
        2.   Amounts received as compensation for *personal injury* or sickness are excluded from income whether received by suit or agreement.
        3.   *Punitive damages* (i.e., amounts received to punish the defendant for gross negligence or the intentional infliction of harm) are taxable *unless* the claim arises out of physical injury or physical sickness.
        4.   Lump-sum awards must be allocated among the various types of damages the award is to cover and are taxed accordingly.
    B.   Workers' Compensation -- Congress has specifically exempted workers' compensation benefits (i.e., fixed amounts for specific job-related injuries) from inclusion in gross income.
    C.   Accident and Health Insurance Benefits -- Such benefits received are excludible from gross income if the premiums are *paid by the taxpayer.*

KEY TERMS
● Gift, Inheritance
● Payments Due to Death
● Employee Fringe Benefits
● Interest, Dividend Income
● Foreign Earned Income
● Tax Benefit Rule

VII.   Employer-Sponsored Accident and Health Plans
    A.   Employees, retired former employees, and their dependents are not required to include in income the amounts *paid by their employer* to keep an accident or health plan in force. Further, the amount paid for such a policy is deductible by the employer.

    B.   As a general rule, *benefits* received by an employee from such plans are includible in income.
    C.   However, payments received for medical care of the employee, spouse, and children are specifically excluded from income, unless the amounts were deducted in a prior year as a medical expense. Payments for expenses that do *not* meet the law's definition of medical care must be included in gross income. In addition amounts received as compensation for permanent loss or use of a *member or function of the body* or permanent disfigurement of the employee, spouse, or dependent are excluded from gross income.
    D.   Medical Reimbursement Plans
        1.   Reimbursements received by an employee from his or her employer to cover medical or hospital costs may be excluded from income if the benefits are received under a plan.
        2.   However, if a self-insured reimbursement plan discriminates, the benefits received are subject to taxation.

VIII. Meals and Lodging
    A.   Furnished for the Convenience of the Employer

1. The *value of meals* provided to an employee and the employee's spouse and dependents is excluded from the taxpayer's income if the following three requirements are met.
    a. The meals are *furnished* by the employer.
    b. The meals are provided on the employer's *business premises*.
    c. The meals are provided for the *convenience of the employer*.
2. The *value of lodging* is excluded from a taxpayer's income if the three requirements listed above are met and, additionally, if the employee is *required* to accept the lodging as a condition of employment.

B. Other Housing Exclusions
1. In certain situations, an *employee of an educational institution* may be able to exclude the value of campus housing provided by the employer.
    a. No income is reported by the employee if annual rents equal or exceed five percent of the appraised value of the facility.
    b. If rents paid are less than five percent of the facility's value, the deficiency is included in the employee's gross income.
2. *Ministers of the gospel* can exclude from income the rental value of a home furnished or a rental allowance paid to them to the extent the amount is used to rent or provide a home.
3. *Military personnel* are allowed a housing exclusion in various situations.

IX. Other Employee Fringe Benefits
A. Specific Benefits -- Several nontaxable fringe benefits have been enacted by Congress in order to encourage employers to do certain things. These provisions, among others, exclude the following.
1. The value (subject to certain limitations) of *child and dependent care services* provided by an employer to enable an employee to work.
2. The value of the use of certain *on-premises athletic facilities* by employees, their spouses and dependents.
3. *Undergraduate tuition reductions* (and certain graduate tuition reductions) granted to an employee, spouse, or dependents by a nonprofit educational institution.
B. Cafeteria Plans -- The value of certain services or noncash benefits received that are a part of a *cafeteria plan* are excluded.
C. General Classes of Excluded Benefits -- Congress has specified six broad classes of nontaxable employee benefits which include the following.
1. General classes
    a. No-additional-cost services.
    b. Qualified employee discounts.
    c. Working condition fringes.
    d. *De minimis* fringes.
    e. Qualified transportation fringe.
    f. Qualified moving expense reimbursement.
2. For the exclusion of these general classes of fringe benefits to be available, certain requirements must be met. For example, *nondiscrimination provisions* apply to the no-additional-cost services and qualified employee discounts which provide that, if the plan discriminates in favor of highly compensated employees, the exclusion is denied to these key employees. However, the nondiscrimination rules generally do not apply to *de minimis* and working conditions fringe benefits.
D. Taxable Fringe Benefits -- Fringe benefits received from employers that are not excluded from income by statute or do not fit into any of the general classes of excluded benefits are taxable. The amount of income is equal to the benefits'

fair market value.

X.   Foreign Earned Income

     A.   A taxpayer who has *earned income* from personal services from a foreign source may elect *either* of the following options.

         1.   Include the receipts in the gross income computation and then claim a credit for foreign taxes paid on that income.

         2.   Exclude part or all of the foreign income from U.S. gross income.

     B.   To qualify for the *exclusion*, the taxpayer must meet one of the two following tests.

         1.   Be a bona fide resident of the foreign country (or countries).

         2.   Be present in the foreign country for 330 days during any consecutive 12-month period.

     C.   The exclusion is *limited* to $70,000 earned during a tax year but the exclusion must be prorated over the year if the taxpayer is in the foreign country for less than the entire year. For married persons, both of whom have foreign earned income, the exclusion is computed separately for each spouse.

     D.   In addition, *reasonable housing costs* incurred by the taxpayer and the taxpayer's family in a foreign country in excess of a base amount may be excluded from income.

XI.   Interest on Certain State and Local Government Obligations

     A.   Interest income on state and local government obligations is exempt from federal taxation.

     B.   Other types of income are not excluded by this provision, such as interest received on a condemnation award, the overpayment of a state income tax liability, or gains on the sale of tax-exempt securities.

While most municipal bond interest is not subject to federal income tax, capital gain income realized on their sale is. An investor should be aware of this when deciding which bonds to buy, and when to sell them.

XII.   Dividends

     A.   Amounts paid by a corporation to a shareholder with respect to his or her stock is taxable to the extent the payments are made from *current* or *accumulated earnings and profits*.

     B.   Often receipts that are referred to as dividends, such as dividends on deposits with savings and loans, patronage dividends, and dividends paid to policyholders of mutual insurance companies, are *not* dividends for tax purposes.

     C.   A *stock dividend* generally is not taxable. However, if the taxpayer has the *option* of receiving cash in lieu of additional stock, the consideration received is taxable.

XIII.   Educational Savings Bonds

     A.   Interest earned on certain Series EE U.S. government savings bonds may be excluded if the following requirements are met.

         1.   The savings bonds are issued after 1989.

         2.   The bonds are redeemed to pay *qualified higher education expenses*.

         3.   The bonds are issued to an individual who was at least 24 years old at the

time of issuance.

For married taxpayers, the exclusion is not available if a separate return is filed.

B.   Qualified higher education expenses consist of tuition and fees paid to an eligible educational institution for the taxpayer, spouse, or dependents.

C.   If the redemption proceeds exceed the qualified expenses, only a pro-rata amount of the expenses will qualify for the exclusion.

D.   The benefit of the exclusion is phased-out as the taxpayer's *modified adjusted gross income* exceeds $42,300 ($63,450 on a joint return) for 1995.

E.   Modified adjusted gross income is adjusted gross income prior to the foreign earned income exclusion and the educational savings bond exclusion.

With the top marginal income tax rate applicable to individuals at 39.6 percent, certain investors will likely to be attracted to municipal bonds and educational-use savings bonds. Be certain that this decision makes sense after-tax, given the investor's tax rate, and the taxable and exempt rates of return.

XIV. Tax Benefit Rule

A.   If a taxpayer obtains a deduction for an item in one year and in a later year recovers a portion of the amount which caused the prior deduction, the recovery produces income in the year of receipt.

B.   No income must be recognized on the recovery of the deduction or portion of the deduction if a tax benefit was not received in a previous year.

XV.   Income from Discharge of Indebtedness

A.   The transfer of appreciated property in satisfaction of a debt is treated as a sale of the property followed by a payment of the debt. Foreclosure by a creditor is also treated as a sale or exchange of the property. Income is realized in such cases and is generally taxable.

B.   The discharge of indebtedness in the following situations is subject to special treatment.

1.   Creditors' gifts.
2.   Discharges under federal bankruptcy law.
3.   Discharges when the debtor is insolvent.
4.   A solvent farmer whose farm debt is discharged.
5.   Discharge of real estate debt on qualified real property used in a trade or business.
6.   A seller's cancellation of the buyer's indebtedness.
7.   A shareholder's cancellation of the corporation's indebtedness.
8.   Forgiveness of loans to students.

TEST FOR SELF-EVALUATION -- CHAPTER 4

True or False

Indicate which of the following statements are true or false by circling the correct answer.

T   F   1.   It is possible that a beneficiary may exclude more than $5,000 of a death benefit received from a decedent's former employer.

T   F   2.   Life insurance proceeds are always excluded from income.

T   F   3.   If a taxpayer has received various types of income during the year from foreign sources, the taxpayer may either include all of that foreign income in the regular tax computation and then take a foreign tax credit, or the taxpayer may exclude all of such income, subject to an overall limitation.

T   F   4.   A dividend received by a policyholder from a mutual insurance company is not taxable income.

T   F   5.   On the receipt of a simple stock dividend, the taxpayer generally does not recognize income.

T   F   6.   There are currently no interest income exclusion provisions in the law applicable to individuals.

T   F   7.   Interest received on certain state and local government obligations is excluded from federal income taxation.

T   F   8.   A voluntary transfer of property to another where adequate consideration is not exchanged is included in the recipient's gross income if the transfer is made out of affection, respect, admiration, charity, or like impulses.

T   F   9.   Payments received as compensation for services (e.g., for teaching) in certain educational degree programs may be excluded from income if all students are required to engage in the activity.

T   F   10.   The value of a parking space provided by an employer must be included in the income of an employee.

T   F   11.   In order to qualify for exclusion from income, a qualified employee discount for the receipt of services may not exceed 15% of the customer price.

T   F   12.   Alfred is an employee of his employer's car rental business. His employer also operates a regional bus company. As an employee, Alfred may exclude the value of a free bus trip and the use of a rental car received from the company's "vacation plan" fringe benefit package which is available to all employees.

T   F   13.   One of the requirements that must be met for meals and lodging to be excluded from a recipient's income is that they must be provided for the convenience of the employee.

T   F   14.   Interest earned on certain Series EE U.S. government savings bonds may be excluded if the proceeds from a bond's redemption are used to pay qualified higher education expenses.

T   F   15.   A cash payment received by an employee from his or her employer in most cases can qualify for the gift exclusion.

T   F   16.   Gain realized on the sale of a bond issued by a state or municipality is not recognized.

T   F   17.   No portion of a scholarship received that is used for tuition, room, and board is included in income.

T   F   18.   Receipts from illegal sources (e.g., embezzlement) are not taxable because the government would never expect the recipient to voluntarily report the amounts.

T   F   19.   Workers' compensation benefits are not taxable.

T   F   20.   Generally, a debtor whose debt is forgiven has enjoyed the receipt of income that must be recognized for tax purposes.

Fill-in-the-Blanks

Complete the following statements with the appropriate word(s) or amounts(s).

1.   The _____ rule provides that if a taxpayer obtains a benefit from a deduction for an item in one year and later recovers a portion of the prior deduction, the recovery produces taxable income in the year received.

2.   Section 101(b) provides an exclusion of the first _____ paid by an employer to an employee's beneficiary by reason of death of the employee.

3.   The _____ portion, but not the _____ portion of amounts collected on a life insurance policy received in installments are excluded from gross income.

4.   In order for meals provided by the employer to be excluded from income of the employee, three tests must be met. These tests are (1) _____ (2) _____ (3) _____.

5.   For lodging provided by an employer to be excluded from income of the employee, the following additional test (over and above the three tests listed in the preceding question) must be met: _____.

6.   The interest earned from certain _____ and _____ obligations is excluded from federal income tax.

7.   Certain amounts of scholarships may be excluded from income by _____ candidates, but similar amounts may not be excluded by _____ candidates.

8.   The maximum amount of foreign earned income that may be excluded from gross income by a taxpayer is _____.

9.   There are _____ broad categories of nontaxable employee fringe benefits which have been specified by Congress in § 132.

10. A _____ plan provision permits a covered employee to choose one or more benefits from among several taxable or nontaxable fringe benefits that may be offered by the employer.

11. The benefit of the exclusion from Educational Savings Bonds is phased out as a taxpayer's _____ exceeds certain amounts.

12. A scholarship recipient may exclude from gross income the amount used for _____ and _____.

13. Fred gave a corporate bond, valued at $10,000, to Debbie at the beginning of the year. If $800 of interest was generated by the bond during the year, Debbie would have to report _____ of taxable income.

14. Emily gave a municipal bond, valued at $10,000, to David at the beginning of the year. If $800 of interest was generated by the bond during the year, David would have to report _____ of taxable income.

15. While cash dividends are taxable to the recipient, _____ dividends generally are not taxable to the recipient.

Multiple Choice

Choose the best answer for each of the following questions.

_____ 1. A widow and her two sons each received $5,000 from their husband's and father's former employer by reason of the death of their husband and father. What amount of the death benefit must be *included* in the surviving spouse's income in the year of receipt?
  a. $0.
  b. $1,667.
  c. $3,333.
  d. $5,000.
  e. $15,000.

_____ 2. Which of the following items is not normally excluded from an individual's gross income?
  a. Punitive damages.
  b. Life insurance proceeds received by reason of death.
  c. *De minimis* fringe benefits.
  d. A $5,000 employee death benefit.
  e. All of the above are excluded from taxation.

_____ 3. Emily, an undergraduate majoring in tax accounting, received a $5,000 scholarship from the accounting department at the University of Illinois during the year. The amount was spent in the following ways. How much can Emily *exclude* from gross income?

Tuition	$2,000
Room	1,000
Board	1,000
Books	500
Incidental living expenses	500

  a. $5,000.

       b. $3,500.
       c. $2,500.
       d. $2,000.
       e.   Some other amount is excluded.

4. Which of the following statements is true?
   a. The receipt of a scholarship is always taxable.
   b. A limited exclusion is available to nondegree candidates who receive a scholarship.
   c. A deduction for scholarship receipts spent for tuition by a degree candidate is available.
   d. The *de minimis* fringe benefit rule could apply on the receipt of "supper money" by an employee.
   e. None of the above is true.

5. Mr. and Mrs. Peace, who live in Dallas, Texas, received the following distributions from entities in which they held securities during this year.

Mr. Peace	General Motors cash dividends	$125
	City of Dallas bond interest income	200
Mrs. Peace	Xerox Corporation cash dividends	30
	Mexican Foods (a Mexican corporation) bond interest	100
	Continental National Bank (stock dividends paid on common stock)	20

   Mr. and Mrs. Peace file a joint return. What amount of the above income is subject to tax as ordinary income for the year after available exclusions?
   a. $75.
   b. $100.
   c. $200.
   d. $300.
   e. None of the above.

6. In the current year, Mr. Toms died. His wife was named the beneficiary of his $50,000 life insurance policy. Mr. Toms had paid $20,000 in premiums. Ms. Toms elected to collect the proceeds in ten equal installments of $7,500 each. Of the $7,500 Ms. Toms collected in this year, what is the taxable amount?
   a. $1,500.
   b. $2,500.
   c. $5,000.
   d. $7,500.
   e. None of the above.

7. In 1994, Joe had taxable income of $40,000. He is single and had total itemized deductions of $4,340, of which $1,000 was for state income taxes paid. Joe receives a refund in 1995 for all of the state income taxes that he paid in 1994. How much of this refund, if any, is Joe required to include in his income for 1995?
   a. $0.
   b. $540.
   c. $1,000.
   d. None of the above.

_____ 8.   Which of the following employee benefits is always taxable?

     a.   The value of the use of athletic facilities provided by the employer on the employer's premises.

     b.   Free lodging made available to and occupied by hotel employees in lieu of a $300 monthly salary.

     c.   "Supper money" received from the employer because of having to work a 12-hour day.

     d.   Certain employee discounts on employer's merchandise.

     e.   All of the above are taxable.

_____ 9.   If a life insurance contract has been transferred for valuable consideration to another individual who assumes ownership rights, then the proceeds by reason of death are included in income. An exception to this rule includes a transfer to which of the following?

     a.   A partner of the insured.

     b.   A corporation in which the insured is an officer.

     c.   A fellow shareholder of a corporation.

     d.   a. and b.

     e.   All of the above.

_____ 10.   Which of the following employee fringe benefits generally is not excluded from taxation?

     a.   Free parking provided by the employer.

     b.   Personal use of a company car.

     c.   Discounts on employer's merchandise.

     d.   Payment of employee's professional dues.

     e.   All of the above are excluded from taxation as a matter of policy.

_____ 11.   Sarah, a cash basis taxpayer, practices law as an employee of a firm in Virginia where she earns an annual salary of $100,000. She received the following fringe benefits from her employer this year.

Personal use of copying machine	$ 45
Free parking (provided only to highly paid employees and partners)	360
Personal letters typed	105
Membership in the U-R-Fit Athletic Club	500
Personal use of the firm's beach cottage	150

What amount related to the receipt of these fringe benefits must be _included_ in Sarah's gross income?

     a. $500.

     b. $605.

     c. $650.

     d. $695.

     e.   None of the above.

_____ 12.   Which of the following categories of fringe benefits do not qualify for exclusion?

     a.   No-additional-cost services.

     b.   _De minimis_ fringe benefits.

     c.   Qualified tuition reductions.

     d.   Certain working condition fringes.

     e.   All of the above qualify for exclusion.

_____ 13. The maximum amount of foreign earned income that currently may be excluded from a U.S. taxpayer's gross income is limited to the following amount.
     a. $70,000.
     b. $80,000.
     c. $85,000.
     d.   All foreign earned income may be excluded.
     e.   None of the above.

_____ 14. What fringe benefits (if any) will be excludible from an individual's gross income if provided by his employer on a "nondiscriminatory" basis?
     a.   No-additional-cost services.
     b.   Discounts to below cost on goods sold to the public.
     c.   Discounts on services exceeding 25% of the selling price.
     d.   None of the above.
     e.   All of the above.

_____ 15. Lisa received the following interest payments during the year.

Interest on refund of federal income tax for the prior year	$520
Interest on award for personal injuries sustained in an automobile accident last year	460
Interest on municipal bonds	900
Interest on Series H US savings bonds	650

How much should she report as gross income?
     a. $0.
     b. $980.
     c. $1,630.
     d. $2,530.
     e.   None of the above.

_____ 16. Mike sustained serious injuries in the course of his employment as a Washington, D.C. hot dog vendor. As a result of his injuries, Mike received the following payments during the current year.

Damages for personal injuries	$3,250
Worker's compensation	6,400
Reimbursement from his employer's accident and health plan for medical expenses paid by Mike and not deducted by him	2,500

Compute his gross income.
     a. $12,150.
     b. $9,650.
     c. $5,750.
     d. $0.
     e.   None of the above.

_____ 17. Which of the following is *not* excluded from a taxpayer's gross income?
     a.   Earned income from a foreign source in amounts up to $80,000.
     b.   Gifts received from one's parents.
     c.   Interest earned on bonds issued by the State of California.
     d.   A $5,000 employee death benefit.
     e.   All of the above are excluded.

_____ 18.   Carmen, the owner of a $50,000 life insurance policy, decides to cancel the
            policy. She has paid premiums of $12,000 during the years the policy has been in
            force, while the current cash surrender value received on the cancellation is
            $20,000. Carmen must recognize income of what amount?
            a. $0.
            b. $8,000.
            c. $12,000.
            d. $20,000.
            e.   None of the above.

_____ 19.   Ivan, the owner of a $50,000 life insurance policy, had planned to cancel the
            policy. However, he was killed in a tragic automobile accident prior to
            contacting his insurance agent. He had paid premiums totalling $12,000 during
            the years since the policy's acquisition. At the time of Ivan's death, the
            policy had a cash surrender value of $20,000. What amount is taxable on the
            receipt of the $50,000 proceeds?
            a. $0.
            b. $30,000.
            c. $38,000.
            d. $50,000.
            e.   None of the above.

_____ 20.   Jane received a $15,000 scholarship from Boatright College to be used for
            tuition, fees, and related expenses during the 1995-1996 academic year. She
            actually incurred qualifying expenditures as follows.

                        August-December, 1995 $6,000
                        January-May, 1996   7,000

            Compute Jane's gross income.
            a. $1,500 in 1995.
            b. $9,000 in 1995.
            c. $500 in 1996.
            d. $2,000 in 1996.
            e.   All of the above qualify for exclusion.

_____ 21.   Lane received the following compensation and benefits during the year.

                        Salary $60,000
                        Overtime bonus   12,000
                        Value of medical insurance coverage 5,000
                        Medical insurance reimbursements   3,000
                                Total $80,000

            What amount is *included* in Lane's current year tax computation?
            a. $60,000.
            b. $72,000.
            c. $77,000.
            d. $80,000.
            e.   None of the above.

_____ 22.   Rick, a plumber, was fatally injured on the job and his widow, Jane, received the
            following as a result of his death.

                        Accrued earnings $ 5,000

Death benefit paid by the employer	3,000
Group term life insurance proceeds	8,000
Total	$16,000

Compute Rick and Jane's gross income for the year of his death.
- a. $0.
- b. $3,000.
- c. $5,000.
- d. $8,000.
- e. $16,000.
- f.   None of the above.

_____ 23.   Ross, a full time student at Keller College, serves as a teaching assistant in exchange for tuition and board. Normally the tuition is $10,000 per year, while board is $3,000 per year. What must be *included* in income for tax purposes due to this arrangement?
- a. $0, because the value received is classified as a scholarship.
- b. $0, because teaching is a requirement of Ross's degree program.
- c. $3,000, because only $10,000 is classified as a scholarship.
- d. $13,000 must be included in Ross's gross income because it is compensation.
- e.   None of the above.

_____ 24.   Mitchell is employed as the general manager of a local hotel. His employer gave him the choice of two compensation arrangements:

Cash salary of $30,000 per year, *or*
Cash salary of $24,000 per year plus free lodging at the hotel valued at $5,000

If Mitchell chose the second option, what amount would be *included* in his gross income?
- a. $24,000.
- b. $29,000.
- c. $30,000.
- d.   None of the above.

_____ 25.   The provision under § 119 excludes the value of lodging from an employee's gross income if the following requirements are met.
- a.   The lodging is provided for the convenience of the employer.
- b.   The lodging is furnished by the employer.
- c.   The lodging is on the employer's business premises.
- d.   The employee is required to accept the lodging as a condition of employment.
- e.   All of the above must be present.

_____ 26.   The following are dividends generally subject to current taxation.
- a.   Cash dividends on publicly traded stock.
- b.   Stock dividends on publicly traded stock.
- c.   Dividends paid by a mutual insurance company on an unmatured life insurance policy.
- d.   Only a and b.
- e.   Only a and c.
- f.   None of the above.

Code Section Recognition

Several important sections of the Internal Revenue Code are described below. Indicate, by number, the appropriate Code section.

1. _____The general rules for the taxability of scholarships and fellowships are provided here.

2. _____This section excludes the value of meals and lodging from gross income when certain conditions are met.

3. _____Provides guidance regarding the taxation of six categories of fringe benefits.

4. _____Provides an exclusion associated with the funding of higher education with Educational Savings Bonds.

Short Answer

1. Margaret receives a $15,000 scholarship to attend State University during the 1995-96 school year. Her records reflect the following expenditures.

Tuition	$10,000
Books and fees	500
Room	2,000
Board	2,000
	$14,500

   Comment on how the scholarship proceeds are taxed.

2. Identify the six broad classes of nontaxable employee benefits.

SOLUTIONS TO CHAPTER 4 QUESTIONS

True or False

1. T   If the beneficiary can show gratuitous intent on the part of the employer, payments in excess of $5,000 may be excluded.
2. F   Normally this is the case, but exceptions do exist. For example, such proceeds may be income to an assignee to the extent that they exceed the amount paid for the policy plus subsequent premiums paid.
3. F   The special treatment for foreign income is only available for *earned* income.
4. T   Such a receipt is not considered a "dividend" for tax purposes; rather, it is considered a reduction in the premium.
5. T
6. F   Interest received on certain state and local government obligations is exempt from taxation.
7. T
8. F   Gifts are not included in the recipient's gross income.
9. F   Such a receipt is not treated as an excludible scholarship. The amounts received are considered compensation for services rendered.
10. F   Not included because it would qualify as a working condition fringe benefit.
11. F   The discount exclusion may not exceed 20% of the selling price.
12. F   Alfred may exclude the value of the rental car fringe benefit received but may not exclude the value of the free bus trip because of the "line of business" limitation.
13. F   It must be provided for the convenience of the employer to be excluded, not the employee.
14. T
15. F
16. F   The exclusion available pertains to interest income generated by such obligations.
17. F   The portion of the scholarship not used for tuition and related expenses is included in income.
18. F   Such amounts are taxable.
19. T
20. T

Fill-in-the-Blanks

1. tax benefit
2. $5,000
3. principal, interest
4. The meals must be (1) furnished by the employer, (2) furnished on the employer's business premises, and (3) furnished for the convenience of the employer.
5. The employee is required to accept the lodging as a condition of employment.
6. state, municipal
7. degree, nondegree
8. $70,000
9. six
10. cafeteria
11. modified adjusted gross income
12. tuition, related expenses
13. $800
14. $0

15. stock

Multiple Choice

1. c $3,333 = $5,000 - [\dfrac{\$5,000}{\$15,000} \times \$5,000]$

   See Example 5 in the text.

2. a

3. c The cost of tuition ($2,000) and books ($500) may be excluded as a scholarship. See Example 8 in the text.

4. d

5. e $255 = $125 + $30 + $100

6. b $2,500 is the interest element (taxable) and $5,000 is the principal element (nontaxable).

7. b Income to the extent the deduction produced a tax benefit ($4,340 - $3,800 = $540). The standard deduction in 1994 for single individuals was $3,800. See Example 38 in the text.

8. b Because acceptance of the lodging is not a condition of employment, it is taxable.

9. d

10. b

11. c

Athletic club membership	$500
Use of firm's beach cottage	150
Total	$650

12. e

13. a

14. a

15. c $1,630 = $520 + $460 + $650

16. d

17. a The exclusion is available on foreign earned income of up to $70,000.

18. b $8,000 = $20,000 - $12,000. See discussion in the text preceding Example 3.

19. a See Example 1 in the text.

20. d See Example 9 in the text.

21. b Only the salary and the overtime bonus are included in the tax computation. The other items are excluded from taxation.

22. c See Example 5 in the text.

23. d See Example 6 in the text.

24. b See Example 19 in the text.

25. e

26. a

Code Section Recognition

1. 117

2. 119

3. 132

4. 135

Short Answer

1. Of the $15,000 received, the $10,500 spent on tuition, books, and fees is excluded from taxation. The remaining $4,500 ($15,000 - $10,500) is subject to taxation.

2.   No-additional-cost services.
Qualified employee discounts.
Working condition fringes.
De minimis fringes.
Qualified transportation fringe.
Qualified moving expense reimbursement.

CHAPTER 5
DEDUCTIONS AND LOSSES: IN GENERAL

CHAPTER HIGHLIGHTS

The courts have established the doctrine that unless an expenditure is provided by the Code as being deductible, then it is *not* deductible. Generally, however, deductions are allowable for items of expense incurred in a trade or business or in the production of income as well as for some items of a personal nature. These expenditures are deductible in determining taxable income, either as deductions in arriving at adjusted gross income or as deductions subtracted from adjusted gross income. Business and nonbusiness losses are also deductible, but with some limitations. Moreover, a number of disallowance possibilities exist in situations where otherwise deductible items are not deductible in part or in full. This chapter includes discussion of these concepts and issues.

I.   Classification of Deductible Expenses
    A.   Scheme of the Treatment of Deductions and Losses
        1.   Expenditures and losses are *not* deductible unless a provision in the law provides for such deduction.
        2.   Deductible expenses may be deducted *for* adjusted gross income (AGI) (i.e., deductions subtracted from gross income in calculating adjusted gross income) or *from* AGI.
        3.   Deductions *for* AGI may be claimed whether or not the taxpayer itemizes. However, deductions *from* AGI produce a tax benefit only if they exceed the taxpayer's standard deduction. Thus, deductions *for* AGI may be more valuable to the taxpayer than deductions *from* AGI.
        4.   AGI is an important amount because it is used as a factor in the limitation of certain itemized deductions (e.g., medical expenses, charitable contributions).
    B.   Deductions *for* Adjusted Gross Income -- Section 62 specifies those expenses which are deductible *for* adjusted gross income. These items include (among others) the following.
        1.   Trade or business deductions.
        2.   Certain reimbursed employee business expenses.
        3.   Rent and royalty expenses.
        4.   Alimony payments.
        5.   Keogh and IRA deductions.

6.   Losses, within limits, on the sale or exchange of property other than personal use property.

7.   Moving expenses.

C.   Itemized Deductions -- The following lists some of the more commonly encountered expenses deductible *from* adjusted gross income.

    1.   Expenses allowed by § 212 that are paid or incurred.

        a.   For the production or collection of income (other than rent or royalty income).

        b.   For the management, conservation, or maintenance of property held for the production of income (other than rent or royalty income).

        c.   In connection with the determination, collection, or refund of any tax.

    2.   Medical expenses.

    3.   Certain state and local taxes.

    4.   Interest incurred on a personal residence.

    5.   Charitable contributions.

    6.   Personal casualty losses.

D.   Trade or Business Expenses and Production of Income Expenses

    1.   Section 162(a) permits a deduction for all *ordinary and necessary* expenses paid or incurred in carrying on a trade or business. Unfortunately, a clear and unambiguous definition of *trade or business* does not exist. Such expenses are deductible *for* AGI.

    2.   Certain types of expenses, such as charitable contributions, bribes, and fines and penalties, are not classified as trade or business expenses.

    3.   An expense must be both *ordinary* and *necessary* in order to be deductible under § 162. However, the words ordinary and necessary are not defined in the Code; but rather, they have been defined over time by the courts.

    4.   An expense is considered to be *necessary* if a prudent businessperson would incur the same expense and if the expense is expected to be appropriate and helpful in the taxpayer's business.

    5.   An expense is *ordinary* if it is normal, usual, or customary in the taxpayer's business. The amount cannot be capital in nature and it need not be a recurring expenditure.

    6.   Reasonableness Requirement -- Salaries and other compensation for personal services must be of a *reasonable* amount in order to be deducted. Further, the courts have held that for other business expenses to be ordinary and necessary, they must also be reasonable in amount. What constitutes reasonable is a *question of fact*.

E.   Business and Nonbusiness Losses

    1.   Section 165 allows a deduction for the following losses.

        a.   Losses incurred in a trade or business.

        b.   Losses incurred in any transaction entered into for profit.

        c.   Personal casualty losses.

    2.   Personal casualty losses are reduced by $100 *per casualty* and the *aggregate of all casualty losses* is reduced by 10 percent of the taxpayer's adjusted gross income.

    3.   These losses may be deducted either *for* or *from* adjusted gross income, depending on the nature of the loss.

II. Deductions and Losses -- Timing of Expense Recognition
   A. Importance of Taxpayer's Method of Accounting -- The *method of accounting* used by a taxpayer controls as to when an item is includible in income and deductible from income in the determination of taxable income. The method selected must clearly reflect the taxpayer's income and must be applied consistently.
   B. Cash Method Requirements
      1. Expenses are deductible only when an amount is actually or constructively paid with cash or other property. However, payment does not assure a current deduction.
      2. A deduction can be generated by paying with borrowed funds, but issuing a note or promising to pay will not give rise to a deduction.
      3. If an expenditure creates an asset that has a life which extends substantially beyond the close of the tax year, the amount must be capitalized.
      4. Limitations on Who Can Use the Cash Method -- There are several exceptions as to those taxpayers who are allowed to use the cash method (see Chapter 15).
   C. Accrual Method Requirements
      1. To deduct an expense under the accrual method, the *all events test* and the *economic performance test* must be met. A deduction cannot be claimed until (1) all the events have occurred to create the taxpayer's liability and (2) the amount of the liability can be determined with reasonable accuracy.

KEY TERMS
- Deduction For, From AGI
- Trade or Business Expense (§162)
- Income Production Expense (§212)
- Hobby Loss
- Vacation Home

Once these requirements are satisfied, the deduction is permitted only if economic performance has occurred. The economic performance test is met when the service, property, or use of property giving rise to the liability is actually performed for, provided to, or used by the taxpayer.
      2. Exceptions to the economic performance test apply in the case of certain recurring items in some situations.
      3. Reserves for estimated expenses that may be claimed for financial accounting purposes are *not* deductible for tax purposes because the economic performance test cannot be satisfied.

III. Disallowance Possibilities
   A. Public Policy Limitation
      1. A payment that is in *violation of public policy* is not considered a necessary expense and therefore is not deductible.
      2. Several nondeductible expenses fall under this limitation.
         a. Payments for illegal bribes and kickbacks.
         b. Fines and penalties paid to a government for violation of a law.
         c. Two-thirds of the treble damage payments made to claimants

resulting from violation of the antitrust law.

3.   Legal expenses are deductible if they are incurred in connection with trade or business activity or relate to property held for the production of income or relate to the determination of a tax liability. However, legal fees incurred for personal reasons are not deductible.

4.   The normal expenses of operating an illegal business, other than those expenses that are contrary to public policy, are deductible. An exception to this rule applies to ordinary and necessary business expenses incurred with regard to illegal trafficking in drugs. Such expenses are not deductible.

B.   Political Contributions and Lobbying Activities

1.   Generally, a business deduction is not allowed for direct or indirect payments made for political purposes.

2.   Taxpayers may not deduct expenses associated with political campaigns or attempts to influence voters or the public. In addition, any lobbying expenses incurred in attempting to influence state or federal legislation or the actions of high ranking government officials is not deductible. The disallowance also applies to a pro rata portion of the membership dues of trade associations and other groups used for lobbying activities.

3.   The disallowance does not apply to activities devoted solely to monitoring legislation or to lobbying expenses at the local government level.

C.   Excessive Executive Compensation -- The compensation deduction allowable to a publicly held corporation may be limited to $1 million for each covered executive. The provision is applicable to the compensation paid to the chief executive officer and the four other most highly compensated officers. Exceptions to this limitation exist and include (among others) certain performance-based compensation.

D.   Investigation of a Business

1.   If a taxpayer investigating a business is already in a business similar to or the same as the business being investigated, the relevant expenses incurred are deductible.

2.   Investigation expenses incurred are not deductible if the taxpayer who is not in the same or similar business does not acquire the new business. If such new business is acquired, the expenses must be capitalized and then they may be amortized subsequently over a period of 60 months or more.

E.   Hobby Losses

1.   If an individual can show that a business or investment activity (that may have personal pleasure attributes) has been conducted with the purpose of earning a profit, then any losses from the activity are deductible in full.

2.   The *hobby loss* rules under § 183 apply if the activity is considered not to be engaged in for profit.

3.   A rebuttable presumption in the Code provides that if an activity shows a profit in *at least three of any five consecutive years* (two years out of seven for activities involving horses), then the activity is considered to be profit-seeking and the hobby loss rules do *not* apply.

4.   If an activity is deemed to be a hobby, expenses are deductible only to the extent of the income from the hobby. However, some expenses may be

deducted in full as allowed by other sections of the Code (e.g., property taxes). These expenses must be considered before other types of expenses in computing the overall hobby loss limitation. Hobby deductions are deductible *from* AGI as itemized deductions, but only to the extent that they exceed two percent of AGI.

F.   Rental of Vacation Homes

    1.   Depending on the relative amount of time a vacation residence is used for personal and rental purposes, the tax treatment will vary. Three possible classifications exist.

        a.   When the structure is devoted primarily to *personal use*.

        b.   When the home is used primarily for *rental purposes.*

        c.   When the residence is characterized as *personal/rental property*.

    2.   If the residence is rented for less than 15 days in a year, the property is treated as a personal residence. Rental income would be excluded, and mortgage interest and real estate taxes incurred would be itemized deductions. No other expenses would be deductible.

    3.   If the residence is not used for more than 14 days (or more than 10 percent of the total days rented) for personal use, the residence is treated as a rental property. Expenses must be allocated between personal and rental days if there are any personal days. Deductible rental losses may result.

    4.   If the residence is rented for 15 or more days and is used for personal purposes for the greater of more than 14 days or more than 10 percent of the rental days, it is treated as personal/rental property. In such case, the rental expenses are allowed only to the extent of rental income.

One of the very few instances when the law considers income to be nontaxable is where property is rented for less than 15 days. Residents of Augusta, Georgia, for example, have an annual opportunity to rent their houses for a short period during the Masters Golf Tournament and earn income that is not taxable.

G.   Expenditures Incurred for Taxpayer's Benefit or Taxpayer's Obligation -- For an expense to be deductible, it must be incurred for the taxpayer's benefit or arise from the taxpayer's obligation.

H.   Disallowance of Personal Expenditures

    1.   Unless a deduction is provided in the law, no deduction is allowed for personal, living, or family expenses.

    2.   Examples of deductible personal expenses include the following.

        a.   Medical expenses (§ 213).

        b.   Charitable contributions (§ 170).

        c.   Moving expenses (§ 217).

    3.   Legal fees incurred in connection with a divorce are deductible only if they relate solely to tax advice. For example, fees attributable to

the determination of dependency exemptions, or the determination of the tax consequences of a property settlement are deductible.

I. Disallowance of Deductions for Capital Expenditures

1. Amounts paid for new buildings or for permanent improvements which tend to add value or prolong the life of a property or adapt the property to a new or different use, must be *capitalized* rather than being currently deducted.

2. When an item is capitalized rather than expensed, a deduction, is at best, deferred and, at worst, lost forever. However, in some situations, a taxpayer may prefer to capitalize an item (such as when the deduction would create an unusable net operating loss). However, in some situations, a taxpayer may elect to expense an item rather than capitalize it.

J. Transactions between Related Parties

1. Restrictions are placed on the recognition of gains and losses resulting from transactions occurring between *related parties* because of the myriad opportunities to create tax savings from transactions that have no economic substance.

2. Section 267 *disallows* the recognition of losses when property is sold or exchanged between related parties. However, a previously unrecognized loss may *reduce* any realized gain on the subsequent sale of the property to an unrelated person.

3. Section 267 *defers* a deduction by an *accrual basis taxpayer* (when the party to receive a payment is related and is on the *cash basis*) until the period when the amount is included in the income of the recipient.

4. Related parties include the following.

   a. Brothers, sisters (including half-blood), spouse, ancestors, and lineal descendants of the taxpayer.

   b. A corporation owned *more than* 50 percent by the taxpayer.

   c. Two corporations that are members of a controlled group.

5. Constructive ownership rules are applied in order to determine whether taxpayers are related. These rules provide that for loss and expense deduction disallowance purposes, stock owned by certain relatives or related entities is *deemed* to be owned by the taxpayer.

K. Substantiation Requirements

1. Appropriate documentation and substantiation of events and transactions are usually advisable, and generally required by law.

2. The law provides that in order for travel, entertainment, or business gift expenditures to be deductible, the following information must be kept.

   a. The amount of the expense.

   b. The time and place of the travel or entertainment (or date of gift).

   c. The business purpose of such expense.

   d. The business relationship of the taxpayer to the person entertained (or receiving the gift).

Credit card issuers have been responsive to changes in the tax law, in that they provide a form on each charge slip on which the person doing the entertaining can enter all of the Code-required information to substantiate the deduction. Whether taxpayers are conscientious about filling in this required information may be another story.

L.   Expenses and Interest Relating to Tax-Exempt Income
      1.   Generally, expenses incurred for purposes of producing tax-exempt income are *not* deductible.
      2.   It is often very difficult to show a direct relationship between borrowings and investments in tax-exempt securities. Judicial interpretation generally has tried to show "reasonableness" in the disallowance of expenses under this Code section.

TEST FOR SELF-EVALUATION -- CHAPTER 5

True or False

Indicate which of the following statements are true or false by circling the correct answer.

T   F   1.   The courts have established a doctrine which provides that an expenditure is not deductible unless a Code section provides for its deduction.

T   F   2.   Section 212 allows a deduction for "all ordinary and necessary expenses paid or incurred during the taxable year in carrying on any trade or business."

T   F   3.   Section 162 deductions are deductions *for* adjusted gross income and can be taken whether or not an individual taxpayer itemizes.

T   F   4.   To obtain a deduction under § 212, it is necessary for the property to which the deduction relates to be producing income currently.

T   F   5.   For a salary expense to be deductible, it must be ordinary and necessary and also, it must be reasonable in amount.

T   F   6.   Legal fees pursuant to a criminal defense are deductible if the taxpayer is declared not guilty.

T   F   7.   Any deductible loss relating to an asset is limited to the taxpayer's cost basis of the asset involved.

T   F   8.   Section 267 operates to disallow or defer losses and deductions between related parties.

T   F   9.   The amount of deductible travel and entertainment expenses may be estimated if adequate records have not been maintained.

T   F   10.   Interest expense incurred is always deductible by an individual taxpayer.

T   F   11.   An accrual basis taxpayer may claim a deduction for an amount owed to a related cash basis taxpayer if the amount is paid within two and a half months of the accrual taxpayer's year-end.

T   F   12.   Because a rental activity is not considered to be a trade or business, rental expenses are not deductible *for* adjusted gross income.

T   F   13.   The amount of deductions taken *for* adjusted gross income can never have an impact on the amount of itemized deductions.

T   F   14.   Alimony expenditures are deductible *for* adjusted gross income.

T   F   15.   Because they are related to a taxpayer's trade or business, unreimbursed employee expenses are deductible *for* adjusted gross income.

T   F   16.   As a general rule, cash basis taxpayers cannot claim an immediate deduction for capital expenditures.

T   F   17.   Legal and accounting expenses incurred in connection with rental property are itemized deductions.

T   F   18.   If Father pays Son's mortgage interest obligation, Father may then claim a deduction on his return for the amount paid.

T   F   19.   Even if Father pays Son's mortgage interest obligation, Son may claim a deduction on his tax return for the amount paid by Father because the payment pertains to Son's obligation.

T   F   20.   Unrealized losses can in certain situations be deducted.

Fill-in-the-Blanks

Complete the following statements with the appropriate word(s) or amount(s).

1.   For individual taxpayers, deductions are claimed either _____ adjusted gross income or _____ adjusted gross income.

2.   Corporations are not subject to the separate classification scheme of classifying deductions as *for* or *from* because the term _____ does not appear in the corporate tax formula.

3.   A qualifying expenditure will be deductible *from* adjusted gross income as an itemized deduction if the total amount of itemized deductions exceeds the _____.

4.   The _____ rules apply only if an activity which has personal and profit-seeking attributes is not engaged in for profit.

5.   Section 183 provides that hobby expenses are deductible only to the extent of _____.

6.   The Code provides a rebuttable presumption that an activity (that does not involve horses) is profit-seeking if it shows a profit in at least _____ of any _____ consecutive years ending with the taxable year in question.

7.   One of the basic concepts in the tax law is that a deduction can be taken only when a loss has actually been _____.

8.   All income received from the rental of a residence is excluded and all rental expense incurred is disallowed if a residence is rented for less than _____ days.

9.   The period in which an accrual basis taxpayer can deduct an expense is determined by

applying the _____ test.

10. Generally, in order for an expense to be deductible, it must be incurred for the taxpayer's _____ or arise from the taxpayer's _____.

11. Documentary evidence, such as itemized receipts, is required to support all expenditures for lodging while traveling away from home and for any other expenditure of _____ or more.

12. Trade or business expenses are deductible only if they possess the following three attributes. Such expenses should be _____, _____, and _____.

13. Whether and to what an extent an expenditure is deductible depends on a notion referred to as _____.

14. All itemized deductions *from* adjusted gross income are reported on _____ of Form 1040.

15. A vacation home used 10 days for personal purposes and 4 months for rental purposes is treated as _____ property.

Multiple Choice

Choose the best answer for each of the following questions.

_____ 1. Which of the following is not a deduction *for* adjusted gross income?
     a. Alimony payments.
     b. Ordinary and necessary business expenses.
     c. Reimbursed travel expenses incurred in the capacity of an employee.
     d. Charitable contributions made by a sole proprietor.
     e. All of the above are deductions *for* adjusted gross income.

_____ 2. Which of the following expenditures is not deductible?
     a. Expenses incurred for the production or collection of income.
     b. Expenses incurred for the management, conservation, or maintenance of property held for the production of income.
     c. Expenses related to the management, conservation, or maintenance of a personal residence.
     d. Expenses incurred in connection with the determination, collection, or refund of any tax.
     e. All of the above are deductible.

_____ 3. Which of the following expenses is not deductible *from* adjusted gross income?
     a. Alimony payment
     b. Safe deposit box rental.
     c. Investment counseling fee.
     d. Interest on home mortgage.
     e. All of the above are deductible *from* adjusted gross income.

_____ 4. In connection with the hobby loss rules, indicate which of the following is incorrect.

    a.   If a taxpayer can show that an activity has been conducted with the intent to earn a profit, losses from the activity are fully deductible.

    b.   Section 183 provides that hobby expenses are deductible only to the extent of hobby income.

    c.   The Code provides a rebuttable presumption that an activity is profit-seeking if it shows a profit in two of any five consecutive years.

    d.   If an activity is deemed to be a hobby, some expenses incurred may be deductible by virtue of other sections in the Code.

    e.   All of the above are true.

_____ 5.   Irene, not a dealer in securities, sold common stock (basis of $15,000) to her son Victor for $10,000. What is Irene's deductible loss from this transaction?

    a. $0.

    b. $5,000.

    c. $10,000.

    d. $15,000.

    e.   Some other amount.

_____ 6.   Refer to the previous problem. Victor sells the stock subsequently for $12,000 to an unrelated third party. In the year of sale, what amount of gain or loss should Victor recognize for tax purposes?

    a. $2,000 gain.

    b. $3,000 loss.

    c.   No gain or loss.

    d.   None of the above.

_____ 7.   Select the correct statement.

    a.   Reserves for estimated expenses that are frequently employed for financial accounting purposes are also deductible for tax purposes.

    b.   Legal expenses paid to effect a divorce generally are not deductible because they are personal expenditures.

    c.   A father who pays his daughter's home mortgage payments would be able to deduct the related interest expense on his federal income tax return.

    d.   Expenses incurred in connection with municipal bond interest income are deductible within certain limitations.

    e.   None of the above is correct.

_____ 8.   On January 1, Rashad sold stock with a cost of $12,000 to his sister Cora for $10,000, its fair market value. On July 1, Cora sold the same stock to Miguel for $12,500 in an arms-length transaction. What is the result of these transactions?

    a.   Neither Rashad nor Cora has a recognized gain or loss.

    b.   Rashad has a $2,000 recognized loss.

    c.   Cora has a $500 recognized gain.

    d.   Cora has a $2,500 recognized gain.

    e.   None of the above.

_____ 9.   Davidson leases his vacation home for three months and uses it for one month during his vacation. Gross rental income from the property was $12,000.

Davidson incurred the following expenses during the year.

Taxes and interest	$ 8,800
Utilities	1,000
Depreciation	2,000
Maintenance	500
Total	$12,300

Compute the allowable deduction available to offset rental income (i.e., the amount that is not otherwise deductible) assuming that Davidson believes that the IRS's approach to allocating expenses between rental and personal days is appropriate.
a. $0.
b. $9,225.
c. $12,000
d. $12,300.
e.   None of the above.

10. Refer to the preceding problem. If Davidson does not use the property any of the time for personal purposes, what is the allowable deduction that may be claimed (prior to considering possible implications of the passive activity rules)?
a. $0.
b. $9,225.
c. $12,000.
d. $12,300.
e.   None of the above.

11. Which of the following are *not* "related parties" under § 267?
a.   Taxpayer and a great, great grandparent.
b.   Taxpayer and an uncle.
c.   Taxpayer and a child.
d.   Taxpayer and a corporation in which more than 50% of the stock of the corporation is held by the taxpayer.
e.   All of the above are "related parties."

12. Which of the following is deductible when paid by a cash-basis taxpayer who itemizes deductions?
a.   Charitable contributions.
b.   Fines paid by a sole proprietor.
c.   Prepaid interest expense.
d.   Medical expenses paid for a physical examination to be performed next year.
e.   Acquisition of a building by a sole proprietor.

13. Choose the *correct* statement.
a.   A cash basis taxpayer always receives equal tax benefit for an amount paid whether it be deductible *for* or *from* adjusted gross income.
b.   An expense related to the maintenance of a personal residence is deductible as an itemized deduction.
c.   The courts have held that an expense is "necessary" for business

purposes if a prudent businessperson would incur the same expense.

d.   Business prepaid rent is includible in the gross income of the landlord and deductible by the tenant as a deduction *for* adjusted gross income in the year paid.

e.   None of the above.

_____ 14.   Mr. Amor, a self-employed massage parlor owner, incurred the following expenses during the year.

Rent expense	$ 1,000
Wages	20,000
Bribes to police	5,000
Expenses incurred to influence the public on a massage parlor bill in the state legislature	1,000
Interest on loan used to purchase municipal bonds	1,000

Determine the amount of deductions *for* adjusted gross income that Mr. Amor can take currently.

a. $22,000.
b. $23,000.
c. $26,000.
d. $27,000.
e.   None of the above.

_____ 15.   Based on advice from his financial analyst, Tracy made the following long-term investments at par:

$3,000 general obligation bonds of Fairfax County (wholly tax-exempt)
$9,000 debentures of McIntire Corporation (16% effective yield)

Tracy did not have the cash on-hand to finance these purchases so she obtained a $12,000 loan from the Jefferson bank. She paid the following amounts as interest expense during the year.

Home mortgage	$4,500
Jefferson Bank	1,800
	$6,300

What amount can Tracy deduct currently as interest expense?

a. $0.
b. $4,500.
c. $5,850.
d. $6,300.
e.   Some other amount.

_____ 16.   Rich is the president of Masters Corporation and has owned 75 percent of its outstanding stock since its inception. During the year, Rich purchased from the corporation depreciable property with an adjusted tax basis of $60,000 for $45,000, its fair market value. Masters placed this property in service five

years ago. What is the available loss that Masters Corporation can claim for the current year?
a. $11,250 ordinary loss.
b. $15,000 capital loss.
c. $15,000 ordinary loss.
d. $0 loss.
e.   Some other amount.

____ 17.   After 25 years of marriage, Victor and Paula divorced during the year. The settlement included the following payments to Paula from Victor, all of which would cease upon her death or remarriage.

Lump-sum property distribution $60,000
Annual alimony payments   5,000

Victor does not itemize his deductions. How much can he deduct as alimony in the current year?
a. $0.
b. $5,000.
c. $60,000.
d. $65,000.
e.   Some other amount.

____ 18.   Which of the following may be considered a trade or business expense?
a.   Travel expenses incurred by a self-employed CPA.
b.   Charitable contributions or gifts.
c.   Illegal bribes and kickbacks.
d.   Fines and penalties.
e.   All of the above.

____ 19.   An exception to the economic performance requirement for accrual basis taxpayers provides that certain recurring items may be deducted if which of the following conditions are met?
a.   Such items are treated consistently.
b.   Either they are not material in amount or such accrual results in better matching of income and expenses.
c.   The all-events test is met.
d.   Economic performance occurs within a reasonable period but not more than 8 and one-half months after year-end.
e.   All of the above are conditions that must be met.

____ 20.   Choose the *correct* statement.
a.   Personal legal expenses may be deductible if they relate to the determination of a tax liability.
b.   For legal expenses to be deductible *for* adjusted gross income, the taxpayer must be able to show that the origin and character of a related claim pertaining to the legal services rendered are directly related to a trade or business or an income-producing activity.
c.   Legal expenses may be deductible either *for* or *from* adjusted gross income, depending on the circumstances.
d.   Legal expenses that are deductible *from* adjusted gross income only

produce a tax benefit to the extent they exceed 2 percent of adjusted gross income.

 e. Each of the above is correct.

_____ 21. Bonnie incurs $15,000 of travel and other expenses during the investigation of a business opportunity in Bermuda. Specifically, she has heard that the hotel business in that part of the world normally proves to be a wonderful investment. Whether and how the $15,000 expenditure produces a tax benefit is *not* dependent on the following.

 a. The current business of the owner.
 b. The length of time the owner has been in the current business.
 c. The extent to which the investigation has proceeded.
 d. Whether or not the acquisition actually takes place.
 e. Each of the above is a relevant factor.

_____ 22. Which of the following expenditures is deductible *from* adjusted gross income (i.e., an itemized deduction), but the size of the deduction is dependent on the amount of the taxpayer's adjusted gross income?

 a. Mortgage interest expense.
 b. Moving expense.
 c. Casualty loss.
 d. State and local income taxes.
 e. None of the above.

_____ 23. Which of the following is deductible?

 a. Commuting expenses.
 b. Unrealized losses.
 c. Unreimbursed employee business expenses.
 d. Interest expense incurred to purchase a City of Richmond bond.
 e. None of the above is deductible.

_____ 24. Pat, single, had gross income during the year of $22,000 and incurred the following expenses.

IRA contribution	$2,000
Commuting expense	1,000
Mortgage interest expense	2,500
Loss realized on XYZ stock	2,000
Legal fees related to his divorce	500
Total	$8,000

What is Pat's adjusted gross income?

 a. $16,000.
 b. $18,000.
 c. $20,000.
 d. $22,000.
 e. Some other amount.

_____ 25. Bubba owns and operates a very successful automotive service station. Every weekend and during vacations from school, his son Junior (age 12) works full time, earning $35 per hour. During the years, Junior has become very knowledgeable about this type of business. However, on other occasions when Junior cannot work and heavy traffic is anticipated, Bubba hires high school students at $4 per hour. With respect to Junior's wages, what amount is deductible by Bubba's business?

a. $0.
b. $4 per hour.
c. $35 per hour.
d.   None of the above.

Code Section Recognition

Several important sections of the Internal Revenue Code are described below. Indicate, by number, the appropriate Code section.

1. _____Allows a deduction for "all ordinary and necessary" business expenses.

2. _____Provides a deduction for losses incurred in a trade or business, losses incurred in any transaction entered into for a profit, and casualty losses.

3. _____Deductions are allowed for expenses involved in the production or collection of income; for expenses incurred in the management, conservation, or maintenance of property held for the production of income; and for expenses in connection with the determination, collection, or refund of any tax.

4. _____Determines which expenditures are deductible *for* AGI.

5. _____Determines the treatment of expenses incurred in the conduct of an activity not engaged in for profit (i.e., the "hobby loss" rules).

6. _____Disallows losses arising from transactions between related parties.

Short Answer

1.   Indicate whether the following expenses are deductible *for* or *from* AGI.

Expense Item	Deductible *for* AGI	Deductible *from* AGI
Medical expenses		
Rent expenses		
Unreimbursed moving expenses		
Charitable contributions		
Trade or business expenses		

2.   David and Eleanor own a mountain cabin where they live for two months in the summer. However, each fall, their cabin is rented for 2 weeks to Eleanor's mother for $2,000 (an arms-length rental). The vacation home is vacant for the rest of the year. In addition, real property taxes of $600 and utility payments of $500 are incurred during the year. How are these receipts and expenditures treated for tax purpose?

SOLUTIONS TO CHAPTER 5 QUESTIONS

True or False

1.   T
2.   F   Section 162 allows deductions of this nature.
3.   T
4.   F   The property needs only to be *held* for the production of income.
5.   T   In addition, executive compensation is limited in certain situations.
6.   F   They are deductible only if the crime is associated with the taxpayer's trade or business activity.
7.   T
8.   T
9.   F   The law provides that a deduction must be properly substantiated.
10. F   Section 265 disallows a deduction for an expense incurred for the production of tax-exempt income. Further, "consumer interest" deductions are prohibited.
11. F   Such amounts cannot be deducted by the accrual basis taxpayer until payments are made.
12. F   The law specifically provides that rental expenses are deductible *for* AGI.
13. F   For example, as deductions reduce AGI, itemized deductions such as medical expenses and personal casualty and theft losses which are modified by a percentage of AGI, may become deductible to a greater extent.
14. T
15. F   These are always deductible *from* AGI.
16. T
17. F   Expenses related to rental property are deductible *for* AGI.
18. F   Because Father is not obligated to make the payment, he may not claim the deduction.
19. F   In order for Son to qualify to claim a deduction, he must be the one who makes the payment.
20. F   Losses can never be deducted until they are realized.

Fill-in-the-Blanks

1.   for, from
2.   adjusted gross income
3.   standard deduction
4.   hobby loss
5.   hobby income
6.   three, five
7.   realized
8.   15
9.   economic performance
10. benefit, obligation
11. $25
12. ordinary, necessary, reasonable
13. legislative grace
14. Schedule A
15. rental

Multiple Choice

1.	d	These expenses would be deductible as itemized deductions *from* adjusted gross income. See Concept Summary 5-2 in the text.
2.	c	
3.	a	An alimony payment is deductible *for* AGI. See Concept Summary 5-2 in the text.
4.	c	Except for horses, a profit must be shown in three out of five years.
5.	a	Because Irene and Victor are related, the loss realized by Irene on the sale is not deductible. See Example 35 in the text.
6.	c	In this situation, gain is not recognized because the realized gain of $2,000 is reduced by an amount up to the previously disallowed loss ($5,000). See Example 35 in the text.
7.	b	
8.	c	$500 = [($12,500 - $10,000) - $2,000 (previously disallowed loss)] See Example 35 in the text.
9.	b	$9,225 = $12,300 X .75 See Example 29 in the text.
10.	d	Because the property is rental property, a loss may result. See Example 27 in the text.
11.	b	
12.	a	
13.	c	
14.	e	$21,000 (Rent expense and wages)
15.	c	$5,850 = $4,500 + [($9,000/$12,000) X $1,800] The deduction is not limited by the investment interest restrictions (see Chapter 10) assuming $1,440 (i.e., 16% yield) has been received on the McIntire Corporation debentures during the year. Interest expense related to the Fairfax County bond is not deductible.
16.	d	No loss is deductible because Rich and Masters are related parties. See Example 35 in the text.
17.	b	Only the alimony payment is deductible *for* adjusted gross income.
18.	a	
19.	e	
20.	e	
21.	b	
22.	c	See Concept Summary 5-2.
23.	c	See Concept Summary 5-2.

24.   b

Gross income	$22,000
Less: IRA contribution	2,000
Loss on XYZ stock	2,000
Adjusted gross income	$18,000

25.   b   The reasonableness requirement would apply which would undoubtedly prohibit Bubba from deducting Junior's salary at the $35 per hour rate.

Code Section Recognition

1.	162
2.	165
3.	212
4.	62
5.	183
6.	267

Short Answer

1.

Expense Item	Deductible *for* AGI	Deductible *from* AGI
Medical expenses		X
Rent expenses	X	
Unreimbursed moving expenses	X	
Charitable contributions		X
Trade or business expenses	X	

2. Because the property is not rented for at least fifteen days, the $2,000 of income is excluded from taxation, the real property tax is an itemized deduction, and the utility payments are nondeductible personal expenses.

CHAPTER 6
DEDUCTIONS AND LOSSES: CERTAIN BUSINESS EXPENSES AND LOSSES

CHAPTER HIGHLIGHTS

T he discussion relating to certain business expenses and losses is continued in this chapter. Specifically, bad debts, worthless securities, § 1244 stock, casualty and theft losses, research and experimental expenditures, and net operating losses are discussed. As the discussion suggests, while §§ 162 and 165 provide for the deductibility of business expenses and losses in general, additional guidance has been developed in defining the procedural details and limitations that apply to the expenses and losses covered in this chapter.

I. Bad Debts
   A. A bad debt deduction is allowed in the year an account receivable, which was previously included in income, becomes *worthless*. No such deduction is allowed if the taxpayer uses the *cash basis* of accounting.
   B. Specific Charge-Off Method -- Most taxpayers are required to use the *specific charge-off* method. Under the specific charge-off method, a deduction is available when a specific *business debt* becomes either *partially* or *totally worthless*. Further, this method is available when a specific *nonbusiness debt* becomes *wholly worthless*.
   C. Business versus Nonbusiness Bad Debts
       1. A debt is considered to be *nonbusiness* if it is not related to the taxpayer's trade or business either when the debt was created or when it becomes worthless.
       2. A business bad debt is always deductible as an *ordinary loss* in the year incurred. A nonbusiness bad debt, however, is treated as a *short-term capital loss* and is subject to capital loss limitations (i.e., the maximum net short-term loss that is deductible annually is $3,000).
   D. Loans Between Related Parties
       1. A question can be raised whether a transfer of funds made between relatives is a *bona fide loan* or whether it is a *gift*.
       2. Some considerations which would indicate that a debtor-creditor relationship exists include the following.
           a. Whether a note was properly executed.
           b. Whether there is a reasonable rate of interest.

    c.   Whether there is collateral.

    d.   What collection efforts have been made.

    e.   What was the intent of the parties.

E.   Loss of Deposits in Insolvent Financial Institutions

    1.   Qualified individuals may *elect* to deduct a loss from deposits in qualified financial institutions as a casualty loss. The loss is deducted in the year in which the amount of the loss can be reasonably estimated. In such situations, the personal casualty loss rules described below would apply.

    2.   If the individual does not make such election, the loss will be treated as a nonbusiness bad debt.

II.   Worthless Securities

A.   Generally, a loss deduction is allowed for securities (e.g., shares of stock, bonds, notes, or other evidence of indebtedness of a corporation or government) that become *completely worthless* during the year. This loss is considered to have occurred as of the *last day* of the year in which the loss occurred and it is usually considered to be capital.

B.   Small Business Stock

    1.   *Individuals* may receive *ordinary loss* treatment, within limitations, on the sale or exchange of stock if such stock is classified as *§ 1244 stock*. The treatment as an ordinary loss is limited to $50,000 ($100,000 for married individuals filing jointly) per year.

    2.   Were it not for this provision, a shareholder would always receive capital loss treatment on such a disposition of stock. Section 1244 only applies to *losses*.

    3.   Section 1244 stock can be either common or preferred stock.

III.   Losses of Individuals

A.   An individual may deduct a loss in the following circumstances.

    1.   For losses incurred in a trade or business.

    2.   For losses incurred in a transaction entered into for profit.

    3.   For losses caused by fire, storm, shipwreck, or other casualty or by theft.

B.   A *casualty* is usually defined as destruction of property resulting from an event due to some *sudden, unexpected*, or *unusual* cause. Further, the loss must result from an event that is identifiable and damaging to the property. However, a deduction for a casualty loss from an automobile accident can be taken only if the damage was not caused by the taxpayer's willful act or willful negligence.

C.   Events That Are Not Casualties -- Not all "acts of God," such as erosion, are casualty losses for income tax purposes; they must be sudden, unusual, or unexpected to qualify.

D.   Theft Losses

    1.   Theft includes larceny, embezzlement, and robbery. However, the term does *not* include lost or misplaced items.

    2.   A theft loss is taken in the year of *discovery,* not in the year of theft, if the two are different.

    3.   If in the year of discovery a claim exists, such as against an insurance company, and there is a reasonable expectation of recovering the fair market value of the asset, no deduction is allowed.

    4.   A partial deduction may be available if a recovery is less than the otherwise deductible amount.

E.   When to Deduct Casualty Losses

    1.   General Rule

a.   Usually, a casualty loss is deducted in the year during which the loss occurs.

b.   A casualty loss is not permitted if a reimbursement claim exists with a *reasonable prospect of (full) recovery*.

c.   If a reimburse-ment is received for a loss previously sustained and deducted, the taxpayer must include the amount in gross income when received to the extent that the previous deduction produced a tax benefit.

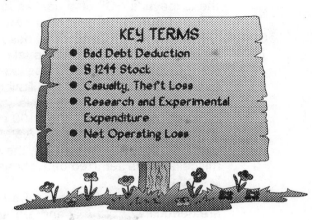

KEY TERMS
* Bad Debt Deduction
* S 1244 Stock
* Casualty, Theft Loss
* Research and Experimental Expenditure
* Net Operating Loss

2.   Disaster Area Losses -- An exception to the general rule allows a taxpayer to *elect* to deduct a loss in the year *preceding* the taxable year in which a disaster occurred if the loss results from a casualty sustained in an area designated as a disaster area by the President of the United States.

F.   Measuring the Amount of Loss

1.   Amount of Loss

a.   The computation of the amount of a casualty loss depends on whether the property is held for personal use or for business use and whether the property was partially or completely destroyed.

b.   The amount of the deduction for *partial losses* to both business and personal-use property and for the *complete* destruction of personal-use property is the *lesser* of the following.

(1)   The adjusted basis of the property.

(2)   The difference between the fair market value of the property before the casualty and the fair market value immediately after the casualty.

c.   If *business* property is *completely* destroyed, the deduction is equal to the property's adjusted basis at the time of the destruction.

d.   Any insurance recovery reduces the loss for business and personal-use casualties. However, if the taxpayer chooses not to file a timely claim against the insurance company, a deduction will *not* be allowed. If insurance proceeds exceed the amount of the loss, a taxable gain results.

If a taxpayer plans to claim a deduction for a casualty or theft loss, it is important that as much supporting evidence as possible be gathered. Newspaper clippings about a storm, police reports, and insurance reports may all be helpful in proving the nature of the casualty or theft and when it occurred. Remember, the taxpayer has the burden of proof that a casualty occurred and that the loss was a direct result of the casualty.

2.   Reduction for $100 and 10 Percent-of-AGI -- A casualty loss on *personal-use* property must be reduced by a $100 statutory floor when computing the deduction. Further, an additional floor, which is equal to 10 percent of the taxpayer's AGI, also applies to the *aggregate* of all personal losses incurred during the year after reducing *each* loss by the $100 floor.

G.   Statutory Framework for Deducting Losses of Individuals

1.   Losses incurred by an individual in connection with a trade or business are deductible *for* AGI. These losses are not subject to the $100 per event and 10 percent-of-AGI limitations.

2.   Losses incurred by an individual in a transaction entered into for profit are not subject to the $100 per event and 10 percent-of-AGI limitations. If such losses relate to rents and royalties, they are deducted *for* AGI. Otherwise, they are deducted *from* AGI as miscellaneous itemized deductions and subject to the two percent-of-AGI limitation.

3.   Casualty and theft losses incurred which pertain to personal property are deductible *from* AGI and are subject to the $100 per event floor and the 10 percent-of-AGI limitation.

H.   Personal Casualty Gains and Losses

1.   If *personal casualty gains* exceed *personal casualty losses*, the gains and losses will be treated as dispositions of capital assets. The result can be either long-term or short-term, depending on the length of time that the taxpayer held the various assets involved in the casualty.

2.   If the losses exceed the gains, all of the gains and losses will be treated as ordinary items. In this case, the losses, to the extent of the gains, will offset the gains in computing AGI while the excess losses will be deductible *from* AGI to the extent they exceed 10 percent-of-AGI.

IV.   Research and Experimental Expenditures

A.   The law permits three alternatives for handling *research and experimental expenditures*.

1.   The expenditures may be expensed in the year paid or incurred.

2.   They may be deferred and amortized.

3.   The costs may be capitalized.

B.   In addition, a credit to encourage research and experimentation activities may be claimed equal to 20 percent of certain *incremental* research and experimentation expenditures.

The incremental research credits and deductions are aimed at encouraging cash expenditures related to manufacturing and other industries that create physical products. No such incentive exists to bolster the software, publishing, or other "intellectual property" industries at this time.

V.   Net Operating Losses

A.   A net operating loss deduction is allowed which is designed to provide partial relief from potential inequitable tax treatment that may arise because of the requirement that every taxpayer is to file an income tax return annually.

B.   Carryback and Carryover Periods -- Generally, a net operating loss must be applied initially to the three taxable years preceding the loss. If the loss is not fully used up in the carryback period, it may be carried forward for up to 15 years. A taxpayer may elect to only carry forward a net operating loss.

C.   Computation of the Net Operating Loss

    1.   A net operating loss is intended as a relief provision for *business* income and losses. Therefore, in its computation, an individual must make several adjustments in the net operating loss computation for personal items taken in arriving at taxable income (e.g., personal exemption, standard deduction).

    2.   The net operating loss must reflect the taxpayer's *economic* loss.

TEST FOR SELF-EVALUATION -- CHAPTER 6

True or False

Indicate which of the following statements are true or false by circling the correct answer.

T   (F)   1.   The reserve method for bad debts is available for all taxpayers who sell goods or services on credit and use the accrual method of accounting.

(T)   F   2.   Assuming a timely insurance claim is filed, a personal casualty loss is potentially deductible only to the extent that it is not covered by insurance.

(T)   F   3.   A nonbusiness bad debt is deductible by individuals as a short-term capital loss.

(T)   F   4.   The net operating loss provisions for individuals apply only to business-related or economic losses.

T   (F)   5.   Personal casualty losses are never deductible in the year prior to the actual occurrence of the casualty event.

T   (F)   6.   A taxpayer who qualifies to obtain a tax benefit for bad debts incurred in a trade or business may in all cases use either the specific write-off method or the reserve method.

T   (F)   7.   An individual taxpayer who recognizes a loss from the disposition of stock held as an investment always would recognize a capital loss assuming the stock is a capital asset in the taxpayer's hands.

                         1244 - ordinary loss

T   (F)   8.   A deduction may be claimed by an individual when stock held for investment becomes partially worthless.

(T)   F   9.   Items that are lost or misplaced may not be deducted as a personal casualty or theft loss.

T   (F)   10.   The measure of a personal casualty loss deduction is always the decline in the property's fair market value as a result of the casualty event.

(T)   F   11.   Personal casualty and theft loss deductions are subject to the $100 per event and 10 percent-of-AGI limitations.

T   (F)   12.   Business and nonbusiness bad debts receive the same tax treatment.

               ordinary loss   *short term cap loss*

(T)   F   13.   The business bad debt deduction may not be claimed if the taxpayer uses the cash method of accounting.

(T)   F   14.   The reserve method for computing deductions for bad debts is allowed for certain financial institutions.

T   (F)   15.   A taxpayer may deduct a casualty loss for termite damage incurred on her personal residence over a ten-year period.

(T)   F   16.   A taxpayer may elect to not carry back a net operating loss, but instead to carry it forward only to future years.

T   F   17.   A deduction is allowed on the partial worthlessness of a business bad debt.

T   (F)   18.   Because the deduction for a theft loss must be claimed in the year in which the loss occurs, filing an amended income tax return may sometimes be necessary.

T   (F)   19.   Research and experimental expenditures must be expensed in the year in which they are incurred.

T   (F)   20.   The special treatment available for § 1244 stock applies equally to gains and losses.

Fill-in-the-Blanks

Complete the following statements with the appropriate word(s) or amount(s).

1.   A business bad debt is deductible as a(n) _ordinary_ loss in the year incurred, whereas a nonbusiness bad debt is always treated as a(n) _short term capital_ loss.

2.   A shareholder may claim an ordinary loss rather than a capital loss on the sale or exchange of stock if the stock has been classified as _small business_, which is also known as _1244 stock_.

3.   If business property or property held for the production of income is completely destroyed, the measure of the deduction is always the _adjusted basis of the property_ at the time of the destruction.

4.   A taxpayer may deduct an ordinary loss of up to _50,000_ (_100,000_ if filing a joint return) in the year of disposition of § 1244 stock.

5.   The amount of a personal casualty loss deduction is the lesser of its _adjusted basis_ or the decline in its _fair market value_.

6.   A net operating loss deduction may be carried back _3_ years and then any unused amounts may be carried forward _15_ years.

7.   Assuming no capital asset transactions, a nonbusiness bad debt may be deducted in an amount of up to _3,000_ in any given year.

8.   The amount of a casualty loss for personal use property must be reduced by a _100_ per event floor as well as the _10%_ percent-of-AGI aggregate floor.

9.   If personal casualty gains and losses net to a gain, all of the assets involved in the casualty events will be considered to be _capital_ assets.

10.   Casualty losses connected to rental or royalty property are deductible _for_ AGI.

11.   Transfers of funds between related parties raise the issue of whether the transfers were bona fide loans or _gifts_.

12.   A nonbusiness bad debt incurred by a taxpayer is always treated as a _short term capital loss_.

13. If the securities of an affiliated corporation become worthless, the corporate taxpayer's loss will be treated as a(n) ordinary loss.

14. The loss on a deposit in a qualified financial institution may by taken as either a personal casualty loss or a nonbusiness bad debt.

15. No deduction is allowed for the partial worthlessness of a nonbusiness bad debt.

Multiple Choice

Choose the best answer for each of the following questions.

a. 1. John, single and over 65, uses the cash receipts and disbursements method in his business and has the following income, expenses and deductions during the year.

Gross receipts	$30,000
Business expenses	32,000
Uncollectible customer accounts	4,000

Compute his bad debt deduction.
- a. $0.
- b. $1,000.
- c. $2,000.
- d. $4,000.
- e. None of the above.

d. 2. Refer to the preceding problem. If John uses the accrual method of accounting, what would be his bad debt deduction?
- a. $0.
- b. $1,000.
- c. $2,000.
- d. $4,000.
- e. None of the above.

e. 3. During the year, Wayne had the following personal casualty losses which were fully covered by an insurance policy and which all resulted from the same casualty. His AGI for the year was $20,000.

		Fair Market Value	
Asset	Adjusted Basis	Before	After
Auto	$5,000	$3,000	$ 0
Boat	1,600	2,400	1,900
Television	600	700	0

What is Wayne's casualty loss deduction for the year, assuming he had not requested a reimbursement from his insurance company?
- a. $1,800.
- b. $2,000.
- c. $4,100.
- d. $6,100.
- e. None of the above.

b. 4. Assume the same facts as in the problem above, except Wayne did not have insurance coverage for the assets. What is Wayne's casualty loss deduction?

    a. $1,800.
    b. $2,000.
    c. $4,100.
    d. $6,100.
    e.   None of the above.

_a._ 5.   Assume the same facts as in the preceding problem, except each of the casualties occurred in separate events. What is Wayne's casualty loss deduction?
    a. $1,800.
    b. $2,000.
    c. $4,100.
    d. $6,100.
    e.   None of the above.

_d_ 6.   Which of the following would be deductible as a personal casualty loss before considering any ceilings or limitations?
    a.   Termite damage to the foundation of your home.
    b.   Moth damage to out-of-style clothes that you had in storage.
    c.   Reduction in the value of your home because it was near a disaster area.
    d.   A car window broken due to vandalism.
    e.   All of the above are personal casualty losses.

_b_ 7.   Select the correct statement.
    a.   Harry bought Ivy Corporation stock on December 1, 1995. Ivy Corporation went bankrupt on March 15, 1996. Harry may take a short-term capital loss for 1996.
    b.   A deduction for theft is allowed in the year in which the taxpayer discovers the loss, and not necessarily in the year during which the loss actually occurred.
    c.   The nature of a debt depends on whether the borrower was engaged in a business or used the loan for a nonbusiness reason.
    d.   Misplaced or lost valuables that have value greater than $100 and the 10 percent-of-AGI limitation may be allowed as casualty loss deductions.
    e.   None of the above is correct.

_e_ 8.   Robert, the sole stockholder in his corporation, suffered the following uninsured casualty losses. His AGI is $10,000.

Asset	Basis	Fair Market Value Before Casualty	After Casualty
Company car	$1,000	$1,500	$ 300
Theft of wife's diamond ring	2,000	3,000	0
Company boat (shipwreck)	1,100	1,700	1,400

3000 - 100 - 1000
900

What is Robert's *personal* casualty loss deduction?
    a. $2,300.
    b. $2,400.
    c. $3,300.
    d. $3,400.
    e.   None of the above.

_c_ 9.   On October 1, 1994, Holkham Corporation and Ed (a single taxpayer) each purchased $75,000 worth of stock in the newly formed Johnson Corporation. On September 1, 1995, the company suddenly went bankrupt and the stock became totally worthless. The stock was § 1244 stock. How should the loss be reported?

	Holkham Corporation	**Ed**
a.	$25,000 LTCL $50,000 Ordinary Loss	$75,000 STCL
b.	$25,000 Ordinary Loss	$75,000 Ordinary Loss
c.	$75,000 LTCL	$50,000 Ordinary Loss $25,000 LTCL
d.	$50,000 Ordinary Loss $25,000 LTCL	$50,000 Ordinary Loss $25,000 LTCL
e.	None of the above.	

10. Louie, who had an AGI of $20,000 during the year, suffered a theft loss of a ring worth $6,000 (adjusted basis was $7,000) and a $3,000 casualty loss due to a boat accident. What amount would be deductible (assuming no insurance coverage)?
    a. $6,800.
    b. $6,900.
    c. $8,800.
    d. $8,900.
    e. $9,000.

    9,000 - 100 - 100 - 2,000 = 6800

11. On Thanksgiving Day of last year, Bill was seriously injured when he was riding on rugged terrain in the Blue Ridge Mountains on his all-terrain vehicle. Unfortunately, because of the seriousness of the accident, he had to be flown to the trauma center at the closest local hospital for care. The all-terrain vehicle, which cost Bill $2,000, had a FMV of approximately $1,600 immediately before the accident. After his release from the hospital on January 5 of the current year, Bill traded in the all-terrain vehicle for a new set of snow skis and was given an allowance of $600. Bill also received a settlement of $500 under his homeowners insurance policy on February 26. What amount can he deduct as a casualty loss before the 10 percent-of-AGI limitation, and in which year should the deduction be taken?
    a. $400 last year.
    b. $400 this year.
    c. $500 last year.
    d. $500 this year.
    e. None of the above.

    1600 - 600 - 500 - 100 = 400

12. Womack and Co., a professional accounting corporation, extended a loan ($10,000) last year to one of its trusted employees, Charles, who promptly and permanently left the country at the beginning of this year. As a consequence, the loan will never be collected. Womack and Co. may deduct what amount?
    a. $10,000 ordinary loss this year.
    b. $3,000 short-term loss this year and has a $7,000 carryover.
    c. $10,000 ordinary loss on last year's tax return.
    d. $3,000 short-term loss last year, $3,000 short-term loss this year, and has a $4,000 carryover.
    e. None of the above.

13. Margaret operates a pet shop that specializes in the sale of rare breeds of cats. During the year, she has sales of $300,000. However, she has determined that $8,000 will never be collected from some of her customers who have moved out of town. Assuming Margaret uses the accrual method of accounting in her business, she may claim the following bad debt deduction.
    a. $0.
    b. $8,000.
    c. A specified percentage of her sales.

d.   Some other amount.

_b_   14.   Assume the facts of the preceding problem, but Margaret misjudged the integrity
of one of her best customers, Sue, whose account had been written-off. Sue made
payment on her $2,400 debt in the following year. Margaret must report the
following amount of income.
a. $0.
b. $2,400.
c. $8,000.
d   The $2,400 multiplied by Margaret's gross profit percentage.
e.   Some other amount.

_b_   15.   Meghan and Travis loaned $4,000 to their next door neighbor, Dan, so that he
could buy some new living room furniture. Dan's business, his sole source of
income, fell on "hard times" and he informed Meghan and Travis that he could not
repay the loan. What are the tax consequences to Meghan and Travis in the year of
the loss, assuming the only other items on their income tax return are their
salaries?
a.   No deduction is available.
b. $3,000 STCL.
c. $4,000 STCL.
d. $4,000 ordinary loss.
e. $4,000 itemized deduction.
f.   Some other treatment.

_c_   16.   Select the correct statement.
a.   Individuals could never be in a situation that would generate a net
operating loss deduction.
b.   A net operating loss must be carried back before it is carried forward to
offset income of future years.
c.   A business loss incurred by an individual may create a net operating
loss.
d.   An individual's net operating loss for a year is the excess of all of the
taxpayer's deductions for and from AGI over gross income.
e.   None of the statements is correct.

_d_   17.   An individual may deduct the following types of losses.
a.   Losses incurred in a trade or business.
b.   Losses incurred in a transaction entered into for profit.
c.   Losses caused by fire, storm, shipwreck, or other casualty or by theft.
d.   Any of the above types may be deducted.
e.   None of the above may be deducted.

_d_   18.   The law allows which of the following alternatives for the handling of research
and experimental expenditures:

Option I.   Expensing in the year paid or incurred.
Option II.   Deferral and amortization.
Option III.   Capitalization.

a.   Only Option III.
b.   Option II or III.
c.   Only Option II
d.   Options I, II, or III.
e.   None of the above.

_b_ 19.   During 1994, Champaign Corporation incurred research and experimental expenses
          of $10,000. In 1995, the business incurred another $40,000 of such expenditures
          and began to enjoy benefits from the project on July 1, 1995. If the taxpayer
          elects the deferral and amortization method, what amount may be deducted in
          1995?
          a. $4,000.
          b. $5,000.
          c. $8,000.
          d. $10,000.
          e.   None of the above.

_d_ 20.   During 1994, Champaign Corporation incurred research and experimental
          expenditures of $10,000. In 1995, the business incurred another $40,000 of such
          expenditures and began to enjoy benefits from the project on July 1, 1995. If
          the taxpayer uses the expense method for the research and experimental
          expenditures, what amount may be deducted?
          a. $10,000 in 1994.
          b. $40,000 in 1995.
          c. $50,000 in 1995.
          d.   Both a and b are correct.
          e.   None of the above.

_b._ 21. Pedro is in the business of lending money. Two years ago Pedro lent $3,000 to
          Abby for nonbusiness purposes. Last year, Abby declared bankruptcy, but
          expected to be able to pay all her creditors at the rate of $.60 on the dollar.
          However, this year, Abby was only able to pay in final settlement $.10 on the
          dollar. How should Pedro have treated the loss on *last year's* return?
          a.   No deduction is available.
          b. $1,200 ordinary loss.
          c. $1,200 short-term capital loss.
          d. $2,700 ordinary loss.
          e.   None of the above.

_b_ 22.   Ross is in the business of lending money. Two years ago Ross lent $3,000 to
          Carlos for nonbusiness purposes. Last year, Carlos declared bankruptcy, but
          expected to be able to pay all of his creditors at the rate of $.60 on the dollar.
          However, this year, Carlos was only able to pay in final settlement $.10 on the
          dollar. How should Ross treat the loss on *this year's* return?
          a.   No deduction is available.
          b. $1,500 ordinary loss.
          c. $1,500 short-term capital loss.
          d. $2,700 ordinary loss.
          e.   None of the above.

_a_ 23.   On November 30, 1994, Kathleen acquired Concord Corporation § 1244 stock from
          the corporation for $5,000. On October 31, 1995, the stock was considered to be
          worthless. How is the loss treated?
          a. $5,000 ordinary loss.
          b. $5,000 short-term capital loss.
          c. $5,000 long-term capital loss.
          d.   No loss is available in any year because this was a personal investment.
          e.   Some other amount.

_c_ 24.   On November 30, 1994, Kathleen acquired Concord Corporation stock (not § 1244
          stock) from the corporation for $5,000. On October 31, 1995, the stock was

considered to be worthless. How is the loss treated?
a. $5,000 ordinary loss.
b. $5,000 short-term capital loss.
c. $5,000 long-term capital loss.
d.   No loss is available in any year because this was a personal investment.
e.   Some other amount.

_a._ 25.   Molly suffered the following casualty events, in a year when her AGI totalled $20,000.

Personal casualty gain (asset held 4 years) $2,000
Personal casualty loss (after $100 floor)   6,000

= 4,000 - 0 - 3,000

10,000 × 10% = 7000

What is her casualty loss deduction?
a. $2,000.
b. $3,800.
c. $4,000.
d. $6,000.
e.   None of the statements is correct.

Code Section Recognition

Several important sections of the Internal Revenue Code are described below. Indicate, by number, the appropriate Code section.

1.   _166_ Provides for a bad debt deduction.

2.   _1244_ Rules relating to small business stock.

3.   _165_ Provides for the deduction for worthless securities and net operating losses.

4.   _165_ Provides for a deduction for personal and casualty theft losses.

Short Answer

1.   Hector, who is single, owns 100 shares of stock in Blue Corporation which he purchased four years ago for $200,000. The stock meets all of the requirements of § 1244. How will the following transactions be treated for tax purposes under the following scenarios?

a.   In the current year, he sold the stock for $75,000.

125,000   50,000 ordinary loss
75,000 LTCL

b.   In the current year, he sold the stock for $225,000.

25,000 gain

2.   Molly incurs the following personal casualty losses in separate incidents during the year. Calculate the casualty loss for each item before application of the 10% of AGI limitation.

Asset	Adjusted Basis	FMV Before Casualty	FMV After Casualty	Insurance Recovery
A	$500	$600	$400	$200
B	$500	$600	$ 50	$150
C	$500	$600	$400	$400
D	$500	$600	$250	$300

A   ∅

B.   350 -100 = 250

C.   200

D.   50 -100 = ∅

SOLUTIONS TO CHAPTER 6 QUESTIONS

True or False

1.	F	The reserve method is not available for most income tax purposes by taxpayers.
2.	T	
3.	T	
4.	T	
5.	F	A taxpayer may elect to deduct the amount in the prior year if the President of the United States declares the area in which the casualty occurred a disaster area.
6.	F	Under current law, only the specific write-off method may be used by most taxpayers.
7.	F	Dispositions of § 1244 stock at a loss will produce an ordinary loss within certain limitations.
8.	F	The stock must be fully worthless in this situation.
9.	T	A taxpayer may not claim a loss due to negligence.
10.	F	The deduction is equal to the property's adjusted basis if such amount is less than the decline in fair market value.
11.	T	
12.	F	Business bad debts are treated as ordinary losses while nonbusiness bad debts are considered short-term capital losses.
13.	T	
14.	T	
15.	F	Such damage would not likely meet the suddenness test.
16.	T	
17.	T	
18.	F	The theft loss deduction is claimed in the year in which the loss is discovered.
19.	F	Three alternatives are available: expensing, deferral and amortization, and capitalization.
20.	F	The special treatment only applies to losses.

Fill-in-the-Blanks

1. ordinary, short-term capital
2. small business stock, § 1244 stock
3. adjusted basis of the property
4. $50,000, $100,000
5. adjusted basis, fair market value
6. 3, 15
7. $3,000
8. $100, 10
9. capital
10. for
11. gifts
12. short-term capital loss
13. ordinary
14. personal casualty loss, nonbusiness bad debt
15. nonbusiness

Multiple Choice

1. a   A bad debt expense deduction is not available to cash basis taxpayers. See Example 1 in the text.
2. d   See Example 1 in the text.
3. e   No deduction for such a loss would be allowed unless a timely insurance claim is filed.
4. b

Auto ($3,000 - $0)	$3,000
Boat ($2,400 - $1,900)	500
Television	600
	$4,100
Statutory floor per event	- 100
10% of AGI	-2,000
Deduction	$2,000

See Example 17 in the text.
5. a

Auto ($3,000 - $100)	$2,900
Boat ($500 - $100)	400
Television ($600 - $100)	500
	$3,800
10% of AGI	-2,000
Deduction	$1,800

See Example 17 in the text.
6. d
7. b
8. e $900; the loss from the theft of the diamond ring is the only *personal* casualty loss incurred [$2,000 - $100 - 10%($10,000) = $900]. The other casualties would be reported by Robert's corporation. See Example 17 in the text.
9. c   See Example 8 in the text.
10. a $6,800 = [($6,000 - $100) + ($3,000 - $100)] - ($20,000 X 10%) See Example 17 in the text.
11. a $1,000 decline in FMV (net of allowance) - $500 insurance reimbursement - $100 floor = $400. The deduction would be taken last year (i.e., the year of the accident) because the anticipated insurance recovery would not be enough to offset the entire amount of the loss. See Example 11 in the text.
12. a   Business bad debts produce ordinary loss deductions. See Example 5 in the text.
13. b   The specific write-off method is required in this situation. See Example 1 in the text.
14. b   Income must be recognized in the year of recovery to the extent the amount produced a tax benefit in a previous year.
15. b   The nonbusiness bad debt is treated as a STCL and limited to $3,000 in the year of the loss. See Example 4 in the text.
16. c
17. d
18. d
19. b $5,000 = ($10,000 + $40,000) / 60 months X 6 months. See Example 20 in the text.
20. d
21. b   See Example 3 in the text.
22. b

Total loss	$2,700
Less: Loss claimed last year	1,200
Current year's loss	$1,500

23. a   See Example 8 in the text.
24. c   See Example 7 in the text.
25. a

Casualty loss in excess of casualty gain	$4,000
Less: 10% of AGI (10% X $20,000)	2,000
Allowable deduction	$2,000

See Example 19 in the text.

Code Section Recognition

1.   166
2.   1244
3.   165
4.   165

Short Answer

1.   a.   Of the total $125,000 loss on the sale of § 1244 stock, §1244 treats $50,000 as an ordinary loss while the remaining $75,000 loss is capital.

      b.   The stock is sold at a $25,000 gain. The gain is treated as a capital gain because the stock is a capital asset to Hector. Section 1244 does not apply when stock is sold at a gain.

2.

Asset	Loss	Insurance Recovery	Net Gain/Loss before $100 floor	$100 floor	Net Gain or Loss
A	($200)	$200	$ 0	$ 0	$ 0
B	($500)	$150	($350)	$100	($250)
C	($200)	$400	$200	$ 0	$200
D	($350)	$300	($ 50)	$100	$ 0

CHAPTER 7
DEPRECIATION, COST RECOVERY, AMORTIZATION, AND DEPLETION

CHAPTER HIGHLIGHTS

*M*any assets acquired for use in a trade or business or held for the production of income do not produce a tax benefit equal to their costs in the year of acquisition because their lives extend substantially beyond the close of the particular tax year. This chapter discusses the procedures by which a tax benefit is received over an asset's useful life or over a specified period of time. The write-off of the cost (or other adjusted basis) of an asset is known as the process of depreciation, cost recovery, amortization, or depletion. Depreciation and cost recovery are associated with tangible property, amortization pertains to intangible property, and depletion relates to certain natural resources. These provisions have been changed numerous times since the early 1980s and, as a result, have produced something of a nightmare for taxpayers who own long-lived assets. Further, distinctions such as whether an asset has a business or personal use, whether it is realty or personalty, or whether it is tangible or intangible, are important when determining the tax treatment of an asset.

I.   Overview
   A.   The frequent changes in the depreciation and cost recovery provisions have increased complexity and made it more difficult for taxpayers to compute write-offs for long-lived assets. A summary of the provisions that apply to such assets is provided in Exhibit 7-1. The selection of the appropriate depreciation or cost recovery provision depends on when a particular asset is placed into service.
   B.   Taxpayers may write off the cost of certain assets that are used in a trade or business or held for the production of income. The write-off takes the form of either depreciation, depletion, or amortization. Generally, no deduction is allowed for an asset that does not have a determinable useful life.
   C.   ACRS and MACRS provide separate tables for *realty* (real property) and *personalty* (personal property).
   D.   Personalty includes furniture, machinery, and equipment. Personalty should not be confused with *personal use* property. Personal use property includdes assets *not* put to a business or income producing use. Personal use property may not be written off.

Exhibit 7-1
DEPRECIATION AND COST RECOVERY: RELEVANT TIME PERIODS

System	Date Property is Placed in Service
Section 167 depreciation (pre-ACRS)	Before January 1, 1981 and certain property placed in service after December 31, 1980
Accelerated cost recovery system (ACRS)	After December 31, 1980 and before January 1, 1987
Modified accelerated cost recovery system (MACRS)	After December 31, 1986

II. Accelerated Cost Recovery System (ACRS and MACRS)
    A. General Considerations
        1. Generally, the ACRS rules apply to those assets placed into service after December 31, 1980 and before 1987. However, the pre-ACRS rules may still apply to assets in certain situations.
        2. Under ACRS, the cost of an asset is recovered over a predetermined period which generally is shorter than the useful life of the asset or the period over which the asset is used to produce income.
        3. The basis of cost recovery property must be reduced by the cost recovery allowed and by not less than the allowable amount.
        4. The basis for cost recovery purposes generally is the adjusted cost basis used to determine gain if the property is sold or otherwise disposed of. However, if personal use assets are converted to business or income-producing use, the basis for cost recovery and for loss is the *lower* of the adjusted basis or the fair market value at the time the property was converted.
    B. Personalty: Recovery Periods and Methods
        1. The cost of eligible personalty subject to ACRS is recovered over 3, 5, 10, or 15 years, depending on the classification of the property.
        2. Taxpayers had a choice of (1) using the *straight-line method* over the regular or an optional recovery period or (2) a prescribed accelerated method over the regular recovery period (the *statutory percentage method*).
        3. The statutory percentage method applicable used the half-year convention and the 150 percent declining balance method, and assumed a zero salvage value.
        4. If a taxpayer acquired regular investment tax credit property after 1982 and before 1986, the asset's basis was to be reduced by 50 percent of the credit claimed unless the election was made to claim a reduced investment credit. Under the reduced credit election, no basis reduction was made. For property placed in service after 1985, the basis reduction is not required because the TRA of 1986 repealed the ITC.
        5. The classes and methods shown in Exhibit 7-2 are available under the MACRS rules for personalty placed in service *after* 1986. In each class, a switch-over is made to the straight-line method in the latter years of an asset's class life when it yields a larger amount of cost recovery. Procedurally, however, the cost recovery deduction is computed by multiplying the asset's basis by the percentages found in the appropriate table.
        6. Taxpayers may *elect* the straight-line method to compute cost recovery allowances for these classes of property. Further, certain assets do not

qualify to be depreciated using the accelerated methods and must be depreciated using the alternative depreciation system (ADS) discussed below.

Exhibit 7-2
CLASSIFICATION OF PERSONAL PROPERTY UNDER MACRS

Class	Method
3-year	200%DB
5-year	200%DB
7-year	200%DB
10-year	200%DB
15-year	150%DB
20-year	150%DB

7. Under MACRS, all personalty is subject to the half-year convention in the year of acquisition *and* in the year of disposition or retirement. Thus, in a practical sense, the write-off periods are 4, 6, 8, 11, 16, and 21 years.

8. An exception applies, however, if more than 40 percent of the value of property other than real estate is placed in service during the last quarter of the year. In this situation, the *mid-quarter convention* applies whereby the asset acquisitions are grouped and depreciated depending on the quarter during which the assets were acquired. (See Exhibit 7-3 below.)

Exhibit 7-3
MID-QUARTER CONVENTION

Assets Acquired in	Amount of Depreciation
1st Quarter	10.5 months
2nd Quarter	7.5 months
3rd Quarter	4.5 months
4th Quarter	1.5 months

C.   Realty: Recovery Periods and Methods
    1.   Under the original ACRS rules, realty acquired before March 16, 1984 was assigned a 15-year recovery period.
    2.   The half-year convention does not apply to 15-year real property. Instead, the cost recovery deduction is based on the month the asset is placed in service.
    3.   Except for low-income housing, realty placed into service after March 15, 1984 and before May 9, 1985 was assigned an 18-year recovery period. Further, 18-year real property placed in service after June 22, 1984 is subject to a mid-month convention.
    4.   The minimum recovery period for real property (except low-income housing) is 19 years for property placed in service after May 8, 1985 and before 1987.
    5.   Real property placed in service after December 31, 1986 is subject to MACRS rules which vary depending on whether the assets are *residential rental property* or *nonresidential real estate.*
    6.   For residential rental property (property for which 80 percent or more of the gross rental revenues are from non-transient dwelling units), costs are recovered over 27.5 years on a straight-line basis using the mid-month convention. Low-income housing is also subject to the residential rental property rules.
    7.   Nonresidential real estate has a life of 31.5 years, during which the straight-line method and the mid-month convention are used if placed in service on or before May 12, 1993. For nonresidential realty placed in service after May 12, 1993, the recovery period is 39 years.

> By carefully analyzing the tax benefits associated with cost recovery deductions, a taxpayer may find it more advantageous to make a planned acquisition in one year rather than another. In addition, the effect of various elections and methods of cost recovery on taxable income must be carefully assessed.

D.   Straight-Line Election under ACRS and MACRS
    1.   The straight-line method could be *elected* for assets subject to ACRS rather than using the statutory percentage method.
        a.   Allowable straight-line recovery periods for each class of property are summarized in Exhibit 7-4.
        b.   If the straight-line method was elected for ACRS personalty, the half-year convention was used. Also, there is no cost recovery deduction in the year of disposition.
        c.   When the straight-line method is selected for personalty, the election applies to *all* assets in a *particular class* that are placed into service in the year of the election.

Exhibit 7-4
STRAIGHT-LINE ELECTION UNDER ACRS

Class	Recovery Period
3-year property	3, 5, or 12 years
5-year property	5, 12, or 25 years
10-year property	10, 25, or 35 years
15-year property	15, 35, or 45 years
18-year property	18, 35, or 45 years
19-year property	19, 35, or 45 years

2. Although straight-line depreciation is currently required under MACRS for all eligible real property, a taxpayer may *elect* to depreciate MACRS personalty using the straight-line method instead of using the statutory percentage method. In this situation, the taxpayer uses the straight-line method, with a half-year or mid-quarter convention, over the entire class life of the asset. The election is available on a class-by-class, year-by-year basis.

E. Election to Expense Assets

1. Up to $17,500 of cost of an investment in tangible personal property which is used in a trade or business may be written off in the year the property is placed into service under § 179. This provision is elective and the amount expensed is not capitalized.

2. In addition to the $17,500 ceiling on the deduction, two other limits apply.

    a. The ceiling amount on the deduction is reduced dollar-for-dollar when property (other than eligible real estate) placed in service during the taxable year exceeds $200,000.

    b. The amount expensed under this election cannot exceed the aggregate amount of taxable income derived from the conduct of any trade or business by the taxpayer.

3. If expensed property is converted to personal use, recapture income results.

The §179 election is designed to expense immediately the full extent of acquisitions by the typical small business in a typical year. While not directly indexed to inflation, the maximum amount of the "first year bonus" depreciation has been adjusted upward periodically, although not as quickly or as broadly as some might like.

F. Business and Personal Use of Automobiles and Other Listed Property

1. ACRS and MACRS deductions are limited for automobiles and other listed property put to a business and personal use.

2. If the property is used *predominantly for business*, the statutory percentage method may be taken. Otherwise, costs are recovered using the straight-line method.

3. *Listed property* includes the following.

    a. Any passenger automobile.

    b. Any other property used as a means of transportation.

c.   Any property of a type generally used for entertainment, recreation, or amusement.

    d.   Any computer or peripheral equipment unless used exclusively at a regular business establishment.

    e.   Any cellular telephone or other similar telecommunications equipment.

    f.   Any other property specified by the Regulations.

4.   Listed property is used predominantly for business if it is used *more than 50 percent* of the time in business (not including the time spent for the production of income).

5.   Special limitations apply to *passenger automobiles* used for business. For passenger automobiles, the annual MACRS deduction, which is adjusted each year for inflation, is limited as shown in Exhibit 7-5.

Exhibit 7-5
COST RECOVERY DEDUCTION LIMITS FOR PASSENGER AUTOMOBILES

First year	$3,060
Second year	$4,900
Third year	$2,950
Each succeeding year	$1,775

6.   The dollar caps must be reduced if qualified business use is less than 100 percent. In addition, the limitation includes any amount expensed under § 179. If the regular MACRS percentages produce a lesser amount of cost recovery, the lesser amount is used.

7.   If listed property is *not* used predominantly for business, its costs must be recovered using the straight-line method. Under MACRS, the straight-line method used is that required under the alternative depreciation system (ADS) described below. This system requires a five-year recovery period for automobiles. Further, the cost recovery limitations listed above for passenger automobiles cannot be exceeded.

8.   *Cost recovery recapture* is triggered if an asset, which has been used predominantly for business, is not continued to be used in business for more than 50 percent of the time. The amount recaptured is included in the taxpayer's income tax return as ordinary income.

9.   A taxpayer who leases a passenger automobile must report an *inclusion amount* (computed from an IRS table) in gross income. This provision is intended to prevent taxpayers from circumventing the cost recovery limitations by leasing.

10.   Listed property is subject to the substantiation requirements of § 274. However, the substantiation requirements do not apply to vehicles that are not likely to be used more than a *de minimis* amount for personal purposes.

The purchase of business equipment and its related maintenance are generally deductible to a business. Rather than an individual attempting to deduct the business use of a personal computer at home, a taxpayer should negotiate with the company to supply a home computer based on its ability to increase productivity for the business.

G.   Alternative Depreciation System (ADS)

    1.   The *ADS* rules must be used to calculate cost recovery in the following situations.

        a.   For the portion of depreciation treated as an adjustment for purposes of the alternative minimum tax.

        b.   For the depreciation expense for the following assets.

            (1)   Used predominantly outside of the US.

            (2)   Leased or otherwise used by tax-exempt entities.

            (3)   Financed with proceeds from tax-exempt bonds.

            (4)   Imported from certain foreign countries.

        c.   For depreciation expense allowances for corporate E&P purposes.

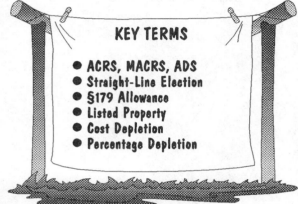

    2.   In general, ADS depreciation is computed using the straight-line method without regard to salvage value. However, the computation for alternative minimum tax purposes for personalty is computed using the 150 percent declining balance method, followed by a switch to straight-line.

    3.   The half-year or the mid-quarter convention applies to all property other than real estate. For real property, the mid-month convention is used.

    4.   The ADS recovery periods follow.

        a.   Personalty: ADR mid-point life if not in the 5-year (e.g., technological equipment, automobiles, and light-duty trucks) or the 12-year (e.g., personal property with no class life) class.

        b.   Realty: 40 years.

    5.   A taxpayer may elect to use the ADS provisions on assets that otherwise would qualify under the regular MACRS rules.

III. Amortization

    A.   Intangible property used in a trade or business or in the production of income may be *amortized* if the property has a limited life that can be determined with reasonable accuracy.

    B.   Generally, intangible property is amortized using a straight-line method.

    C.   Under current law, taxpayers who acquire goodwill, going-concern value, and certain other customer-based intangibles are permitted under § 197 to amortize the costs of these assets over a 15-year period.

IV. Depletion

    A.   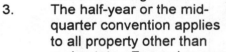 Intangible Drilling and Development Costs -- These costs may be treated in *either* one of two ways by the taxpayer.

        1.   They may be charged off as an expense in the year they are incurred.

        2.   They may be capitalized and written off through depletion.

    B.   Depletion Methods

        1.   The owner of an interest in a wasting asset is entitled to deduct depletion. Like depreciation, depletion is a deduction *for* adjusted gross income.

        2.   There are two methods of calculating depletion: cost depletion and percentage depletion. The choice between the two methods is made by an annual election

and generally the method producing the *higher* expense would be taken.

3.   The *cost depletion* per unit is calculated by using the adjusted basis of the natural resource. The depletion per unit is then multiplied by the number of units *sold* to arrive at the cost depletion deduction for a given year.

4.   The *percentage depletion* amount is calculated by multiplying a specified percentage provided in the Code by the gross income received from the property during a given year. In no event should the depletion deduction computed by this method exceed 50 percent of taxable income from the property before the allowance for depletion.

5.   IDC affects the depletion deduction in two ways: the depletion deduction may be increased if the IDC are capitalized; whereas, if the IDC are expensed, the taxable income from the property would be reduced and could invoke the depletion limitation of 50 percent of taxable income as described above.

TEST FOR SELF-EVALUATION -- CHAPTER 7

True or False

Indicate which of the following statements are true or false by circling the correct answer.

T   (F)   1.   Taxpayers must use the statutory percentage method of depreciation under MACRS.

(T)   F   2.   To be depreciable, property must be used in a trade or business or held for the production of income.

(T)   F   3.   The amount that currently may be expensed under § 179, Election to Expense Certain Depreciable Assets, generally is limited to $17,500.

T   (F)   4.   For all real property placed in service after March 15, 1984, the 15-year cost recovery period has been lengthened to either 18 or 19 years.

T   (F)   5.   Limitations exist relating to the aggregate amount of depreciation deductions that may be claimed for automobiles.

T   (F)   6.   Goodwill is amortizable for tax purposes over a period that is arbitrarily determined by the taxpayer.

(T)   F   7.   Under the MACRS depreciation rules, the estimated salvage value of an asset is ignored.

(T)   F   8.   The depletion deduction calculation can be based either on the cost depletion or percentage depletion methods.

(T)   F   9.   For real property placed in service in the current year, a straight-line method of depreciation *must* be used.

(T)   F   10.   Depreciation on real property placed in service after December 31, 1993 may be claimed in the years of acquisition and disposition.

T   (F)   11.   A mid-quarter convention applies to the depreciation of personal tangible property placed in service during the year if more than 40 percent of the property is placed in service during the last 4 months of the year.

T   (F)   12.   The use of the alternative depreciation system is in all cases elective.

T   (F)   13.   For tangible personal property placed in service in the current year, a straight-line method of depreciation *must* be used.

(T)   F   14.   For intangible property placed in service in the current year, a straight-line method of amortization *must* be used.

(T)   F   15.   The mid-quarter convention would apply whether or not the taxpayer uses an accelerated method or the straight-line method of cost recovery.

(T)   F   16.   Assuming the mid-quarter convention does not apply, only one-half year's worth of depreciation is available during a tangible personalty's year of acquisition if it is placed in service on January 1, 1995.

T   (F)   17.   Only one-half year's worth of depreciation is available during a tangible realty's year of acquisition if it is placed in service on January 1, 1995.

(T)   F   18.   The amount expensed under § 179 cannot exceed the aggregate amount of taxable income derived from the conduct of any trade or business by the taxpayer.

(T)   F   19.   The amount of the § 179 deduction otherwise available is not affected by the amount of real estate placed into service during the year.

(T)   F   20.   A passenger automobile is classified as listed property even if it is used exclusively for business.

Fill-in-the-Blanks

Complete the following statements with the appropriate word(s) or amount(s).

1. When a personal use asset is converted to business or income producing use, the basis for depreciation purposes is the lower of its __Adjusted basis__ or __fair market value__ on the date of conversion.

2. The basis of a depreciable asset is reduced by the depreciation actually __allowed__, but never by a lesser amount than that __allowable__.

3. Under the pre-ACRS rules, the period over which an asset's cost is recovered is its __estimated useful life__.

4. The two methods available to compute depletion are the __cost__ method and the __percentage__ method.

5. The regular cost recovery periods under ACRS for personal property are __3__ years, __5__ years, __10__ years, and __15__ years. The recovery periods for such assets subject to MACRS are __3__ years, __5__ years, __7__ years, __27.5__ years, __31.5__ years, and __39__ years.

6. For __personal__ property placed in subject to ACRS, depreciation may be deducted in the year of acquisition, but not in the year of disposition.

7. The reduction of an asset's depreciable basis because of investment credit taken applies only to personalty placed into service after __1962__ and before __1986__.

8. Under the ACRS rules, realty is normally assigned a __15__ year, __18__ year, or __19__ year recovery period. For such property after 1986, the normal recovery period for residential realty is __27.5__ years, but for nonresidential realty, the recovery period is __31.5__ or __39__ years.

9. The half-year convention applies to __personal__ property, but not to __real__ property under ACRS.

10. The election to expense immediately up to $17,500 in the year of acquisition applies only to purchased tangible __personal__ property used in a trade or business.

11. In order to claim any portion of the $17,500 immediate expensing deduction, the aggregate acquisitions (excluding real estate) for the year may not exceed __$17,500__.

12. Listed property that is not used predominantly for business must be depreciated using the __straight line__ method.

13. For listed property to be considered as predominantly used in business, the percentage of use for business must exceed __50__ percent.

14.   _Percentage_ depletion is computed without regard to basis.

15.   All cost recovery deductions for ___real___ property are calculated using the mid-month convention.

Multiple Choice

Choose the best answer for each of the following questions.

_b_   1.   On April 1 of this year, Robert acquired equipment for $120,000 for use in his business. The equipment has a 5-year recovery period. Robert elects straight-line depreciation. Given this was his sole acquisition for the year, Robert desires to maximize his first year write-off on the equipment. Calculate the maximum Robert may deduct due to the purchase and use of the machine during the year, assuming the mid-quarter convention is not appropriate.
       a. $38,000.
       b. $27,750.
       c. $19,000.
       d. $12,000.
       e.   None of the above.

handwritten: 120,000 / 17,500 / 102,500 ÷ 5 = 20500 · ½ = 10,250 / 17,500 / 27,750

_b._   2.   On April 1 of this year, Robert acquired equipment for $120,000 for use in his business. The equipment has a 5-year recovery period. Robert desires to use § 179 and the MACRS provisions to recover the cost of his investment. If this was his sole acquisition for the year, determine the total depreciation expense for the year, assuming the mid-quarter convention is not appropriate.
       a. $41,500.
       b. $38,000.
       c. $27,750.
       d. $24,000.
       e.   None of the above.

handwritten: 120,000 / 17,500 / 102,500 × .20 = 20500 / .17,500 / 38,000

_c_   3.   On April 1 of this year, Robert acquired equipment for $220,000 for use in his business. The equipment has a 5-year recovery period. Robert desires to use § 179 and the MACRS provisions to recover the cost of his investment. If this was his sole acquisition for the year, determine the total depreciation expense for the year, assuming the mid-quarter convention is not appropriate.
       a. $54,000.
       b. $52,000.
       c. $44,000.
       d. $42,000.
       e.   None of the above.

handwritten: 220,000 · 20 = 44,000,000 ... 17,500 ... 20 = 40,500...

_d._   4.   Which of the following statements is not true?
       a.   The recovery of the costs of automobiles is subject to special limitations that affect the timing of the available deductions.
       b.   Personal/business use assets are subject to rules that affect the timing of the deduction.
       c.   For personal/business use assets, the straight-line method of depreciation is required if business use is not more than 50%.
       d.   If a personal/business use asset is used for business more than 50% of the time, no restrictive rules are applicable.   *luxury*
       e.   All of the above statements are correct.

_e_　5.　The definition of "listed property" excludes which of the following?
  a.　Passenger automobiles.
  b.　Entertainment, recreation, or amusement facilities.
  c.　Computer and peripheral equipment.
  d.　Other property specified by Regulations.
  e.　All of the above are listed property.

_d_　6.　Zane Corporation purchased and placed into service a new car, which cost $20,000. It is used 100% for business. What is the maximum amount that Zane Corporation can expense on this car in the year of acquisition?
  a.　$4,000.
  b.　$5,000.
  c.　$3,200.
  d.　$3,060. max
  e.　None of the above.

_d_　7.　Christy purchased improved real property as an investment this year. Which of the following is true?
  a.　The property's cost may be recovered over a 15-year period.
  b.　The mid-month convention is not required.
  c.　An accelerated write-off based on the 175% declining balance is available.
  d.　A distinction is made between residential and nonresidential real property for depreciation purposes.
  e.　None of the above.

_b_　8.　Which taxpayer described below is allowed to write off real property used in a trade or business over 15 years?
  a.　Ann placed real property in service in July 1985.
  b.　Bill placed low-income housing in service in July 1984.
  c.　Chris placed real property in service in July 1984.
  d.　Both b and c.
  e.　None of the above.

_e_　9.　Jason purchased a microcomputer in January for $10,000. He uses the computer for business exactly 50% of the time. What is the maximum depreciation deduction that he can take currently, assuming a five-year classification?
  a.　$10,000.
  b.　$5,000.
  c.　$2,000.
  d.　$1,000.
  e.　None of the above.

_b_　10.　Jason purchased a microcomputer in January for $10,000. He uses the computer for business exactly 60% of the time. What is the maximum depreciation deduction that he can take currently, assuming a five-year classification and assuming the § 179 election is not available?
  a.　$2,000.
  b.　$1,200.
  c.　$1,000.
  d.　$600.
  e.　None of the above.

_e_　11.　Which statement concerning the alternative depreciation system is not true?
  a.　There is only one depreciation class for all types of real property.
  b.　In certain situations, a taxpayer may elect to use ADS.

    c.   The half-year convention is required for all assets other than realty under ADS.

    d.   ADS must be used to compute the depreciation adjustment amount for alternative minimum tax purposes.

    e.   All of the above are true.

12.   A new automobile was acquired by Emily on January 1. The automobile, which cost $20,000, is used 80 percent for business. Determine the maximum depreciation that may be taken in the year of acquisition.

    a. $10,000.

    b. $8,000.

    c. $4,000.

    d. $3,200.

    e. $3,060.

    f. $2,448.

    g.   Some other amount.

13.   In the previous problem, assume instead that the automobile was used 20 percent of the time for business. Calculate the depreciation deduction for the year of acquisition.

    a. $4,000.

    b. $3,060.

    c. $800.

    d. $612.

    e.   Some other amount.

14.   On February 26 of the current year, Ivy Corporation placed in service a *new* warehouse costing $1 million. Determine the cost recovery for the year.

    a. $34,850.

    b. $31,820.

    c. $27,780.

    d. $22,470.

    e.   Some other amount.

15.   On February 26 of the current year, Ivy Corporation placed in service a *used* warehouse costing $1 million. Determine the cost recovery for the year.

    a. $34,850.

    b. $31,820.

    c. $27,780.

    d. $22,470.

    e.   Some other amount.

16.   On March 15 of the current year, Crozet Corporation placed in service a new apartment building costing $1 million. Calculate the cost recovery deduction for this year.

    a. $18,181.

    b. $28,790.

    c. $34,850.

    d. $36,360.

    e.   None of the above.

17.   On March 15 of the current year, Crozet Corporation placed in service a new apartment building costing $1 million. Calculate the cost recovery deduction for the second year.

    a. $18,181.

    b. $28,790.

    c. $34,850.

d. $36,360.
e.   None of the above.

18.   On March 15 of the current year, Crozet Corporation placed in service a new apartment building costing $1 million. Assuming the taxpayer elected ADS, calculate the cost recovery deduction for the year of acquisition.
a. $18,181.
b. $28,790.
c. $34,850.
d. $36,360.
e.   None of the above.

19.   On March 15, 1995, Crozet Corporation placed in service a new apartment building costing $1 million. The taxpayer elected ADS. Assuming the building is sold on October 31, 1999, determine the cost recovery deduction for the year of disposition.
a. $12,500.
b. $19,792.
c. $21,875.
d. $25,000.
e.   None of the above.

20.   Crystal Corporation acquired a machine (7-year property) on May 15, 1995 for $100,000. Assuming neither the § 179 election nor the straight-line method is used, determine the cost recovery for the current year.
a. $7,145.
b. $14,290.
c. $20,000.
d. $33,330.
e.   Some other amount.

21.   Crystal Corporation acquired a machine (5-year property) on December 15, 1995 for $100,000, which was its sole acquisition for the year. Assuming that neither the § 179 election nor the straight-line method is used, calculate the cost recovery deduction for the current year.
a. $5,000.
b. $10,000.
c. $14,290.
d. $20,000.
e.   Some other amount.

22.   Canary Corporation acquired an asset (5-year property) on March 15 for $100,000. The asset is listed property (not an automobile) and it is used 35 percent for business, 50 percent for the production of income, and the remainder of the time it is used for personal use. Assuming the § 179 election is not made, calculate the cost recovery for the current year.
a. $8,500.
b. $10,000.
c. $17,000.
d. $20,000.
e.   Some other amount.

23.   Canary Corporation acquired an asset (5-year property) on March 15 for $100,000. The asset is listed property (not an automobile) and it is used 50 percent for business, 35 percent for the production of income, and the remainder of the time it is used for personal use. Assuming the § 179 election is not made, determine the cost recovery for

the current year.
a. $8,500.
b. $10,000.
c. $17,000.
d. $20,000.
e.   Some other amount.

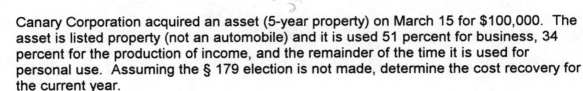

C

24.   Canary Corporation acquired an asset (5-year property) on March 15 for $100,000. The asset is listed property (not an automobile) and it is used 51 percent for business, 34 percent for the production of income, and the remainder of the time it is used for personal use. Assuming the § 179 election is not made, determine the cost recovery for the current year.
a. $8,500.
b. $10,000.
c. $17,000.
d. $20,000.
e.   Some other amount.

25.   On February 26, Jennifer purchased the rights to a depletable asset for $1,000,000. At the time of its acquisition, it was estimated that the number of tons that could be mined would be 250,000. During the year, 50,000 tons were mined and 30,000 tons were sold for $750,000. Expenses other than depletion totaled $500,000. If the depletion rate is 22 percent, calculate the maximum depletion deduction.
a. $120,000.
b. $125,000.
c. $165,000.
d. $200,000.
e.   Some other amount.

$$\frac{1,000,000}{250,000} = 4 \times 30,000 = 120,000$$

$$22\% \times 750,000 = 165,000$$

$$(750,000 - 500,000) \times 50\% = 125,000$$

Code Section Recognition

Several important sections of the Internal Revenue Code are described below. Indicate, by number, the appropriate Code section.

1. _167_ This section permits a deduction for the exhaustion, wear and tear, and obsolescence of business property.

2. _168_ The MACRS rules appear in this section.

3. _280F_ Describes the limitations on depreciation for luxury automobiles.

4. _274_ Provides substantiation requirements for listed property.

Short Answer

1. Identify the MACRS cost recovery period for the following assets:
   a. Automobile. 5 yr
   b. Copier. 5 yr
   c. Office furniture. 7 yr
   d. Land improvements. 15 yr
   e. Computer. 5 yr

2. Betty acquires commercial real estate and residential real estate for $100,000 each in March of 1995. Assuming that each asset is depreciable, compute the annual cost recovery deduction under MACRS and under ADS for the assets' first two years of use.

	MACRS	ADS
Commercial		
Year 1	2033	1979
Year 2	2564	2506
Residential		
Year 1	2679	1979
Year 2	3636	2500

SOLUTIONS TO CHAPTER 7 QUESTIONS

True or False

1.   F   A taxpayer may use a method other than the statutory percentage method, such as the unit-of-production method of depreciation, if appropriate, or may elect to use either the ADS system or the straight-line method over the ACRS or MACRS recovery period. Further, no assets placed in service prior to 1981 may be depreciated using ACRS.

2.   T

3.   T

4.   F   An exception is available for low-income housing whose recovery period is 15 years; and for certain real property placed in service after December 31, 1986, the recovery period is either 27.5 years (for residential realty) or 31.5 years (for nonresidential). For nonresidential realty placed in service after May 12, 1993, the recovery period is 39 years.

5.   F   The limitation concerns the *timing* of the deductions and not the total or aggregate *amount* claimed.

6.   F   Goodwill is amortizable over a 15-year period.

7.   T

8.   T

9.   T

10. T

11. F   The convention applies if more than 40 percent is placed in service during the last 3 (not 4) months of the year.

12. F   The ADS rules are required in several situations, including the alternative minimum tax and earning and profits computations.

13. F   Accelerated methods of cost recovery are available under MACRS for tangible personal property.

14. T

15. T

16. T

17. F   The mid-month convention applies.

18. T

19. T

20. T

Fill-in-the-Blanks

1.   adjusted basis, fair market value
2.   allowed, allowable
3.   estimated useful life
4.   cost, percentage
5.   3, 5, 10, 15; 3, 5, 7, 10, 15, 20
6.   personal
7.   1982, 1986
8.   15, 18, 19; 27.5, 31.5, 39
9.   personal, real
10. personal
11. $217,500
12. straight-line
13. 50
14. Percentage
15. real

Multiple Choice

1. b $27,750 = $17,500 + [($102,500 / 5 yrs.) X 1/2] See Examples 21 and 22 in the text.
2. b $38,000 = $17,500 + ($102,500 X .20) See Example 22 in the text.
3. c   Robert may not elect to use § 179 because the cost of his acquisition exceeded the $217,500 ceiling amount. Therefore, the total cost recovery for the year is $44,000 ($220,000 X .20).
4. d   Luxury automobiles are subject to special restrictions even when they are used predominantly (i.e., more than 50%) for business.
5. e
6. d   The deduction is limited to $3,060 in the year of acquisition. This deduction is less than the amount that would otherwise be available ($20,000 X 20% = $4,000). See Example 26 in the text. Note that these amounts are indexed annually.
7. d
8. b
9. e $500 = $10,000 X .50 X .10. The half-year convention is used in the year of acquisition; the straight-line method is required. See Example 28 in the text.
10. b $1,200 = $10,000 X .60 X .20. Because the taxpayer uses the computer predominantly for business, it may be depreciated using an accelerated method (MACRS). See Example 25 in the text.
11. e
12. f $2,448 -- Lesser of:
             $20,000 X .80 X .20 = $3,200 or
             $3,060 X .80 = $2,448
         See Example 26 in the text. Note that these amounts are indexed annually.
13. e $400 -- Lesser of:
             $20,000 X .20 X .10 = $400 or
             $3,060 X .20 = $612
         The half-year convention is used in the year of acquisition. See Example 28 in the text. Note that these amounts are indexed annually.
14. d $22,470 = $1,000,000 X .02247. See Example 15 and the related discussion in the text.
15. d $22,470 = $1,000,000 X .02247. There is no distinction between new and used property in the cost recovery calculation. See Example 15 and the related discussion in the text.
16. b $28,790 = $1,000,000 X .02879.
17. d $36,360 = $1,000,000 X .03636.
18. e $19,790 = $1,000,000 X .01979.
19. b $19,792 = $1,000,000 X .025 X 9.5/12.
20. b $14,290 = $100,000 X .1429.
21. a $5,000 = $100,000 X .05. The mid-quarter convention applies.
22. a $8,500 = $100,000 X .10 X .85. The property is listed property; straight-line depreciation must be used because the business usage test is not met.
23. a $8,500 = $100,000 X .10 X .85. The property is listed property; straight-line depreciation must be used because the business usage test is not met.
24. c $17,000 = $100,000 X .20 X .85. The property is listed property; however, the straight-line depreciation need not be used because the business usage test is met.
25. b $1,000,000/250,000 tons = $4/ton.
         30,000 tons X $4/ton = $120,000 cost depletion.
         22% X $750,000 = $165,000 percentage depletion.
         Percentage limit ($750,000 - $500,000) X 50% = $125,000.

Code Section Recognition

1.   167
2.   168
3.   280F
4.   274

Short Answer

1.   a.   Automobile -- 5-year property.
          b.   Copier -- 5-year property.
          c.   Office furniture -- 7-year property.
          d.   Land improvements -- 15-year property.
          e.   Computer -- 5-year property.

2.

	MACRS	ADS
Commercial		
Year 1	$2,033	$1,979
Year 2	$2,564	$2,500
Residential		
Year 1	$2,879	$1,979
Year 2	$3,636	$2,500

CHAPTER 8
DEDUCTIONS: EMPLOYEE EXPENSES

CHAPTER HIGHLIGHTS

Discussions concerning the deductibility and treatment of many commonly incurred employee-related expenses are included in this chapter. Specifically, the provisions which govern transportation, travel, moving expenses, education, entertainment, and certain other employee expenses are explained and illustrated. In addition, the substantiation requirements that must be met to support an employee deduction are discussed. Finally, the rules governing the classification of deductions as either *for* or *from* adjusted gross income are discussed in detail.

I. Employee versus Self-Employed
    A. Expenses incurred by self-employed taxpayers (i.e., independent contractors) in a trade or business are deductible *for* adjusted gross income; whereas, expenses incurred as a result of an employment relationship generally may be deductible *from* adjusted gross income.
    B. Generally, an employer-employee relationship exists when the employer has the right to specify the end result of a task and the ways and means by which the end result is to be achieved.
    C. *Statutory employees*, a special category of employees (e.g., full-time insurance salespersons, homeworkers, traveling salespersons), are allowed to deduct expenses *for* adjusted gross income.

II. Employee Expenses -- In general, once employee status has been established, employee expenses fall into one of the following categories. These expenses are not necessarily limited to employees.
    A. Transportation.
    B. Travel.
    C. Moving.
    D. Education.
    E. Entertainment.
    F. Other.

III. Transportation Expenses
    A. Qualified Expenditures

1.   An employee is allowed a deduction *from* adjusted gross income for transportation expenses incurred for the purpose of transporting him/herself from one place to another in the course of business when the employee is not *away from home* in a travel status.

2.   *Commuting expenses* are nondeductible. However, certain costs incurred by an employee who uses an automobile to transport heavy tools to work may be deductible. Further, expenses incurred for transportation from one job to another are deductible as are expenses incurred for transportation associated with *temporary* or minor assignments beyond the general area of the tax home.

B.   Computation of Automobile Expenses

   1.   A taxpayer may compute the deduction for automobile expenses in *either* one of two ways.

      a.   The taxpayer may deduct the actual operating expenses incurred in the pursuit of business.

      b.   The taxpayer may deduct 30 cents per business mile driven during 1995 (29 cents for 1994). Parking fees and tolls are also allowed when using the automatic mileage method.

   2.   Actual operating expenses include depreciation (cost recovery), gas, oil, repairs, licenses, and insurance. Records must be kept to document the automobile's personal and business use. Complex depreciation rules apply if the actual expense method is used.

IV.   Travel Expenses

A.   Definition of Travel Expenses -- Travel expenses are more broadly defined in the law than transportation expenses. In addition to transportation expenses, travel expenses include meals and lodging while away from home in pursuit of business. In contrast to transportation expenses, the taxpayer must be *away from home overnight* in order to deduct travel expenses. Unreimbursed meals and entertainment are subject to the 50 percent rule outlined below.

B.   Away-from-Home Requirement

   1.   To be deductible, travel expenses must be incurred by a taxpayer for a period while away from home substantially longer than an ordinary day's work, and for a period where rest, sleep or a relief-from-work period is required.

KEY TERMS
- Statutory Employee
- 2%-of-AGI Floor
- Travel and Entertainment
- Accountable Plans
- Travel Transportation
- Office in the Home

   2.   Under ordinary circumstances, there is no problem in determining the location of a taxpayer's tax home. However, in some circumstances, controversy may exist.

C.   Restrictions on Travel Expenses

   1.   Deductions related to attending a convention, seminar, or similar meeting are disallowed unless they are associated with the taxpayer's trade or business. The restrictions do not apply to trade or business conventions and seminars. In addition, stringent restrictions on the

deductibility of travel expenses of the taxpayer's spouse or dependent exist.

    2.   No deduction is allowed for travel that by itself is considered by the taxpayer to be educational.

D.   Combined Business and Pleasure Travel -- If a trip combines both business and personal objectives, the following points are relevant.

    1.   Transportation expenses are deductible (for domestic trips) only if the trip is *primarily for business*.

    2.   No transportation expenses may be deducted if the trip is *primarily for personal pleasure*; however, other expenses incurred which specifically relate to business are deductible.

    3.   If the trip is *outside the United States*, special rules apply.

    4.   Special restrictive rules apply to the deductibility of expenses paid or incurred to attend conventions held in locations outside the North American area.

V.   Moving Expenses

A.   General Requirements -- Moving expenses incurred (either as an employee or as a self-employed individual) in connection with the commencement of work at a new principal place are deductible. To be deductible, the *distance and time tests* must be met. Unreimbursed moving expenses are deductible *for* AGI. Employer reimbursements are excludible from income to the extent the amounts are otherwise deductible. Meals are *not* deductible as moving expenses.

B.   Distance Test

    1.   For moving expenses to be deductible, the taxpayer's new job location must be *at least* 50 miles farther from the old residence than the old residence was from the former place of employment.

    2.   This test eliminates the deduction for taxpayers who purchase a new home in the same general area without acquiring new employment, if a new job in the same general area does not necessitate a move, or if the move is for personal reasons.

C.   Time Test -- To be eligible for the moving expense deduction, an employee must be employed on a full-time basis for 39 weeks in the 12-month period following the move; or if the person is self-employed, he or she must work for 78 weeks during the next two years in the new location.

D.   Treatment of Moving Expenses

    1.   What is Included -- Qualified moving expenses include *reasonable* expenses incurred for the following purposes.

        a.   Moving household goods and personal effects.

        b.   Traveling from the former residence to the new place of residence. Traveling for this purpose includes lodging, but not meals, for the taxpayer and members of the household. It does not include the cost of moving servants or others who are not members of the household. The taxpayer can elect to use actual auto expenses (no depreciation is allowed) or the automatic mileage method. In this case, moving expense mileage is limited to nine cents per mile for each automobile. These expenses are also limited by the reasonableness standard.

    2.   How treated

        a.   Qualified moving expenses that are paid (or reimbursed) by the employer are not reported as part of the gross income of the employee.

        b.   Moving expenses that are paid (or reimbursed) by the employer which are not qualified moving expenses are included in the employee's gross income and are not deductible.

        c.   The qualified expenses that are not reimbursed or those of self-employed taxpayers are shown as deductions *for* AGI.

VI.   Education Expenses
    A.   General Requirements
        1.   An employee may deduct education expenses if they are incurred in either of the following situations.
            a.   To maintain or improve existing skills required in the present job.
            b.   To meet the stated requirements of the employer or to meet requirements imposed by law to retain his or her employment status.
        2.   In no instances are education expenses deductible in the following situations.
            a.   If they are incurred to meet the minimum educational standards for qualification in the taxpayer's existing job.
            b.   If they qualify the taxpayer for a new trade or business.
    B.   Requirements Imposed by Law or by the Employer for Retention of Employment -- Teachers often qualify under this provision, which provides for the deduction of education expenses incurred if they are required by their employer or by law to take additional courses. However, if the required education is the minimum required for the job, no deduction is allowed.
    C.   Maintaining or Improving Existing Skills -- This requirement has been difficult for taxpayers and the courts to interpret. The successful application of the rule is often dependent on subtleties of the particular case under consideration.
    D.   Classification of Specific Items -- Educational expenses include expenses for books, tuition, typing, transportation, and travel. Unless the expenses are reimbursed by the taxpayer's employer, the amounts are deductible as miscellaneous itemized deductions, subject to the two percent-of-AGI floor. In addition, the 50 percent rule applies to meals.

VII.   Entertainment Expenses
    A.   Dollar Limitations
        1.   Only 50 percent of meal and entertainment expenses are allowed as a deduction. The limitation applies in both the context of employment or self-employment status.
        2.   Although the reduction can apply to *either* the employer or the employee, it will *not* apply twice.
        3.   Transportation expenses are not affected by this provision.
        4.   The 50 percent limitation does not apply in the following situations.
            a.   Where the full value of the meals or entertainment is included in the compensation of the employee (or independent contractor).
            b.   Where the *de minimis* fringe benefit rule is met.
            c.   Employer-paid recreational activities for employees (e.g., spring picnic).
    B.   Classification of Expenses -- Entertainment expenses may be categorized as follows.
        1.   Those *directly related to business* -- related to an actual business meeting or discussion.
        2.   Those *associated with business* -- must serve a specific business purpose.
    C.   Restrictions Upon Deductibility
        1.   The cost of business meals are deductible only in certain situations.
            a.   The meal is directly related to or associated with the active

        conduct of a trade or business.

    b. The expense is not lavish or extravagant under the circumstances.

    c. The taxpayer (or employee) is present at the meal.

  2. No deduction is allowed for *club dues* for any type of club organized for business, pleasure, or any other purpose. However, this prohibition does not apply to clubs whose primary purpose is public service and community volunteerism (e.g., Kiwanis, Lions, Rotary). This limitation is true regardless of the business usage of the club. However, meals and entertainment expenses incurred at a club may be deductible.

  3. Ticket Purchases for Entertainment

    a. The deduction for the cost of an entertainment event is subject to several limitations. Assuming an expenditure is otherwise deductible, its deduction is limited to 50 percent of the face value of the ticket (including any ticket tax). Thus, to the extent a premium is paid for a ticket (e.g., to a "scalper"), none of the excess over face value would be deductible.

    b. A special rule for skyboxes provides that expenditures for the rental or use of a luxury skybox at a sports arena are deductible only to the extent of the face value of the regular tickets.

  4. Business gifts are deductible to the extent of $25 per donee per year. Records must be maintained to substantiate business gifts.

VIII. Other Employee Expenses

 A. Office in the Home

  1. No deduction is allowed unless a portion of the residence is used *exclusively* and on a *regular basis* in either of the following two ways.

    a. As the principal place of business for any trade or business of the taxpayer.

    b. As a place of business which is used by patients, clients, or customers.

  2. Employees must meet an additional test: the use must be for the *convenience of the employer* as opposed to being merely *appropriate and helpful*.

  3. The allowable home office expense may not exceed the gross income from the business reduced by all other business expenses attributable to the activity.

 B. Miscellaneous Employee Expenses -- Other employee expenses, which are generally deductible *from* adjusted gross income and subject to the two percent-of-AGI limitation, include the following.

  1. Union dues.

  2. Professional expenses (e.g., dues).

  3. Certain employment agency fees.

  4. Special clothing.

 These expenses are deductible *for* AGI only if they are reimbursed.

 C. Contributions to Individual Retirement Accounts

  1. Employees not covered by another qualified plan may establish their own tax deductible IRAs. The annual deduction is limited to the *lesser* of $2,000 (or $2,250 for spousal IRAs) or 100 percent of compensation.

  2. If the taxpayer or spouse is an active participant in another qualified plan, the IRA deduction limitation is phased out *proportionately* between certain adjusted gross income ranges.

  3. When a deduction for the contribution is available, it is deducted *for* AGI.

  4. To the extent that an individual is ineligible to make a deductible

contribution to an IRA, nondeductible contributions may be made to separate accounts.

Congress limited the deduction for contributions to IRAs in the 1986 tax act, allowing deductions only for those who have access to no other qualified retirement plan, because so many taxpayers were making use of the deduction, and the 1986 act essentially became revenue neutral based upon the repeal of this deduction. An IRA deduction for all taxpayers would (a) move the income tax toward a consumption tax model, (b) encourage citizens to save for the future, and (c) create sizable tax liabilities in the future, when the funds and the related investment income are withdrawn from the account.

IX.   Classification of Employee Expenses
   A.   If employee expenses are reimbursed by an employer under an accountable plan, they are not reported by the employee.
   B.   If the expenses are reimbursed under a nonaccountable plan or are not reimbursed at all, then they are classified as deductions *from* AGI and can only be claimed if the employee-taxpayer itemizes.
   C.   Moving expenses and the employment-related expenses of a qualified performing artist are deductible *for* AGI.
   D.   Accountable Plans
      1.   An *accountable plan* requires the employee to satisfy the following requirements.
         a.   The employee must adequately account for, or substantiate, the expenses.
         b.   The employee must return any excess reimbursement or allowance to the employer.
      2.   Proper *substantiation* of expenses involves maintaining adequate records which contain the following information.
         a.   The amount of the expense.
         b.   The time and place of travel or entertainment, or date of gift.
         c.   The business purpose of such expense.
         d.   The business relationship of the taxpayer to the person entertained or receiving the gift.
      3.   To reduce paperwork, some employers reimburse employees for travel away from home based on a flat dollar amount per day of business travel (a *per diem*). The amount *deemed substantiated* is equal to the *lesser* of the per diem allowance or the amount of the federal per diem rate.
         a.   Use of the standard federal per diem for meals constitutes an adequate accounting. Further, an employee who receives a reimbursement of not more than the standard mileage rate allowed for tax purposes for the use of an automobile will be treated as rendering an adequate accounting.
         b.   Only the *amount* of the expense is considered substantiated under the deemed substantiated method. The other substantiation requirements mentioned above must also be met.
         c.   Limitations apply which prohibit the use of the per diem method as an adequate accounting for certain parties related to the employer.
   E.   Nonaccountable Plans -- A *nonaccountable plan* is one in which an adequate

accounting or return of excess amounts is not required, or both. All reimbursements are fully included as income and deductible in the same manner as unreimbursed expenses.

    1.   Unreimbursed employee expenses -- Meals and entertainment expenses are subject to the 50% limit. Total unreimbursed employee business expenses are reported as miscellaneous itemized deductions subject to the 2%-of-AGI floor.

    2.   Failure of an employee to follow the rules of an accountable plan causes nonaccountable plan treatment.

F.   Reporting Procedures -- Requirements range from no reporting at all (accountable plans when all requirements are met) to the use of some or all of three forms (i.e., Form W-2, Form 2106, and Schedule A) for nonaccountable plans and unreimbursed expenses.

The value of a deduction depends on the tax bracket of the taxpayer incurring an expense. For example, if a taxpayer who incurs an employee business expense of $100 is in the 15 percent tax bracket, the net after-tax cost of a deductible expenditure to the employee is $85. That is, the taxpayer is out-of-pocket by $85. A better approach would be for the taxpayer to seek reimbursement from his or her employer of any business related expenses incurred, reducing the out-of-pocket cost to the employee to zero. If the reimbursement is not granted, then the taxpayer should claim the appropriate deduction.

X.   Limitations on Itemized Deductions

A.   *Miscellaneous itemized deductions* are classified as members of either one of two groups. Certain of these miscellaneous itemized deductions are aggregated and reduced by two percent- of-AGI, while certain other itemized deductions are not subject to this limitation.

B.   Other itemized deductions that are not miscellaneous itemized deductions *may* be subject to their own limitations. Such deductions include charitable contributions, interest expenses, taxes, medical expenses, and certain casualty losses (see Chapters 5 and 9).

C.   Miscellaneous itemized deductions which must be aggregated and then reduced by two percent- of-AGI include the following.

    1.   All § 212 expenses, except expenses of producing rent and royalty income. (Rent and royalty expenses are deductible *for* AGI.)

    2.   All unreimbursed employee expenses (after the 50 percent reduction for meals and entertainment expenditures, if applicable) except moving expenses.

    3.   Professional dues and subscriptions.

    4.   Union dues and work uniforms.

    5.   Employment-related educational expenses.

    6.   Malpractice insurance premiums.

    7.   Expenses of job hunting.

    8.   Home office expenses.

    9.   Legal, accounting, and tax return preparation fees.

    10.   Hobby expenses (up to hobby income).

    11.   Investment expenses.

    12.   Custodial fees relating to income-producing property.

13.   Any fees paid to collect interest or dividends.
14.   Appraisal fees incurred to establish a casualty loss or charitable contribution.

D.   Other miscellaneous itemized deductions are not subject to the two percent-of-AGI floor. Included in this group are the following.

1.   Impairment-related work expenses of handicapped individuals.
2.   Gambling losses to the extent of gambling winnings.

TEST FOR SELF-EVALUATION -- CHAPTER 8

True or False

Indicate which of the following statements are true or false by circling the correct answer.

(T)   F   1.   Expenses of self-employed individuals incurred in a trade or business are always deductible *for* adjusted gross income.

T   **(F)**   2.   An employee may never deduct employee related expenses *for* adjusted gross income.

T   **(F)**   3.   For tax purposes, transportation expenses and travel expenses incurred by an employee are always deductible *for* adjusted gross income.

(T)   F   4.   For persons who qualify, payments to Individual Retirement Accounts are deductible *for* adjusted gross income.

T   **(F)**   5.   Transportation expenses and travel expenses are synonymous terms.

T   **(F)**   6.   Moving expenses are deductible without limit if they are related to an employee's trade or business.

T   **(F)**   7.   A taxpayer's daily cost of traveling from his home in Richmond, VA to his job in Washington, D.C. are deductible because he is traveling out of town.

(T)   F   8.   Special clothing, such as that worn by a police officer, may be deductible as a miscellaneous employee expense.

T   **(F)**   9.   All employee expenses reimbursed under a nonaccountable plan by an employer are deductible *for* adjusted gross income.

(T)   F   10.   A taxpayer may compute the deduction for automobile expenses in either one of two ways: the taxpayer may deduct the actual operating expenses incurred in the pursuit of business, or the taxpayer may deduct a standard allowance for every business mile driven.

T   **(F)**   11.   Like other employee expenses deductible *from* adjusted gross income as miscellaneous itemized deductions, moving expenses are subject to the two percent-of-adjusted gross income limitation.

T   **(F)**   12.   The deduction for meals and entertainment is always limited to 50 percent of the cost incurred.

T   **(F)**   13.   The tax treatment of business expenses applicable to employees and independent contractors is essentially the same.

(T)   F   14.   Statutory employees are allowed to deduct related expenses *for* adjusted gross income.

(T)   F   15.   Unreimbursed employee expenses, such as for travel, are miscellaneous itemized deductions subject to the two percent-of-AGI floor.

T (F) 16. Lavish or extravagant expenses are excluded after application of the 50 percent rule.

T (F) 17. For a plan to be an accountable plan, participating employees only must render an adequate accounting of expenses.

T (F) 18. Commuting expenses are never deductible.

(T) F 19. The law disallows all deductions related to attending a convention, seminar, or similar meeting unless the expenses are related to a trade or business of the taxpayer.

T (F) 20. An example of a qualifying educational expense is one that enables an employee to meet the minimum educational standards for qualification in the taxpayer's existing job.

Fill-in-the-Blanks

Complete the following statements with the appropriate word(s) or amount(s).

1. If a taxpayer utilizes the automatic method in computing the allowable automobile expense deduction for 1995, the deduction is based on ____30____ cents per mile.

2. Unreimbursed moving expenses are deductible ____for____ adjusted gross income.

3. To be eligible for the moving expense deduction, a taxpayer must meet two basic tests: ___distance___ and ___time___.

4. Moving expenses incurred by a self-employed taxpayer are deductible ____for____ AGI.

5. In order to be deductible, entertainment expenses must be categorized as either ___direct___ or ___associated___

6. Business gifts generally are deductible to the extent of ___25___ per donee per year.

7. In order for ___travel___ expenses to be deductible, a taxpayer must meet the "away from home" requirement.

8. An absence by a taxpayer of more than ___1 year___ from his/her tax home automatically causes a change in the tax home.

9. A single individual may contribute up to ___2,000___ per year to an IRA.

10. Certain miscellaneous itemized deductions are deductible *from* AGI to the extent that they exceed ____2____ percent of the taxpayer's AGI.

11. No deduction is allowed for a home office unless the office space is used ___exclusively___ and ___regularly___ for trade or business activity.

12. The tax treatment of employee business expenses depends on whether the expenses are ___reimbursed___ or ___unreimbursed___ and, if reimbursed, whether the expenses are reimbursed under an ___accountable___ plan or a ___nonaccountable___ plan.

13. In most situations, ___meal___ and ___entertainment___ expenses are reduced by 50 percent of the

amount incurred.

Multiple Choice

Choose the best answer for each of the following questions.

_____ 1. Kathleen incurred the following expenses when her employer transferred her from Chicago to New York.

Continental Movers	$1,900
House-hunting trip to NYC	1,400
Loss on sale of old residence	5,000
Installation of carpeting in new home	800
Real estate commissions on residences	1,000
Lodging costs enroute to new residence	400

Assuming Kathleen is not reimbursed by her employer, she may deduct what amount as her moving expenses?
a. $9,700.
b. $8,900.
c. $6,100.
d. $5,700.
e.   None of the above.

_____ 2. David, an employee of Able Accountants, Inc., incurs a total of $4,500 in business expenses, consisting of the following.

Transportation (other than commuting)	$1,200
Lodging while away from home	1,800
Professional dues	750
Dues and subscriptions	750
Total	$4,500

David received a reimbursement of $3,000 from his employer under an accountable plan. His itemized deductions, based on the above and before any limitations, would be what amount?
a. $1,500.
b. $1,000.
c. $500.
d. $250.
e.   None of the above.

_____ 3. Matt had incurred the following expenses at the Thursday Society Social Club. Matt was not reimbursed by his employer for any of these expenses.

Annual dues	$5,500
Business meals "directly related to"	1,700
Business meals "associated with"	300
Personal meals and charges	2,000
Days directly related to business	120
Days associated with business	30
Days of personal use	70

The deduction attributable to the above before the two percent-of-AGI limitation and the 50 percent limitation is what amount?

a. $2,000.
b. $5,000.
c. $5,750.
d. $7,500.
e. None of the above.

_d_   4.   James, a traveling sales representative (i.e., a statutory employee), incurred the following job related expenses as an employee of J. Jones, Inc.

Transportation	$3,000
Travel	1,000
Entertainment and dues	2,000

His employer reimbursed him to the extent of $4,000, which was intended to cover all of James's expenses. Before the 50 percent limitation, what amount may James deduct as a deduction *for* adjusted gross income?

a. $4,000.
b. $4,667.
c. $5,333.
d. $6,000.
e. None of the above.

_C_   5.   Steve moved to Dallas during the year. He moved from Wyoming after getting a Masters in Tax degree. On concluding he could apply his tax expertise, he accepted the job of managing the Cowboys' Cheerleaders. During the move from Wyoming, Steve incurred the following expenses.

Truck Rental	$250
New grips on golf clubs	50
Cost of shipping pet Bengal Tiger	1,000
Lodging during trip	500
House-hunting costs after securing new job	1,000
Hotel, first 60 days in Dallas	1,100
Miles traveled in car	1,000

Assuming Steve's AGI is $30,000, what is the deduction *for* AGI for moving expenses?

a. $840.
b. $890.
c. $1,840.
d. $3,940.
e. None of the above.

_a_   6.   Nancy teaches French at Central High School. The local school board requires that she take professional development courses to maintain her professional status--and to retain her position on the faculty. The expenses incurred in meeting this requirement during the year at a college in another city are as follows.

Transportation	$600
Meals (while out of town)	200
Lodging	300
Trip to France to maintain general	

familiarity with the culture	1,500
Tuition and books	700
Total	$3,300

Unfortunately, the school board does not reimburse its employees for such expenditures. Nancy's AGI is $40,000. What is her deduction *from* AGI?

a. $900.
b. $1,000.
c. $1,700.
d. $1,800.
e. $2,500.
f. None of the above.

7. In celebration of the oldest locally-owned hardware store's 95th anniversary, the owners decide to make some business gifts to its valued employees. Because the 10 employees had served for varying lengths of time, gifts of different values were presented to the employees. These gifts, which were not considered to be compensation, had the following fair market values: two at $20 each, three at $25 each, three at $50 each, and two at $500 each. What amount pertaining to these gifts is deductible as a business expense?

a. $1,265.
b. $250.
c. $240.
d. $115.
e. $0.

8. Tami is a CPA who works as a public accountant for Lincolnshire and Company, CPAs. During the current year she incurred and paid the following expenses. Her employer's reimbursement procedure is pursuant to the terms of an accountable plan.

Airfare for business trips (reimbursed in full by employer)	$800
Use of personal auto for company business (reimbursed by employer for $400)	500
Professional dues	300
Safety deposit box rental where she keeps US Savings Bonds	50
Cost of preparing her will	100

If Tami were to itemize her personal deductions, what amount should she claim as miscellaneous deductible expenses, without considering any limitations?

a. $450.
b. $850.
c. $950.
d. $1,750.
e. None of the above.

9. Mary and Joseph decided that it was time to take a second honeymoon to Niagara Falls. However, Joseph decided to incorporate some business into the trip in order to be able to deduct a portion of the costs. Luckily, the headquarters office of one of his business clients was located in Niagara Falls. Roundtrip airfare from their home to Niagara Falls was $260 per passenger. Of the ten days out of town, Joseph consulted with his client for two days. How much of the airfare may Mary and Joseph deduct?

a. $520.
b. $260.

    c. $104.
    d. $52.
    e.   None of the above.

10. Which of the following expenses is *not* classified as a miscellaneous itemized deduction subject to the two percent-of-AGI floor?

    a.   Moving expense.
    b.   Home office expense.
    c.   Investment expense.
    d.   Unreimbursed employee expense.
    e.   All of the above are miscellaneous itemized deductions subject to the two percent-of-AGI floor.

11. Select the *correct* statement.

    a.   Meals and entertainment deductions are always subject to the 50 percent limitation.
    b.   Reimbursed employee expenses are deductible *for* AGI.
    c.   Commuting expenses may be deducted by an employee if the distance between the taxpayer's home and employment exceeds 50 miles.
    d.   The terms transportation expense and travel expense are synonymous.
    e.   None of the above is correct.

12. Sam and Susan are both employed and earn $35,000 and $37,000, respectively. Neither of them are active participants in a qualified retirement plan. They file a joint federal income tax return. What is the maximum amount that may be contributed to an IRA and deducted by Sam and Susan?

    a. $0 and $0.
    b. $2,000 and $2,000.
    c. $2,250 and $2,250.
    d. $2,250 allocated between Sam and Susan as they agree.
    e.   None of the above.

13. Ramon and Alicia are both employed and earn $35,000 and $37,000, respectively. Ramon, but not Alicia, is an active participant in his employer's qualified retirement plan. They file a joint federal income tax return. What is the maximum amount that may be contributed to an IRA and deducted by Ramon and Alicia?

    a. $0 and $0.
    b. $2,000 and $2,000.
    c. $2,250 and $2,250.
    d. $2,250 allocated between Ramon and Alicia as they agree.
    e.   None of the above.

14. Select the *correct* statement below.

    a.   The tax treatment of employee business expenses generally depends on whether the expenses are reimbursed or unreimbursed.
    b.   The tax treatment of reimbursed employee business expenses depends on whether the expenses were reimbursed under an accountable plan or a nonaccountable plan.
    c.   A reimbursement plan is considered an accountable plan if the employee renders an adequate accounting of the expenses and returns any excess reimbursement or allowance.
    d.   Only the amount of an employee business expense is considered substantiated under the deemed substantiated method.
    e.   All of the above statements are correct.

_b_   15.   The following does *not* qualify as a deductible employee education expense.
        a.   Expenses incurred to maintain or improve existing skills required in the present job.
        b.   Fees incurred for professional qualification exams.
        c.   Amounts incurred to meet the express requirements of the employer to retain employment status.
        d.   Amounts incurred to meet the express requirements imposed by law to retain employment status.
        e.   All of the above qualify as deductible education expenses.

_d_   16.   Which of the following is *not* a miscellaneous itemized deduction subject to the two percent-of-AGI floor?
        a.   Unreimbursed employee expenses.
        b.   Union and professional dues.
        c.   Employment-related educational expenses.
        d.   Moving expenses.
        e.   All of the above are miscellaneous itemized deductions subject to the two percent-of-AGI floor.

_✓_   17.   The following is *not* an exception to the 50 percent rule for meals and entertainment.
        a.   Where the full value of meals or entertainment is included in the compensation of an employee.
        b.   Where the full value of meals or entertainment is included in the compensation of an independent contractor.
        c.   Where the expense relates to traditional employer-paid recreation expenses for employees.
        d.   Where the taxpayer can prove the validity of the expense in the conduct of the business.
        e.   All of the above are exceptions.

_a_   18.   Dena incurs unreimbursed employee meals and entertainment expenses of $2,400 in her job as an accountant. If her AGI is $45,000 and she has no other miscellaneous itemized deductions, what is the amount of her deduction?
        a. $300.
        b. $600.
        c. $900.
        d. $1,200.
        e.   None of the above.

_c_   19.   Harry, whose AGI is $90,000 this year (without considering the expenditures below), incurs the following expenses.

Unreimbursed moving expenses	$3,000
Tax return preparation fee	500
Unreimbursed employee expenses	1,000
Safe deposit rental	100
Total	$4,600

        Assuming Harry itemizes his deductions, the total amount deductible resulting from the above expenditures is what amount?
        a. $1,600.
        b. $2,800.
        c. $3,000.
        d. $4,600.

e.   None of the above.

a

20.   Harry, whose AGI is $90,000 this year (without considering the expenditures
        below), incurs the following expenses.

Deductible moving expenses	$3,000
Tax return preparation fee	500
Unreimbursed employee expenses	1,000
Safe deposit rental	100
Total	$4,600

Assuming Harry itemizes his deductions, what is the total itemized deductions
resulting from the above expenditures?
a. $0.
b. $2,800.
c. $3,000.
d. $4,600.
e.   None of the above.

e

21.   Records which are to substantiate expenses incurred need not include which of
        the following items?
a.   The amount of the expense.
b.   The time and place at which the expense was incurred.
c.   The business purpose of the expense.
d.   The business relationship of the taxpayer to the person for whom the
        expense was incurred.
e.   All of the above are necessary.

a

22.   Which of the following is *not* deductible employee expenses?
a.   Expense incurred for daily travel from home in Baltimore to office in
        Washington, D.C.
b.   Expense of traveling from taxpayer's office to client's office.
c.   Expense of traveling from one job (day-time job) to another job (evening
        job).
d.   All of the above are deductible.
e.   None of the above is deductible.

d

23.   Which of the following is *not* true?
a.   Travel expenses are allowed if the taxpayer clearly demonstrates a
        realistic expectation as to the temporary nature of the job.
b.   If an assignment is indefinite in length rather than temporary, no
        deduction will be allowed for the travelling expenses.
c.   For travel expenses to be deductible, the taxpayer must be away from home
        overnight.
d.   If a trip is primarily for pleasure, the amount of deductible
        transportation expenses are determined based on the relative time spent
        on personal and business matters.
e.   All of the above are true.

b

24.   A self-employed accountant attended a tax seminar and incurred the following
        expenses.

Air transportation	$ 500
Local transportation	50
Airport parking	50

Meals	320
Lodging	275
Dry cleaning	25
Total	$1,220

The taxpayer may claim a deduction *for* AGI for the following amount.

a. $1,035.
b. $1,060.
c. $1,075.
d. $1,220.
e. None of the above.

25. A self-employed physician attended a tax seminar and incurred the following expenses.

Air transportation	$ 500
Local transportation	50
Airport parking	50
Meals	320
Lodging	275
Dry cleaning	25
Total	$1,220

The taxpayer may claim a deduction *for* AGI for the following amount.

a. $1,035.
b. $1,060.
c. $1,075.
d. $1,220.
e. None of the above.

Code Section Recognition

Several important sections of the Internal Revenue Code are described below. Indicate, by number, the appropriate Code section.

1. _____ The location of employee related expenses on the tax return and the definition of adjusted gross income are discussed here.

2. _____ Restrictions on the deductibility of entertainment expenses.

3. _____ Provides the rules which govern the deductibility of moving expenses.

Short Answer

1. James, an employee of Wren Corporation, accepts a promotion which requires a move to another city. In the move, the following expenses are incurred.

Transportation costs during the move	$ 500
Cost of meals enroute to new location	200
Charge for professional movers	3,000
House-hunting expenses	1,200
Temporary housing expenses at new location (four nights)	400
Real estate commission on sale of old home	1,600

Compute the amount of the moving expense deduction James may claim on his income tax return, assuming the expenses are not reimbursed by his employer.

2.   Jane, is an employee of an accounting firm in Gainesville, Florida and is need of CPE credit to maintain her certification to practice in Florida. Therefore, she attends the AICPA National Tax Education Program held at the University of Illinois and incurs the following expenses, none of which are reimbursed by her employer.

Transportation	$600
Tuition and materials	1,200
Meals	300
Lodging	500

Compute the amount Jane may treat as an itemized deduction and describe how the deduction is treated (i.e., is it subject to any limitations?).

SOLUTIONS TO CHAPTER 8 QUESTIONS

True or False

1.   T
2.   F   Unreimbursed employee expenses *generally* are deducted *from* AGI, but such expenses which are reimbursed by the employer are deducted *for* AGI, assuming the reimbursement is under an accountable plan. In addition, unreimbursed moving expenses are deducted *for* AGI.
3.   F   Such expenses are deductible *for* AGI only if they have been reimbursed by the employer.
4.   T
5.   F   Travel expenses are incurred when the taxpayer is away from home, whereas the away from home status is not required for transportation expenses. Further, the term travel expenses has a broader meaning than does the term transportation expenses.
6.   F   Only qualifying unreimbursed moving expenses of a reasonable amount are deductible. Indirect moving expenses (e.g., commissions on the sale of an old residence) and meals are not deductible.
7.   F   Commuting expenses are not deductible.
8.   T
9.   F   The deductions are classified as deductions *from* AGI and can only be claimed if the employee-taxpayer itemizes.
10. T
11. F   Unreimbursed moving expenses are deductible *for* AGI.
12. F   Several exceptions to the 50 percent rule exist.
13. F   Expenses incurred by self-employed taxpayers are deductible *for* AGI while similar expenses incurred by employees are deductible either *for* or *from* AGI, depending on the circumstances.
14. T
15. T
16. F   Such expenses are excluded *before* application of the 50 percent rule.
17. F   In addition, the employee must return any excess reimbursement or allowance.
18. F   While commuting expenses generally are not deductible, several exceptions exist (e.g., to transport heavy tools, to travel to a second job).
19. T
20. F   Educational expenses incurred that enable an employee to meet minimum educational standards are not deductible.

Fill-in-the-Blanks

1.   30
2.   *for*
3.   distance, time
4.   *for*
5.   directly related to business, associated with business
6. $25
7.   travel
8.   one year
9. $2,000
10. two
11. exclusively, on a regular basis
12. reimbursed, unreimbursed, accountable, nonaccountable

13.   meals, entertainment

Multiple Choice

1.   e   Continental Movers $1,900
           Lodging costs enroute to new residence   400
           Total deductible moving expenses $2,300
           See Example 23 in the text.
2.   a   The unreimbursed expenses ($1,500 = $4,500 - $3,000) subject to limitation are
           deductible *from* AGI as itemized deductions.
3.   a $2,000 = $1,700 + $300 See Example 33 in the text.
4.   d   Statutory employee expenses are deductible *for* AGI.
5.   c   Truck Rental $ 250
           Cost of shipping pet   1,000
           Lodging during trip   500
           Mileage (1,000 miles X $.09)   90
           Total moving expense deduction $1,840
           See Example 23 in the text.
6.   a   Transportation $ 600
           Meals (50% X 200)   100
           Lodging   300
           Tuition and books   700
           Subtotal $1,700
           Less: $40,000 X .02   800
           Total education expense deduction $ 900
           See Example 25 in the text.
7.   c $240 = (2 X $20) + (8 X $25)
8.   a $450 = $100 (unreimbursed auto expense) + $300 (professional dues) + $50 (safety
           deposit box rental) See Example 42 in the text.
9.   e   Nothing may be deducted, because the trip was not *primarily* for business. Of the
           ten days out of town, only two were devoted to business. See Example 20 in the
           text.
10.   a   Moving expenses are deductible *for* AGI.
11.   b
12.   b
13.   a
14.   e
15.   b
16.   d
17.   d
18.   a   Expenses incurred $2,400
           Less: 50%   1,200
           Subtotal $1,200
           Less: 2%-of-AGI   900
           Deduction $ 300
           See Example 42 in the text.
19.   c   Deduction *for* AGI
               Moving expense $3,000
           Deduction subject to the 2%-of-AGI floor
               ($500 + $1,000 + $100) $1,600
           Less: 2%-of-AGI [($90,000 - $3,000 moving
               expense deducted *for* AGI) X 2%]   1,740   0
           Total deduction $3,000
           See Example 42 in the text.

20.   a   Moving expenses are deductible *for* AGI. The other expenditures ($1,600) are not deductible because they are offset by the 2 percent-of-AGI floor [($90,000 - $3,000 moving expense deducted *for* AGI) X 2% = $1,740].

21.   e

22.   a

23.   d

24.   b $1,060 = $500 + $50 + $50 + ($320 X .50) + $275 + $25

25.   e   None of the expenses are deductible. The law disallows all deductions related to attending a seminar unless the expenses are related to the taxpayer's trade or business.

Code Section Recognition

1.   62
2.   274
3.   217

Short Answer

1.   Only certain moving expenses are deductible *for* AGI.

Transportation costs during the move	$ 500
Charge for professional movers	3,000
Total deductible moving expenses	$3,500

2.

Transportation	$600
Tuition and materials	1,200
Meals ($300 X 50%)	150
Lodging	500
Total	$2,450

The deduction of $2,450 is subject to the 2%-of-AGI floor limitation. Therefore, the amount actually deducted by Jane must be reduced by 2% of her AGI.

CHAPTER 9
DEDUCTIONS AND LOSSES:
CERTAIN ITEMIZED DEDUCTIONS

CHAPTER HIGHLIGHTS

ection 262 of the Code specifically provides that personal expenditures are not allowed as deductions in computing taxable income. However, there are certain expenses that are essentially personal in nature which become deductible in the tax computation because of *legislative grace*. These personal expenses, which are deductible *from* adjusted gross income as itemized deductions, include medical expenses, certain taxes, interest expenses on a home mortgage, charitable contributions, personal casualty and theft losses, and certain miscellaneous expenditures. The details relating to the nature of these deductible items and the required computational procedures and limitations are discussed in this chapter.

I.   General Classification of Expenses
   A.   As a general rule, personal expenditures are disallowed by statute as deductions in arriving at taxable income. If the Code does not specifically provide for a deduction of a personal expenditure, then it is *not* deductible.
   B.   There are some personal expenses that, because of *legislative grace*, are deductible. These amounts are deductible *from* adjusted gross income (in lieu of claiming the standard deduction) and are referred to as *itemized deductions*.

II.   Medical Expenses
   A.   General Requirements -- Within limitations (to the extent eligible expenses *exceed* 7.5 percent of adjusted gross income) and to the extent not reimbursed by insurance or otherwise, medical expenses paid for the care of the taxpayer, spouse, and dependents are allowed as an itemized deduction.
   B.   Medical Expenses Defined
      1.   The term *medical care* includes expenditures incurred for the "diagnosis, cure, mitigation, treatment, or prevention of disease, or for the purpose of affecting any structure or function of the body."
      2.   Deductible expenses are expenses that are incurred to cure any specific ailment or disease and do not include those expenses incurred for enhancing the general health of the taxpayer. However, costs incurred as a preventive measure (e.g., annual physical exam) are deductible. The cost of prescription drugs and insulin is included as a medical expense.
      3.   Amounts paid for discretionary *cosmetic surgery* are not deductible medical expenses. Such surgery would only be considered necessary when it ameliorates the following.

    a. A deformity arising from a congenital abnormality.

    b. A personal injury.

    c. A disfiguring disease.

  4. The deductibility of *nursing home expenses* depends on the medical condition of the patient and the nature of the services rendered.

  5. *Tuition expense* of a dependent at a special school may be deductible as a medical expense if the individual's condition is such that the resources of the school for alleviating such infirmities are a principal reason for the individual's presence there.

C. Capital Expenditures for Medical Purposes

  1. A capital expenditure that qualifies as a medical expense is deductible in the year incurred.

  2. A capital improvement (e.g., swimming pool, elevator) which would otherwise qualify as a medical expenditure is deductible to the extent that the expenditure *exceeds* the increase in value of the related property.

  3. The full cost of certain home-related capital expenditures incurred for the benefit of a physically handicapped individual qualifies as a medical expense. Qualifying costs include the following.

    a. Construction of entrance and exit ramps to the residence.

    b. Widening doorways at a residence's entrances and exits.

    c. Modifying (i.e., widening) doorways and hallways to accommodate wheelchairs.

    d. Installation of railings, support bars, etc. in bathrooms to accommodate handicapped individuals.

    e. Modifying kitchen cabinets and equipment to accommodate access by handicapped individuals.

    f. Adjustment of electrical outlets and fixtures.

D. Medical Expenses Incurred for Spouse and Dependents

  1. A taxpayer's medical expense deduction includes medical expenses paid or incurred on behalf of a spouse and dependents.

  2. In determining dependency status for medical expense purposes, neither the gross income nor the joint return tests apply (see Chapter 2).

  3. Medical expenses paid on behalf of a former spouse may be deductible as a medical expense or as alimony, depending on the circumstances.

  4. Special rules apply to a noncustodial parent in the situation of divorced persons with children.

E. Transportation, Meal, and Lodging Expenses for Medical Treatment

  1. Expenditures incurred for *transportation* (for the patient and parent or other attendant) to and from a point of treatment are deductible. The IRS currently allows a deduction of nine cents per mile instead of actual out-of-pocket expenses if an automobile is used in such transit.

  2. *Lodging* expenses of up to $50 *per* night for *each* person (i.e., for the patient, and in some situations another person) may be deducted in certain cases while receiving medical care away from home.

F. Amounts Paid for Medical Insurance Premiums -- Medical insurance premiums paid by the taxpayer are treated like any other medical expense and are subject to the 7.5 percent-of-AGI limit. If a taxpayer is self-employed, up to 25 percent of certain insurance premiums paid for medical coverage is deductible as a business expense. Any excess can be treated as a medical expense. (The 25 percent deduction for self-employed taxpayers expired for tax years after 1993, but many commentators expect that Congress will reenact it.)

G. Year of Deduction

  1. Medical expenses are deductible in the year *paid*, regardless of the taxpayer's method of accounting.

  2. In most situations, lump-sum prepayments for medical services are not

deductible in the year of payment if the services are to be received in future years. However, exceptions may exist if the taxpayer is under an obligation to make such prepayments.

H.   Reimbursements

1.   When an insurance reimbursement has been received for medical expenses which were deducted in a previous year, the reimbursement must be included in gross income to the extent a *tax benefit* was received in the earlier year.

KEY TERMS
● Medical Expense
● Personal Interest
● Investment Interest
● Home Mortgage Interest
● Charitable Contributions
● Miscellaneous Itemized Deductions

2.   If the taxpayer did not itemize deductions in the year the expenses were incurred, a subsequent reimbursement is *not* included in gross income.

III.   Taxes -- The deduction of certain state, local, and foreign taxes paid or accrued by a taxpayer is allowed in order to relieve the burden of multiple taxes upon the same source of revenue.

A.   Deductibility as a Tax

1.   A distinction is made between a *tax* and a *fee*. Certain taxes (i.e., enforced contributions) are deductible, whereas fees are not deductible *unless* they are incurred as ordinary and necessary business expenses or for the production of income.

2.   The following taxes are listed in the Code as being deductible.

a.   State, local, and foreign real property taxes.

b.   State and local personal property taxes.

c.   State, local, and foreign income taxes.

d.   The environmental tax.

3.   Taxes that may *not* be deducted include the following.

a.   Federal income taxes, including any social security and railroad retirement taxes paid by the employee.

b.   Estate, inheritance, and gift taxes.

c.   General sales taxes.

d.   Federal, state, and local excise taxes.

e.   Foreign income taxes, if the foreign tax credit is claimed.

f.   Taxes on real property to the extent that such taxes are apportioned and treated as imposed on another taxpayer.

B.   Property Taxes

1.   Real and personal property taxes are generally deductible by the person against whom the tax is imposed.

2.   Personal property taxes must be *ad valorem* (i.e., assessed in relation to the value of the property).

3.   As a general rule, real property taxes do not include amounts assessed for local benefits (e.g., sidewalks, curbing in front of a taxpayer's home). Such assessments are added to the adjusted basis of the taxpayer's property.

4.   Assessments are deductible as taxes if the taxpayer can show that the amounts are incurred for the purpose of maintenance or repair, or for the purpose of meeting interest charges with respect to such benefits.

5.   Real estate taxes for the entire year must be apportioned between a buyer and seller of real property, regardless of who actually pays the tax and without

     regard to a proration in the purchase agreement, based on the number of days the property was held by each party during the real property tax year.

  6. In making such an apportionment, the real estate tax year serves as the basis for apportionment, and the assessment and lien dates are disregarded.

C. State and Local Income Taxes

  1. State, local, or foreign income taxes imposed on individuals can only be deductible as itemized deductions, even if the taxpayer's sole source of income is from business, rents, or royalties.

  2. The amounts are deductible in the year withheld by a taxpayer's employer or paid by an individual, even if the amounts paid relate to a prior or subsequent year.

  3. A refund received in a later year due to excessive withholdings and/or estimated tax payments must be included in gross income to the extent that a deduction provided a *tax benefit* in the prior year.

> A taxpayer should be careful not to include too much of a state tax refund in income. State tax refunds may not be taxable if the taxpayer did not get a tax benefit from the previous year's deduction. For example, if a taxpayer used the standard deduction in the year the taxes were paid, the refunded amount is not included in income.

IV. Interest

 A. Disallowed and Allowed Items

  1. Generally, only certain types of interest paid or accrued on indebtedness within the taxable year are deductible. However, even when a certain type of interest is allowable as a deduction, restrictions may be present in the law which limit the amount of its deductibility.

  2. *Interest* has been defined as compensation for the use or forbearance of money.

  3. The general rule is that *personal (consumer) interest* is *not* deductible. Personal interest generally is any interest other than the following.

   a. Trade or business interest.

   b. Investment interest.

   c. Interest on passive activities.

   d. Home mortgage interest to a limited extent if it is qualified residence interest.

  4. The amount of *investment interest* expense (i.e., interest incurred on funds borrowed to acquire investment assets) that may be deducted for the year is limited to net investment income.

   a. *Net investment income* is the excess of investment income over investment expenses.

   b. When investment expenses fall into the category of miscellaneous itemized deductions that are subject to the two percent-of-AGI floor, some may not enter into the calculation of net investment income because of the floor.

  5. *Qualified residence interest* is interest paid or accrued on indebtedness (subject to limitations) secured by a *qualified residence* of the taxpayer. Qualified residence interest falls into two categories: interest on *acquisition indebtedness* and interest on *home equity* loans. A qualified residence includes the *principal residence* and *one other residence* of the taxpayer or spouse.

  6. In most cases, qualified interest is fully deductible; however, limitations

apply.

    a.   The interest deduction is restricted on indebtedness secured by a qualified residence of $1,000,000 or less ($500,000 married, filing separate returns). Acquisition indebtedness is debt incurred in acquiring, constructing, or substantially improving a qualified residence of the taxpayer. Debt in excess of these limits generates interest expense that is not deductible under these rules.

    b.   In addition, interest on aggregate home equity indebtedness of up to $100,000 ($50,000 for married persons filing separate returns) is deductible. However, the deductible interest is limited to home equity loans that do not exceed the fair market value of the residence reduced by the acquisition indebtedness. The use to which the proceeds from home equity indebtedness are put is irrelevant insofar as the deductibility of the related interest expense, even if the proceeds are used for personal purposes.

7.   The deductibility of interest paid on mortgages secured by a third or more residences or on indebtedness that exceeds the allowable limitations depends on the use of the proceeds. If the proceeds are used for personal purposes, the interest is nondeductible. However, if the proceeds are used for business, the interest may be fully deductible. Alternatively, if the proceeds are used for investment purposes or in passive activities, the restrictions pertaining to those types of activities apply.

8.   Interest Paid for Services

    a.   To qualify as deductible interest, *points* paid by a borrower (i.e., buyer) must be considered compensation to a lender solely for the use or forbearance of money as opposed to being a form of service charge or compensation for specific services. A buyer also may deduct seller-paid points in the year they are paid in certain situations.

    b.   In contrast to points paid in connection with the purchase or improve-ment of the residence, points incurred when refinancing a residential mortgage are not deductible in a lump sum. Such expenditures should be capitalized, and then amortized and deducted over the life of the loan.

9.   Prepayment penalties which may be incurred if loans are paid off early are considered to be interest (e.g., personal, qualified residence, investment) in the year paid.

10.   If related parties are involved where the debtor is an accrual basis taxpayer and the creditor is a cash basis taxpayer, the interest expense must be actually paid by the accrual basis taxpayer in order for a deduction to be taken.

11.   An interest deduction is not allowed when the related indebtedness is incurred to *purchase or carry* tax-exempt securities.

B.   Restrictions on Deductibility and Timing Considerations

1.   For interest expense to be deductible, the related debt must be a bona fide obligation of the taxpayer. Additionally, there must be an intent to repay the loan.

2.   Unless the taxpayer uses the accrual method, payment must be made to secure the deduction. Under the accrual method, interest is deductible ratably over the life of the loan.

3.   Prepaid interest payments must be capitalized and allocated to the subsequent periods to which the interest payments relate, even if the taxpayer otherwise uses the cash basis.

C.   Classification of Interest Expense

1.   If indebtedness is incurred in connection with a business or for the production of rent or royalty income, the related interest expense is deductible *for* adjusted gross income.

2.   Otherwise, the related interest expense is deductible *from* adjusted gross income.

V.   Charitable Contributions

    A.   Overview -- Charitable contributions made to qualified domestic organizations may be deducted *from* adjusted gross income. The government, by allowing this deduction, believes that it encourages charitable giving by individuals and corporations.

    B.   Criteria for a Gift

        1.   A *charitable contribution* is defined as a gift made to a qualified organization.

        2.   The following major elements are needed to qualify a contribution as a gift.

            a.   Donative intent.

            b.   Absence of consideration received by the donor.

            c.   Acceptance of the contribution by the donee.

        3.   Generally, to the extent a tangible benefit is derived from a contribution, the value of such benefit cannot be deducted.

        4.   However, if a taxpayer contributes an amount and receives in return the right to purchase athletic tickets from a college or university, then 80 percent of the amount paid to or for the benefit of the institution qualifies as a charitable contribution deduction.

        5.   A deduction is not allowed for a contribution of one's services to a qualified charitable organization. However, unreimbursed expenses related to the services rendered are deductible.

        6.   The following do not qualify as charitable contributions.

            a.   Country club dues, fees, and bills.

            b.   Raffle, bingo, and lottery tickets.

            c.   Gifts to individuals.

            d.   The rental value of property used by a qualified charity.

    C.   Qualified Organizations

        1.   To qualify as a deductible charitable contribution, a payment must be made to one of the following organizations.

            a.   A state or possession of the United States, or any subdivision thereof.

            b.   Certain organizations situated in the United States organized and operated exclusively for religious, charitable, scientific, literary or educational purposes or for the prevention of cruelty to children or animals.

            c.   A veteran's organization.

            d.   A fraternal organization operating under the lodge system.

            e.   A cemetery company.

        2.   Gifts made to a donee in an individual capacity rather than as a representative of a qualifying organization are *not* deductible.

    D.   Time of Deduction

        1.   A charitable contribution generally is deductible, by either cash or accrual basis individual taxpayers, in the year payment is made. A contribution made by check is considered paid on the date of mailing.

        2.   An *accrual basis corporate taxpayer* may claim a charitable contribution deduction in the year prior to payment if the actual payment or contribution is made within two and one-half months of the close of the taxable year *and* the board of directors has authorized such payment prior to the end of the year.

    E.   Recordkeeping and Valuation Requirements

        1.   No deduction is allowed for a contribution of $250 or more unless the taxpayer obtains *contemporaneous written substantiation* from the charitable organization.

        2.   Additional information is required if the value of the donated property is over $500 but not over $5,000. If the noncash contribution exceeds $5,000 in

claimed value ($10,000 in the case of nonpublicly traded stock), an appraisal of the property's fair market value must be obtained by the taxpayer.

3. Donated property is generally valued at its *fair market value* at the time of the gift.

4. The only guidance provided in the Code and Regulations with respect to the meaning of the term fair market value is as follows: "The fair market value is the price at which the property would change hands between a willing buyer and a willing seller, neither being under any compulsion to buy or sell and both having reasonable knowledge of relevant facts."

F. Limitations on Charitable Deductions

1. Individual taxpayers are subject to overall ceiling limitations on the aggregate amount that may be deducted for the tax year.

    a. If the qualifying contributions for the year total 20 percent or less of adjusted gross income, they are fully deductible.

    b. If the contributions are more than 20 percent of adjusted gross income, the deductible amount may be limited to either 20 percent, 30 percent, or 50 percent of adjusted gross income, depending on the type of property given and the type of organization to which the donation is made.

    c. In any case, the maximum charitable contribution deduction may not exceed 50 percent of adjusted gross income for the tax year.

2. Corporations also are subject to an overall limitation (see Chapter 16). Moreover, in some situations, the deduction allowed is less than the fair market value of the property contributed.

3. If *ordinary income property* is contributed, the deduction is equal to the fair market value of the property less the amount of ordinary income which would have been recognized if the property had been sold. Ordinary income property is any property which, if sold, would result in the recognition of ordinary income (e.g., inventory).

4. As a general rule, the deduction for a contribution of *capital gain property* (i.e., property that would have produced a long-term capital gain or § 1231 gain if it had been sold) is equal to the fair market value of the property.

5. If capital gain property is contributed to a private *nonoperating* foundation, then the contribution is reduced by the long-term capital gain that would have been recognized had the property been sold. Such reduction is generally not required for contributions of intangible or real tangible capital gain property to public charities.

6. With respect to capital gain *tangible personalty* given to a public charity, the deduction must be reduced by the long-term capital gain element if the property is put to an *unrelated use* by the charity.

Especially with respect to large, national charities, it may be difficult for the benefactor to determine exactly what the charity is going to do with the donated property, let alone determine whether the asset is put to a related or unrelated use. Often, boards of the donee charities have specific policies about what to do with gifts of in-kind assets, such as immediate liquidation into cash, or review by an investment committee. None of these contingencies makes it easy to determine the amount of the donor's deduction by the due date of the tax return.

7. Contributions made to public charities, all private operating foundations, or

certain other private nonoperating foundations may not exceed 50 percent of an individual's adjusted gross income for the year. Excess contributions may be carried over for five years.

8. If appreciated *capital gain property* is contributed to an organization to which the 50 percent limitation applies or if a contribution of cash or ordinary income property is made to a private nonoperating foundation, then the deduction is limited to 30 percent of the adjusted gross income. Any unused or excess contribution may be carried forward for up to five years.

9. Contributions of appreciated long-term capital gain property made to private nonoperating foundations are limited to 20 percent of adjusted gross income. Any unused excess contribution may be carried forward for up to five years.

VI. Miscellaneous Itemized Deductions

A. A number of miscellaneous itemized deductions are allowed to be reported on Schedule A for expenditures related to employment. Examples of such miscellaneous deductions include the following.

    1. Unreimbursed business expenses.
    2. Professional dues.
    3. Tax return preparation fees.
    4. Job-hunting expenses.
    5. Safe deposit box rental.
    6. Hobby losses to the extent of hobby income.
    7. Subscription costs to professional journals.
    8. Uniforms.

B. These expenses are deductible only to the extent that they exceed two percent of the taxpayer's adjusted gross income.

VII. Other Miscellaneous Deductions -- If a taxpayer itemizes deductions and incurs the following costs, then they may be deducted without being subject to the two percent-of-AGI limitation.

A. Gambling losses to the extent of gambling earnings.
B. Impairment-related work expenses of a handicapped person.
C. Federal estate tax on income in respect of a decedent.
D. Deduction for repayment of amounts under a claim of right if more than $3,000.
E. Unrecovered investment in an annuity contract when the annuity ceases by reason of death.

VIII. Overall Limitation on Certain Itemized Deductions

A. High-income taxpayers are subject to a limitation on itemized deductions when their AGI exceeds certain levels. The *threshold amount* (the figure where the limitation begins to take effect) for 1995 is $114,700 ($57,350 for married persons filing a separate return). For 1994, the threshold amounts were $111,800 and $55,900, respectively.

B. The limitation applies to all itemized deductions *except* the following.

    1. Medical expenses.
    2. Investment interest.
    3. Nonbusiness casualty and theft losses.
    4. Gambling losses.

C. The limitation requires itemized deductions to be reduced by three percent of AGI to the extent of its excess over the threshold amount. However, in no case may the reduction be more than 80 percent of the covered itemized deductions.

D. This adjustment is applied *after* taking into account other Code provisions that reduce allowable deductions (e.g., the two percent-of-AGI limitation that applies to miscellaneous itemized deductions).

TEST FOR SELF-EVALUATION -- CHAPTER 9

True or False

Indicate which of the following statements are true or false by circling the correct answer.

T   F   1.   Personal expenditures are specifically disallowed by the Code as deductions in arriving at taxable income.

T   F   2.   Tuition expenses of a dependent at a special school are never deductible as a medical expense.

T   F   3.   A capital improvement, such as a swimming pool at one's personal residence which would otherwise qualify as a medical expenditure, is fully deductible.

T   F   4.   The term "medicine and drugs" includes only prescribed drugs or insulin.

T   F   5.   Fees paid or incurred for automobile inspection, automobile titles and registration, and bridge and highway tolls are never deductible because they are not taxes.

T   F   6.   Both the environmental tax and the federal income tax are deductible under the Code.

T   F   7.   The real estate taxes incurred in a year of sale are apportioned between the buyer and the seller of a property on the basis of the number of days the property was held by each party.

T   F   8.   State income taxes imposed on an individual are deductible only as an itemized deduction except if the taxpayer's sole source of income is from business, rents, or royalties.

T   F   9.   Service charges are not deductible as an interest expense.

T   F   10. The amount of interest on investment indebtedness that may be deducted is unlimited.

T   F   11. Charitable contributions made in any one year which are in excess of the appropriate limitation may be carried over for up to four years.

T   F   12. The limitation percentage applicable to charitable contributions made to private nonoperating foundations varies depending on the type of property contributed.

T   F   13. The unrealized appreciation related to real property contributed to a charitable organization may produce a charitable contribution deduction in certain situations.

T   F   14. Qualifying medical expenditures incurred by an individual are normally deductible only to the extent that they exceed two percent of the taxpayer's adjusted gross income.

T   F   15. Cosmetic surgery could never qualify as a deductible medical expense.

T   F   16.   Property taxes are deducted in the year paid whether or not the taxpayer uses the cash or accrual method of accounting.

T   F   17.   All taxes must be *ad valorem* in order to be deductible.

T   F   18.   The investment interest expense deduction can never include amounts paid to enable a taxpayer to purchase a tax-exempt bond.

T   F   19.   Interest paid on a home equity line may be deducted only if the loan proceeds are used on home improvement projects.

T   F   20.   No deduction is allowed for a contribution of one's services to a qualified charitable organization.

Fill-in-the-Blanks

Complete the following statements with the appropriate word(s) or amount(s).

1.   The deduction for property donated to a charity is generally measured by its _____ at the time the gift is made.

2.   A distinction must be made between a fee and a tax because a _____ is not deductible unless it is incurred as a business expense or incurred in the production of income.

3.   When apportioning real estate taxes between a buyer and a seller of property, the _____ date and the _____ date are disregarded.

4.   Many miscellaneous itemized deductions may not be deducted unless they exceed _____ perce of adjusted gross income.

5.   All of the itemized deductions of individual taxpayers are reported on Schedule _____ of Form _____.

6.   _____ expense has been defined by the Supreme Court as compensation for the use or forbearance of money.

7.   The deductibility of investment interest is limited to the amount of the taxpayer's _____.

8.   The major elements needed to qualify a contribution as a gift are _____, _____, and _____.

9.   An individual may claim a charitable contribution deduction only _____, regardless of whether the cash or accrual method of accounting is used.

10.   For charitable contribution purposes, _____ property is any property which, if sold, will result in the recognition of ordinary income.

11.   Generally, when making a charitable contribution of property (other than publicly traded securities) which has a claimed value exceeding _____, an independent appraisal must be conducted.

12.   Interest expense on a home equity loan of up to _____ may be fully deducted regardless of the use to which the loan proceeds are put.

13.   Transportation for medical purposes is deductible at ____9____ per mile while transportation
       for charitable contribution purposes is deductible at ___12___ per mile.

14.   The threshold amount for 1995 for the overall limitation of certain itemized deductions is
       __114700__ (__57350__ for married persons filing separate returns).

15.   While the overall limitation of certain itemized deductions adjustment is ___3___ percent of
       the excess of AGI over the threshold amount, in no case may the reduction be for more than
       ___80%___ percent of the covered itemized deductions.

Multiple Choice

Choose the best answer for each of the following questions.

____d____   1.   Which of the following taxes are not deductible?
                  a.   State, local or foreign income taxes.
                  b.   Personal and real property taxes.
                  c.   The environmental tax.
                  d.   Estate, inheritance, and gift taxes.
                  e.   All of the above are deductible.

____c____   2.   The tax year for real property taxation in Albemarle County is January 1 to December
                  31. The assessment date is April 1 and the lien date is October 1. Steve sold his home
                  to Penny on May 1 of this year and it was agreed that Penny would pay the property taxes
                  of $800 when due. How much of the tax payment is attributed to Penny assuming that this
                  year is not a leap year?
                  a. $197.
                  b. $263.
                  c. $537.
                  d. $603.
                  e. $800.

____d____   3.   Which of the items listed is not deductible as interest?
                  a.   Points paid by a purchaser of a personal residence.
                  b.   Mortgage interest on primary residence.
                  c.   Mortgage interest on a taxpayer's second home.
                  d.   Finance charges on a homeowner's utility bill.
                  e.   All of the above are deductible.

____a____   4.   Which of the items listed is deductible as interest?
                  a.   Mortgage prepayment penalty.
                  b.   Interest on a student loan.
                  c.   Interest expense incurred to buy or carry tax-exempt securities.
                  d.   Service charges.
                  e.   None of the above are deductible.

____a____   5.   During the current year, Gene contributed stock to a qualifying private nonoperating
                  foundation which he had purchased as an investment four years ago for $1,000. The fair
                  market value of the stock on the date of contribution was $1,600. What is Gene's
                  current charitable contribution deduction based on the above information assuming that
                  his adjusted gross income is $7,500?
                  a. $1,000.
                  b. $1,240.
                  c. $1,500.

d. $1,600.
e.   None of the above.

6.   Assuming the same facts as in the preceding question, except he contributed the stock to the University of Virginia, how much may Gene deduct currently as a charitable contribution?
a. $1,000.
b. $1,240.
c. $1,500.
d. $1,600.
e.   None of the above.

7.   Mary Ann paid $1,545 to various parties during the year, as follows.

State cigarette tax	$50
State gasoline tax	90
Real estate tax on vacation home	400
State income tax	900
City personal property tax (*ad valorem*)	60
State driver's license and car license	45

Mary Ann's Federal income tax return should include a deduction for taxes paid in the following amount.
a. $850.
b. $900.
c. $1,360.
d. $1,450.
e.   None of the above.

8.   Bill made the following charitable contributions during the current year.

▸   Allowed the United Way to use a building he owned, without requiring the normal $3,000 rent payment
▸   Gift of $10,000 cash to his alma mater, the University of Richmond
▸   Gift of his services as a CPA to his church audit committee (valued at $2,000)

Assuming Bill's AGI this year is $30,000, calculate his charitable contribution deduction.
a. $10,000.
b. $12,000.
c. $13,000.
d. $15,000.
e.   None of the above.

9.   During the year, Elizabeth and Bruce incurred the following expenses.

Prescription drugs	$300
Medical insurance premiums	600
Illegal drugs	200
Hospital bills	1,000
Doctors bills	800
Foreign real property tax	1,000
Mortgage interest expense	4,200
Reimbursed employee travel expenses	500

If Elizabeth and Bruce's AGI is $20,000, calculate their itemized deductions for the year.
- a. $0.
- b.) $6,400.
- c. $6,700.
- d. $6,900.
- e. $7,200.

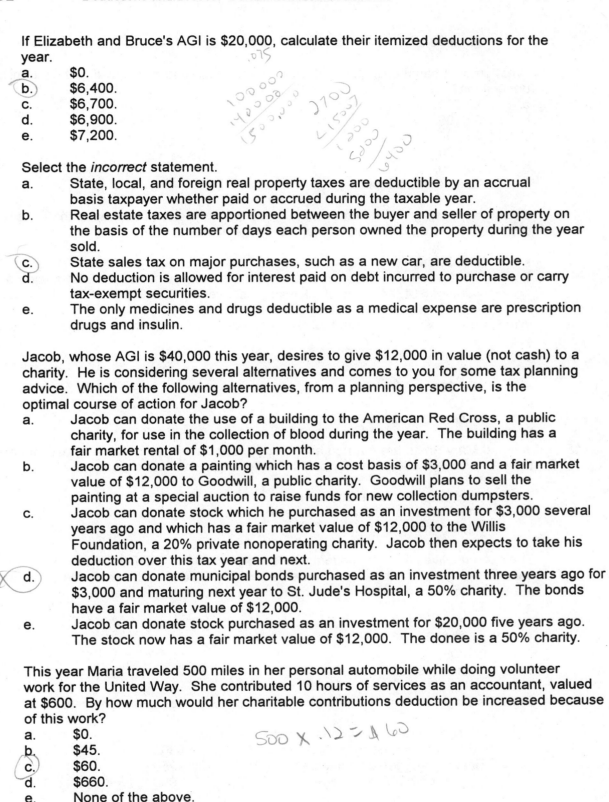

10.   Select the *incorrect* statement.
- a.   State, local, and foreign real property taxes are deductible by an accrual basis taxpayer whether paid or accrued during the taxable year.
- b.   Real estate taxes are apportioned between the buyer and seller of property on the basis of the number of days each person owned the property during the year sold.
- c.)   State sales tax on major purchases, such as a new car, are deductible.
- d.   No deduction is allowed for interest paid on debt incurred to purchase or carry tax-exempt securities.
- e.   The only medicines and drugs deductible as a medical expense are prescription drugs and insulin.

11.   Jacob, whose AGI is $40,000 this year, desires to give $12,000 in value (not cash) to a charity. He is considering several alternatives and comes to you for some tax planning advice. Which of the following alternatives, from a planning perspective, is the optimal course of action for Jacob?
- a.   Jacob can donate the use of a building to the American Red Cross, a public charity, for use in the collection of blood during the year. The building has a fair market rental of $1,000 per month.
- b.   Jacob can donate a painting which has a cost basis of $3,000 and a fair market value of $12,000 to Goodwill, a public charity. Goodwill plans to sell the painting at a special auction to raise funds for new collection dumpsters.
- c.   Jacob can donate stock which he purchased as an investment for $3,000 several years ago and which has a fair market value of $12,000 to the Willis Foundation, a 20% private nonoperating charity. Jacob then expects to take his deduction over this tax year and next.
- d.)   Jacob can donate municipal bonds purchased as an investment three years ago for $3,000 and maturing next year to St. Jude's Hospital, a 50% charity. The bonds have a fair market value of $12,000.
- e.   Jacob can donate stock purchased as an investment for $20,000 five years ago. The stock now has a fair market value of $12,000. The donee is a 50% charity.

12.   This year Maria traveled 500 miles in her personal automobile while doing volunteer work for the United Way. She contributed 10 hours of services as an accountant, valued at $600. By how much would her charitable contributions deduction be increased because of this work?
- a. $0.
- b. $45.
- c.) $60.
- d. $660.
- e.   None of the above.

13.   Mr. and Mrs. Burke made the following payments during the year.

Interest on loan to purchase auto	$1,000
Interest on home mortgage	2,700
Prepayment penalty on home mortgage	800

3500

Finance charges on bank credit card   1,000

What amount can the Burkes deduct as interest expense in calculating their itemized deductions?

a. $2,700.
b. $3,100.
c. $3,700.
d. $3,900.
e. $5,500.
f.   None of the above.

_____ 14.   Betsy's adjusted gross income was $80,000 for the year and she made the following contributions to qualified public charitable organizations.

▸ $6,000 cash
▸   1,500 shares of common stock of the Crenshaw Corporation with a fair market value of $14,000. The stock was purchased for $10,000 in 1973.

What is the maximum amount that Betsy can deduct for charitable contributions this year?

a. $6,000.
b. $16,000.
c. $20,000.
d. $30,000.
e.   None of the above.

_____ 15.   Jim and Mary Smith are married and file a joint return. Their adjusted gross income for the year was $40,000, and they paid the following in medical expenses.

Physician bills for themselves	$1,200
Physician bills for Mary's mother	3,420
Physician bill for their son	175

Their son qualifies as a dependent, while Mary's mother would qualify as their dependent except for the fact that she earned $3,500 during the year. What amount can the Smiths deduct as qualifying medical expenses on their joint return?

a. $1,200.
b. $1,375.
c. $1,795.
d. $4,795.
e.   Some other amount.

_____ 16.   James is single and made the following cash expenditures during the year.

Interest on loan to purchase taxable securities (net investment income = $1,500)	$300
Finance charges on bank credit card	250
Interest on home mortgage	900

How much interest expense can James include on his schedule of itemized deductions?

a. $0.
b. $900.
c. $1,200.
d. $1,450.
e.   None of the above.

17. Mimi made the following cash outlays during the current tax year.

State and local sales taxes paid	$400
State and local real property taxes paid	900
State income taxes paid for last year	450
Federal gift taxes paid	325

How much can Mimi deduct as taxes on her schedule of itemized deductions for the year?

a. $0.
b. $1,350.
c. $1,750.
d. $2,075.
e. None of the above.

18. During 1995, Megan's records reflect the following information.

Salary	$100,000
Interest income	39,700
Qualified residence interest expense	10,000
Charitable contributions	12,000
State income taxes	13,000

Assuming Megan is single, compute the amount of itemized deductions that she may claim on her federal income tax return.

a. $31,250.
b. $32,750.
c. $34,250.
d. $35,000.
e. None of the above.

19. During 1995, Hal's records reflect the following information.

Salary	$225,000
Interest income	39,700
Medical expenses (after the 7.5%-of-AGI floor)	15,000
Qualified residence interest expense	5,000
Investment interest expense	15,000

Assuming Hal is single, compute the amount of itemized deductions that he may claim on his federal income tax return.

a. $29,000.
b. $30,500.
c. $31,000.
d. $35,000.
e. None of the above.

20. During the year, Warner incurred medical expenses of $6,000. But in addition, his physician recommended that he install a home dust elimination system to help mitigate his breathing problems. The cost of the new system was $3,500, but it increased the home's fair market value by only $2,000. Assuming Warner's AGI was $20,000, what is the amount of his medical expense deduction?

a. $4,500.
b. $6,000.
c. $7,500.

d. $8,000.
e.   None of the above.

_____ 21.   Which of the following taxes is deductible?
a.   Federal income taxes.
b.   FICA taxes imposed on employees.
c.   Foreign real property taxes.
d.   General sales taxes.
e.   None of the above.

_____ 22.   Tami is single and employed as controller of a major industrial company. Her financial
records for the year reflect the following.

Net investment income	$23,000
Investment interest expense	25,000
Mortgage interest expense	5,000
Home equity line interest expense (proceeds used to fund a vacation to Florida)	2,000
Bank credit card interest expense	1,000

How much interest expense can Tami deduct currently?
a. $30,000.
b. $31,000.
c. $32,000.
d. $33,000.
e.   None of the above.

_____ 23.   Ray made a contribution to Central State University's athletic booster club for
$1,000. This payment provided Ray the right to purchase tickets in a preferred part of
the football and basketball facilities; and in addition, Ray would be invited to the
coaches' luncheons every Monday. The value of these benefits were immeasurable in
Ray's view. In addition, Ray forwarded $500 to the school for season football and
basketball tickets. What amount may Ray deduct on his return for these expenditures?
a. $0.
b. $800.
c. $1,000.
d. $1,500.
e.   None of the above.

_____ 24.   Which of the following is deductible as a charitable contribution?
a.   Country club fees.
b.   Raffle or bingo tickets.
c.   Donation of blood.
d.   Gifts to homeless individuals.
e.   None of the above.

_____ 25.   Which of the following miscellaneous itemized deductions is subject to the two
percent-of-AGI floor?
a.   Job-hunting costs.
b.   Moving expenses.
c.   Casualty and theft losses.
d.   Medical expenses.
e.   None of the above.

Code Section Recognition

Several important sections of the Internal Revenue Code are described below. Indicate, by number, the appropriate Code section.

1. _262_ Personal expenditures are specifically disallowed as deductions in arriving at adjusted gross income.

2. _213_ Determines the medical expense deduction.

3. _164_ Lists a number of taxes that are deductible if they are paid or accrued during a taxable year.

4. _265_ Provides that an interest deduction is not allowed for interest on debt incurred to purchase or carry tax-exempt securities.

5. _170_ Determines the deduction for charitable contributions.

Short Answer

1. Sandra made the following contributions to bonafide public charitable organizations during the year.

    Cash--$1,000.
    Green Corporation stock--Cost, $1,200; FMV, $1,000; held for 3 years.
    Blue Corporation stock--Cost, $1,200; FMV, $1,500; held for 2 years.
    Old clothing to the Salvation Army--Cost, $500; FMV, $200.
    Value of services rendered serving on her church's finance committee--$500.

    1,000
    1,000
    1500
    200

    3,700

    Determine the amount that may be deducted on her return before any AGI limitations.

2. Indicate whether each of the following is subject to the 2%-of-AGI limitation.
    a. Moving expense. NO
    b. Professional dues. yes
    c. Tax return preparation fees. yes
    d. Medical expenses. no
    e. Safe deposit box used to store investment-related records. yes
    f. Hobby loss expenses up to the amount of hobby income. yes

SOLUTIONS TO CHAPTER 9 QUESTIONS

True or False

1.   T   However, in certain situations, several Code sections exist which override this general disallowance of personal expenditures.
2.   F   In certain situations, such expenditures are deductible.
3.   F   In the acquisition of an item such as a swimming pool, the cost is deductible to the extent that the expenditure exceeds the increase in value of the related property.
4.   T
5.   F   They would be deductible if they were incurred as a business expense under § 162 or for the production of income under § 212.
6.   F   The federal income tax is not deductible. However, the environmental tax is deductible.
7.   T
8.   F   State income taxes imposed on individuals are always deductible as itemized deductions.
9.   T
10.   F   The amount deductible generally is limited to net investment income.
11.   F   A five-year carryover provision is available.
12.   T
13.   T
14.   F   A 7.5 percent of adjusted gross income threshold applies.
15.   F   Cosmetic surgery may be deductible if it is considered *necessary* (i.e., when it ameliorates a deformity arising from a congenital abnormality, a personal injury, or a disfiguring disease).
16.   F   An accrual basis taxpayer may deduct property taxes in the year that fixes the right to deductibility.
17.   F   The restriction only applies to personal property taxes.
18.   T
19.   F   The use of the proceeds is irrelevant.
20.   T

Fill-in-the-Blanks

1.   fair market value
2.   fee
3.   assessment, lien
4.   two
5.   A, 1040
6.   Interest
7.   net investment income
8.   donative intent, the absence of consideration, acceptance by donee
9.   in the year of payment
10.   ordinary income
11. $5,000
12. $100,000
13.   nine cents, twelve cents
14. $114,700, $57,350
15.   three, 80

Multiple Choice

1. d   See Exhibit 9-2 in the text.
2. c $537 = $800 - (120/365 X $800) Steve used the property for 120 days while Penny used the property for 245 days. See Example 14 in the text.
3. d
4. a
5. a $1,000--Limited to the stock's basis because the contribution is made to a private nonoperating foundation. The AGI limit is moot in this case. See Example 30 in the text.
6. d   Limited to 30% X $7,500 (AGI). Therefore, the entire $1,600 contribution is deducted. See Example 32 in the text.
7. c $1,360 = $400 + $900 + $60. See Exhibit 9-2 in the text.
8. a $10,000 cash
9. b   Medical expense deduction (net of 7.5%-of-AGI floor)

[$2,700 - (7.5% X $20,000)]	$1,200
Foreign real property tax	1,000
Mortgage interest expense	4,200
Total	$6,400

The $500 of reimbursed employee expenses are deductible *for* AGI. See Example 12, Exhibit 9-1, and Exhibit 9-2 in the text.

10. c   See Exhibit 9-2 in the text.
11. d
12. c $60 = 500 miles X $0.12; value of services rendered are not deductible. See discussion preceding Example 28 in the text.
13. f $3,500 = $2,700 + $800
14. c $20,000 = $6,000 + $14,000 See Example 32 in the text.
15. c $1,795 = [$1,200 + $3,420 + $175 - ($40,000 X 7.5%)] See Example 7 in the text.
16. c $1,200 = $900 + $300
17. b $1,350 = $900 + $450 See Exhibit 9-2 in the text.
18. c $34,250 = $35,000 - .03[$139,700 (AGI) - $114,700 (threshold amount)] See Example 35 in the text.
19. c   Deductions *not* subject to the 3 percent limitation

Medical expenses	$15,000	
Investment interest expense	15,000	
Deductions subject to the 3 percent limitation		
Qualified residence interest expense	5,000	
Less: The smaller of--		
.03($264,700 - $114,700) [3% rule]	$4,500	
.80($5,000) [80% rule]	4,000	-4,000
Allowable itemized deductions		$31,000

See Example 35 in the text.

20. b

Medical expenses		$6,000
Cost of dust elimination system, net of the increase		
in the home's value ($3,500 - $2,000)		1,500
Total medical expenses		$7,500
Less: 7.5% of AGI		-1,500
Medical expense deduction		$6,000

21. c   See Exhibit 9-2 in the text.
22. a $30,000 = $23,000 + $5,000 + $2,000
23. b $800 = $1,000 X 80%   See Example 27 in the text.
24. e
25. a

Code Section Recognition

1.   262
2.   213
3.   164
4.   265
5.   170

Short Answer

1.

Cash	$1,000
Green Corporation stock	1,000
Blue Corporation stock	1,500
Old clothing to the Salvation Army	200
Value of services rendered	0
Total	$3,700

2.   a.   Moving expense--No, this expense is deductible *for* AGI and not as an itemized deduction.
       b.   Professional dues--Yes.
       c.   Tax return preparation fees--Yes.
       d.   Medical expenses--No.
       e.   Safe deposit box used to store investment-related records--Yes.
       f.   Hobby loss expenses up to the amount of hobby income--Yes.

CHAPTER 10
PASSIVE ACTIVITY LOSSES

CHAPTER HIGHLIGHTS

*T*he tax law includes a set of complex rules which limit the numerous opportunities that were available to taxpayers under prior law to avoid or reduce their income tax liability through tax shelter investments. These rules, the at-risk limitations and the passive loss limitations, are the topics included in this chapter. In essence, the at-risk rules limit a taxpayer's deductions from an investment to the amount the taxpayer would stand to lose if the investment became worthless. The passive loss rules stipulate that deductions attributable to passive activities may, as a general rule, be used only to offset passive income. Thus, in most situations passive losses may not be used to offset active or portfolio income.

I. The Tax Shelter Problem
    A. Under prior law, *tax shelter* investments were successfully used for tax avoidance purposes (i.e., to either avoid or reduce the income tax liability).
    B. The *at-risk limitations* and the *passive activity rules* are now included in the law to curb such abuse. As a result, the term *tax shelter* is now almost obsolete.

II. At-Risk Limits
    A. Rules apply to individuals and closely held corporations which limit the amount of deductible losses to the amount that the taxpayer has at risk (i.e., the amount the taxpayer could actually lose) in the activity. These rules apply to losses from business and income-producing activities.
    B. The initial amount considered at risk includes the following.
        1. Cash and the adjusted basis of property contributed to the activity.
        2. Amounts borrowed for use in the activity for which the taxpayer has personal liability or has pledged as security property not used in the activity.
        However, the amount at risk varies as the entity recognizes income and losses, obtains and pays down qualifying debt, and distributes assets (e.g., cash withdrawals) to the owners.

C. Any losses disallowed for any given year by the at-risk rules may be deducted in the first succeeding year in which the rule does not prevent the deduction. However, such losses will be subject to the passive loss limitations if incurred in a passive activity.

D. Recapture of previously allowed losses is required to the extent the at-risk amount is reduced below zero.

III. Passive Loss Limits
   A. Classification and Impact of Passive Income and Losses
      1. Classification -- The passive loss rules require the classification of income and losses into three categories: active, passive, and portfolio.
         a. *Active income* includes the following.
            (1) Amounts for services rendered (e.g., salary, commissions).
            (2) Profit from a trade or business in which the taxpayer is a material participant.
            (3) Gain on the disposition of an asset used in a trade or business.
            (4) Income from intangible property if the taxpayer's personal efforts significantly contributed to the creation of the property.
         b. *Portfolio income* includes the following.
            (1) Interest, dividends, annuities, and royalties not derived in the ordinary course of a trade or business.
            (2) Gain or loss from the disposition of property that produces portfolio income or that is held for investment purposes.
         c. *Passive income or loss* includes the following.
            (1) Income or loss from any trade or business or production of income activity in which the taxpayer does not materially participate.
            (2) Any rental activity regardless of whether the taxpayer materially participates, with the exception of certain real estate rental activities discussed later in the chapter.
      2. General Impact
         a. Deductions or expenses generated by passive activities can be deducted only to the extent of income from all of the taxpayer's passive income. Unused passive losses are suspended and carried forward to future years to offset passive income in those years.
         b. A loss is suspended under the passive loss rules only after the application of the at-risk rules as well as other provisions relating to the measurement of taxable income.
         c. Suspended losses that exist when a taxpayer disposes of his or her entire interest in an activity may offset active and portfolio income.
      3. Impact of Suspended Losses -- On the disposition of an entire interest of a passive activity in a fully taxable disposition, any realized but suspended losses may be recognized and used to offset nonpassive income.
      4. Carryovers of Suspended Losses
         a. The suspended loss for an activity is determined by allocating the passive activity losses among all activities in which the taxpayer has an interest.
         b. Suspended losses are carried over indefinitely and are deducted

from the activities to which they relate in the immediately succeeding taxable year.

5. Passive Credits -- Passive credits are limited much like passive losses and can be utilized only against regular tax attributable to passive income.

6. Carryovers of Passive Credits -- While unused passive credits can generally be carried forward indefinitely, they can be lost forever when the activity is disposed of in a taxable transaction.

B. Taxpayers Subject to the Passive Loss Rules

1. The passive loss rules apply to the following taxpayers.

    a. Individuals.
    b. Estates.
    c. Trusts.
    d. Closely held C corporations.
    e. Personal service corporations.

2. For investments in partnerships or S corporations that are passive activities, the passive activity rules are applied at the owner level.

3. Application of the passive loss limitation to personal service corporations is intended to prevent taxpayers from sheltering personal service income by creating personal service corporations and acquiring passive activities at the corporate level.

4. Application of the passive loss rules to closely held (non-personal service) corporations also is intended to prevent individuals from incorporating to avoid the passive loss limitations.

C. Passive Activities Defined -- Passive activities are defined to include the following.

1. Any *trade or business* or *production of income* activity in which the taxpayer does not *materially participate*.

2. Subject to certain exceptions, all *rental activities*.

D. Identification of an Activity

1. Identifying what constitutes an *activity* is of critical importance in applying the passive loss limitations.

2. Regulations provide a set of rules for grouping a taxpayer's trade or business activities and rental activities for purposes of applying the passive loss limitations. The rules provide a *facts and circumstances test* to determine whether a taxpayer's activities constitute an *appropriate economic unit*. Taxpayers may use *any reasonable method* in applying the facts and circumstances test.

3. In general, one or more trade or business or rental activities will be treated as a single activity if the activities constitute an appropriate economic unit. Five factors are applied in determining whether activities constitute an appropriate economic unit.

    a. Similarities and differences in types of business conducted in the various trade or business or rental activities.
    b. The extent of common control over the various activities.
    c. The extent of common ownership of the activities.
    d. The geographical location of the different units.
    e. Interdependencies among the activities.

4. Regrouping of activities

    a. Once activities have been grouped, they cannot be regrouped unless the original grouping was clearly inappropriate or there has been a material change in the facts and circumstances.
    b. In certain situations, the IRS is allowed to regroup activities.

5. Special rules deal specifically with the grouping of rental activities. These provisions are designed to prevent taxpayers from grouping rental

activities, which are generally passive, with other businesses in a way that would result in a tax advantage.

E.   **Material Participation** -- To be a material participant, the taxpayer must participate on a *regular*, *continuous*, and *substantial* basis. If a taxpayer does not materially participate in a nonrental trade or business activity, any loss will be treated as a passive loss. Temporary Regulations provide seven tests for determining whether a taxpayer is a material participant.

1.   *Tests Based on Current Participation* -- Four quantitative tests of a taxpayer's participation require measurement in terms of hours of activity during the year.

2.   *Tests Based on Prior Participation* -- Two tests allow a taxpayer in certain situations to be classified as a material participant, even though a high level of activity is no longer maintained, if the taxpayer was formerly a material participant.

3.   *Facts and Circumstances Test* -- The criteria of regular, continuous, and substantial participation are used in applying this test. However, the definition of these terms has not yet been fully developed.

4.   Participation Defined -- Participation generally includes any work done by an individual in an activity that he or she owns. However, work done in an individual's capacity as an investor is not counted in applying the material participation tests.

5.   Limited Partners -- While exceptions exist, a *limited partner* generally is not deemed to materially participate.

F.   **Rental Activities Defined**

1.   Rental activities generally are treated as passive activities.

KEY TERMS
- At-Risk Limitation
- Passive Activity Rules
- Material Participation
- Active Participation
- Suspended Loss on Taxable Disposition

2.   A *rental activity* is defined as any activity where payments are received principally for the use of tangible property.

3.   However, Temporary Regulations provide six exceptions involving rentals of real and personal property that are *not* to be treated as rental activities. However, such activities will be subject to the material participation tests for final determination as to their passive status. The exceptions involve the following circumstances.

a.   The average period of customer use for such property is seven days or less.

b.   The average period of customer use for such property is 30 days or less, and significant personal services are provided by the owner of the property.

c.   Extraordinary personal services are provided by the owner of the property.

d.   The rental of such property is treated as incidental to a nonrental activity of the taxpayer.

e.   The taxpayer customarily makes the property available during defined business hours for nonexclusive use by various customers.

f. The property is provided for use in an activity conducted by a partnership, S corporation, or joint venture in which the taxpayer owns an interest.

Tax planning regarding passive activity losses might include (a) finding assets that generate passive income in an amount that roughly offsets the suspended passive losses, (b) using the Regulations' definitions of passive activity to one's advantage, e.g., in counting hours spent in generating passive income and loss, and (c) turning over the assets more frequently, so as to access any suspended losses fairly frequently and preserve the value of resulting deductions.

G. Interaction of the At-Risk and Passive Activity Limits -- The determination of whether a loss is suspended under the passive loss rules is made after application of the at-risk rules, as well as other provisions relating to the measurement of taxable income. In other words, a loss that is not allowed for the year because the taxpayer is not at risk with respect to it is suspended under the at-risk provisions and not under the passive loss rules.

H. Special Passive Activity Rules for Real Estate Activities -- Two exceptions allow all or part of rental real estate losses to be used to offset active or portfolio income even though the activity is a passive activity.

1. Material Participation in a Real Property Trade or Business -- Losses from real estate rental activities are not treated as passive losses for certain real estate professionals. In order to qualify for nonpassive treatment, a taxpayer must satisfy the following requirements.

a. More than half of the personal services that the taxpayer performs in trades or businesses are performed in real property trades or businesses in which the taxpayer materially participates.

b. The taxpayer performs more than 750 hours of services in these real property trades or businesses as a material participant.

Since the interest costs incurred when borrowing to finance a passive investment are not deductible, a taxpayer should try to realign his or her personal finances so the unnecessary borrowing costs are not incurred.

2. The second exception allows individuals to deduct up to $25,000 of losses on rental real estate activities against active and portfolio income.

a. The annual $25,000 deduction is reduced to zero by 50 percent of the taxpayer's adjusted gross income in excess of $100,000. In the case of a married taxpayer not filing a joint return and living apart for the entire year, the allowable $12,500 deduction is reduced by 50 percent of the adjusted gross income in excess of $50,000. Married individuals who live together at any time during the taxable year and file separate returns receive no benefit of the $25,000 allowance. For this purpose, adjusted gross income is computed without regard to IRA contributions, the taxable Social Security benefits amount, and the net losses from passive activities. The loss allowance is phased out completely once AGI exceeds $150,000 ($75,000 for married couples filing separately).

    b.   In order for the relief provision to be available, a taxpayer must meet the following criteria.

        (1)   Actively participate in the real estate rental activity.

        (2)   Own at least 10 percent of the value of all interests in the activity during the entire tax year or the period during which the taxpayer held an interest.

    Note that the *active participation* requirement is different (and less rigorous) than the *material participation* requirement.

    c.   The $25,000 allowance is an aggregate of both deductions and credits in deduction equivalents (i.e., the amount of deductions that would reduce the tax liability for the taxable year by an amount equal to the credit).

I.   Dispositions of Passive Interests -- Special rules apply to dispositions of passive activities other than those that are fully taxable transactions.

    1.   Disposition of a passive activity at death.

    2.   Disposition of a passive activity by gift.

    3.   Installment sale of a passive activity.

    4.   Passive activity changes to active.

    5.   Nontaxable exchange of a passive activity.

TEST FOR SELF-EVALUATION -- CHAPTER 10

True or False

Indicate which of the following statements are true or false by circling the correct answer.

T **F** 1. Net losses from passive activities never produce a deduction.

T F 2. The passive activity rules apply to the limitation of net losses and tax credits.

T **F** 3. Net passive income is recognized to the extent of passive losses incurred.

T F 4. The passive loss rules disallow all of the net losses from passive activities held by an individual taxpayer.

T F 5. The at-risk rules limit a taxpayer's tax deductions from an activity for any taxable year to the amount the taxpayer has at risk at the end of the year.

T **F** 6. An interest in a limited partnership is automatically characterized as an interest in a passive activity.

T **F** 7. An individual is considered to be a material participant if he/she participates in an activity for 400 or more hours during the year.

                 500

T F 8. Rental activities include both real estate rentals and rentals of tangible personal property.

T **F** 9. Generally, up to $25,000 of losses on rental real estate or rental tangible personal property activities of an individual may be deducted against active or portfolio income.

T **F** 10. Suspended losses related to a passive activity may be used to offset gains realized on a fully taxable disposition of a portion of the taxpayer's interest.

                    All

T **F** 11. In order for a taxpayer to qualify for the rental real estate exception, which provides for deductions of up to $25,000, the taxpayer must be a material participant in the activity.

    Act. in

T F 12. The passive activity limitations apply only to individuals, estates, trusts, closely held C corporations, and personal service corporations.

T **F** 13. The at-risk provisions only limit an individual's ability to claim deductions for losses from business and income-producing activities.

T **F** 14. The amount that a taxpayer has at risk is always limited to the amount the taxpayer has invested in the business or income producing venture.

T **F** 15. The at-risk rules are an important limitation because if a taxpayer is denied losses for a particular year by the at-risk rules, they can never be deducted in future years.

(T)   F   16.   Recapture of previously allowed losses is required to the extent the at-risk amount is reduced below zero.

(T)   F   17.   Closely held corporations (other than personal service corporations) may offset passive losses against active income, but not against portfolio income.

T   (F)   18.   If a taxpayer actively participates in a nonrental activity, any loss from that activity can be offset against active income.

(T)   F   19.   The law stipulates that material participation must entail regular, continuous, and substantial involvement in the operations of an activity.

T   (F)   20.   By virtue of the definition of a limited partner, such a taxpayer could never be a material participant in an activity.

Fill-in-the-Blanks

Complete the following statements with the appropriate word(s) or amount(s).

1.   On real estate rental activities, in certain situations an individual taxpayer may deduct up to 25,000 of losses against nonpassive income. However, for a single individual or for a taxpayer who files a joint return, the allowance is completely phased out once the taxpayer's AGI exceeds 150,000

2.   Suspended losses _____ are recognized on the taxable disposition of an entire interest in a passive activity.

3.   In terms of the interaction of the at-risk and passive activity limits, the determination of whether a loss is suspended under the passive loss rules is made after application of the at-risk rules.

4.   The passive activity rules require classification of income into three categories: Active income, portfolio income, and passive income.

5.   To be a material participant, the taxpayer must participate on a regular, continuous, and substantial basis.

6.   The passive activity rules apply to any trade or business if the taxpayer does not materially participate

7.   If a taxpayer materially participates in an activity, income or loss from the activity is considered active, not passive

8.   Credits _____ arising from passive activities are limited much like passive losses.

9.   In terms of levels of participation in an activity by a taxpayer, material participation requires more involvement than does active participation.

10.   A closely held corporation (other than a personal service corporation) may offset passive losses against active income, but not against portfolio income.

11.   Identifying what constitutes an activity is a necessary first step in applying the

passive loss limitations.

12. As required by the passive loss rules, interest, dividends and annuities are classified as _portfolio_ income.

13. As a general rule, taxpayers who are subject to the passive loss limitations cannot offset passive losses against _active_ income or _portfolio_ income.

14. The _at-risk_ rules apply to individuals and closely held corporations, while the _passive activity_ rules apply to individuals, estates, trusts, closely held C corporations, and personal service corporations.

15. The _at-risk_ rules are designed to prevent a taxpayer from deducting losses in excess of the actual economic investment in an activity.

Multiple Choice

Choose the best answer for each of the following questions.

_e_ 1.   The rules restricting losses and credits from passive activities apply to the following taxpayers.
   a.   Individuals.
   b.   Trusts or estates.
   c.   Personal service corporations.
   d.   Closely held C corporations.
   e.   All of the above.

_____ 2.   A passive activity is defined as any of the following.
   a.   Any trade or business in which the taxpayer does not materially participate.
   b.   Any rental activity, subject to certain exceptions.
   c.   Both a and b are passive activities.
   d.   None of the above.

_____ 3.   If a taxpayer materially participates in an activity, income or loss from the activity is considered active, and not passive. Material participation is achieved by meeting any one of seven tests. Which of the following is not one of those tests?
   a.   The individual participates in the activity for more than 500 hours during the year.
   b.   The individual's participation in the activity for the taxable year constitutes substantially all of the participation in the activity of all individuals for the year.
   c.   The individual participates in the activity for more than 100 hours during the year, and the individual's participation in the activity for the year is not less than the participation of any other individual for the year.
   d.   Based on all of the facts and circumstances, the individual participates in the activity on a regular, continuous, and substantial basis during such year.
   e.   Each of the above is a qualifying test.

_____ 4.   Margaret has investments, acquired during the current year, in three passive activities with the following income and losses for the year.

Activity X	($40,000)
Activity Y	(30,000)
Activity Z	20,000
Net passive loss	($50,000)

Which of the following statements is true?
a.   Current deductible losses total $70,000.
b.   The deductible losses are allocated equally among Activities X, Y, and Z.
c.   The deductible losses are allocated equally between Activities X and Y.
d.   The total suspended loss is $50,000.
e.   None of the above are true.

_____ 5.   Sue disposed of her entire interest in a passive activity at a $20,000 gain while she continues to hold investments in several other passive activities. Associated with the activity disposed of were suspended losses of $50,000. Which of the following describes the tax result of the disposition?
a.   None of the suspended losses are deductible because she continues to hold investments in other passive activities.
b.   All $50,000 of suspended losses may be used this year.
c.   Only $20,000 of the $50,000 in the suspended losses may be used this year.
d.   The amount of the $50,000 loss that may be used this year depends on the returns from the other passive activities during the current year.
e.   None of the above.

_____ 6.   Assume the same facts as in the previous problem, except that a $10,000 suspended credit also exists at the time of disposition. The suspended tax credit is treated as follows.
a.   All of the credit may be used in the year of disposition.
b.   None of the credit may be used in the year of disposition or in future years.
c.   A portion of the credit may be used in the year of disposition.
d.   None of the credit may be used in the year of disposition, but it may be carried forward and used in future years.
e.   None of the above is true.

_____ 7.   Woody, who files a joint return with his wife, actively participates in a rental activity (a beach cottage) that has reported a $60,000 loss from current operations. Assuming he owns a 50 percent interest in this property and that his other AGI (solely from salary) totals $75,000, his current deduction from this property is what amount?
a. $0.
b. $25,000.
c. $30,000.
d. $60,000.
e.   None of the above.

_____ 8.   Assume the same facts as in the preceding problem, except Woody's AGI (solely from salary) this year, exclusive of the rental loss, is $125,000. What amount of the loss is currently deductible?
a. $0.
b. $25,000.
c. $30,000.
d. $60,000.

(e)   None of the above.

____ 9.   Assume the same facts as in the preceding problem, except that Woody and his wife
           file separately instead of jointly, even though they continue to be married and
           live together for the entire year. What amount may Woody deduct on his return
           this year?
           a. $0.
           b. $25,000.
           c. $30,000.
           d. $60,000.
           e.   None of the above.

____ 10.   A taxpayer in the 28 percent tax bracket with $10,000 of tax credits from a
           passive activity would have a deduction equivalent of what amount?
           a. $0.
           b. $2,800.
           c. $10,000.
           d. $35,714, but limited to $25,000.
           e. $35,714.

____ 11.   During the year, a taxpayer in the 28 percent tax bracket realized a $10,000 tax
           credit from a passive activity. In addition, the following is noted.

           •   The taxpayer's share of passive income or loss during the current year
                    from the activity (or any others) is zero.
           •   The tax credit arises from an investment in a rental real estate venture
                    in which the taxpayer actively participates.

           Based on the above, what is the maximum deduction equivalent that may be used
           currently by the taxpayer?
           a. $0.
           b. $2,800.
           c. $10,000.
           d. $25,000.
           e. $35,714.

____ 12.   The at-risk limitations apply to which of the following types of taxpayers?
           a.   Partnerships.
           b.   Individuals.
           c.   Closely held corporations.
           d.   Publicly held corporations.
           e.   b and c.
           f.   a, b, and c.
           g.   All of the above.

____ 13.   Samantha made an investment in three passive activities during the current year.
           The following income and losses resulted from operations during the year.

                         Activity X   ($60,000)
                         Activity Y   (40,000)
                         Activity Z   50,000
                         Net passive loss   ($50,000)

           What is the amount of suspended loss allocated to Activity Y?
           a. $0.

b. $20,000.
c. $25,000.
d. $40,000.
e. $50,000.
f.   Some other amount.

                                                                    40,000

_____ 14.   Tom sold a boarding house during the year that had an adjusted basis of $80,000.
             The sales price of the property was $120,000. Suspended losses associated with
             the rental property totaled $60,000. Assuming Tom has no other passive
             activities, which of the following is true?
             a.   Suspended losses of $40,000 reduce the gain recognized to zero and
                   $20,000 of the suspended losses are lost.
             b.   Suspended losses of $40,000 reduce the gain recognized to zero and
                   $20,000 of the suspended losses remain suspended until passive income of
                   at least $20,000 is generated.
             c.   The total gain of $40,000 is offset by the suspended losses and the
                   remaining $20,000 suspended losses are used to offset Tom's active and
                   portfolio income.
             d.   The total gain recognized on the transaction is $40,000 because the
                   suspended losses are not relevant.
             e.   None of the above is true.

_____ 15.   Molly, who earned a salary of $80,000, invested $25,000 for a 50 percent interest
             in a partnership venture. The entity acquired assets worth $3 million through
             the use of $2,400,000 in nonrecourse financing. Molly's share of the
             partnership's loss for the current year was $80,000. Assuming she was a material
             participant, how much may Molly deduct this year?
             a. $0.
             b. $25,000.
             c. $40,000.
             d. $80,000.
             e.   None of the above.

_____ 16.   Molly, who earned a salary of $80,000, invested $25,000 for a 50 percent interest
             in a partnership venture. The entity acquired assets worth $3 million through
             the use of $2,400,000 in recourse financing (i.e., Molly is personally liable
             for one-half of the debt). Molly's share of the partnership's loss for the
             current year was $80,000. Assuming she was a material participant, how much may
             Molly deduct this year?
             a. $0.
             b. $25,000.
             c. $40,000.
             d. $80,000.
             e.   None of the above.

_____ 17.   Darlene, who earned a salary of $20,000 and portfolio income of $60,000,
             invested $25,000 for a 50 percent interest in a partnership venture. The entity
             acquired assets worth $3 million through the use of $2,400,000 in recourse
             financing (i.e., Darlene is personally liable for one-half of the debt).
             Darlene's share of the partnership's loss for the current year was $80,000.
             Assuming she was a material participant, how much may Darlene deduct this year?
             a. $20,000.
             b. $25,000.
             c. $40,000.
             d. $80,000.

e.   None of the above.

____ 18.   Because of the at-risk limitations, Iris has been unable to deduct $30,000 from previous years' operations of an oil partnership investment. However, this year, Iris invests an additional $5,000 in cash and the partnership generates a net income, of which her share is $10,000. What amount of the loss carryover from previous years remains, after accounting for this year's activities?
a. $0.
b. $15,000.   10,000
c. $20,000.
d. $30,000.
e.   None of the above.

____ 19.   Orange Corporation, a closely held C corporation (not a personal service corporation), has $45,000 of passive losses from a rental activity, $30,000 of active income, and $15,000 of portfolio income. What amount of the passive losses may be deducted this year by Orange?
a. $0.
b. $15,000.
c. $30,000.
d. $45,000.
e.   None of the above.

____ 20.   Blue Corporation, a personal service corporation, has $45,000 of passive losses from a rental activity, $30,000 of income generated from personal services, and $15,000 of portfolio income. What amount of the passive losses may be deducted this year by Blue?
a. $0.
b. $15,000.
c. $30,000.
d. $45,000.
e.   None of the above.

____ 21.   Sarah owns the following businesses and participates in each of the indicated activities.

Activity	Hours of Participation
1	100
2	130
3	300
4	250

In which activities is Sarah considered to be a material participant?
a.   None of them.
b.   Only activities 3 and 4.
c.   Activities 2, 3, and 4
d.   All of them.
e.   Some other answer.

____ 22.   Sarah owns the following businesses and participates in each of the indicated activities.

Activity	Hours of Participation
1	101
2	130

3	300
4	250

In which activities is Sarah considered to be a material participant?

a. None of them.
b. Only activities 3 and 4.
c. Activities 2, 3, and 4
d. All of them.
e. Some other answer.

_____ 23.   Sarah owns the following businesses and participates in each of the indicated activities.

Activity	Hours of Participation
1	101
2	130
3	250

In which activities is Sarah considered to be a material participant?

a. None of them.
b. Only activities 2 and 3.
c. All of them.
d. Some other answer.

_____ 24.   Suzanne's adjusted basis in a passive activity is $20,000 at the beginning of the year. Her loss from the activity during the year is $15,000. She has investments in no other passive activities. Which of the following is true?

a. $5,000 year-end basis; $0 deductible loss.
b. $20,000 year-end basis; $0 deductible loss.
c. $5,000 year-end basis; $15,000 deductible loss.
d. $20,000 year-end basis; $15,0000 deductible loss.
e. None of the above is true.

Code Section Recognition

Several important sections of the Internal Revenue Code are described below. Indicate, by number, the appropriate Code section.

1. _____   Prescribes limitations on the deduction of losses to the extent that a taxpayer is at risk.

2. _____   Provides that net losses and credits from passive activities are limited.

Short Answer

1.   Identify those taxpayers who are subject to the passive loss rules.

2.   What activities or endeavors are considered to be passive?

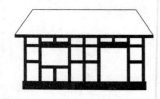

SOLUTIONS TO CHAPTER 10 QUESTIONS

True or False

1. F   A carryover of net passive losses is available to offset passive income in future years; further, special rules allow up to a $25,000 loss deduction from real estate rental activities and deductions for real estate rental losses of certain real estate professionals.
2. T
3. F   There is no limitation on the recognition of passive income.
4. T
5. T
6. F   Generally, a limited partner is not deemed to materially participate unless certain exceptions apply. However, if the exceptions are met, losses from such an interest would not be subject to the passive activity rules.
7. F   The standard provided in the Regulations requires more than 500 hours of participation during the year.
8. T
9. F   The exception applies only to rental real estate activities.
10. F   In order to utilize suspended losses, the taxable disposition must be of the taxpayer's *entire* interest.
11. F   The taxpayer must be an *active* participant.
12. T
13. F   The provisions apply to individuals and closely held corporations.
14. F   The amount at risk is adjusted periodically to reflect the taxpayer's share of income, losses, and withdrawals from the activity.
15. F   Losses disallowed under the at-risk rules generally can be carried over and used in future years to the extent an at-risk basis becomes available.
16. T
17. T
18. F   The taxpayer must be a *material* participant to deduct such losses against active income.
19. T
20. F   Such a taxpayer could be a material participant if Test 1, 5, or 6 as described in the text is met.

Fill-in-the-Blanks

1. $25,000, $150,000
2. Suspended losses
3. passive loss, at-risk
4. active, portfolio, passive
5. regular, continuous, substantial
6. materially participate
7. passive
8. Credits
9. material, active
10. active, portfolio
11. activity
12. portfolio
13. active, portfolio
14. at-risk, passive activity
15. at-risk

Multiple Choice

1. e
2. c
3. e
4. d   See Example 9 in the text.
5. b   Since the taxpayer disposes of her *entire* interest in the passive activity, all
          of the suspended losses may be utilized in the year of disposition. See Example
          8 in the text.
6. b   See Example 12 in the text.
7. b   This loss qualifies under the real estate rental activity exception, but only
          $25,000 of his share of the current loss (i.e., $30,000) is deductible this year.
          See Example 46 in the text.
8. e $12,500 = $25,000 - (50% [$125,000 - $100,000]). See the discussion in the text
          preceding Example 46.
9. a   If married individuals file separately, the $25,000 deduction is reduced to zero
          unless they lived apart for the entire year. See the discussion in the text
          preceding Example 46.
10. e $35,714 = $10,000 / 28%. See the discussion in the text following Example 46.
11. d
12. e
13. b $20,000 = $50,000 X ($40,000 / $100,000). See Example 9 in the text.
14. c   See Example 8 in the text.
15. b   The loss deduction is limited to the amount at risk, the $25,000 investment. See
          Example 4 in the text.
16. d   The amount at risk includes the taxpayer's share of the recourse debt.
17. d   Because the taxpayer is a material participant in the venture, the passive
          activity rules do not limit the amount of the deduction.
18. b   See Example 5 in the text.
19. c   Passive losses may be used to offset active income, but not portfolio income.
          See Example 15 in the text.
20. a   See Example 14 in the text.
21. c   Material participation is achieved based on Test 4. See Example 27 in the text.
22. d   See Example 27 in the text.
23. a   See Example 28 in the text.
24. a   See Example 41 in the text.

Code Section Recognition

1. 465
2. 469

Short Answer

1. The passive loss rules apply to individuals, estates, trusts, closely held C
    corporations, and personal service corporations.

2. The following types of activities are treated as passive.
    - Any trade or business or income-producing activity in which the taxpayer does
      not materially participate.
    - Subject to certain exceptions, all rental activities.

CHAPTER 11
TAX CREDITS

CHAPTER HIGHLIGHTS

ax credits are used by Congress at times to implement its tax policy objectives. Tax credits have a substantially different impact in the determination of a tax liability than do tax deductions: tax credits offset a tax liability dollar for dollar, whereas tax deductions merely reduce the tax base on which a tax liability is calculated. Some observers contend that tax credits provide benefits to taxpayers on a more equitable basis than those benefits received as a result of tax deductions. Numerous tax credits are available to individuals and businesses. The attributes of the various credits differ: the calculations for some of the credits are complex and some are not; some credits are refundable and some are nonrefundable. Many of these tax credits and their attributes are discussed in this chapter.

I. Tax Policy Considerations
    A. A tax credit should not be confused with an income tax deduction. A tax credit is generally worth substantially more to a taxpayer than a deduction of a similar amount since a credit directly offsets the tax liability. On the other hand, a deduction merely reduces taxable income.
    B. Tax credits, as opposed to deductions, generally provide benefits to taxpayers on a more equitable basis.
    C. Generally, tax credits are used by Congress to achieve social or economic objectives or to provide equity between different groups of taxpayers.
    D. Congress has used the tax credit provisions liberally in implementing tax policy. However, over time budget constraints and economic considerations have often dictated whether a credit would survive or be repealed. For example, in recent years, several important credits have been repealed, reduced, or allowed to expire (e.g., regular investment tax credit, political contributions credit). However, other credits have been retained, or even strengthened, based on economic or equity considerations (e.g., earned income credit).

II.   Overview and Priority of Credits
   A.   Refundable versus Nonrefundable Credits
      1.   Two basic types of credits exist: refundable and nonrefundable. *Refundable credits* (e.g., taxes withheld on wages, earned income credit) are paid to the taxpayer even if they exceed the taxpayer's tax liability; whereas, *nonrefundable credits* (e.g., foreign tax credit, tax credit for the elderly or disabled) are not paid if the credits exceed the tax liability.
      2.   Some of the nonrefundable credits are subject to carryover provisions if they cannot be used in a given year (e.g., foreign tax credit), while some of the nonrefundable credits are lost forever if they cannot be used in the year in which they arise (e.g., tax credit for the elderly or disabled).
      3.   A prioritized ranking by which tax credits are utilized to reduce a tax liability is specified by law and shown in the text in Exhibit 11-1.
   B.   General Business Credit -- This credit is comprised of a number of other credits, each of which is computed separately under its owns set of rules. This credit combines these credits into one amount to limit the amount of business credits that can be used of offset a taxpayer's income tax liability. Special rules apply to the general business credit.

KEY TERMS
- Refundable, NonRefundable Credit
- Investment Tax Credit
- Rehabilitation Credit
- Child Care Credit
- Earned Income Credit
- Research Credit

      1.   Any unused credit must first be carried back 3 years, then forward 15 years.
      2.   The general business tax credit is limited for any tax year: the maximum allowable credit is limited to the taxpayer's *net income tax* reduced by the greater of the following.
         a.   The *tentative minimum tax*.
         b.   25 percent of *net regular tax liability* that exceeds $25,000.
   C.   Treatment of Unused General Business Credits -- Unused credits are initially carried back for three years. Any remaining unused credits are then carried forward for 15 years. The FIFO method is applied to the carrybacks, carryovers, and utilization of credits earned during a specific year.

III.   Specific Business-Related Tax Credit Provisions
   A.   Investment Tax Credit: Introduction
      1.   The investment tax credit (ITC) currently is comprised of the credit for rehabilitation expenditures and the business energy credit.
      2.   Under prior law, the regular ITC also was a component. Prior to its repeal, the regular ITC was allowed for most tangible business personalty placed in service before 1986.
      3.   The ITC has had a checkered history, as it has been suspended, reinstated, repealed, and reenacted in response to various conditions and pressures.
   B.   Regular Investment Tax Credit
      1.   Although the credit has been repealed, tax professionals will have to deal with the credit carryover provisions for years into the future. Therefore,

some familiarity with the basic ITC rules is required.

2. Qualifying Property
    a. The regular ITC generally was available for tangible personal property (e.g., automobiles, machinery, and furniture) used in a trade or business.
    b. The regular ITC was not available for most real property (e.g., land and buildings).
3. Computation of Qualified Investment and Amount of the Credit
    a. The credit was computed on the aggregate amount of qualifying property placed in service during a year. Limited amounts of used property acquired also qualified for the credit.
    b. The regular ITC was calculated based on the rates given in Exhibit 11-1.

Exhibit 11-1
INVESTMENT TAX CREDIT RATES

Recovery Period (in years)	Full Credit Rate	Reduced Credit Rate
3	6%	4%
5, 10, or 15	10%	8%

    c. Taxpayers computed the credit using either the full or reduced credit. If the full credit rate was used, the related property's depreciable basis was reduced. If the reduced credit was claimed, no basis reduction was required.
4. Reduction of Investment Tax Credit -- A 35 percent reduction of the ITC is required for carryovers of the regular ITC from pre-1986 years.

C. Tax Credit for Rehabilitation Expenditures
1. A tax credit is available for rehabilitation expenditures incurred on industrial and commercial buildings and on certified historic structures. However, no credit is allowed for the rehabilitation of personal use property.
2. The operating features are summarized in Exhibit 11-2.

Exhibit 11-2
REHABILITATION TAX CREDIT RATES

Rate of Credit for Rehabilitation Expenses	Nature of Property
10%	Nonresidential buildings and residential rental property, other than certified historic structures, originally placed in service before 1936
20%	Nonresidential and residential certified historic structures

3.   The basis of a rehabilitated building must be reduced by the amount of the credit taken, and the taxpayer is required to depreciate the rehabilitated structure using the straight-line method.

4.   To qualify for the credit, the building must be substantially rehabilitated. The building is considered to have been substantially rehabilitated if the rehabilitation expenditures exceed the greater of the following.

    a.   The adjusted basis of the property.

    b. $5,000.

5.   If the rehabilitated building is disposed of prematurely (before five years) or if it ceases to be qualifying property, part or all of the credit must be recaptured.

D.   Business Energy Credits

1.   For many years, business energy credits have been allowed to encourage the conservation of natural resources and the development of alternative energy sources. While many of these energy credits have expired, two remain.

2.   Business energy credits are available at a 10% rate for the acquisition of solar energy property and geothermal property.

E.   Jobs Credit

1.   The jobs credit was enacted to encourage employers to hire individuals from one or more of several target groups listed below.

    a.   Vocational rehabilitation individuals.

    b.   Economically disadvantaged youths (age 18 to 22).

    c.   Economically disadvantaged Vietnam-era veterans.

    d.   Recipients of certain Social Security supplemental security income benefits.

    e.   General assistance recipients.

    f.   Youths (age 16 to 19) participating in cooperative education programs.

    g.   Economically disadvantaged ex-convicts.

    h.   Eligible work incentive employees.

    i.   Qualified summer youth employees (age 16 and 17).

2.   Computation of the Regular Jobs Credit

    a.   The regular jobs credit is equal to 40 percent of the first $6,000 of wages (per eligible employee) for the first year of employment for employees who start work on or before December 31, 1994.

    b.   To qualify the employer for the credit, the unemployed individual must be certified by a local jobs service office of a state employment security agency.

    c.   The employer's tax deduction for wages must be reduced by the amount of the credit.

    d.   Wages will qualify only if the employee has worked for at least 90 days or has completed at least 120 hours of work.

3.   Computation of the Jobs Credit for Qualified Summer Youth Employees

    a.   The credit for summer youth employees is only available for wages paid for any 90-day period between May 1 and September 15, but only if the employee is hired on or before December 31, 1994. Such employees must be age 16 or 17 on the hiring date.

    b.   The maximum amount of wages paid which qualify for the credit is $3,000 per summer youth employee, and the rate of the credit is 40 percent. Thus, the maximum credit is $1,200 per eligible summer youth employee.

       c.   If the employee qualifies as a member of another target group, the regular jobs tax credit may be available to a limited extent.

       d.   The employer's tax deduction for wages must be reduced by the amount of the credit.

F.   Research Activities Credit

    1.   A credit is allowed for the purpose of encouraging research and experimentation. It is available for qualifying expenditures paid or incurred through June 30, 1995. The credit is the *sum* of two components: an incremental research activities credit and a basic research credit.

    2.   Incremental Research Activities Credit

       a.   The credit applies at a 20 percent rate to the *excess* of *qualified research expenses* for the current taxable year over the *base amount*.

       b.   A statutory rule defines the nature of expenditures qualifying for the credit.

       c.   The credit may be claimed on these expenditures and, in addition, the taxpayer may choose among several alternatives insofar as their deduction is concerned. One of the following options may be used.

          (1)   Use the full credit and reduce the expense deduction for research expenses by 100 percent of the credit.

          (2)   Retain the full expense deduction and reduce the credit by the product of 50 percent times the maximum corporate tax rate.

          (3)   Use the full credit, and capitalize the research expenses and amortize them over 60 months or more.

    3.   Basic Research Credit

       a.   A credit is allowed for *basic research expenditures* incurred in *excess* of a base amount, at the rate of 20 percent. *Basic research* payments are amounts paid in cash to a qualified basic research organization, such as a college or university.

       b.   Basic research is any original investigation for the advancement of scientific knowledge not having a specific commercial objective.

G.   Low-Income Housing Credit

    1.   Owners of qualified low-income housing may claim a credit which is intended to encourage the provision of affordable housing to low-income individuals. The credit may be claimed annually in equal amounts for ten years if the property continues to meet the required conditions.

    2.   Several important characteristics of the credit follow.

       a.   The appropriate rate for computing the credit is set monthly by the IRS.

       b.   The amount of the credit is based on the qualified basis of the property, which depends on the number of units rented to low-income tenants.

       c.   Once declared eligible, the property must meet the required conditions continuously throughout an extended period. Recapture rules apply in the case of noncompliance.

H.   Disabled Access Credit

    1.   The disabled access credit is designed to encourage small business taxpayers to make their businesses more accessible to disabled individuals.

    2.   The credit is available for *eligible access expenditures* paid or incurred by an *eligible small business* (i.e., certain sole proprietorships, partnerships, and regular or S corporations).

    3.   The credit is calculated at the rate of 50 percent of the eligible expenditures that exceed $250 but do not exceed $10,250.

4. To the extent the credit is available, no deduction or credit is allowed under any other provision of the tax law (e.g, for depreciation).

IV. Other Tax Credits
    A.   Earned Income Credit
        1.   The earned income credit has been part of the tax law for many years. It is intended to provide equity to the working poor. Since 1994, the credit has been more generous and simpler than the previous version of the law.

> The earned income credit is unusual in several ways: (a) the taxpayer need not spend money to obtain it, (b) he or she can collect the credit throughout the year through a withholding adjustment, and (c) the credit is available as a "negative income tax," (i.e., if the credit exceeds the tax due for the year, the Treasury still pays the difference).

        2.   For 1995, the *earned income credit* is determined by multiplying a maximum amount of earned income ($6,160, if the taxpayer has one child; or $8,640, if the taxpayer has two or more children) by the appropriate credit percentage (either 34 percent, if the taxpayer has one child; or 36 percent, if the taxpayer has two or more children). However, the maximum earned income credit is phased out, beginning when the taxpayer's earned income or adjusted gross income exceeds $11,290. The phase-out rates are 15.98 percent and 20.22 percent, depending on the number of the taxpayer's qualifying children.
        3.   The IRS issues a table that may be used to determine the proper amount of the credit.
        4.   In general, to be *eligible* for the credit, not only must certain income thresholds not be exceeded, but the taxpayer must also have a *qualifying child*. To have a qualifying child, the following three tests must be met.
            a.   Relationship test.
            b.   Residency test.
            c.   Age test.
        5.   The earned income credit is available for low-income workers who do not have any qualifying children, as long as the worker (or his or her spouse) is over age 25 (and under 65) and is not claimed as a dependent on another return. The credit is 7.65 percent of the first $4,100 of earned income, and is phased out at the rate of 7.65 percent for each dollar of earned income (or AGI, if larger) exceeding $5,130.
        6.   The earned income credit is refundable to the extent that it exceeds the taxpayer's tax liability.
    B.   Tax Credit for the Elderly or Disabled Taxpayers
        1.   The retirement income credit, which was originally enacted in 1954, is a relief provision for certain elderly (age 65 and over) taxpayers and/or certain taxpayers who are permanently and totally disabled.
        2.   Individuals under age 65 also are eligible for this credit, but only if they retire with a permanent and total disability and have disability income from a public or private employer on account of that disability.

3.   The *maximum* allowable credit is $1,125 (15% X $7,500 of qualifying income).

4.   The credit is based on an initial ceiling amount of $5,000 (designated as the base amount) for a single taxpayer. The base amount is also $5,000 for married taxpayers filing a joint return when only one spouse is 65 or older. However, this amount increases to $7,500 for married taxpayers filing jointly when both spouses are 65 or older. If married taxpayers file separately, the base amount is $3,750.

5.   This initial ceiling amount is *reduced* by (1) social security, railroad retirement, and certain excluded pension benefits and (2) one-half of the taxpayer's adjusted gross income in excess of $7,500. To compute the credit, the remainder is multiplied by 15 percent.

6.   The adjusted gross income factor of $7,500 for single taxpayers described above, is increased to $10,000 for married taxpayers filing jointly. For married taxpayers filing separately, the amount is $5,000. The amount is also $7,500 for a head of household or a surviving spouse.

C.   Foreign Tax Credit

1.   A tax credit (as an alternative to a deduction) may be claimed by individual or corporate taxpayers on income earned and subject to a tax in a foreign country or U.S. possession.

2.   The credit, which is generally more favorable than a deduction, is designed to mitigate double taxation.

3.   The credit is computed using the following formula.

$$\frac{\text{Foreign-source taxable income}}{\text{Worldwide Taxable Income}} \quad X \quad \begin{array}{c}\textit{US tax before}\\ \textit{the FTC}\end{array} = \begin{array}{c}\textit{Overall}\\ \textit{limitation}\end{array}$$

The foreign tax credit is the *lesser* of the foreign taxes actually imposed or the overall limitation amount. Only foreign income taxes, war profits taxes, and excess profits taxes qualify for the credit.

4.   Unused foreign tax credits may be carried back two years and then forward five years.

D.   Credit for Child and Dependent Care Expenses

1.   This credit was enacted to benefit taxpayers who incur employment-related expenses for child or dependent care. The credit is equal to a specified percentage of expenses incurred to enable the taxpayer to work or seek employment.

2.   To be eligible, an individual taxpayer must maintain a household for a qualifying individual(s).

     a.   A dependent under age 13.

     b.   A dependent or spouse who is physically or mentally incapacitated.

3.   Eligible expenses include amounts paid for household services and care of a qualifying individual(s) which are incurred to enable a taxpayer to be employed. The amount of employment-related expenses that may be considered in the computation of the credit are limited to an individual's earned income. For married taxpayers, this limitation applies to the spouse with the *lesser* amount of earned income.

4.   The credit is equal to a percentage (ranging from 20 to 30 percent) of employment-related expenses up to $2,400 for one qualifying individual and $4,800 for two or more individuals. The rate used to compute the credit is dependent on the taxpayer's adjusted gross income.

5.   A taxpayer is not allowed to exclude an amount from gross income under a qualifying dependent care assistance program and compute the child and

dependent care credit on the same amount. Thus, the allowable child and dependent care expenses are reduced by any amount received pursuant to a dependent care assistance program.

TEST FOR SELF-EVALUATION -- CHAPTER 11

True or False

Indicate which of the following statements are true or false by circling the correct answer.

T   F   1.   A tax credit is always worth more than a tax deduction of equal dollar amount.

T   F   2.   One rationale for the use of tax credits as a means of implementing tax policy is that tax credits provide benefits on a more equitable basis than do tax deductions.

T   F   3.   For a building to qualify as being substantially rehabilitated for purposes of the rehabilitation tax credit, the rehabilitation expenditures must exceed the greater of the adjusted basis of the property or $10,000. *5,000*

T   F   4.   To qualify for the tax credit for the elderly or disabled taxpayers, an individual under 65 years of age need only be retired with a permanent and total disability.

T   F   5.   Rehabilitation tax credit recapture may be triggered on disposing of property on which the rehabilitation tax credit had been claimed.

T   F   6.   Unused foreign tax credits may be carried back two years and forward 5 years.

T   F   7.   The maximum amount of employment-related expenses that qualify for purposes of computing the credit for child and dependent care expenses for a taxpayer is $2,400. *4400*

T   F   8.   The earned income tax credit is a form of negative income tax.

T   F   9.   Eligible employment-related expenses allowable in computing the credit for child and dependent care expenses include amounts paid for household services.

T   F   10. The amount of the earned income credit may be dependent on the number of the taxpayer's qualifying children.

T   F   11. Unused general business tax credits must first be carried back for 3 years and then carried forward for 15 years.

T   F   12. In order to be eligible for the earned income credit the taxpayer must have at least one qualifying child.

T   F   13. Refundable credits are paid to the taxpayer even if the amount of the credit (or credits) exceeds the taxpayer's tax liability.

T   F   14. The low-income housing credit is an example of a refundable credit.

T   F   15. A LIFO method is applied to the carryovers, carrybacks, and utilization of unused general business credit used in a particular year. *FIFO*

T   (F)   16.   The jobs credit is one of the components of the investment tax credit.

T   (F)   17.   The rehabilitation tax credit must be recaptured if the property is disposed of or ceases to be qualifying property within ten years of incurring the rehabilitation expenditures.

(T)   F   18.   An economically disadvantaged ex-convict is one of the types of individuals targeted by the jobs credit.

(T)   F   19.   The research activities credit is the sum of two components: an incremental research activities credit and a basic research credit.

(T)   F   20.   Qualified research and experimentation expenditures not only are eligible for the 20 percent credit but also can be expensed in the year incurred.

Fill-in-the-Blanks

Complete the following statements with the appropriate word(s) or amount(s).

1.   While a tax deduction merely reduces ___tax inc.___, a tax credit reduces the ___tax liab___.

2.   A tax credit is available for rehabilitation expenditures incurred on certain commercial and industrial buildings as well as ___hist. b___.

3.   The _____ method is applied to the carryovers, carrybacks, and the utilization of general business credits earned during a particular year.

4.   The regular jobs credit is equal to ___40%___ percent of the first ___6,000___ of wages per eligible employee for the first year of employment.

5.   A ___20%___ percent tax credit for rehabilitation expenditures is allowed on certified historic structures.

6.   The disabled access credit is available at the rate of ___50___ percent of the eligible expenditures that exceed ___250___ but do not exceed ___10,250___.

7.   A taxpayer may either claim a ___deduction___ or a ___credit___ with respect to taxes paid on income earned from foreign sources.

8.   The maximum child care credit allowable to a taxpayer who maintains a household for one dependent is ___720___.   2400 x 30%

9.   In computing the tax credit for the elderly or disabled taxpayers, after the initial ceiling amount is reduced for certain items, the remainder is multiplied by ___15___ percent.

10.   The credit for child and dependent care expenses is a percentage of the employment-related expenses, ranging from ___20___ to ___30___ percent.

11.   A regular jobs credit will be available to an employer if an individual from a qualifying target group is employed for at least ___90___ days or ___120___ hours.

12.   The research activities credit is the sum of two components: an _____ and a _____ .

13.   All tax credits are of one or two types: they are either ___refund___ or ___nonrefund___ .

14.   The ___rehab___ credit was introduced as a part of tax law to discourage the relocation of businesses from older, economically distressed areas to newer locations and to preserve historic structures.

15.   For the incremental research activities credit, if research is conducted by persons outside the taxpayer's business (i.e., under contract), only ___65___ percent of the amount paid qualifies for the credit.

Multiple Choice

Choose the best answer for each of the following questions.

_____   1.   Which of the following is a refundable tax credit?
        a.   Earned income credit.
        b.   Foreign tax credit.
        c.   Credit for the elderly or disabled.
        d.   Disabled access credit.
        e.   None of the above is a refundable tax credit.

_____   2.   Which of the following statements regarding the energy credit is true?
        a.   The energy credit is available for business and residential energy conservation endeavors.
        b.   The amount of the energy credit ranges from 5 to 25 percent of qualifying expenditures.
        c.   Solar panels and storm doors are examples of the type of expenditures that give rise to the energy credit.
        d.   The credit is limited to expenditures for solar energy property and geothermal property.
        e.   None of the above.

_____   3.   Two and one-half years ago, Westphal placed in service a non-historic building on which expenditures were incurred which qualified for the rehabilitation tax credit. Qualifying rehabilitation expenditures incurred were $800,000. If Westphal sold the building at a loss this year, what amount of rehabilitation tax credit recapture is due?   held 2½ yrs!
        a. $32,000.
        b. $48,000.
        c. $80,000.
        d.   None because the building was disposed of at a loss.
        e.   None of the above.

_____   4.   Select the *correct* statement.
        a.   The only taxpayer eligible to claim the earned income credit would be one who either is married and entitled to a dependency exemption for a child, or is a surviving spouse.
        b.   Because of the ceiling limitation imposed, the foreign tax credit may not

eliminate completely the effect of multiple taxation.

c.   The LIFO method is applied to the carryovers, carrybacks and utilization of general business tax credits earned during a particular year.

d.   An intangible asset used in a trade or business with a useful life of three years or more would have been eligible for the regular investment tax credit.

e.   None of the above is correct.

_____ 5.   Select the *incorrect* statement below pertaining to the research activities credit.

a.   The research credit is the sum of two components: an incremental credit and a basic research credit.

b.   The incremental research activities credit is 20 percent of the amount of qualified research expenses that exceed the base amount.

c.   Qualifying expenditures not only are eligible for the research credit, but also can be expensed in the year incurred.

d.   Corporations, but not S corporations or personal service corporations, are eligible for the basic research credit.

(e)   Each of the above statements is correct.

_____ 6.   Sam and Tanya, married filing a joint return, have two children. In 1995, their earned income is $13,000. Calculate their earned income credit for 1995.

a. $2,173.90.

(b) $2,764.64.

c. $2,915.77.

d. $3,110.40.

e.   Some other amount.

_____ 7.   John and Susie are married, file jointly, and have one dependent daughter, Sarah. Qualifying child care expenditures of $3,000 were incurred in order that both parents could work outside the home. John earned $7,500 and Susie earned $17,000; however, their adjusted gross income was $25,000. What is the allowable credit for child and dependent care expenses?

(a) $528.

b. $660.

c. $720.

d. $900.

e.   Some other amount.

_____ 8.   Assume the same facts as in the previous problem, except that John and Susie have two dependent daughters, Sarah and Emily. What is the allowable credit for child and dependent care expenses?

a. $528.

(b) $660.

c. $720.

d. $900.

e.   Some other amount.

_____ 9.   Tami and Bobby have three dependent children aged 3, 5, and 14. Tami has been physically disabled since March 1, 1995 and unable to work or care for the children. Since March 1, 1995, Tami and Bobby have incurred $7,200 of child care expenses. Bobby's salary was $30,000. Tami had no earnings in January or February, 1995. Bobby and Tami may claim a child care credit for 1995 of what amount?

  a. $1,440.
  b. $960.
  c. $800.
  d. $0.
  e. None of the above.

10. Good Hands Company hires six economically disadvantaged Vietnam veterans on May 6, 1994, to work at its summer camp for inner-city youth. The veterans worked for four months. Their wages totaled $8,000 each. What is the jobs credit and the wages deduction available to Good Hands?
  a. $19,200; $28,800.
  b. $19,200; $48,000.
  c. $14,400; $48,000.
  d. $14,400; $33,600.
  e. None of the above.

11. In 1995, Burk Corporation had $250,000 in income from Scotland which imposes a 50% income tax on income earned within its borders. Burk also had income of $500,000 from within the United States. The tentative U.S. tax on the $750,000 total income is $255,000. How much is Burk's foreign tax credit for 1995?
  a. $0.
  b. $41,667.
  c. $85,000.
  d. $125,000.
  e. None of the above.

12. Which of the following taxes *do* qualify for purposes of calculating the foreign tax credit?
  a. VAT (value added taxes).
  b. War profits taxes.
  c. Property taxes.
  d. Sales taxes.
  e. None of the above qualify.

13. Which of the following statements concerning the earned income credit is true?
  a. The credit can only be subtracted from any net tax liability after considering withholdings and estimated tax payments.
  b. The credit can result in a refund only when the taxpayer has had taxes withheld.
  c. The credit can result in a refund even if the taxpayer has had no taxes withheld and has no tax liability.
  d. None of the above is true.

14. The general business credit is *not* comprised of which of the following?
  a. Tax credit for rehabilitation expenditures.
  b. Jobs credit.
  c. Low-income housing credit.
  d. Foreign tax credit.
  e. All of the above are components of the general business credit.

15. Herold Corporation's general business credit for the year is $85,000. The business's net income tax is $125,000, while the tentative alternative minimum tax

is $50,000. Assuming Herold Corporation has no other credits for the year, the general business credit allowed for the year is what amount?

   a. $50,000.
   b. $75,000.
   c. $85,000.
   d. $100,000.
   e.   Some other amount.

16.   Herold Corporation's general business credit for the year is $85,000. The business's net income tax is $125,000, while the tentative alternative minimum tax is $15,000. Assuming Herold Corporation has no other credits for the year, the general business credit allowed for the year is what amount?

   a. $15,000.
   b. $85,000.
   c. $100,000.
   d. $110,000.
   e.   Some other amount.

17.   Traylor Corporation spent $75,000 to rehabilitate a building that had originally been placed in service in 1921 in the inner city. Traylor had acquired the building early this year for $100,000. The amount of the rehabilitation expenditures credit available to the taxpayer is the following.

   a. $7,500.
   b. $15,000.
   c. $17,500.
   d. $35,000.
   e.   None of the above.

18.   Traylor Corporation spent $75,000 to rehabilitate a historic structure located in the inner city. Traylor had acquired the building early this year for $50,000. The amount of the rehabilitation expenditures credit available to the taxpayer is the following.

   a. $7,500.
   b. $12,500.
   c. $15,000.
   d. $25,000.
   e.   None of the above.

19.   Blue Corporation hired Sally as a qualified summer youth employee beginning May 15, 1994. Sally continued working for Blue Corporation through Labor Day when she returned to college. Sally was paid $4,500 for her efforts. Blue Corporation is eligible for a jobs credit of what amount?

   a. $0.
   b. $600.
   c. $1,200.
   d. $1,800.
   e.   None of the above.

20.   Skyline Corporation, desiring to make their business more accessible to disabled individuals, incurred $8,000 in eligible access expenditures. The amount of disabled access credit arising from these expenditures is what amount?

a. $0.
b. $3,875. $(8,000-250) × 50%$
c. $4,000.
d. $5,000.
e. Some other amount.

_____ 21. Skyline Corporation, desiring to make their business more accessible to disabled individuals, incurred $18,000 in eligible access expenditures. The amount of disabled access credit arising from these expenditures is what amount?
a. $3,875.
b. $5,000. $10,250-250 × 50%$
c. $8,875.
d. $9,000.
e. Some other amount.

_____ 22. Viola, a single taxpayer who is 26 years old, is not claimed as a dependent on another tax return. During 1995, her earned income was $6,000. She qualifies for the following amount of earned income credit.
a. $247.09.
b. $313.65.
c. $392.44.
d. $459.00.
e. None of the above.

_____ 23. During the current year, Green Hills Corporation had $250,000 in income from Ireland which imposes a 10% income tax on income earned within its borders. Green Hills also had income of $500,000 from within the United States. The tentative U.S. tax on the $750,000 total income is $255,000. How much is Green Hill's foreign tax credit for the year?
a. $0.
b. $8,333.
c. $25,000.
d. $85,000.
e. None of the above.

_____ 24. To qualify for the credit for child and dependent care expenses, the taxpayer must maintain a household for which of the following individuals?
a. A dependent under age 13.
b. A dependent of any age.
c. A dependent or spouse who is physically or mentally incapacitated.
d. a or b.
e. a or c.
f. All of the above qualify.

Code Section Recognition

Several important sections of the Internal Revenue Code are described below. Indicate, by number, the appropriate Code section.

1.   _____   Requires recapture of the rehabilitation tax credit in certain situations.

2.   ____   Provides a tax credit to multinational taxpayers to relieve double taxation.

3.   ____   Taxpayers who incur qualifying child care expenditures may claim a credit.

Short Answer

1.   Bob and Tami incur child care expenses of $4,000 on behalf of their two sons, Mitchell and
      Lane. Bob's earnings for the year are $3,800 and Tami's earnings total $22,000. Assuming
      they had no other income, determine their credit for child and dependent care expenses.

_25,800_
_.22_

_3800_

_434_

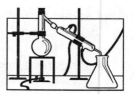

SOLUTIONS TO CHAPTER 11 QUESTIONS

True or False

1. T
2. T
3. F   The expenditures must exceed the greater of the adjusted basis or $5,000.
4. F   The taxpayer must also have disability income from a public or private employer on account of that disability.
5. T
6. T
7. F   The maximum amount is $4,800 if expenditures are incurred on behalf of two or more dependents.
8. T
9. T
10. T
11. T
12. F   While this generally may be the situation, a reduced earned income credit is available for a low-income taxpayer if he/she (or his or her spouse) is over 25 and under age 65 and is not claimed as a dependent on another return.
13. T
14. F   The low-income housing credit is not a refundable credit.
15. F   A FIFO method is used.
16. F   The current components of the investment tax credit are the rehabilitation expenditures credit and the business energy credit.
17. F   The amount recaptured is based on a holding period requirement of five years.
18. T
19. T
20. T

Fill-in-the-Blanks

1. taxable income, tax liability
2. certified historic structures
3. FIFO
4. 40, $6,000
5. 20
6. 50, $250, $10,250
7. deduction, credit
8. $720 (i.e., $2,400 X 30%)
9. 15
10. 20, 30
11. 90, 120
12. incremental research activities credit, basic research credit
13. refundable, nonrefundable
14. rehabilitation expenditures
15. 65

Multiple Choice

1. a
2. d
3. b   Original credit ($800,000 X .10) $80,000
         Less: Amount of credit earned ($80,000 X .40)   32,000
         Recapture tax $48,000
         See Example 12 in the text.
4. b
5. e
6. b   Maximum credit ($8,640 X 36.0%) $3,110.40
         Less: 20.22% ($13,000 - $11,290)   345.76
         Allowable earned income credit $2,764.64
         See Example 23 in the text.
7. a $528 = $2,400 X 22%   See Example 28 in the text and related discussion.
8. b $660 = $3,000 X 22%   See Example 28 in the text and related discussion.
9. c $800 = $4,800 X 10/12 X .20 See Example 28 in the text and related discussion.
10. d $14,400 credit = 6 X $6,000 X 40%
         $33,600 wage deduction = $48,000 - $14,400   See Example 13 in the text.
11. c $85,000 = $250,000/$750,000 X $255,000 See Example 26 in the text.
12. b   In general, qualifying taxes must be based on income (e.g., war profits).
13. c   The earned income credit is a "refundable" credit.
14. d
15. b   Net income tax $125,000
         Less: The greater of
                ▸ $50,000 (tentative minimum tax)
                ▸ $25,000 [25% X ($125,000 - $25,000)]   50,000
         Allowable business credit $ 75,000
         See Example 7 in the text.
16. b   Net income tax $125,000
         Less: The greater of
                ▸ $15,000 (tentative minimum tax)
                ▸ $25,000 [25% X ($125,000 - $25,000)]   25,000
         Maximum business credit allowed $100,000
         Allowable business credit limited to
           amount of credit available $ 85,000
         See Example 7 in the text and related discussion.
17. e   The rehabilitation expenditures credit is not available because the building has not
         been substantially rehabilitated (i.e., the amount of the expenditures incurred did
         not exceed the greater of $5,000 or the adjusted basis of the building prior to the
         rehabilitation).
18. c $15,000 = $75,000 X 20%   See Example 11 in the text.
19. c $1,200 = $3,000 (maximum wages eligible for the credit) X 40%   See Example 15 in the
         text.
20. b $3,875 = ($8,000 - $250) X 50%   See Example 22 in the text.
21. b $5,000 = ($10,250 - $250) X 50%   See Example 22 in the text.
22. a   Initial credit ($4,100 X 7.65%) $313.65
         Less: 7.65% ($6,000 - $5,130)   66.56
         Allowable earned income credit $247.09
         See Example 24 in the text.
23. c $85,000 = $250,000/$750,000 X $255,000. But, the maximum credit is limited to the

amount of foreign tax actually paid (i.e., $25,000). See Example 26 in the text.

24.   e

Code Section Recognition

1.   50
2.   901
3.   21

Short Answer

1.   Qualifying expenses--$4,000, but limited to Bob's earnings $3,800
       Rate (based on AGI of $25,800)   X 22%
       Credit amount $ 836

CHAPTER 12
PROPERTY TRANSACTIONS: DETERMINATION OF GAIN OR LOSS, BASIC CONSIDERATIONS, AND NONTAXABLE EXCHANGES

CHAPTER HIGHLIGHTS

Tax consequences generally result when a sale or other disposition of property occurs. In such cases, any gain or loss realized is recognized for tax purposes. Thus, income tax would be payable on the gain realized or a loss deduction would be available on the loss realized in the year of sale or disposition. However, in some situations gains or losses realized are not recognized for tax purposes in the year of disposition. Examples of transactions in which gains or losses realized may not be currently recognized for tax purposes include like-kind exchanges, involuntary conversions, and sales of personal residences. Thus, these nonrecognition provisions, which may or may not be mandatory, can provide for temporary deferral of gain or loss recognition. Further, one provision, the election to exclude up to $125,000 of gain realized on the sale of a personal residence by taxpayers at least 55 years old, provides for a permanent forgiveness of gain recognition.

I. Determination of Gain or Loss
   A. Realized Gain or Loss
       1. A *realized gain* or *loss* is measured by the difference between the amount realized from the sale or other disposition of property and its adjusted basis on the date of disposition.
       2. A realized gain results if the amount realized exceeds the property's adjusted basis. A loss is realized if the adjusted basis exceeds the amount realized.
       3. The term *sale or other disposition* includes virtually any disposition of property, such as trade-ins, casualties, sales and exchanges, or condemnations.
       4. The *amount realized* from the disposition of property is the sum of money received, plus the fair market value of property received, plus the release of any liability on the property disposed of, less selling expenses relating to the sale.
       5. The *adjusted basis* of property disposed of is the original basis (usually cost), plus capital additions or improvements, less capital recoveries. The result reflects the unrecovered cost or other basis of the property on the date of disposition.

6.   Capital additions, which may be distinguished from ordinary repair and maintenance expenditures, include the cost of capital improvements and betterments made to property by a taxpayer.

7.   The following are examples of capital recoveries (i.e., reductions in an asset's basis).

       a.   Depreciation and cost recovery allowances.

       b.   Casualties and thefts.

       c.   Certain corporate distributions.

       d.   Amortizable bond premium.

B.   Recognized Gain or Loss

1.   *Recognized gain* is an amount of realized gain that is included in a taxpayer's gross income.

2.   A *recognized loss* is an amount of realized loss that is deductible for tax purposes.

3.   As a general rule, all realized gains and losses are recognized.

C.   Nonrecognition of Gain or Loss -- Several situations where realized gains and/or losses are not recognized include the following.

1.   Nontaxable exchanges.

2.   Losses realized on personal use assets, except in the case of thefts or casualties.

3.   On making an election, gains of up to $125,000 realized on the sale of a personal residence by a taxpayer 55 or more years of age.

4.   Realized losses on certain transactions between related parties.

D.   Recovery of Capital Doctrine

1.   A taxpayer is entitled to recover the cost or other original basis of property acquired and, therefore, is not taxed on that amount.

2.   The cost or other original basis is recovered through annual depreciation deductions.

3.   On a sale or other disposition, it is the unrecovered cost that is compared to the amount realized to determine realized gain or loss.

II.   Basis Considerations

A.   Determination of Cost Basis

1.   The basis of property is generally its cost -- the amount paid for the property in cash or other property. However, the basis of property received in a *bargain purchase* is its fair market value.

2.   Cost identification problems are frequently encountered in securities transactions. Unless a taxpayer can adequately identify the particular stock that has been sold, a security sold is presumed to come from the first lot or lots purchased (i.e., a FIFO presumption).

3.   It is often necessary to allocate the lump-sum purchase price of multiple assets acquired for the purpose of determining the basis of each individual asset involved. The lump-sum cost is allocated on the basis of the relative fair market value of the individual assets acquired. If a business is purchased and *goodwill* is involved, a special allocation rule applies. Further, a special allocation may be required in the case of *nontaxable stock dividends*.

When selling shares of stock or interests in a mutual fund, be certain that the asset's basis is properly stated. Income and capital gains distributions that have been reinvested in more stock over the years increase the investment's basis. The effect of these adjustments is to reduce the amount of gain or increase the amount of loss to be reported.

B. Gift Basis
1. Because there is no cost to the recipient on the receipt of a gift, a basis must be assigned to the property. However, the basis for gain and the basis for loss may not be the same amount. In general, the donee's basis depends on the following.
   a. The date of the gift.
   b. The basis of the property to the donor.
   c. The amount of the gift tax paid.
   d. The fair market value of the property.
2. The basis rules for gifts made in 1921 or after require the following.
   a. If the donee subsequently disposes of the property and a gain is realized, the basis to the donee is the same as the donor's adjusted basis.
   b. If the donee subsequently disposes of the property in a transaction which results in a loss, the basis to the donee is the lower of the donor's adjusted basis or the fair market value on the date of the gift.
3. If, on a sale by the donee, the amount of sales proceeds is between the basis for gain and the basis for loss, then no gain or loss is recognized.
4. Gift taxes paid by the donor are often added, in part or in full, to the basis of property given to the donee.
   a. For gifts made after 1976, the amount of the gift tax added is that amount attributed to the *net unrealized appreciation* up to the date of the gift.
   b. For gifts made prior to 1977, the full amount of the gift tax paid is added to the donor's basis, up to the fair market value of the property.
5. If the donor's adjusted basis of property received by gift is the basis to the donee, then the *holding period* begins on the date the property was acquired by the donor. The holding period begins on the date of the gift if the fair market value is the basis to the donee.
6. The basis for depreciation on depreciable gift property is the donor's adjusted basis (i.e., the donee's basis for gain).

C. Property Acquired from a Decedent
1. The basis of property acquired from a decedent is generally its fair market value at the date of the decedent's death. In some situations, an estate's executor or administrator may *elect* the *alternate valuation amount*, which generally, is the property's fair market value six months after the decedent's death.
2. Survivor's Share of Property
   a. With *community property*, both the decedent's share and the survivor's share assume a basis equal to fair market value on the date of the decedent's death.
   b. With property in a *common law* state, only one-half of jointly held property of spouses is included in the decedent's estate. No adjustment of the basis is permitted for the excluded property

interest.

3. The holding period of property acquired from a decedent is *deemed* to be *long-term* (i.e., held for the required long-term holding period).

D. Disallowed Losses
    1. Related Taxpayers
        a. Direct and indirect losses realized from sales or exchanges of property between certain related parties are *not* recognized.

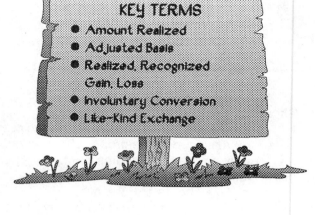

KEY TERMS
• Amount Realized
• Adjusted Basis
• Realized, Recognized Gain, Loss
• Involuntary Conversion
• Like-Kind Exchange

   b. The basis of business or income producing property to the transferee in a related party transaction is its cost.
   c. The original transferee may reduce any realized gain on a subsequent disposition of the property to the extent of the previously disallowed loss.
   d. The holding period includes only the period of time the property was held.
2. Wash Sales -- A realized loss will not be recognized if the taxpayer sells or exchanges stock or securities and, within 30 days before or after such sale or exchange, acquires *substantially identical* stock or securities. Any realized loss not recognized is added to the basis of the substantially identical stock or securities acquired. The holding period of the new stock or securities includes the holding period of the old stock or securities. These rules relate to transactions known as *wash sales*.

E. Conversion of Property From Personal Use to Business or Income-Producing Use
    1. The *original basis for loss* on personal use assets converted to business or income-producing use is the *lower* of the property's adjusted basis or fair market value on the date of conversion.
    2. The *gain basis* for converted property is equal to its adjusted basis on the date of conversion.
    3. The basis for loss serves as the basis for depreciating the converted property.

III. Nontaxable Exchanges
    A. In a *nontaxable exchange*, realized gains or losses are not recognized until the property received in the nontaxable exchange is subsequently disposed of in a taxable sale or exchange. That is, the recognition of such gains and losses are *postponed* or *deferred*.
    B. Gain or loss is not recognized in a nontaxable exchange based on the theory that a taxpayer merely has changed the *form*, but not the *substance*, of his or her relative economic position. That is, the property received is viewed as being a continuation of the old investment.

IV. Like-Kind Exchanges -- § 1031
    A. Section 1031 provides that "no gain or loss shall be recognized if property held for productive use in a trade or business or for investment is exchanged solely for property of a *like-kind* to be held either for productive use in a trade or business or for investment."

B.   Property held for personal use, inventory, partnership interests, or securities do *not* qualify for deferral of gain or loss under the like-kind provisions. Further, US real property and foreign real property are not like-kind under these provisions.

C.   The like-kind provisions are not elective -- they are *mandatory* if the following requirements are satisfied.

     1.   The form of the transaction is an exchange.

     2.   Both the property transferred and the property received are held either for productive use in a trade or business or for investment.

     3.   The property is like-kind property.

D.   However, in most situations, a like-kind exchange between related parties loses its nonrecognition status if, within two years of the exchange, one of the parties disposes of the property it acquired in the exchange.

E.   Like-Kind Property

     1.   The words *like-kind* have reference to the nature or character of the property and not to its grade or quality.

     2.   Under this definition, real estate may be exchanged only for other real estate, and personalty may be exchanged only for other personalty. It is irrelevant whether the real estate is improved or unimproved.

F.   Exchange Requirement

     1.   To qualify as a like-kind exchange, a transaction must involve a direct exchange.

     2.   The sale of old property and the purchase of new property, even though like-kind, is generally not an exchange. However, the IRS may treat the two transactions as a like-kind exchange if the transactions are mutually dependent.

G.   Boot

     1.   *Boot* is cash or property other than like-kind property.

     2.   Realized gain is recognized to the extent of any boot *received*; however, boot received has no effect on the recognition of realized losses.

     3.   Cash *given* in a like-kind exchange has no effect on the recognition of realized gains or losses. However, if appreciated or depreciated non like-kind property (i.e., boot) is given, realized gain or loss will be recognized.

H.   Basis of Property Received

     1.   The basis of the property received in a like-kind exchange must be adjusted to reflect any postponed gain or loss.

     2.   The basis may be computed using either of the two methods shown in Exhibit 12-1.

Exhibit 12-1
LIKE-KIND EXCHANGE BASIS CALCULATIONS

Method 1	The basis of the property received in the exchange is its _fair market value less postponed gain_ or _plus postponed loss_
Method 2	_Adjusted basis of property surrendered_
Plus:	_Adjust basis of boot given_
Plus:	_Gain recognized_
Less:	_Fair market value of boot received_
Less:	_Loss recognized_
Equals:	_Basis of like-kind property received_

3.   The _holding period_ of the like-kind property given up carries over and "tacks on" to the holding period of the like-kind property received. For any boot received, the holding period will begin from the date of the exchange.

V.   Involuntary Conversions -- § 1033

    A.   General Scheme

        1.   This relief provision specifies that if a taxpayer suffers an involuntary conversion of property, he or she may postpone recognition of _gain_ (but not loss) realized from the conversion.

        2.   The basic rules of the provision follow.

           a.   If the amount realized (e.g., insurance proceeds) exceeds the amount reinvested in replacement property, realized gain is recognized to the extent of the _excess_.

           b.   If the amount reinvested in replacement property equals or exceeds the amount realized, realized gain is _not_ recognized.

    B.   Involuntary Conversion Defined -- An _involuntary conversion_ is the result of the complete or partial destruction, theft, seizure, requisition or condemnation, or the sale or exchange under threat or imminence of requisition or condemnation of the taxpayer's property.

    C.   Computing the Amount Realized -- The amount realized from a condemnation of property generally includes only the amount received as compensation for the property. Amounts designated as _severance damages_ are not generally included as part of the amount realized. Such severance damage awards reduce the basis of the property.

    D.   Replacement Property

        1.   A basic requirement is that the replacement property be _similar or related in service or use_ to the involuntarily converted property. This rule is more restrictive than the § 1031 like-kind rules.

        2.   _Owner-investors_ are subject to the _taxpayer use test_ in selecting qualified replacement property. That is, the replacement property must be used by the taxpayer in a similar endeavor.

        3.   Replacement property is subject to the _functional use test_ if acquired by _owner-users_. This test requires that the taxpayer's use of the replacement property and the involuntarily converted property be the same.

        4.   Business or investment realty need only be replaced by like-kind property if it has been condemned.

    E.   Time Limitation on Replacement -- The taxpayer has a two-year period (three years for condemnation of realty used in a trade or business or held for investment) to replace the property after the close of the taxable year in which any gain is realized from the involuntary conversion.

F.   Nonrecognition of Gain
   1.   If the conversion is made *directly* into replacement property rather than into money, then the nonrecognition of realized gain is *mandatory* and the basis of the replacement property is the same as the adjusted basis of the converted property.
   2.   If the conversion is first into money and then into property, which is the usual situation, then the provision is *elective*. In such case, the basis of the replacement property is its cost *less* postponed gain.
   3.   The provision applies *only* to the nonrecognition of gains. Losses are recognized if the property is held for business or income-producing purposes or the conversion is the result of a personal casualty.

G.   Involuntary Conversion of a Personal Residence
   1.   The tax consequences of an involuntary conversion of a personal residence depend on whether a gain or loss results and whether the conversion is due to a condemnation or a casualty.
   2.   Special tax relief is allowed for taxpayers whose principal residence (and/or its contents) is involuntarily converted in a Presidentially declared Federal disaster area.
   3.   Loss Situations
      a.   If a loss is due to a *condemnation*, the realized loss is not recognized.
      b.   If a loss is due to a *casualty*, the loss is recognized but is subject to the personal casualty loss limitations.
   4.   Gain Situations
      a.   If a gain results from a *condemnation*, the taxpayer may defer the gain under either § 1033 or § 1034.
      b.   If a gain results from a *casualty*, the taxpayer may postpone the gain only under § 1033.

H.   Reporting Considerations -- Even though a taxpayer may have elected to postpone a gain, the facts of the transaction should be disclosed in the taxpayer's return.

VI.   Sale of a Residence -- § 1034
   A.   Section 1034 provides for the *mandatory* nonrecognition (deferral) of gain from the sale of a personal residence. Losses are *never* recognized on the sale of a personal residence. The rationale in support of the deferral provision is that the acquisition of a new residence is substantially a continuation of the original investment.
   B.   Replacement Period
      1.   The taxpayer generally must replace the old residence within the period *beginning two years before* the sale and *ending two years after* the sale in order for the provision to apply.
      2.   The Code, however, generally precludes the application of § 1034 to any sales occurring within two years of the provision's last use.
   C.   Principal Residence
      1.   For these provisions to apply, both the old and new residences must be the taxpayer's *principal residence*.
      2.   Temporarily renting out the old or new residence, however, does not necessarily terminate its status as the taxpayer's principal residence.
   D.   Nonrecognition of Gain Requirements
      1.   The taxpayer must reinvest an amount *at least equal* to the adjusted sales price of the old residence for the realized gain not to be recognized. Therefore, realized gain is recognized to the extent the taxpayer does not reinvest an amount equal to the adjusted sales price in a new residence.
      2.   *Adjusted sales price* is the amount realized less certain fixing-up expenses.

The *amount realized* is the selling price less selling expenses (e.g., commissions, legal fees, advertising). *Fixing-up expenses* are nondeductible expenses incurred, within certain time limitations, to assist in the sale of the old residence (e.g., repairs, painting).

E. Capital Improvements -- Capital improvements are added to the basis of a principal residence for the purpose of computing gain or loss on a subsequent sale or disposition of the property.

F. Basis of the New Residence
1. The *basis* of the new residence is its cost less any postponed or unrecognized gain.
2. If there is any postponed gain, the holding period of the new residence includes the holding period of the old residence.

G. Reporting Procedures -- The taxpayer must report the details of a sale in the year in which gain is realized, even if all of the gain is postponed.

The §§ 1034 and 121 personal residence provisions work to protect the gains accumulated over time by taxpayers who live according to the "American Dream," (i.e., they keep moving into bigger and bigger houses during their working years, and then they retire to an apartment or care facility at the end of their career). Under this scenario, no gain (or loss) on home sales will ever be recognized by the typical homeowner over his or her lifetime.

VII. Sale of Residence -- § 121
A. Taxpayers age 55 years or older may make a *one time only election to exclude* up to $125,000 of realized gain on the sale or exchange of a principal residence. A new residence is *not* required to be purchased.

B. Requirements -- The taxpayer must be at least 55 years of age before the date of the sale and have *owned* and *used* the property as his or her principal residence for at least *three* of the *five years* preceding the date of the sale.

C. Relationship to Other Provisions
1. A taxpayer may treat an involuntary conversion as a sale for purposes of § 121. Any gain not excluded by virtue of this provision is then subject to postponement under § 1033 or § 1034.
2. Any gain from the sale of a residence not excluded by the election of § 121 may then be postponed under § 1034.

D. Making and Revoking the Election -- The election not to recognize gain under this provision may be made or revoked at any time before the statute of limitations expires.

 If two taxpayers are both at least 55 years of age, each own a personal residence with low tax bases, and are planning to marry, they should each consider selling their homes prior to marriage. This way, both of them may take advantage of the one-time $125,000 tax-free exclusion available to qualified taxpayers.

VIII.   Other Nonrecognition Provisions
   A.   Exchange of Stock for Property -- § 1032 -- No gain or loss is recognized by a corporation when it deals in its own stock.
   B.   Certain Exchanges of Insurance Policies -- § 1035 -- No gain or loss is recognized as a result of the following exchanges.
      1.   The exchange of life insurance contracts.
      2.   The exchange of life insurance contracts for endowment or annuity contracts.
      3.   The exchange of certain endowment contracts.
      4.   The exchange of endowment contracts for annuity contracts.
      5.   The exchange of annuity contracts.
   C.   Exchange of Stock for Stock of the Same Corporation -- § 1036 -- No gain or loss is recognized from the exchange of common stock solely for common stock or from the exchange of preferred stock solely for preferred stock.
   D.   Certain Reacquisitions of Real Property -- § 1038 -- Although gain may be recognized to a limited extent, no loss is recognized from the repossession of real property which is sold on an installment basis.
   E.   Transfer of Property Between Spouses Incident to Divorce -- § 1041 -- Property transfers made between *spouses* or *former spouses incident to a divorce* are nontaxable transactions. The recipient has a carryover basis in the property received.
   F.   Rollovers into Specialized Small Business Investment Companies -- § 1044 -- If the amount realized on the sale of publicly traded securities is reinvested in the common stock or partnership interest of a specialized small business investment company, the realized gain, subject to limitations, is not recognized. Any amount not reinvested will trigger the recognition of the realized gain on the sale.

TEST FOR SELF-EVALUATION -- CHAPTER 12

True or False

Indicate which of the following statements are true or false by circling the correct answer.

T   F   1.   Realized gain or loss is measured by the difference between the amount realized from the sale or other disposition of property and the property's adjusted basis on the date of disposition.

T   F   2.   Depreciation is an example of a capital recovery.

T   F   3.   Realized gains and losses are always recognized for tax purposes.

T   F   4.   The basis of property received by a gift is assigned depending on the date of the gift, gift tax paid (if any), the basis of the property to the donor, and the fair market value of the property on the date of the gift.

T   F   5.   The basis of property received by gift is dependent on whether the property is later sold at a gain or a loss.

T   F   6.   The basis of property acquired from a decedent is always its fair market value at the date of the decedent's death.

T   F   7.   The holding period of property acquired from a decedent is always deemed to be long-term.

T   F   8.   The like-kind exchange provisions under § 1031 are mandatory.

T   F   9.   The nonrecognition provisions for involuntary conversions apply only to gains.

T   F   10.   A realized loss on the sale of a personal residence is never recognized.

T   F   11.   Like-kind treatment under § 1031 is not available for exchanges of partnership interests.

T   F   12.   A personal casualty loss deduction pertaining to one's personal residence does not reduce the property's basis.

T   F   13.   The wash sale rules disallow the recognition of realized gains and losses in certain sales or exchanges of stock or securities.

T   F   14.   An exchange of idle farmland for an apartment building could qualify as a nontaxable like-kind exchange.

T   F   15.   A bakery destroyed in a fire could be replaced by its owner-user with idle farm land in a qualifying nontaxable involuntary conversion.

T   F   16.   The use of the involuntary conversion provision allowing for the deferral of gain recognition is always elective.

T   F   17.   The tax consequences of the involuntary conversion of a personal residence depend on whether the conversion is a casualty or condemnation and whether a realized loss or gain results.

(T)   F   18.   The opportunity to defer the recognition of gain under § 1034 is only available if both the old and new residences qualify as the taxpayer's principal residence.

(T)   F   19.   The opportunity available to taxpayers age 55 or older to exclude up to $125,000 of gain on the sale or exchange of their personal residence can be taken only once.

(T)   F   20.   The adjusted sales price of a principal residence is defined as the amount realized on its sale less fixing-up expenses.

Fill-in-the-Blanks

Complete the following statements with the appropriate word(s) or amount(s).

1.   If a taxpayer is age _55,000_ or older and sells his or her principal residence, the taxpayer may elect to exclude up to _125,000_ of the gain from recognition.

2.   On the sale of an old principal residence and the purchase of a new principal residence, realized gain is recognized if the taxpayer does not reinvest an amount at least equal to the _adj. sale price_ in a new residence.

3.   When selling a principal residence, the adjusted sales price is defined as the _amt real. from sell_ less _fixup exp_

4.   The gain realized on the sale of a principal residence is postponed from recognition if a new residence is purchased during a period that begins _two yrs_ before the sale of the old residence and ends _2 yrs_ after the sale of the old residence.

5.   A(n) _involuntary conversion_ is the result of the complete or partial destruction, theft, seizure, requisition or condemnation, or the sale or exchange under threat or imminence of requisition or condemnation of the taxpayer's property.

6.   The basis of like-kind property received in an exchange is its fair market value _less_ postponed gain or _plus_ postponed loss.

7.   In like-kind exchanges, realized gain is recognized if _boot_ is received.

8.   The _wash sale_ rules specify that if a taxpayer sells or exchanges stock or securities and within _30_ days before or after the date of such sale or exchange acquires substantially identical stock or securities, any loss realized from the sale or exchange is not recognized.

9.   The holding period of property acquired by gift begins on the date the property was acquired by the donor if the donor's _adjusted basis_ is the basis to the donee. The holding period begins on the date of the gift if the property's _fair market value_ serves as the basis to the donee.

10.   Section 1031 requires the recognition of gain in some situations, but only if _boot_ is received by the taxpayer and only if _gain_ is realized on the transaction.

11.   A like-kind exchange between related parties may lose its nonrecognition status if, within _two_ years of the exchange, one of the parties disposes of the property it acquired.

12.   For personal property converted to business or income-producing use, the loss basis is the lower of the property's _adj basis_ or _FMV_ on the date of conversion, while the gain basis

is the property's _Adj basis_ on the date of conversion.

13.   _Fixing up_ are expenses that are personal in nature and are incurred by the taxpayer to assist in the sale of the old residence.

14.   Under the involuntary conversion rules, the _functional_ test applies to owner-users and the _taxpayer use_ test applies to owner-investors.

15.   In general, the _recovery of capital_ doctrine provides that a taxpayer is entitled to recover the cost or other original basis of property acquired and is not taxed on that amount.

Multiple Choice

Choose the best answer for each of the following questions.

_____   1.   Edward exchanged an apartment house held for investment for unimproved land to be held for investment. The old property had an adjusted basis of $80,000 and a fair market value of $140,000 and the new property has a fair market value of $100,000. As a part of the exchange, Edward received $10,000 cash and the other party to the exchange assumed a $30,000 mortgage on the old property. Calculate Edward's recognized gain.
    a. $0.
    b. $30,000.
    c. $40,000.
    d. $60,000.
    e.   None of the above.

_____   2.   Refer to the preceding question. What would be Edward's basis in the new property?
    a. $80,000.
    b. $90,000.
    c. $100,000.
    d. $110,000.
    e.   None of the above.

_____   3.   Catherine was given a parcel of land this year. The donor had originally purchased the land in 1920 for $1,500; however, on the date of the gift the land had a fair market value of $20,000. The gift tax paid by the donor on the transaction was $2,000. The basis of the property to Catherine, if the property were to later be sold at a gain, would be what amount?
    a. $1,500.
    b. $3,350.
    c. $3,500.
    d. $20,000.
    e.   Some other amount.

_____   4.   Mr. Mitchell inherited some prime horse grazing land this year from his long-lost uncle. The land had been purchased by the uncle in 1968 for $25,000, and over the years, the uncle had added over $16,000 of improvements to the land. The fair market value of the property at the date of the uncle's death was $75,000. The basis of the property in Mr. Mitchell's hands would be what amount?
    a. $25,000.
    b. $41,000.
    c. $75,000.
    d.   Some other amount.

_____ 5. Assume the same facts as in the preceding problem, except that the fair market value of the land at the date of uncle's death was $40,000. Also, assume that the land was sold five months later by Mr. Mitchell for $45,000 and no special elections were made by the estate. The basis of the property to Mr. Mitchell would be what amount?
    a. $25,000.
    b. $40,000.
    c. $41,000.
    d. $45,000.
    e.   Some other amount.

_____ 6. Refer to the preceding problem. On the sale of the land (assumed to be held for investment), Mr. Mitchell will recognize the following.
    a.   Short-term capital gain of $4,000.
    b.   Short-term capital gain of $5,000.
    c.   Long-term capital gain of $4,000.
    d.   Long-term capital gain of $5,000.
    e.   Some other amount.

_____ 7. The following statement regarding the § 121 exclusion on the sale of a principal residence is true.
    a.   Unlimited in terms of the amount of gain that can be excluded.
    b.   Of a type that could conceivably be used twice by a taxpayer.
    c.   Mandatory on the sale of a taxpayer's principal residence after reaching the age of 55.
    d.   Available on the sale of principal residential property if the property had formerly been the taxpayer's principal residence for three years during the five year period ending on the date of the sale.
    e.   None of the above is true.

_____ 8. The permanent exclusion available to taxpayers over the age of 55 on the sale of a principal residence is limited to what amount?
    a. $100,000.
    b. $125,000.
    c. $150,000.
    d.   The amount of recognized gain.
    e.   None of the above.

_____ 9. Douglas sold an apartment building this year that had an adjusted basis of $150,000. The buyer agreed to pay $60,000 in cash, agreed to take the title to the building subject to the $140,000 mortgage on the building, and agreed to pay $50,000 plus interest at the current market rate one year from the date of the sale. What is Douglas's gain or loss realized on the sale?
    a. $34,000 loss realized.
    b. $40,000 loss realized.
    c. $100,000 gain realized.
    d. $106,000 gain realized.
    e.   None of the above.

_____ 10. Select the *incorrect* statement.
    a.   The cost on the date of acquisition plus capital additions less capital recoveries equals the adjusted basis of property on date of disposition.
    b.   The amount realized from the sale of property includes related liabilities assumed by the buyer.
    c.   When a taxpayer acquires multiple assets in a lump-sum purchase, the taxpayer must allocate the cost among the individual assets because some may be

depreciable and others not.
d. Gift taxes paid by the donor which are attributable to the net unrealized appreciation up to the date of the gift are subtracted from the basis of the property given to the donee.

11. This year, David made gifts to his two daughters, Sarah and Emily. To Sarah he gave 100 shares of ABC stock which had a basis to him of $5,000 and a fair market value of $4,000 at the date of the gift. To Emily he gave XYZ stock which had a basis of $3,000 and a fair market value of $4,000 at the date of the gift. Late in the same year, both Sarah and Emily sold their gifts to unrelated third parties for $3,500 and $4,500, respectively. What gains or losses must Sarah and Emily recognize in the year of disposition?

	Sarah	Emily
a.	$1,500 loss	$1,500 gain.
b.	$500 loss	$500 gain.
c.	$0 gain or loss	$1,500 gain.
d.	$500 loss	$1,500 gain.
e.	$1,500 loss	$500 gain.

12. This year, Mohammed gave his son common stock with a fair market value of $50,000. He had purchased the stock four years earlier for $20,000. The son subsequently sells the stock to an unrelated third party late in the current year for $40,000. The son should recognize a gain or loss this year of the following.
a. No gain or loss.
b. $20,000 gain.
c. $10,000 loss.
d. None of the above.

13. Which of the following statements is *incorrect*?
a. Real business property which has been condemned may be replaced by "like-kind" property within three years and qualify for treatment under involuntary conversion rules.
b. In involuntary conversions and "like-kind" exchanges, the recognized gain may never exceed the realized gain.
c. A taxpayer who sells property because of threat of condemnation may defer gain on a sale under the involuntary conversion rules.
d. A taxpayer who exchanges a tract of land held for investment for an apartment building may elect to either recognize gain on the exchange or defer gain under the like-kind rules.
e. None of the above is incorrect.

14. Robert sells his home for $100,000 on July 1. The real estate agent's commission is 5 percent of the sales price. On July 15 he pays $500 for painting and ordinary repairs. He pays $1,000 more on September 30 for additional fix-up repairs. The adjusted basis of his old home is $50,000. On July 30 he buys a new home for $80,000. All fix-up expenses relate to the old residence and were incurred 45 days prior to the contract date. His realized and recognized gains, respectively, are the following.
a. $50,000, $15,000.
b. $45,000, $15,000.
c. $44,500, $14,500.
d. $45,000 $14,500.
e. None of the above.

15. Refer to the preceding problem. The adjusted basis of Robert's new home is what

amount?
a. $30,500.
b. $44,500.
c. $49,500.
d. $80,000.
e.   None of the above.

_____   16.   Norm sold his personal residence in Houston this year for $350,000. The residence was
purchased five years ago for $200,000. The following expenses relate to the
residence's sale.

Advertising for sale	$2,000
Broker commissions	5,000
Title Clearance Fee	1,000

In addition, the following expenses were incurred 61 days before the contract of sale
and were paid immediately.

Painting living room	$ 500
Wallpapering kitchen	1,000
New swimming pool	15,000

Norm bought a new residence outside of Dallas for $340,000. What is Norm's *postponed*
gain under § 1034?
a. $125,000.
b. $126,500.
c. $127,000.
d. $142,000.
e.   None of the above.

_____   17.   Patrick Co. and Mitchell Co. exchanged machinery used in their separate businesses.
Patrick Co. transferred to Mitchell Co. a machine with an adjusted basis of $150,000
(FMV $300,000) which was subject to a mortgage of $60,000 (assumed by Mitchell Co.).
In return Patrick Co. received a machine with a FMV of $190,000 (adjusted basis
$100,000) and cash of $50,000. What is Patrick Co.'s recognized gain?
a. $50,000.
b. $60,000.
c. $110,000.
d. $150,000.
e.   None of the above.

_____   18.   Joseph purchased stock in Ace Corporation for $45,000 in 1972. In January of 1980,
when the stock was worth $15,000, he gave it to his son, Marvin. In January of 1995,
Marvin sold the stock for $18,500. How much gain or loss should Marvin recognize in
1995?
a. $0 gain or loss.
b. $3,500 gain.
c. $26,500 loss.
d.   None of the above.

_____   19.   An apartment building held for rental purposes owned by Britton was condemned by the
state on September 12, 1992. However, the condemnation award was not received until
February 26, 1993. In order to defer any gain realized on the involuntary conversion,
what is the latest date on which Britton can purchase qualified replacement property?
a.   September 12, 1994.

b.   September 12, 1995.
c.   December 31, 1995.
d.   February 26, 1996.
(e.)   December 31, 1996.
f.   None of the above.

QUESTIONS 20 AND 21 ARE BASED ON THE FOLLOWING INFORMATION

On January 7, 1995, Susan sold a vacant lot for $65,000. She had received the lot from the estate of her father who died on September 9, 1994, when the land had a fair market value of $63,000. Susan's father had purchased the land in 1983 for $47,500.

____   20.   What is Susan's basis in the lot?
(a) $63,000.
b. $47,500.
c. $0.
d.   None of the above.

____   21.   What is Susan's holding period for the lot?
(a)   Long-term.
b.   Short-term.
c.   The classification is always irrelevant in the situation when receiving property from a decedent.
d.   None of the above.

____   22.   The following information applies to the acquisition of a new piece of machinery received by Al in a like-kind exchange. Al is a self-employed bricklayer, and the machine is used 100 percent in his business.

Original cost of machinery traded in	$17,000
Adjusted basis of machinery traded in	7,000
FMV of new machinery	21,000
Cash payment made by Al	12,000

What amount of gain must Al recognize on the exchange?
(a) $0.
b. $2,000.
c. $4,000.
d. $9,000.
e.   None of the above.

____   23.   In October 1976, John bought 50 shares of common stock in BC Coal Co. for $11,000. In December 1982, when the fair market value of the shares was $8,000, he gave them to his son, Bob. This year in January, Bob sold the stock for $14,000. How much gain should Bob report this year?
a. $0.
(b.) $3,000.
c. $6,000.
d.   None of the above.

____   24.   Willie died this year leaving his entire estate to his sister, Beth. The executor of Willie's estate properly made the alternate valuation date election. Willie's estate included 1,000 shares of ABC Co. stock for which Willie's basis was $200,000. The stock was distributed to Beth seven months after Willie's death. Fair market values for the stock were as indicated.

On the date of Willie's death	$356,000
Six months after Willie's death	270,000
Seven months after Willie's death	272,000

What is Beth's basis in the stock?
a. $200,000.
b. $270,000.
c. $272,000.
d. $356,000.
e.   None of the above.

_____ 25.   Joe converted his personal residence to rental property. At the time of the conversion, the property had an adjusted basis of $75,000 (land $5,000, building $70,000) and a fair market value of $50,000 (land $5,000, building $45,000). What is Joe's gain basis, loss basis, and basis for depreciation?
a.   Gain basis $50,000; loss basis $50,000; depreciation basis $50,000.
b.   Gain basis $50,000; loss basis $75,000; depreciation basis $45,000.
c.   Gain basis $75,000; loss basis $50,000; depreciation basis $45,000.
d.   Gain basis $75,000; loss basis $75,000; depreciation basis $70,000.
e.   None of the above.

Code Section Recognition

Several important sections of the Internal Revenue Code are described below. Indicate, by number, the appropriate Code section.

1. _____ Gains and losses are not recognized on a like-kind exchange.

2. _____ Gains are not recognized on involuntary conversions.

3. _____ The deferral of gain recognition on the sale of a principal residence is provided.

4. _____ The permanent exclusion of gain on the disposition of a principal residence is provided.

Short Answer

1. Calculate the gain or loss recognized on the disposition of the properties in the following transactions.

   a. Judy disposes of stock for $5,000 which had been received as a gift 5 years ago when its value was $3,000. The donor purchased the stock for $2,000 and paid no gift tax on the transfer.   3,000

   b. Judy disposes of stock for $5,000 which had been received as a gift 5 years ago when its value was $3,000. The donor purchased the stock for $4,000 and paid no gift tax on the transfer.   1,000

   c. Judy disposes of stock for $2,000 which had been received as a gift 5 years ago when its value was $3,000. The donor purchased the stock for $4,000 and paid no gift tax on the transfer.   1,000

2. Fran, who is 42 years of age, sells her personal residence for $150,000 during the current year. She had received the house as a bequest from her mother when it was worth $115,000. Her mother had purchased the home 20 years prior to her death for $45,000. Fran incurred selling expenses (commissions) of $7,500 and fix-up expenses of $2,000. Following the sale of her old residence, Fran purchases a new residence for $145,000. Calculate the gain or loss recognized on the sale and Fran's basis in her new home.

SOLUTIONS TO CHAPTER 12 QUESTIONS

True or False

1. T
2. T
3. F   There are certain situations (e.g., like-kind exchanges) when realized gains and losses are not recognized on realization.
4. T
5. T
6. F   An election may be made in certain situations to value the estate using the alternate valuation date. In such cases, the basis of property to the recipient normally is its fair market value six months following the decedent's death.
7. T
8. T
9. T
10. T
11. T
12. F
13. F   The wash sale rules apply only to transactions on which *losses* occur.
14. T   It is immaterial whether real estate is improved (apartment building) or unimproved (farmland).
15. F   The functional use test would require owner-users to replace the bakery with another facility of similar functional use.
16. F   If the conversion is made directly into replacement property rather than into money, nonrecognition of realized gain is mandatory.
17. T
18. T
19. T
20. T

Fill-in-the-Blanks

1.   55, $125,000
2.   adjusted sales price
3.   amount realized from the sale, fixing-up expenses
4.   two years, two years
5.   involuntary conversion
6.   less, plus
7.   boot
8.   wash sale, 30
9.   adjusted basis, fair market value
10. boot, gain
11. two
12. adjusted basis, fair market value, adjusted basis
13. Fixing-up expenses
14. functional use, taxpayer use
15. recovery of capital

Multiple Choice

1. c $40,000 ($10,000 cash + $30,000 liability assumed); realized gain ($60,000) is recognized to the extent boot has been received. See Example 38 in the text.

2. a $100,000 (fair market value) - $20,000 (gain not recognized) = $80,000 See Example 42 in the text.

3. b $1,500 + $\dfrac{\$18,500}{\$20,000}$ X $2,000] = $3,350

    See Example 19 in the text.

4. c Fair market value at the date of the uncle's death. See Example 23 in the text.

5. b Fair market value at the date of the uncle's death. See Example 24 in the text.

6. d $5,000 = $45,000 - $40,000   The holding period is assumed to be long-term.

7. d

8. b

9. c

Amount Realized:	Cash	$ 60,000
	Mortgage	140,000
	Note	50,000
	Total	$250,000
Less: Adjusted Basis		150,000
Gain Realized		$100,000

See Examples 2 and 4 in the text.

10. d A portion of the gift taxes paid is *added* to the property's basis.

11. d Sarah: ($500) = $3,500 - $4,000; Emily: $1,500 = $4,500 - $3,000 See Examples 16 and 17 in the text.

12. b Because the stock is sold at a gain, the donee's basis is equal to the donor's basis. See Example 16 in the text.

13. d Because this qualifies as a like-kind exchange, the deferral of gain realized is mandatory, not elective.

14. d

Selling Price	$100,000
Less: Selling Expenses	5,000
Amount Realized	$ 95,000
Less: Adjusted Basis	50,000
Gain Realized	$ 45,000

Amount Realized	$95,000
Less: Qualifying Fix-up Expenses (painting)	500
Adjusted Sales Price	$94,500
Less: Cost of New Residence	80,000
Gain Recognized	$14,500

See Example 58 in the text.

15. c $49,500 = $80,000 (purchase price) - $30,500 (gain not recognized) See Example 58 in the text.

16. b

Selling Price	$350,000
Less: Selling Expenses	8,000
Amount Realized	$342,000
Less: Adjusted Basis (includes pool)	215,000
Gain Realized	$127,000

Amount Realized	$342,000
Less: Qualifying Fix-up Expenses	1,500
Adjusted Sales Price	$340,500
Less: Cost of New Residence	340,000
Gain Recognized	$ 500
Postponed Gain	$126,500

See Example 58 in the text.

17. c   Amount Realized: Machine $190,000
                                Liability   60,000
                                Cash   50,000
                                Total $300,000
         Less: Adjusted Basis   150,000
         Gain Realized $150,000
         Gain Recognized $110,000
         See Example 38 in the text.

18. a   No gain or loss is recognized because the amount realized on the sale is between the
         basis used to compute a gain (i.e., $45,000) and the basis used to compute a loss (i.e.,
         $15,000). See Example 18 in the text.

19. e   Three years from the end of the year in which gain is realized (1993).

20. a   FMV at date of decedent's death. See Example 23 in the text.

21. a   Property received from a decedent's estate is always considered long-term.

22. a $0; $21,000 - ($7,000 + $12,000) = $2,000 gain realized. However, because no boot was
         received by Al, the gain realized is not recognized in the like-kind exchange.

23. b $3,000 = $14,000 - $11,000

24. b   Value as of six months after decedent's death ($270,000), unless distributed earlier -
         See Example 26 in the text.

25. c   See Example 32 in the text. Note that land is not depreciable.

Code Section Recognition

1.   1031
2.   1033
3.   1034
4.   121

Short Answer

1.   a.   Sales price $5,000
          Less: Basis to Judy   2,000
          Gain on the disposition $3,000

     b.   Sales price $5,000
          Less: Basis to Judy   4,000
          Gain on the disposition $1,000

     c.   Sales price $2,000
          Less: Basis to Judy   3,000
          Loss on the disposition $1,000

2.

Amount realized ($150,000 - $7,500)	$142,500
Less: Adjusted basis	115,000
Realized gain	$ 27,500

Adjusted sales price ($142,500 - $2,000)	$140,500
Less: Cost of new residence	145,000
Recognized gain	$ 0

Cost of new residence	$145,000
Less: Unrecognized gain	27,500
Basis of new residence	$117,500

CHAPTER 13

PROPERTY TRANSACTIONS: CAPITAL GAINS AND LOSSES, SECTION 1231, AND RECAPTURE PROVISIONS

CHAPTER HIGHLIGHTS

apital gain provisions were enacted originally with the intent that they would help promote the formation of capital investment and risk-taking by investors. These provisions allow for beneficial treatment of gains for certain taxpayers on the sale or exchange of capital assets. Further, certain non-capital assets (e.g., depreciable and real property used in a trade or business) also may receive the beneficial treatment associated with a net capital gain when a gain results from a sale, exchange, or involuntary conversion. Recapture provisions, however, provide that certain gains, which might have otherwise qualified for the beneficial capital gain treatment, receive ordinary income treatment. The Tax Reform Act of 1986 practically eliminated much of the distinction between capital and ordinary treatment. However, for years after 1990, subsequent legislation has allowed an alternative tax computation for capital gains which produces an advantage to certain noncorporate taxpayers. Thus, the character of gain or loss as capital or ordinary remains important under current law.

I. General Considerations
    A. Rationale for Separate Reporting of Capital Gains and Losses
        1. Long-term capital gains may be taxed at a lower rate than ordinary gains. Therefore, separating capital asset transactions from other types of transactions is important, and required by law.
        2. Capital losses initially offset capital gains. Only *net capital gains* receive preferential treatment. However, if a net loss results, it is deductible by noncorporate taxpayers only to the extent of $3,000 per tax year.
        3. Because of the unique treatment that applies to capital gains and losses, individual income tax forms include very extensive reporting requirements for these transactions.
    B. General Scheme of Taxation
        1. Proper classification of gains and losses depends on the following.
            a. The tax status of the property.
            b. The manner of the property's disposition.
            c. The holding period of the property.

13-1

2.   There are three possible *tax statuses* of property.
     a.   Capital assets.
     b.   Section 1231 assets.
     c.   Ordinary assets.

3.   Capital gain or loss characterization results from the sale or exchange of a capital asset. In addition, capital gain treatment can result from the sale or exchange of § 1231 assets in some cases. Otherwise, ordinary income or loss results.

4.   A capital gain or loss is considered long-term only if a capital asset has been held for more than the required long-term holding period (i.e., more than one year).

II. Capital Assets

A.   Definition of a Capital Asset

1.   A capital asset is property held by a taxpayer that is *not* one of the following types.
     a.   Stock in trade, inventory, or property held primarily for sale in the ordinary course of a trade or business.
     b.   Accounts or notes receivable acquired in the ordinary course of a trade or business.
     c.   Depreciable property or real estate used in a trade or business.
     d.   Certain copyrights, literary, musical, or artistic compositions, letters or memoranda or similar property.
     e.   Certain US government publications.

2.   The principal capital assets held by *individual* taxpayers include personal-use assets, such as a personal residence or an automobile, or assets held for investment purposes, such as land or corporate stock.

B.   Effect of Judicial Action

1.   Because of the way the Code defines the term *capital asset* and because of the requirement of a *sale or exchange*, whether capital asset treatment is appropriate has at times been uncertain. This uncertainty has often been resolved by the courts.

2.   The court decisions often revolve around whether an asset is held for investment purposes (capital asset) or business purposes (ordinary asset). Further, in order to make the distinction between capital and ordinary, the taxpayer's motive, or the *use* to which property has been put, may have to be determined.

C.   Statutory Expansions

1.   To help reduce uncertainty, Congress has statutorily *expanded* the scope of the general definition of a capital asset in several cases.

2.   If a *securities dealer* clearly identifies certain securities as being held for investment purposes by the close of business on *the date of their acquisition*, gain from their sale will normally be capital. Losses are capital if the dealer has *at any time* identified the securities as being held for investment.

3.   *Noncorporate investors* in real estate who engage in limited development activities may receive capital gain treatment, to a limited extent.

III. Sale or Exchange

A.   For a gain or loss to receive capital treatment, a *sale or exchange* of a capital asset must have had occurred. Although the term sale or exchange is not defined by the Code, a sale generally involves the receipt of money and/or the assumption of liabilities for property, and an exchange involves the transfer of property for other property.

B.   Worthless Securities and § 1244 Stock

1.   If a security that is a capital asset in the hands of the taxpayer becomes worthless during a taxable year, it is treated as a sale or exchange of a

capital asset that has occurred on the *last day* of that same taxable year.

2. Section 1244 allows an ordinary loss, rather than a capital loss, on the disposition of qualifying small business corporation stock. However, the ordinary treatment is limited to $50,000 ($100,000 on a joint return) per year.

C. Special Rule -- Retirement of Corporate Obligations

1. Under the general rule, the collection of a debt obligation does *not* constitute a sale or exchange; therefore, capital treatment cannot result if a gain or loss arises on its collection.

KEY TERMS

- Capital Gain, Loss
- Long-Term, Short-Term
- Worthless Security
- §1231 Gain, Loss
- §1231 Look-Back Rule
- Depreciation Recapture

2. However, corporate and certain government obligations usually *are* subject to capital treatment because the retirement of such obligations is considered to give rise to a sale or exchange.

D. Options

1. The sale or exchange of an *option* to buy or sell property generally results in capital gain or loss if the property subject to the option is or would be a capital asset in the hands of the option holder.

2. If an option holder fails to exercise the option, the *lapse* is considered to be a sale or exchange on the option expiration date and a loss is recognized.

3. If an option is *exercised*, the amount paid for the option by the grantee is added to the cost basis of the property subject to the option. With respect to the grantor, the amount paid for the option is added to the selling price of the property subject to the option.

E. Patents

1. If all *substantial rights* relating to a patent are transferred by a qualifying holder, the disposition will be treated as a sale or exchange of a capital asset held for a long-term.

2. If the requirements are met, any gain or loss is *automatically* a long-term capital gain or loss regardless of whether the patent is a capital asset, whether the transfer is a sale or exchange, and how long the patent was held by the transferor.

3. The *holder* of a patent is usually (but not always) the creator of the invention. The creator's employer and certain parties related to the creator do not qualify as holders.

F. Franchises, Trademarks, and Trade Names

1. A *franchise* is an agreement that gives the franchisee the right to distribute, sell, or provide goods, services, or facilities within a specified area.

2. The transfer of a franchise, trademark, or trade name shall be considered a disposition of a capital asset if the transferor does not retain any *significant power, right, or continuing interest*.

3. When the transferor retains a significant power, right, or continuing interest, the transferee's *noncontingent* payments to the transferor will be ordinary income to the transferor. The franchisee capitalizes the payments and amortizes them over 15 years.

4. *Contingent* franchise payments produce ordinary income for the franchisor and ordinary deductions for the franchisee.

5.   The standard franchise rules under § 1253 do not apply to sports franchises.

G.   Lease Cancellation Payments

      1.   Payments received by a *lessee* in consideration of a lease cancellation produce capital gains if the lease is a capital asset.

      2.   Payments received by a *lessor* are always ordinary income because they are considered to be made in lieu of rental payments.

IV.   Holding Period

A.   Property must be held *more than one year* to qualify for long-term capital gain or loss treatment. If the asset is not held for the required long-term holding period, short-term treatment is appropriate.

B.   Review of Special Holding Period Rules

      1.   The holding period of property received in a nontaxable exchange includes the holding period of the former asset if the property which has been exchanged is a capital or a § 1231 asset.

      2.   If a transaction is nontaxable and the basis of the property to the former owner carries over to the new owner, the holding period of a former owner of property *tacks on* to the present owner's holding period.

      3.   In situations involving disallowed losses, a new holding period begins when the property is transferred.

      4.   Property that has been inherited is always treated as long-term.

C.   Special Rules for Short Sales

      1.   A *short sale* occurs when a taxpayer sells borrowed property and repays the lender with *substantially identical property* (e.g., other shares of the same stock) either held on the date of the sale or purchased after the sale.

      2.   The general rule is that the holding period of the property sold short is determined by the how long the property used to close the short sale was held. However, exceptions to the general rule exist.

      3.   The purpose of the special rule has been to prevent taxpayers from engaging in short sales in order to convert short-term capital gains to long-term capital gains or to convert long-term capital losses to short-term capital losses.

Appreciating assets and long-term growth investments may be more attractive than in times past, thanks to the substantial difference between the capital gains and the top ordinary tax rates.

V.   Tax Treatment of Capital Gains and Losses of Noncorporate Taxpayers -- Taxpayers must net all long-term capital gains (LTCG) and losses (LTCL) and then short-term capital gains (STCG) and losses (STCL). The results are a net long-term capital gain (NLTCG) or loss (NLTCL) and a net short-term capital gain (NSTCG) or loss (NSTCL). Then the taxpayer must net any remaining positive and negative amounts which result from the first round of netting. One of six possible results exists after all netting has been completed.

A.   Treatment of Capital Gains

      1.   If a NLTCG exceeds a NSTCL, the result is a *net capital gain* (NCG). A NCG is subject to a maximum tax rate of 28 percent. When taxable income including the NCG does not put the taxpayer into a rate bracket higher than the 28 percent rate bracket, the alternative tax computation does not yield a tax benefit and is not used.

      2.   The *NCG alternative tax* is the sum of the following.

            a.   The tax computed using the regular rates on the *greater* of the following.

          (1)   Taxable income less the net capital gain.

          (2)   The amount of taxable income taxed at a rate below 28 percent.

       b.   Twenty-eight percent of taxable income in excess of taxable income used in a.

    3.   If NSTCG exceeds NLTCL, the net amount is included in the taxpayer's gross income and taxed at the ordinary income rates.

  B.   Treatment of Capital Losses

    1.   The determination of *net capital losses* involves the same netting process as described above.

    2.   Net capital losses are deductible by noncorporate taxpayers generally up to a maximum of $3,000.

    3.   Individual taxpayers may carry over any unused capital losses for an *indefinite* period. Unused capital losses carried over retain their original nature as short-term or long-term.

    4.   If a taxpayer has both a capital loss deduction and negative taxable income, a special computation of the capital loss carryover is required.

VI.   Tax Treatment of Capital Gains and Losses of Corporate Taxpayers -- The treatment of a corporation's capital gains and losses is different from that of an individual taxpayer.

  A.   The capital gains are taxed at the ordinary corporate tax rates. Long-term gains are subject to a maximum rate of 35 percent.

  B.   No deduction against ordinary income is allowed for capital losses. Capital losses offset only capital gains.

  C.   There is a three-year carryback and a five-year carryforward allowed for net capital losses. The carrybacks and carryforwards are always treated as short-term, regardless of their original nature.

VII. Section 1231 Assets

  A.   Relationship to Capital Assets

    1.   Under current law, it is necessary to identify § 1231 assets and to make the special § 1231 computations in relevant sales and exchanges.

    2.   Section 1231 provides that on the sale or exchange or involuntary conversion of depreciable personal property or real property used in business, *capital gain treatment* may be allowed if the transaction results in a *net gain* and the assets have been held for a period of time which meets the long-term holding period requirement. Therefore, capital gain treatment may result even though the applicable assets are not capital assets.

    3.   *Net losses* on such property, however, are recognized as *ordinary losses* rather than as capital losses. These losses are deductible *for* adjusted gross income.

  B.   Justification for Favorable Tax Treatment -- The scheme of § 1231 and the dichotomy of capital gain/ordinary loss treatment evolved due to economic considerations existing in 1938 and in 1942.

  C.   Property Included -- Property covered by § 1231 *includes* the following.

    1.   Depreciable or real property used in business or for the production of income.

    2.   Timber, coal, or domestic iron ore.

    3.   Livestock held for draft, breeding, dairy, or sporting purposes.

    4.   Unharvested crops on land used in business.

    5.   Certain nonpersonal use capital assets used in business, such as patents, goodwill, and intangible assets.

  D.   Property Excluded -- Section 1231 property does *not* include the following.

    1.   Property *not* held for the normal long-term holding period (except unharvested crops and certain livestock).

    2.   Properties which produce casualty losses in excess of casualty gains.

    3.   Inventory and property held primarily for sale to customers.

    4.   Other property such as copyrights, literary compositions and certain U.S.

Government publications.
E.   Special Rules for Nonpersonal Use Capital Assets
1.   If casualty or theft *gains* from *nonpersonal use* assets held for the long-term holding period which were used in business or for the production of income exceed casualty or theft *losses* from such assets, then the gains and losses are § 1231 transactions. If they net to a loss, then § 1231 does not apply.
2.   Gains *recognized* from an *involuntary conversion* due to condemnation on assets held for the long-term holding period and used in business or for the production of income are given § 1231 treatment.
F.   General Procedure for § 1231 Computation
1.   Net all gains and losses from casualties and thefts of nonpersonal use property held for the long-term holding period. Personal use property casualty gains and losses are not subject to the § 1231 rules.
a.   If gains exceed losses, add the excess to the other § 1231 gains for the year.
b.   If losses exceed gains, exclude from any further § 1231 computation. Business casualty losses are deductible *for* adjusted gross income.
2.   After adding any net casualty gains from above, net all of the § 1231 gains and losses.
a.   If gains exceed losses, the excess is treated as a long-term capital gain.
b.   If losses exceed gains, all gains produce ordinary income and all losses are deductible either *for* or *from* adjusted income, as appropriate.
3.   In addition, net § 1231 gains must be offset by the *nonrecaptured* net § 1231 losses for the five preceding years (i.e., the *§ 1231 lookback*). Capital gain treatment results only after the *non-recaptured § 1231 losses* from the preceding years have been offset.

VIII.   Section 1245 Recapture
A.   Section 1245 was enacted to prevent taxpayers from receiving the dual benefits of depreciation deductions which offset ordinary income plus long-term capital gain treatment provided under § 1231.
B.   Section 1245 recapture provides in general that the portion of recognized gain from the sale or other disposition of § 1245 property is treated as *ordinary income* to the extent of depreciation taken. Any gain in excess of the amount not recaptured as ordinary income may be § 1231 gain.
C.   Section 1245 Potential
1.   Recapture is limited to the amount of recognized gain which represents depreciation claimed on the disposed property.
2.   Depreciation recapture rules do not apply to *losses*. Generally, the loss will be a § 1231 loss unless the form of the disposition is a casualty.

Very few depreciable assets generate § 1231 gain upon their disposal. This results only when the market value of the asset increases during its period of use. In most cases, application of an asset in a business setting consumes the asset's utility, thereby depleting its market value. Then, any gain realized is recognized fully as ordinary-income depreciation recapture. Recapture potential typically is a very large number, approaching the full purchase price. Only unusual assets, such as those that become antiques or prototypes, show an increase in value between acquisition and disposal dates.

D.   Section 1245 Property -- Section 1245 property includes the following.
    1.   All depreciable personalty.
    2.   Livestock on which depreciation has been claimed.
    3.   Amortizable personalty such as goodwill, patents, copyrights, leaseholds, professional football and baseball player contracts.
    4.   Amortization of reforestation expenditures and expensing of costs to remove certain barriers to the handicapped and elderly.
    5.   Immediate expensing of costs under § 179.
    6.   Elevators and escalators acquired before January 1, 1987.
    7.   Certain depreciable tangible real property employed as an integral part of the manufacturing and production process.
    8.   Pollution control facilities, railroad grading and tunnel bores, on-the-job training, and child care facilities on which amortization is taken.
    9.   Single purpose agricultural and horticultural structures and petroleum storage facilities.
    10.   Certain real property placed in service after 1980 and before 1987, including 15-year, 18-year, or 19-year nonresidential real property if the statutory percentage ACRS method is used, which is not subject to § 1250 (see below).

E.   Observations on Section 1245
    1.   Section 1231 gain will not result unless the § 1245 property is disposed of for *more* than its original cost.
    2.   Recapture applies to the total amount of depreciation allowed or allowable.
    3.   Recapture applies regardless of the holding period of the property.
    4.   Losses normally receive § 1231 treatment.
    5.   Gains from the disposition of § 1245 assets may also be treated as passive gains.

IX.   Section 1250 Recapture
A.   Section 1250 recapture was enacted for *depreciable real property* for reasons similar to those supporting the enactment of § 1245. Section 1250 provides for the recapture of a percentage of *additional depreciation* deducted by the taxpayer. Additional depreciation is the *excess* of accelerated depreciation actually taken over the depreciation that would have been allowed had the straight-line method been used. Section 1250 does not apply to dispositions of real property that was depreciated using the straight-line method. Thus, *since real property placed in service after 1986 can only be depreciated using the straight-line method, there will be no § 1250 depreciation recapture on such property*. Further, the recapture provisions do not apply in situations where a loss is recognized; rather, § 1231 or casualty loss treatment generally would be appropriate. Generally, § 1250 property is depreciable real property that is not subject to § 1245.
B.   Computing Recapture on Nonresidential Real Property
    1.   The amount treated as ordinary income is limited to the *lesser* of the gain recognized or the additional depreciation (i.e., depreciation taken in excess of straight-line).
    2.   If the property is held for one year or less, *all* depreciation taken, even under the straight-line method, is additional depreciation.
    3.   Any gain not recaptured as ordinary income is treated under § 1231.
C.   Computing Recapture on Residential Rental Housing
    1.   The computation of depreciation recapture on the disposition of residential realty acquired before 1987 differs from the depreciation recapture rules for nonresidential realty.
    2.   The post-1975 additional depreciation is recaptured in full while the post-1969 through 1975 additional depreciation recapture potential may be only

partially recaptured.

3.   If straight-line depreciation is used, there is no § 1250 recapture potential unless the property is disposed of in the first year of use. Thus, for real property placed in service after 1986, § 1250 will have no application unless it is disposed of in the year of its acquisition.

D.   Section 1250 Recapture Situations
1.   Residential real estate acquired before 1987.
2.   Nonresidential real estate acquired before 1981.
3.   Real property used predominantly outside the United States.
4.   Certain government-financed or low-income housing described in § 1250(a)(1)(B).

X.   Considerations Common to Sections 1245 and 1250 -- Exceptions -- Recapture under §§ 1245 and 1250 does not apply to the following transactions.
A.   Gifts -- However, the recapture potential carries to the donee.
B.   Death -- Recapture potential does *not* carry over from a decedent to an estate or heir.
C.   Charitable Transfers -- The recapture potential reduces the amount of the charitable contribution deduction.
D.   Certain Tax-free Transactions -- In certain tax-free transactions, the recapture potential carries over to the transferee.
E.   Like-kind Exchanges and Involuntary Conversions -- To the extent gain is recognized, the nature of such gain may be governed by §§ 1245 and 1250.

XI.   Special Recapture Provisions
A.   Special Recapture for Corporations
1.   Corporations (other than S corporations) may have ordinary income in addition to that required by § 1250 when selling depreciable real estate.
2.   The provisions call for an *ordinary income adjustment* equal to 20 percent of the excess of the § 1245 potential recapture over the § 1250 recapture amount.
B.   Gain from Sale of Depreciable Property between Certain Related Parties
1.   In general, in the case of a sale or exchange, directly or indirectly, of depreciable property between an individual and his or her controlled corporation or partnership, any gain recognized is ordinary if the property is depreciable in the hands of the *transferee*.
2.   Control for purposes of this section means ownership of *more* than 50 percent in the value of the corporation's outstanding stock or *more* than 50 percent of the capital interest or profits interest of a partnership. Constructive ownership rules apply in such circumstances.
C.   Intangible Drilling Costs
1.   *Intangible drilling and development costs* (IDC) are subject to recapture when the property is disposed of.
2.   Recapture does not apply if the property is disposed of at a loss.

XII.   Reporting Procedures -- Noncapital gains and losses are reported on Form 4797, Sales of Business Property. Form 4684, Casualty and Thefts, will also be required if such transactions have occurred.

TEST FOR SELF-EVALUATION -- CHAPTER 13

True or False

Indicate which of the following statements are true or false by circling the correct answer.

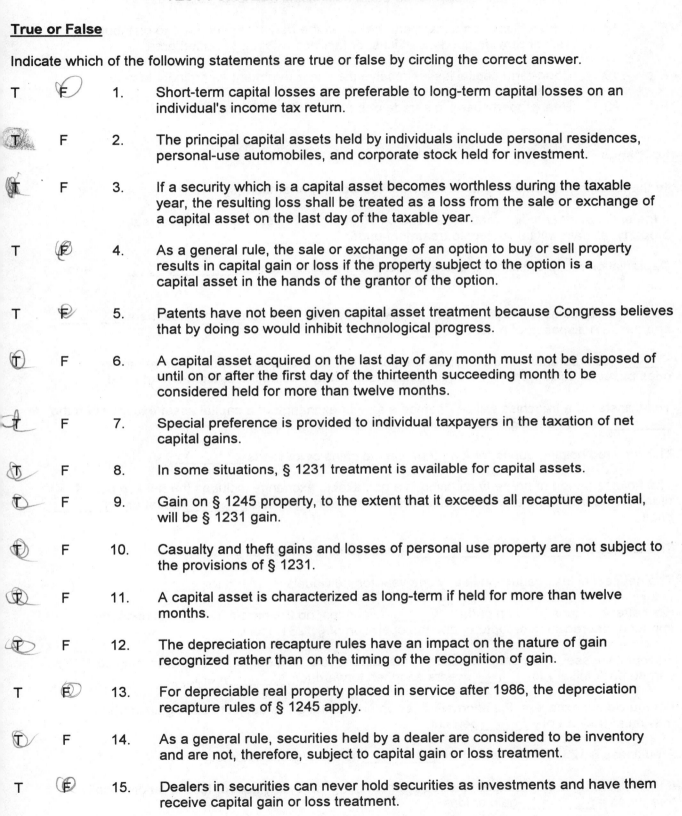

T   **F**   1.   Short-term capital losses are preferable to long-term capital losses on an individual's income tax return.

T   F   2.   The principal capital assets held by individuals include personal residences, personal-use automobiles, and corporate stock held for investment.

T   F   3.   If a security which is a capital asset becomes worthless during the taxable year, the resulting loss shall be treated as a loss from the sale or exchange of a capital asset on the last day of the taxable year.

T   **F**   4.   As a general rule, the sale or exchange of an option to buy or sell property results in capital gain or loss if the property subject to the option is a capital asset in the hands of the grantor of the option.

T   **F**   5.   Patents have not been given capital asset treatment because Congress believes that by doing so would inhibit technological progress.

T   F   6.   A capital asset acquired on the last day of any month must not be disposed of until on or after the first day of the thirteenth succeeding month to be considered held for more than twelve months.

T   F   7.   Special preference is provided to individual taxpayers in the taxation of net capital gains.

T   F   8.   In some situations, § 1231 treatment is available for capital assets.

T   F   9.   Gain on § 1245 property, to the extent that it exceeds all recapture potential, will be § 1231 gain.

T   F   10.   Casualty and theft gains and losses of personal use property are not subject to the provisions of § 1231.

T   F   11.   A capital asset is characterized as long-term if held for more than twelve months.

T   F   12.   The depreciation recapture rules have an impact on the nature of gain recognized rather than on the timing of the recognition of gain.

T   **F**   13.   For depreciable real property placed in service after 1986, the depreciation recapture rules of § 1245 apply.

T   F   14.   As a general rule, securities held by a dealer are considered to be inventory and are not, therefore, subject to capital gain or loss treatment.

T   **F**   15.   Dealers in securities can never hold securities as investments and have them receive capital gain or loss treatment.

T   **F**   16.   The treatment provided to capital gains and losses is identical for both corporate and noncorporate taxpayers.

T   (F)   17.   For individual taxpayers, personal use assets are never capital assets.

(T)   F   18.   A franchise is an agreement that gives the franchisee the right to distribute, sell, or provide goods, services, or facilities within a specified area.

T   (F)   19.   Short-term capital losses receive the same treatment as ordinary losses.

(T)   F   20.   Real property used in a trade or business is § 1231 property.

Fill-in-the-Blanks

Complete the following statements with the appropriate word(s) or amount(s).

1. If the optional straight-line method is used on 15-, 18-, or 19-year nonresidential real property, all gain will be subject to treatment under § __1231__ .

2. Depreciation recapture is not triggered in certain situations such as _____, _____, and _____.

3. To obtain capital asset treatment, two things are required: the transaction must be a _____ and the item disposed of must be a _____.

4. _Real property_ acquired after 1986 and sold at a gain is not subject to the depreciation recapture rules because such property is required to be depreciated using the straight-line method.

5. The transfer of a franchise will be deemed a sale or exchange of a capital asset except when the _transferor_ retains any significant power, right or continuing interest.

6. The required holding period for long-term capital gains or losses is __more than 1 yr.__

7. The holding period of property received in a nontaxable exchange includes the holding period of the former asset if the property which has been exchanged is a _capital_ asset or a __1231__ asset.

8. The excess of _net LTCG_ over _N STCL_ is defined as a net capital gain.

9. The net capital loss deduction in any one year for individuals is limited to __3,000__ .

10. Only after the consideration of the _passive_ loss rules, do the normal rules of taxation, the impact of depreciation recapture, and the operation of § 1231 apply.

11. Net capital losses that cannot be used in the current year by a corporate taxpayer, may be carried back initially for __3__ years and then forward for __5__ years.

12. For individual taxpayers, the alternative tax on net capital gains subjects such gains to a maximum tax rate of __28__ percent.

13. A business § 1231 loss is deductible _for_ adjusted gross income.

14. If the transfer of a patent meets the requirements of § 1235, any gain or loss is automatically treated as a _long term_ gain or loss.

15. To the extent that any § 1231 gain remains after the required netting and consideration of the lookback rules and the depreciation recapture provisions, this gain is treated as _long term cap gain_ .

Multiple Choice

Choose the best answer for each of the following questions.

_____   1.   In the current year, Nancy had the following capital transactions.

Long-term gain	$ 4,000
Long-term loss	6,000
Short-term gain	8,000
Short-term loss	11,000

(handwritten: (2,000) and (3,000))

Before consideration of the above capital transactions Nancy had taxable income of $12,500. Calculate (1) Nancy's current taxable income or loss after considering the capital transactions and (2) the capital loss carryforward.

   a. $7,500, $0 carryforward.
   b. $9,500, $2,000 long-term carryforward.
   c. $9,500, $0 carryforward.
   d. $12,500, $2,000 long-term carryforward and $3,000 short-term carryforward.
   e.   None of the above.

_____   2.   Select the *correct* statement.
   a.   Noncorporate dealers in real estate treat gains and losses from their business as capital transactions.
   b.   The holding period of property received in a nontaxable exchange includes the holding period of the former asset if the exchanged property is a capital or § 1231 asset.
   c.   With a short sale of stock, if substantially identical property is acquired after the date of the short sale and on or before the closing date, the gain or loss may be long-term.
   d.   In general, the sale or exchange of an option to buy or sell property could result in a capital gain or loss if the property subject to the option is not a capital asset to the holder of the option.
   e.   None of the above.

_____   3.   Elizabeth had the following recognized gains and losses during the year.

   ▸ Theft loss of a Picasso painting from her home, owned for six months, net of $100 floor, $700   *(handwritten: 700 ordin—)*
   ▸ Gain from an insurance recovery on a business machine, owned for two years and assuming no recapture potential, $3,000   *(handwritten: 3,000)*
   ▸ Sale of a business machine for $40,000. The machine was purchased six years ago for $45,000. Depreciation of $8,000 was taken on the machinery prior to sale.   *(handwritten: 3,000)*

Calculate Elizabeth's net § 1231 gain or loss. Assume the § 1231 lookback procedure does not apply.
   a. $6,000.
   b. $5,300.
   c. $2,300.
   d. $3,000.
   e.   None of the above.

_____   4.   Mitchell had the following capital gains and losses.

LTCG $15,000   STCG $20,000
LTCL   5,000   STCL   5,000

Calculate Mitchell's net long-term and net short-term capital gains.
a.   NLTCG $15,000; NSTCG $20,000.
b.   NLTCG $20,000; NSTCG $25,000.
c.   NLTCG $35,000; NSTCG $0.
d.   NLTCG $10,000; NSTCG $15,000.
e.   NLTCG $10,000; NSTCG $25,000.

_____ 5.   Ida and Woody are married, and both are under 65 years of age. They have no dependents.
            The current year's income tax facts are as follows.

Ida's salary $ 9,000
Woody's salary   26,000
Interest income   2,000
Short-term capital gain   5,000
Long-term capital loss carryover from the previous year   4,000

What is their adjusted gross income for the year?
a. $37,400.
b. $38,000.
c. $40,000.
d. $42,000.
e.   Some other amount.

_____ 6.   Carpenter Corporation sold an automobile on March 27 for $5,000 when its adjusted basis
            was $2,000. The automobile had originally been purchased on the previous December 31
            for $4,000. How should Carpenter Corporation report the transaction?
a. $2,000 § 1231 gain and $1,000 ordinary income.
b. $1,000 § 1231 gain and $2,000 ordinary income.
c. $3,000 § 1231 gain.
d. $3,000 ordinary income.
e.   None of the above.

_____ 7.   Refer to the preceding problem. Assume the same facts except the automobile was sold
            for $4,500. How should Carpenter Corporation report the transaction?
a. $2,500 ordinary income.
b. $2,500 capital gain.
c. $2,500 § 1231 gain.
d. $2,500 § 1231 gain and $2,000 ordinary income.
e.   Some other answer.

_____ 8.   Robert acquired nonresidential real property in 1986 to be used in his business. The
            building cost $70,000. During the time he had held the building, he utilized the
            statutory percentage method of cost recovery and claimed $23,000 of cost recovery
            deductions. If Robert had used the optional straight-line method over the appropriate
            period, the cost recovery deduction would have totalled $17,000. If the building is
            sold during the year for $80,500, before considering the § 1231 lookback rules, how
            should Robert report the transaction?
a. $33,500 ordinary income.
b. $33,500 § 1231 gain.
c. $23,000 ordinary income and $10,500 § 1231 gain.
d. $6,000 ordinary income and $27,500 § 1231 gain.
e.   None of the above.

_____ 9. Otto gives his mother § 1245 property which was used in his business. He bought the
property for $50,000 and took $25,000 in accelerated depreciation before gifting it to
her this year. Which of the following statements is correct?
   a. Otto will recapture $25,000 as ordinary income on the gift to his mother.
   b. When the mother later sells the property, Otto will recapture $25,000 as
       ordinary income.
   c. The mother will recapture the excess of accelerated depreciation over
       straight-line depreciation as ordinary income on the sale of the property.
   d. The first $25,000 of the realized gain over the basis of the property will be
       ordinary income to the mother when she sells the property.
   e. The first $25,000 of proceeds received on the sale of the property will be
       ordinary income to the mother.

_____ 10. Which of the following is *false* regarding § 1245 recapture?
   a. It can reduce the amount of charitable contribution deduction if § 1245
       property is donated.
   b. It can apply to like-kind exchanges.
   c. It does not apply to any real property.
   d. It can apply to involuntary conversions.
   e. None of the above are false.

_____ 11. Caroline had the following transactions during 1995.

   January 15   Theft of new bicycle she purchased for $250 on 11/15/94. It was not
                 insured.   (150)
   February 21   Sale of personal auto for $1,000; it was purchased on 1/1/85 for
                 $6,000.
   March 1   Sold 100 shares of IBM stock for $3,000; the stock was purchased on   1500 STCL
                 9/1/94 for $1,500.
   March 15   Theft of a diamond necklace she received from her friend Oscar on
                 2/15/94; it had a fair market value of $75,000, and an adjusted basis of   person
                 $60,000; $70,000 was received as reimbursement from the insurance   n
                 company.   10,000 basn

   What should Caroline report on her 1995 return under the assumption that the § 1231
   lookback rule does not apply?
   a. Section 1231 gain $11,500; itemized deduction $150.
   b. Section 1231 gain $ 6,500; itemized deduction $150.
   c. Section 1231 gain $10,000; STCG $1,500; itemized deduction $150.
   d. Section 1231 gain $ 5,000; LTCG $1,500; itemized deduction $150.
   e. None of the above.

_____ 12. Which is not or could not be § 1245 property?
   a. Elevators and escalators.
   b. Professional baseball and football contracts.
   c. Buildings and their structural components.
   d. A copyright on § 1245 property.
   e. All are or could be § 1245 property.

_____ 13. On December 15, 1994, Alfred acquired 3,000 shares of stock in Heights Corporation,
   which is not a "small business corporation," for $50 per share. On March 29, 1995 the
   Heights Corporation stock was considered worthless. What type and amount of deduction
   should Alfred take for 1995 assuming no other capital transactions?   150,000 LTCL
   a. $3,000 loss deduction and $147,000 STCL carryforward.
   b. $50,000 ordinary loss deduction and $100,000 LTCL carryforward.

c. $3,000 loss deduction and $147,000 LTCL carryforward.

d. $3,000 loss deduction and $144,000 LTCL carryforward.

e.   None of the above.

14.   On January 6 of this year, Jason sold some § 1245 business equipment which had an
adjusted basis of $5,000. He purchased the equipment for $10,000 five years ago. If he
sold it for $8,000, how should Jason treat the transaction?

a.   Section 1231 gain of $3,000.

b.   Section 1245 gain of $3,000.

c.   Section 1231 loss of $2,000.

d.   Capital gain of $3,000.

e.   None of the above.

3,000 gain

15.   On January 1, Rose Marie sold machinery for $68,000. The machinery was purchased on
January 1, four years earlier, for $60,000 and using accelerated depreciation had an
adjusted basis of $30,000. Using the straight-line method, the adjusted basis would
have been $40,000. In the year of sale, Rose Marie should report the following.

a.   Section 1231 gain of $28,000.

b.   Section 1231 gain of $38,000.

c.   Ordinary income of $38,000.

d.   Section 1231 gain of $8,000; ordinary income of $20,000.

e.   Section 1231 gain of $8,000; ordinary income of $30,000.

38,000

16.   Last year, Emily sustained a § 1231 loss of $4,000 and was able to deduct the loss in
full as an ordinary loss. This year, Emily realized a $5,000 gain on the disposition of
a § 1231 asset. Assuming there were no other property transactions, how should this
year's transaction be treated?

a. $5,000 capital gains.

b. $5,000 ordinary income.

c. $4,000 capital gain and $1,000 ordinary income.

d. $4,000 ordinary income and $1,000 capital gain.

e.   Some other answer.

17.   The following assets were among those owned by the Gray Corporation at year end.

Delivery Truck	$11,000
Inventory	15,000
Trade Accounts Receivable	6,000

The capital assets total the following.

a. $0.

b. $11,000.

c. $17,000.

d. $32,000.

e.   Some other answer.

18.   If a § 1231 gain is incurred in the tax year 1995, to how many years must a taxpayer
"look back" in order to determine whether any nonrecaptured net § 1231 losses exist?

a.   0. The lookback rule has been repealed.

b.   3.

c.   4.

d.   5.

e.   None of the above.

19.   Black Corporation had § 1231 gains of $5,000 in the current year. The taxpayer also

had "nonrecaptured net § 1231 losses" from the previous five years of $3,500. What is the character of the gain recognized this year?

    a. $3,500 § 1231 gain and $1,500 ordinary income.
    b. $5,000 ordinary income.
    c. $1,500 § 1231 gain and $3,500 ordinary income.
    d. $5,000 § 1231 gain.
    e.   None of the above.

____ 20.   Gary and Gail are married and file a joint return. After offsetting their capital gains, what is the most that they can deduct as capital losses this year?

    a. $0.
    b. $1,000.
    c. $1,500.
    d. $3,000.
    e.   None of the above.

____ 21.   On January 1 of the current year, Freddie owned the following assets.

Personal residence	$65,000
ABC Corporation stock	6,000
Antique automobile	12,000

What amount do his capital assets total?

    a. $83,000.
    b. $77,000.
    c. $71,000.
    d. $18,000.
    e.   None of the above.

____ 22.   Charlie owned an apartment building since 1980 which had been depreciated on an accelerated basis. Straight-line depreciation would have produced deductions of $50,000 less than what was actually claimed. In the current year, when Charlie's basis in the building was $150,000, he exchanged it for an office building worth $275,000. What is Charlie's reportable gain on this transaction?

    a. $50,000 § 1250 gain.
    b. $125,000 § 1231 gain.
    c. $125,000 long-term capital gain.
    d. $0.
    e.   None of the above.

____ 23.   Which of the following is a capital asset?

    a.   Inventory.
    b.   Machinery and equipment.
    c.   Land used as a parking lot.
    d.   Personal use automobile.
    e.   None of the above.

____ 24.   Craft Timber Company purchased an option to buy 100 acres of nearby farmland. Craft Timber Company purchased the option for $2,000 which gave it the right to buy the property at $200,000 at anytime during the next 3 months. If the option is exercised, the following treatment results.

    a.   Craft Timber Company increases its basis in the land purchased by $2,000 to $202,000.
    b.   Craft Timber Company deducts the $2,000 as an ordinary business expense.
    c.   The grantor of the option treats the $2,000 as the receipt of ordinary income

because the land had been used to produce inventory (i.e., crops for sale).

    d.   Craft Timber Company holds an asset that can never be recovered for tax purposes until the business is liquidated.

    e.   None of the above.

____   25.   Brown Company purchased an option to buy 10,000 shares of stock that it planned to hold as an investment. Brown Company purchased the option for $2,000 which gave it the right to buy the stock at $200,000 at anytime during the next 3 months. If the option lapses, the following treatment results.

    a.   Brown Company has an ordinary loss of $2,000.

    b.   Brown Company has a long-term capital loss of $2,000.

    c.   Brown Company has a § 1231 loss of $2,000.

    (d.)   Brown Company has a short-term capital loss of $2,000.

    e.   None of the above.

Code Section Recognition

Several important sections of the Internal Revenue Code are described below. Indicate, by number, the appropriate Code section.

1.   _____   Defines a capital asset.

2.   _____   Provides detailed rules for determining the holding period of an asset.

3.   _____   Provides that in certain cases, long-term capital gain treatment applies to sales and exchanges of certain business assets.

4.   _____   Provides for depreciation recapture on the disposition of all depreciable personal property.

5.   _____   Provides for depreciation recapture on the disposition of depreciable residential realty acquired before 1987.

Short Answer

1.   A number of possibilities result after all possible netting of capital gains and losses occurs. Describe how each possibility is treated by noncorporate taxpayers.

    a.   NLTCG. 14 90

    b.   NSTCG. ordinary rates

    c.   NLTCG and NSTCG.

    d.   NLTCL. 3,000 max

    e.   NSTCL 3,000 max

    f.   NLTCL and NSTCL.

    g.   NCG. 28

    h.   NCL. 3,000

2.   Calf Mountain Company sells depreciable property during the year which is subject to § 1245 recapture. The property had been used for three years. The relevant data follow:

Original cost $10,000
Depreciation taken   4,000

Determine the amount and nature of the gain or loss in the following situations.

    a.   The property is sold for $8,000.   2,000 ord

    b.   The property is sold for $12,000.   4,000 ord 2,000 1231

    c.   The property is sold for $4,000.   2,000 loss 1231

SOLUTIONS TO CHAPTER 13 QUESTIONS

True or False

1.	F	Both types of net capital losses may be used by individuals to offset up to $3,000 of other income.
2.	T	
3.	T	
4.	F	This is true with respect to the option holder, not the option's grantor.
5.	F	Gains from the disposition of patents *do* receive capital asset treatment.
6.	T	
7.	T	
8.	T	
9.	T	However, one must remember to consider the § 1231 lookback procedure.
10.	T	Such gains and losses of personal use property are netted separately rather than being netted with § 1231 gains and losses.
11.	T	
12.	T	
13.	F	The disposition of depreciable real property placed in service after 1986 is not subject to depreciation recapture.
14.	T	
15.	F	
16.	F	
17.	F	
18.	T	
19.	F	Short-term capital losses are initially netted against capital gains. Further, if a net loss results, its current deductibility may be limited.
20.	T	

Fill-in-the-Blanks

1.	1231
2.	gifts, charitable transfers, certain tax-free transactions. Also, death, like-kind exchanges, and involuntary conversions.
3.	sale or exchange, capital asset
4.	Real property
5.	transferor
6.	more than one year
7.	capital, § 1231
8.	net long-term capital gain, net short-term capital loss
9.	$3,000
10.	passive
11.	three, five
12.	28
13.	for
14.	long-term capital
15.	long-term capital gain

Multiple Choice

1. b   See Example 37 in the text.
2. b
3. d   The theft of personal use property and sale of depreciable property (which is subject to depreciation recapture) are not included. See Example 43 in the text.
4. d   See Example 32 in the text.
5. b

Salary and Interest		$37,000
STCG	$5,000	
Less: LTCL carryover	4,000	1,000
AGI		$38,000

See Example 38 in the text.
6. d   All of the gain is ordinary income because the automobile was not held for more than one year. See Example 43 in the text.
7. a   See Example 43 in the text.
8. c   Recapture potential equals *all* depreciation claimed since the property's acquisition because an accelerated method of depreciation was used. This realty is § 1245 property. See Example 51 in the text.
9. d   See Example 55 in the text.
10. c
11. e   STCG $1,500 on the sale of stock; net personal casualty gain $9,850 (gain $10,000 from the necklace - loss $150 from the bicycle, net of $100 floor). The loss on the sale of the personal auto is not deductible. See Example 43 in the text.
12. e
13. c
14. b   See Example 47 in the text.
15. e   See Example 48 in the text.
16. d   The lookback rules apply. See Example 45 in the text.
17. a
18. d   1990, 1991, 1992, 1993, 1994
19. c   See Example 45 in the text.
20. d   See Example 37 in the text.
21. a
22. d   The transaction qualifies for like-kind treatment under § 1031. Further, any depreciation recapture potential does not trigger the recognition of any realized gain. See Example 58 in the text.
23. d
24. a
25. d

Code Section Recognition

1.   1221
2.   1223
3.   1231
4.   1245
5.   1250

Short Answer

1. a.   NLTCG--subject to a maximum rate of 28%.
    b.   NSTCG--subject to ordinary income rates.
    c.   NLTCG and NSTCG--the NLTCG portion is subject to a 28 percent maximum tax rate and the NSTCG is subject to ordinary income rates.
    d.   NLTCL--deductible up to a maximum of $3,000 per year.
    e.   NSTCL--deductible up to a maximum of $3,000 per year.
    f.   NLTCL and NSTCL--deductible up to a maximum of $3,000 per year, with the NSTCL treated first against the annual limitation.
    g.   NCG (the excess of NLTCG over NSTCL)--subject to a maximum rate of 28%.
    h.   NCL (the excess of capital losses over capital gains)--deductible up to a maximum of $3,000 per year.

2. a.   The property is sold for $8,000:

Amount realized	$8,000
Less: Adjusted basis	6,000
Amount of gain recognized	$2,000

Nature of gain recognized

§ 1245	$2,000
§ 1231	$ 0

   b.   The property is sold for $12,000:

Amount realized	$12,000
Less: Adjusted basis	6,000
Amount of gain recognized	$ 6,000

Nature of gain recognized

§ 1245	$4,000
§ 1231	$2,000

   c.   The property is sold for $4,000:

Amount realized	$4,000
Less: Adjusted basis	6,000
Amount of loss recognized	$2,000

Nature of loss recognized

§ 1245	$ 0
§ 1231	$2,000

CHAPTER 14
ALTERNATIVE MINIMUM TAX

CHAPTER HIGHLIGHTS

For most taxpayers, there are no special considerations required when they compute their income tax liability. For those taxpayers, the regular income tax formula applies. However, some taxpayers may be subject to the alternative minimum tax, which was designed to insure that every taxpayer pays at least a minimum amount of tax. The alternative minimum tax applies to individuals, corporations, trusts, and estates, and in essence, represents a parallel tax system, separate and distinct from the regular income tax system. In order to determine which tax system applies, the tax liability, based on the regular income tax system is calculated along with the alternative minimum tax liability, and the taxpayer's liability to the government is the higher of the two amounts.

I.   Introduction: Alternative Minimum Tax
   A.   The tax law contains incentives to encourage economically and socially beneficial behavior, and to provide relief for taxpayers in certain situations. Examples of these incentives include: accelerated depreciation, immediate expensing of research and experimentation expenses, and exclusion of interest received on debt obligations of state and local governmental units.
   B.   Because some taxpayers with large economic incomes had been so successful in reducing (or eliminating) their tax liabilities due to their use of these and other incentives, Congress felt compelled to institute a system which would alleviate the resulting sense of inequity.
   C.   The *alternative minimum tax* (AMT) was enacted to insure that taxpayers who benefit from such preferential treatment under the income tax laws pay at least a minimum amount of tax.

II.   Individual Alternative Minimum Tax
   A.   AMT Formula for Alternative Minimum Taxable Income (AMTI)
      1.   The AMT is separate from, but parallel to, the income tax system. Consequently, alternative minimum taxable income (AMTI) will differ from taxable income.
      2.   In some cases, certain items are considered in both the income tax and AMT computations, but the amounts are different (e.g., income from some long-term contracts).
      3.   Most income and expense items are treated the same way for both income tax and AMT purposes (e.g., salary and alimony).

4.   On the other hand, some income and expense items are treated differently for income tax and AMT purposes (e.g., personal and dependency exemptions).

5.   The approach taken by the tax forms to calculate AMTI uses taxable income as the starting point and essentially reconciles taxable income to AMTI by accounting for the differences between the income tax provisions and AMT provisions. These reconciling items are referred to as AMT *adjustments* and *tax preferences*. The AMTI computation is shown in Exhibit 14-1.

Exhibit 14-1
FORMULA FOR ALTERNATIVE MINIMUM TAXABLE INCOME (AMTI)

Taxable income

Plus: Positive AMT adjustments

Minus: Negative AMT adjustments

Equals: Taxable income after AMT adjustments

Plus: Tax preferences

Equals: Alternative minimum taxable income

6.   Adjustments may *increase or decrease* taxable income in the AMTI formula.

a.   Many of the adjustments arise as a result of *timing differences* related to deferral of income or acceleration of deductions. Examples include differences related to depreciation calculations and immediate expensing options.

b.   When these timing differences reverse, *negative adjustments* are made.

c.   A few adjustments do not relate to timing differences and result in a permanent difference between taxable income and AMT.

7.   Tax preferences are tax benefits that have been singled out in the AMTI formula. The presence of tax preferences in a given year always increases the AMTI base. Examples include excess depreciation on certain assets, interest on certain private activity bonds, and the 50% exclusion from gross income associated with gains on the sale of certain small business stock.

B.   AMT Formula: Other Components

1.   Other formula components must be considered in the conversion of AMTI to AMT as shown in Exhibit 14-2.

2.   If the regular tax liability exceeds tentative AMT, then the AMT is zero. If the tentative AMT exceeds the regular tax liability, the amount of the excess is the AMT.

Exhibit 14-2
ALTERNATIVE MINIMUM TAX FOR NONCORPORATE TAXPAYERS

Regular taxable income

Plus or minus: *Adjustments*

Equals: *Taxable income after AMT adjustments*

Plus: *Tax Preferences*

Equals: *Alternative minimum taxable income*

Minus: *Exemption*

Equals: *Alternative minimum tax base*

Times: *26% rate on first $175,000 plus 28% rate on amounts in excess of $175,000*

Equals: *Tentative minimum tax before foreign tax credit*

Minus: *Alternative minimum tax foreign tax credit*

Equals: *Tentative minimum tax*

Minus: *Regular tax liability*

Equals: *Alternative minimum tax (if amount is positive)*

3. Exemption amount
    a. An exemption of one of the following amounts is allowed in the computation of the AMT.
        (1) Married taxpayers filing a joint return -- $45,000.
        (2) Single taxpayers -- $33,750.
        (3) Married taxpayers filing separate returns -- $22,500.
    b. However, the exemption amount is phased out at a rate of 25 cents on the dollar, beginning when the AMTI exceeds a specified amount.
        (1) Married taxpayers filing a joint return -- $150,000.
        (2) Single taxpayers -- $112,500.
        (3) Married taxpayers filing separate returns -- $75,000.
4. AMT rate schedule -- The AMT rates for noncorporate taxpayers are 26 percent for the first $175,000 of the tax base and 28 percent for the tax base in excess of $175,000.
5. Regular Tax Liability -- The AMT is equal to the tentative minimum tax minus the *regular tax liability*. The regular tax liability for AMT purposes is equal to the gross income tax liability reduced *only* by the allowable foreign tax credit. Thus, in an AMT year, the taxpayer's total tax liability is equal to the tentative minimum tax.

C.   AMT Adjustments

1.   Direction of Adjustments -- With each of the adjustments required, it is necessary to determine not only the *amount* of the adjustment, but also whether the adjustment is *positive or negative*.

2.   Circulation expenditures may be expensed in the year incurred for regular income tax purposes; however, such expenses must be capitalized and amortized ratably over a three-year period for AMT purposes. The difference between the regular income tax deduction and the amount allowed to be amortized for AMT purposes is the required adjustment for circulation expenditures.

3.   Depreciation of Post-1986 Real Property -- The difference between AMT depreciation and regular tax depreciation is treated as an adjustment for real property placed in service after 1986. The AMT depreciation is computed using a life (i.e., 40 years) that is longer than that which is used for the regular depreciation

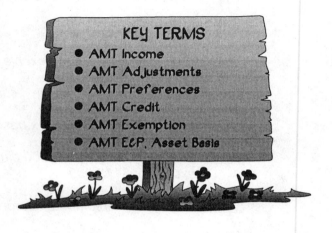

computation (i.e., 27.5, 31.5, or 39 years). Therefore, after an asset has been fully depreciated for income tax purposes it continues to be depreciated for AMT purposes, resulting in a negative adjustment.

4.   Depreciation of Post-1986 Personal Property -- The adjustment for post-1986 personal property is equal to the difference between the MACRS deduction and the amount of depreciation computed using the *alternative depreciation system* (ADS), which assumes longer lives and a lower rate. The taxpayer may *elect* to use ADS for regular income tax purposes. If the election is made, no adjustment is required, because the depreciation deduction for both purposes is the same.

5.   The adjustment for certified pollution control facilities placed in service after 1986 is equal to the difference between the regular tax deduction (i.e., the cost may be amortized over a 60-month period) and the deduction allowed for the calculation of AMT (i.e., depreciated using the ADS over the appropriate class life).

6.   Mining exploration and development costs may be deducted for regular tax purposes in the year paid or incurred for exploration. However, for AMT purposes, these costs must be capitalized and amortized ratably over a 10-year period. The excess of what was deducted under the regular tax system and what would have been amortized over 10 years is the AMT adjustment. The taxpayer may *elect* the same treatment for regular tax purposes as is required for AMT purposes.

7.   With respect to research and experimental expenditures which are expensed for regular income tax purposes in the year paid or incurred, the AMT adjustment is equal to the amount that is in excess of the amount that would have been allowed if the expenditures had been capitalized and amortized ratably over a 10-year period. This adjustment may be avoided if the

taxpayer *elects* to write the expenditures off over the 10-year period for regular income tax purposes.

8. Because the completed contract method is not allowed for AMT purposes, an adjustment is required if that method is used for regular tax purposes. The adjustment is equal to the difference between the income that would have been reported under the percentage of completion method and the amount reported using the completed contract method.

9. For taxpayers with incentive stock options, the excess of the fair market value of stock over the exercise price is treated as an adjustment in the first taxable year in which the rights in the stock are freely transferable or are not subject to a substantial risk of forfeiture.

10. Adjusted gain or loss -- Because the basis of property may be different for regular income tax purposes than for AMT purposes, the gain or loss for regular income tax purposes will be different than gain or loss for AMT purposes. Consequently, a positive or negative adjustment will be required in the year of a sale or disposition.

11. Losses incurred on passive activities are not deductible in computing *either* the income tax or the AMT. However, this does not eliminate the possibility of adjustments attributable to passive activities.

12. The regular income tax NOL is modified for AMT adjustments and tax preferences with the result being the ATNOLD. Preferences and adjustment items that have benefitted the taxpayer in computing the income tax NOL are added back, thereby reducing or eliminating the ATNOLD.

13. Itemized Deductions

   a. Itemized deductions allowed for AMT purposes are limited to casualty losses, gambling losses, charitable contributions, medical expenses in excess of 10 percent of AGI, estate tax on income in respect of a decedent, and qualified interest. Therefore, the effect of any other itemized deductions claimed for regular income tax purposes must be removed from the AMT calculation.

   b. The 3 percent cutback adjustment that disallows a portion of high-income taxpayer's itemized deductions for income tax purposes, does not apply for AMT purposes.

   c. For AMT purposes, medical expenses are deductible only to the extent they exceed 10 percent of AGI while for regular income tax purposes, they are deductible to the extent that they exceed 7.5 percent of AGI.

   d. The AMT itemized deduction for interest expense includes only *qualified housing interest* and *investment interest to the extent of net investment income that is included in the determination of AMTI*. The AMT term qualified housing interest has a different meaning than the regular income tax term *qualified residence interest*.

Taxpayers living in high-tax-rate states, such as Minnesota, Massachusetts, and Wisconsin might be especially vulnerable to the AMT, as they depend upon the itemized deduction for taxes paid to reduce their regular tax liability. This shows how a broader AMT tax base can affect taxpayers with similar income situations in different ways.

14. Other adjustments may be necessary in the computation of AMTI. Taxpayers who do not itemize deductions must include the standard deduction as an adjustment in computing AMTI. In addition, a positive adjustment is required for personal and dependency exemptions.

D. AMT Preferences -- Tax preferences *increase* the AMT base.

1. The percentage depletion preference is equal to the excess of the regular tax deduction for depletion over the adjusted basis of the property at the end of the taxable year.

2. Excess intangible drilling costs (IDC) for the year are treated as a preference item.

3. Tax-exempt interest on private activity bonds is a tax preference item.

4. Depreciation preference -- For real property and leased personal property placed in service before 1987, the preference is equal to the excess of accelerated depreciation over straight-line depreciation, computed on an item-by-item basis.

5. Excess amortization of certified pollution control facilities placed in service before 1987 is a preference item.

6. Fifty percent of the gain on the sale of certain small business stock is excludible from gross income for regular income tax purposes. The excluded amount is a tax preference for AMT purposes.

E. AMT Credit

1. A credit is allowed to provide equity for taxpayers when timing differences that have given rise to AMT adjustments (and an AMT liability) reverse. The regular tax liability may be reduced by the alternative minimum tax credit for prior years' alternative minimum tax liability attributable to timing differences. The alternative minimum tax credit may be carried over indefinitely.

2. The AMT credit is not available in connection with the following.

   a. The standard deduction.
   b. Personal exemptions.
   c. Medical expenses, to the extent deductible for income tax purposes but not deductible in computing AMT.
   d. Other itemized deductions not allowable or AMT purposes.
   e. Excess percentage depletion.
   f. Tax-exempt interest on specified private activity bonds.

If a high-bracket taxpayer is subject to the AMT in one year and is expected to be subject to the regular tax the next year, income should be accelerated into the AMT year (when the income tax rate is relatively lower) and deductions should be deferred into the regular income tax year (when the income tax rate is relatively higher. This is the opposite of the classic income tax planning strategy of deferring income and accelerating deductions.

III.   Corporate Alternative Minimum Tax -- The corporate AMT is very similar to the individual AMT with many (but not all) of the adjustments and preferences being the same. While the corporate AMT rates and exemptions are different than those for the individual AMT, the objectives of the taxes are identical. The formula for computing the corporate AMT follows in Exhibit 14-3.

     A.   AMT Adjustments

         1.   Adjustments applicable to individuals *and* corporations include the following.

             a.   Excess depreciation on property placed in service after 1986.

             b.   Excess recovery for pollution control facilities placed in service after 1986.

             c.   Excess mining and exploration expenditures.

             d.   Income on long-term contracts -- the percentage of completion method is required for AMT purposes instead of the completed contract method.

             e.   Dispositions of assets (if gain or loss for AMT purposes differs from gains or loss for income tax purposes).

             f.   Allowable ATNOLD (which cannot exceed 90 percent of AMTI before deduction for ATNOLD).

         2.   Adjustments applicable *only* to corporations

             a.   The Merchant Marine capital construction fund adjustment.

             b.   The adjustment for special deductions allowed to Blue Cross/Blue Shield organizations.

             c.   The *adjusted current earnings* (ACE) adjustment.

                 (1)   Corporations are subject to an AMT adjustment equal to 75 percent of the excess of ACE over AMTI before the ACE adjustment.

                 (2)   The adjustment can be either a positive or negative amount. Any negative adjustment is limited to the aggregate of the positive adjustments under ACE for prior years reduced by the previously claimed negative adjustments.

                 (3)   While ACE is similar to current earnings and profits, certain variations do exist.

                 (4)   The starting point for computing ACE is AMTI, which is defined as regular taxable income after AMT adjustments (other than the ATNOLD and ACE adjustments) and tax preferences. However, other types of adjustments are also required.

     B.   Tax Preferences -- Tax preference items that apply to individuals also apply to corporations.

C.   Exemption
1.   The tentative AMT, calculated at 20 percent times the AMT base, results only if the tax base exceeds the corporate exemption amount.
2.   The exemption amount for a corporation is $40,000 reduced by 25 percent of the amount by which AMTI exceeds $150,000. The exemption phases out entirely when AMTI reaches $310,000.
D.   Other Aspects of the AMT
1.   Foreign tax credits can be applied against only 90 percent of tentative AMT liability.
2.   All of a corporation's AMT is available for carryover as a minimum tax credit.

Exhibit 14-3
AMT FORMULA FOR CORPORATIONS

Taxable income

Plus: Income tax NOL deduction

Plus or minus: AMT adjustments

Plus: Tax Preferences

Equals: Alternative minimum taxable income before
     ATNOLD

Minus: ATNOLD (limited to 90% of AMTI before
     ATNOLD)

Equals: AMTI

Minus: Exemption

Equals: Alternative minimum tax base

Times: 20% rate

Equals: Tentative minimum tax before AMT foreign tax credit

Minus: AMT foreign tax credit (possibly limited to 90% of
     AMT before AMT foreign tax credit)

Equals: Tentative alternative minimum tax

Minus: Regular tax liability before credits minus regular
     foreign tax credit

Equals: Alternative minimum tax (if amount is positive)

TEST FOR SELF-EVALUATION -- CHAPTER 14

True or False

Indicate which of the following statements are true or false by circling the correct answer.

(T)   F   1.   The maximum tax rate for individual taxpayers subject to the alternative minimum tax is 28 percent.

T   (F)   2.   The alternative minimum tax exemption amount for all married taxpayers filing a joint return is set at $45,000.

(T)   F   3.   "Adjustments" to taxable income in arriving at the alternative minimum taxable income may be either positive or negative.

T   (F)   4.   The adjustments that apply to individuals for AMT purposes also apply to corporations and the adjustments that apply to corporations also apply to individuals.

(T)   F   5.   Itemized deductions for state and local taxes and miscellaneous deductions are examples of adjustments required in the calculation of the alternative minimum taxable income.

T   (F)   6.   A tax preference item would arise in the AMT computation if an asset acquired this year is depreciated using the MACRS method.

T   (F)   7.   For individual taxpayers, the personal exemption is allowed in the computation of AMTI.

T   (F)   8.   Both adjustments and preference items can either increase or decrease taxable income in arriving at AMTI.

T   (F)   9.   Interest expense incurred by individuals is fully deductible for AMT purposes.

T   (F)   10.   Any tax-exempt interest earned by a taxpayer is a tax preference item.

T   (F)   11.   The corporate AMT is calculated using the same tax rate as with the individual AMT.

(T)   F   12.   The tax preferences that apply to individuals also apply to corporations.

(T)   F   13.   The AMT applies only if it produces a higher tax liability than the regular income tax computation.

(T)   F   14.   The AMT is based on a modification of the regular taxable income by preferences and adjustments.

T   (F)   15.   A negative AMT adjustment is required in the amount of the difference between qualified residence interest allowed as an itemized deduction for regular tax purposes and qualified housing interest allowed in the determination of

AMTI.

T F   16.   Alternative minimum taxable income minus the exemption equals the alternative minimum tax base.

T F   17.   To provide equity for the taxpayer when timing differences reverse, the regular tax liability may be reduced by the minimum tax credit for prior years' minimum tax liability attributable to timing differences.

T   **F**   18.   The AMT exemption for corporations is $30,000 ~~reduced by 25 percent of the~~ *40,000* amount by which AMTI exceeds $150,000.

T F   19.   The adjusted current earnings adjustment is applicable only to C corporations.

T F   20.   The ATNOLD is limited to 90 percent of AMTI before the ATNOLD.

Fill-in-the-Blanks

Complete the following statements with the appropriate word(s) or amount(s).

1.   A two-tier rate schedule applies to a noncorporate taxpayer's alternative minimum tax base: __26__ percent of the tax base up the first $175,000 and __28__ percent of the tax base in excess of $175,000.

2.   The alternative minimum tax exemption amount is _45,000_ for married taxpayers filing joint returns, _33,750_ for single taxpayers, and _22,500_ for married taxpayers filing separate returns.

3.   In the context of the alternative minimum tax computation, the excess tax depreciation on post-1986 realty is known as a(n) _Adjustment_

4.   The corporate alternative minimum tax rate is __20__ percent of the alternative minimum tax base.

5.   The exemption amount for a single taxpayer is phased out entirely by the time AMTI reaches _247,500._

6.   _AMTI_ is the sum of the regular taxable income, plus or minus adjustments, plus tax preferences.

7.   The tentative AMT is calculated only if the tax base exceeds the _exemption_ amount.

8.   The _AMT credit_ is allowed as an offset against the regular tax liability to provide equity to taxpayers when timing differences that have given rise to AMT adjustments reverse.

9.   The adjustment for depreciable property acquired after 1986 is equal to the difference between _MACRS_ depreciation deducted for income tax purposes and _ADS_ depreciation deductible for AMT purposes.

10.   _Excess depreciation_ could be either an adjustment or a tax preference item, depending on when the related

property was placed in service.

11.   The _preferences_ applicable to noncorporate taxpayers are also applicable to corporate taxpayers, but some _adjustments_ differ.

12.   Corporations are subject to an AMT adjustment equal to ___75___ percent of the excess of ACE over AMTI before the ACE adjustment.

13.   A bond that produces interest income which is exempt for regular income tax purposes but which is a preference for AMT purposes is known as a _Private activity bond_

14.   The AMT exemption for individuals and corporations is phased out at a rate of ___25___ cents on the dollar for alternative minimum taxable income in excess of specified amounts.

15.   Interest on certain private activity bonds has the effect of _increasing_ alternative minimum taxable income.

Multiple Choice

Choose the best answer for each of the following questions.

_____ 1.   Which of the following is *not* a preference item or an adjustment for purposes of computing the alternative minimum tax?
   a.   Unrealized appreciation element on charitable contributions to public charities made during the year.
   b.   Passive activity losses utilized in computing taxable income.
   c.   Depreciation expense claimed for income tax purposes versus depreciation expense calculated over a longer life using a slower rate.
   d.   The difference between the income reported under the percentage of completion method and the amount reported using the completed contract method.
   e.   Each of the above is either a preference or an adjustment.

_____ 2.   A married taxpayer filing a joint return has alternative minimum taxable income of $200,000. For purposes of the alternative minimum tax computation, what is the amount of the exemption?
   a. $45,000.
   b. $35,000.
   c. $32,500.
   d. $20,000.
   e.   None of the above.

_____ 3.   Assume the above facts, except that the taxpayer is a single individual and not a married taxpayer. What is the amount of the exemption?
   a. $35,625.
   b. $33,750.
   c. $25,625.
   d. $11,875.
   e.   None of the above.

_____ 4.   Which of the following is *not* true with respect to the alternative minimum tax?

      a.   The individual AMT rate is 20 percent.
      b.   The amount of interest (other than qualified housing interest) that may be deducted in arriving at alternative minimum taxable income is limited to the taxpayer's investment income.
      c.   The corporate AMT rate is 20 percent.
      d.   All of the above are true.

5. Before any limitation, the AMT exemption amounts for taxpayers filing as single, married filing jointly, and married filing separately, respectively, are as follow.
      a. $33,750; $45,000; $0.
      b. $112,500; $150,000; $75,000.
      c. $33,750; $60,000; $33,750.
      d. $33,750; $45,000; $22,500.
      e.   None of the above.

6. Timothy's alternative minimum tax base for 1995 is $292,500. As a result, determine the tentative minimum tax liability.
      a. $58,500.
      b. $76,050.
      c. $78,400.
      d. $81,900.
      e.   Some other amount.

7. Bobby and Tami's regular income tax liability on their joint return is $15,000 for the year before considering the AMT. Their AMTI is $145,000. Determine the total amount of their tax liability for the year.
      a. $11,000.
      b. $17,000.
      c. $26,000.
      d. $41,000.
      e.   None of the above.

8. From your review of Fran's income tax data, you note the following.

AGI	$40,000
Medical expenses incurred	5,000
Taxable income	33,000

Assuming that Fran is subject to the AMT this year, what is the adjustment due to the information presented above?
      a. $0.
      b. $1,000.
      c. $2,000.
      d. $4,000.
      e.   None of the above.

9. Bill, a calendar year single taxpayer, had the following transactions.

Taxable income	$200,000
Net capital gain (included in taxable income)	50,000
Receipt of incentive stock option -- excess of current FMV over exercise price (exercisable next year)	10,000

Excess depreciation on fixed assets	50,000
Excess depletion	40,000

Based on the above, what is Bill's AMTI?
- a. $240,000.
- b. $290,000.
- c. $300,000.
- d. $350,000.
- e. Some other amount.

_____ 10. Which of the following is not allowed as an itemized deduction for the individual AMT calculation?
- a. Charitable contributions.
- b. State income taxes.
- c. Medical expenses in excess of 10 percent of AGI.
- d. Qualified interest.
- e. All of the above are allowable.

_____ 11. Which of the following is not an adjustment that applies only to corporations?
- a. The adjustment for excess mining and exploration expenditures.
- b. The Merchant Marine capital construction fund adjustment.
- c. The adjustment for special deductions allowed to Blue Cross/Blue Shield organizations.
- d. The adjusted current earnings adjustment.
- e. Some other amount.

_____ 12. Which of the following is an AMT adjustment?
- a. Itemized deductions allowed for income tax purposes but not for AMT.
- b. Net appreciation on contribution of long-term capital gain property to public charities.
- c. Excess of accelerated over straight-line depreciation on real property placed in service before 1987.
- d. Excess of accelerated over straight-line depreciation on leased personal property placed in service before 1987.
- e. None of the above.

_____ 13. Which of the following is an AMT preference?
- a. Standard deduction if the taxpayer did not itemize.
- b. Percentage depletion in excess of the property's adjusted basis.
- c. Excess of MACRS depreciation over alternative depreciation on all personal property placed in service after 1986.
- d. Excess of MACRS depreciation over alternative depreciation on all real property placed in service after 1986.
- e. All of the above are true.

_____ 14. If Green Corporation placed an office building into service this year which cost $500,000 and claimed MACRS depreciation for regular income tax purposes, which of the following is true?
- a. No adjustment is required this year.
- b. No preference item arises from this transaction.
- c. A negative adjustment arises this year.
- d. If the property is held for 39 years, the adjusted basis for regular tax

            purposes and AMT purposes will be the same.
- e.   None of the above.

15.   AMT adjustments for which of the following items can be avoided if the taxpayer elects to write off the expenditures for regular income tax purposes using the same method as that required for AMT purposes?
- a.   Circulation expenditures.
- b.   Depreciation of post-1986 personal property.
- c.   Mining exploration and development costs.
- d.   Accounting for long-term contracts.
- e.   All of the above.

16.   In 1995, Kelly, a magazine publisher, incurs $33,000 of deductible circulation expenditures. This amount may be deducted in full in 1995 for income tax purposes. Which of the following is correct?
- a.   No amount is deductible for AMT purposes.
- b.   A negative adjustment of $11,000 is required in 1995.
- c.   A positive adjustment of $11,000 is required in 1996.
- d.   A negative adjustment of $11,000 is required in 1997.
- e.   None of the above.

17.   In 1993, Richard exercised an incentive stock option (ISO) that had been granted by his employer. He had acquired 500 shares of his employer's stock for $5,000 at a time when the stock's fair market value was $15,000. The restrictions that the employer had placed on Richard's ownership of the stock lapsed in 1995. Which of the following correctly describes the treatment to Richard?
- a.   Taxable income of $10,000 is recognized in 1993.
- b.   Taxable income of $10,000 is recognized in 1995.
- c.   An AMT adjustment of $10,000 occurs in 1993.
- d.   An AMT adjustment of $10,000 occurs in 1995.
- e.   None of the above.

18.   In 1993, Richard exercised an incentive stock option (ISO) that had been granted by his employer. He had acquired 500 shares of his employer's stock for $5,000 at a time when the stock's fair market value was $15,000. The restrictions that the employer had placed on Richard's ownership of the stock lapsed in 1995. In 1996, the stock is sold for $20,000. Which of the following correctly describes the treatment to Richard from the sale?
- a.   There is an income tax gain of $5,000.
- b.   There is an AMT gain of $5,000.
- c.   There is an AMT gain of $15,000.
- d.   There is no gain recognized for either regular income tax or AMT purposes because of the beneficial attributes of an ISO.
- e.   None of the above.

19.   In 1995, Joyce had a net operating loss for regular income tax purposes of $50,000. This amount included the deduction for accelerated depreciation of $60,000 on real property acquired prior to 1987. Straight-line depreciation acceptable for AMT purposes would have been $45,000. Calculate Joyce's ATNOLD carryover to 1996.
- a. $0.
- b. $35,000.   15,000
- c. $50,000.

       d. $60,000.
       e.   None of the above.

20.   Blue Corporation, an oil and gas company, incurred IDC of $75,000 during the year. The amount was expensed for regular income tax purposes. During the year, Blue Corporation's net oil and gas income was $100,000. What is Blue Corporation's tax preference for IDC?

       a. $0.
       b. $2,500.
       c. $10,000.
       d. $67,500.
       e.   Some other amount.

Code Section Recognition

Several important sections of the Internal Revenue Code are described below. Indicate, by number, the appropriate Code section.

1.   _55_   Requires a taxpayer in certain situations to pay the alternative minimum tax.

2.   _57_   All of the alternative minimum tax preference items are prescribed here.

Short Answer

1. Indicate whether the following items are adjustments or preference items used in the calculation of AMTI.
      a.   Certain itemized deductions.   Adj
      b.   Tax-exempt interest on private activity bonds.   pref
      c.   Excess depreciation over straight-line depreciation on real property placed in   pref service before 1987.
      d.   Excess ACRS depreciation over ADS depreciation on property placed in service after 1986.   Adj
      e.   Standard deduction (if taxpayer does not itemize).   Adj

2. Shaletha, who is single, calculates her AMTI to be $230,000. Calculate her tentative minimum tax.

                  230,000
                    (4375)
                 ─────────
                  225,625

                         59,675

SOLUTIONS TO CHAPTER 14 QUESTIONS

True or False

1. T
2. F   The exemption amount of $45,000 is phased out at a rate of 25 cents on the dollar when the alternative minimum taxable income exceeds $150,000. No exemption is available after the taxpayer's AMTI exceeds $330,000.
3. T
4. F   Differences (e.g., ACE adjustment) do exist between the two.
5. T
6. F   In such situation, an adjustment would arise, not a preference item.
7. F   The preference for personal exemptions allowed for regular income tax purposes increases AMTI.
8. F   Tax preferences always are added to taxable income in arriving at AMTI while adjustments may be either positive or negative.
9. F   Only qualified housing interest and investment interest are deductible for AMT purposes.
10. F   Only tax-exempt interest earned on specified private activity bonds is a tax preference item.
11. F   The individual rates are 26 percent on the first $175,000 of the tax base and 28 percent on the tax base in excess of $175,000, while the corporate rate is 20 percent.
12. T
13. T
14. T
15. F   The adjustment would be positive, not negative.
16. T
17. T
18. F   The corporate exemption amount is $40,000 reduced by 25 percent of the amount by which AMTI exceeds $150,000.
19. T
20. T

Fill-in-the-Blanks

1. 26, 28
2. $45,000, $33,750, $22,500
3. adjustment
4. 20
5. $247,500
6. Alternative minimum taxable income
7. exemption
8. AMT credit
9. MACRS, ADS
10. Excess depreciation
11. preferences, adjustments
12. 75
13. private activity bond
14. 25

15.   increasing

Multiple Choice

1. a
2. c $32,500 = $45,000 - [($200,000 - $150,000) X .25] See Example 5 in the text.
3. d $11,875 = $33,750 - [($200,000 - $112,500) X .25] See Example 5 in the text.
4. a
5. d
6. c

AMT Base	$292,500
Tentative minimum tax liability:	
$175,000 X 26%	$45,500
($292,500 - $175,000) X 28%	32,900
Tentative minimum tax	$78,400

7. c

AMTI	$145,000
Less: Exemption	45,000
AMT Base	$100,000
Rate	X 26%
Tentative AMT	$ 26,000

Because the tentative AMT is higher than the regular income tax liability, the tentative AMT amount is payable.

8. b $1,000 = [$5,000 - ($40,000 X 7.5%)] - [$5,000 ($40,000 X 10%)] See Example 20 in the text.

9. b   AMTI = $290,000 = Taxable income $200,000 + Excess depreciation on fixed assets $50,000 + Excess depletion $40,000 See Example 29 in the text.

10. b
11. a
12. a
13. b
14. b   See Examples 7 and 8 and related discussion.
15. e
16. d   See Example 1 in the text.
17. d   See Example 10 in the text.
18. b   See Example 11 in the text.
19. b $35,000 = $50,000 regular tax NOL - $15,000 tax preference item. See Example 17 in the text.
20. b

Intangible drilling costs expensed in the year incurred	$75,000
Minus: Deduction if IDC were amortized over ten years	7,500
Equals: Excess of IDC expense over amortization	$67,500
Minus: 65% of net oil and gas income	65,000
Equals: Tax preference item	$ 2,500

See Example 27 in the text.

Code Section Recognition

1.   55
2.   57

Short Answer

1.   a.   Adjustment.
       b.   Preference.
       c.   Preference.
       d.   Adjustment.
       e.   Adjustment.

2.

AMTI	$230,000
Less: Exemption	
$33,750 - [($230,000 - $112,500) X 25%]	4,375
Alternative minimum tax base	$225,625
Times: 26% X $175,000	$ 45,500
28% X ($225,625 - $175,000)	14,175
Tentative minimum tax	$ 59,675

CHAPTER 15
ACCOUNTING PERIODS AND METHODS

CHAPTER HIGHLIGHTS

T he computation of the income tax liability may be affected by various accounting periods and methods that are available or required to be used by taxpayers. In particular, requirements exist for the adoption and change of a tax year, various methods of accounting are available, procedures exist for changing accounting methods, and numerous requirements impact the use of the installment method and the methods of reporting long-term contracts. These issues relate to *when* income and deductions are reported by a taxpayer. These issues and the relevant restrictions which apply are discussed in this chapter.

I. Accounting Periods
    A. In General
        1. The federal income tax determination and collection system is based on the concept of an *annual reporting* by the taxable entity. Most individuals use a *calendar year* to report income; however, a noncalendar fiscal year may be selected if the taxpayer's books are maintained on the basis of that same *fiscal year*.
        2. Partnerships and S corporations are subject to restrictions designed to prevent owners from shifting income from one period to another.
            a. A partnership tax year must be the same as the tax year of the *majority interest partners*. If the majority owners do not have the same tax year, the entity must have the same tax year as its *principal partners*. Otherwise, the partnership must use a year which results in the *least aggregate deferral* of income.
            b. Generally, S Corporations must adopt a calendar year.
            c. However, partnerships and S Corporations can *elect* an otherwise *impermissible* year in any of the following situations.

      (1)   A business purpose for the year can be demonstrated.

      (2)   The desired year results in a deferral of not more than three months' income and the entity agrees to make required tax payments.

      (3)   The entity retains the same year as was used for the fiscal year ending in 1987, provided the entity agrees to make required tax payments.

3.   The IRS's position is that the only business purpose which would justify a fiscal year relates to the need to conform reporting to the natural business year of a business. Generally, only seasonal businesses have a natural business year.

4.   Required tax payments of a partnership or an S corporation, which are due April 15 of each year, are computed by applying the highest individual tax rate plus one percent to an estimate of the deferral period income. The deferral period runs from the end of the fiscal year to the end of the calendar year. The amount due is reduced by the amount of required tax payments for the previous year.

5.   If certain requirements are met, a personal service corporation (i.e., a corporation whose shareholder-employees provide personal services, such as medical, dental, legal, accounting, engineering, actuarial, consulting, or performing arts) may *elect* a fiscal year instead of the normally required calendar year.

B.   Making the Election -- A taxpayer makes an election for a particular tax year by the timely filing of its initial return. For all subsequent years, the same period must be used unless prior approval for change is obtained from the IRS.

C.   Changes in the Accounting Period

1.   Consent must be obtained from the IRS before a taxpayer may change his or her tax year. An application for permission to change tax years must be filed on or before the fifteenth day of the second calendar month following the close of the short period that results from the change in accounting period.

2.   The taxpayer must be able to show a substantial business purpose (e.g., a change to a tax year that coincides with the *natural business year*) before permission for the change is granted by the IRS.

3.   To establish the existence of a natural business year, the IRS applies an objective *gross receipts* test which requires that 25 percent of the entity's gross receipts for the 12-month period be realized in the final *two months* of the 12-month period for *three consecutive years*.

4.   The IRS usually establishes certain conditions that the taxpayer must accept if the approval for change is to be granted.

To operate on a fiscal year accounting basis, a taxpayer must keep his or her books and records based on that fiscal year. Since most individual taxpayers keep their personal financial records on a calendar year basis, it is easier to use a calendar year period. It would be virtually impossible for an individual to change to a fiscal year without justification. Such justification may exist, however, when the primary or sole source of income comes from self-employment or partnership income from a cyclical business.

D.   Taxable Periods of Less Than One Year
1.   A *short year* (or short period) is a period of less than 12 calendar months. A taxpayer may have a short year in the following situations.
a.   The first income tax return.
b.   The final income tax return.
c.   A change in the tax year.
2.   If a short period results from a change in the taxpayer's annual accounting period, the taxpayer is required to annualize.
3.   Once the taxable income is annualized, the tax is computed on an annualized basis and then converted to a short period tax.
4.   Rather than annualize the short period *income*, the taxpayer can elect to calculate the tax for a 12-month period beginning on the first day of the short period and then *allocate* the portion of the *tax* attributable to the short period.
5.   Special adjustments are required to be made by individuals when annualizing.
a.   Deductions must be itemized for the short period. The standard deduction is not allowed.
b.   Personal and dependency exemptions must be prorated.

E.   Mitigation of the Annual Accounting Period Concept -- Relief is provided by the tax law to mitigate harsh treatment resulting from the effects of an arbitrary accounting period and a progressive rate structure. Examples include the following.

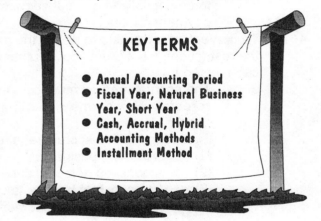

KEY TERMS

● Annual Accounting Period
● Fiscal Year, Natural Business Year, Short Year
● Cash, Accrual, Hybrid Accounting Methods
● Installment Method

1.   Net operating loss carryback and carryover rules.
2.   Restoration of amounts received under a claim of right -- If the *claim of right doctrine* requires income to be recognized on receipt of an amount, a later repayment will generally give rise to a deduction. In situations where the deduction for the amount previously included in income exceeds $3,000, the taxpayer may claim the deduction in the year that would produce the greater tax benefit (i.e., either the year of original receipt or the year of repayment).

II.   Accounting Methods
A.   Permissible Methods
1.   Taxable income must be computed using the method of accounting regularly used by the taxpayer, provided that the method *clearly reflects income*.
2.   Three permissible overall methods are allowed by the Code.
a.   The cash receipts and disbursements method.
b.   The accrual method.
c.   A hybrid method (a combination of cash and accrual).
3.   Special methods of accounting are also permitted or required in certain situations. The taxpayer *must* use the accrual method to report sales and cost of goods sold if inventories are an income-producing factor in business. Special methods are permitted for installment sales, for long-term construction contacts, and for farmers.

4.   A taxpayer who has more than one trade or business may use a different method of accounting for *each* trade or business activity.

5.   The IRS may require a taxpayer to change his method of accounting if that method does not clearly reflect income.

B.   Cash Receipts and Disbursements Method -- Cash Basis

1.   The popularity of this method can be largely attributed to its simplicity and flexibility. Income is recognized when the taxpayer actually or constructively receives cash or its equivalent. Deductions are generally permitted in the year of payment.

2.   An item of income must be included in income if it has been *constructively* received. An item has been constructively received if it has been made available to a taxpayer so that he or she could draw on it.

3.   While a deduction generally is allowed in the year of payment, there are exceptions to this rule.

   a.   A taxpayer must capitalize and amortize an asset over its useful life if the asset has a useful life that extends substantially beyond the tax year.

   b.   Many items that have been prepaid (e.g., rent, interest) are required to be capitalized and subsequently deducted in the years to which the payment relates.

4.   To prevent opportunities to distort the measurement of income, in addition to the restrictions mentioned above, other limitations apply in the use of the cash method.

   a.   The accrual method must be used by a corporation (other than an S corporation), a partnership with a corporate partner, and a tax shelter.

   b.   Exceptions to this accrual requirement apply in certain situations.

      (1)   A farming business.

      (2)   A qualified personal service corporation.

      (3)   An entity that is not a tax shelter whose average annual gross receipts for the most recent three-year period is $5 million or less.

5.   Although farming operations may generally use the cash method even though inventories normally are material to farming operations, exceptions to this treatment do exist. The cash method may not be used by certain farming corporations and limited partnerships. In addition, capitalization of costs is generally required when the preproduction period of certain assets (e.g., apple farmer) is greater than two years. A farmer may elect out of this capitalization requirement, but only if the alternative depreciation system is used for all farming property. Further, while the cost of purchasing an animal must be capitalized, the cost of raising an animal may be expensed by a cash basis farmer.

C.   Accrual Method

1.   All Events Test for Income -- Under the accrual method, an item of income is included in income for the year in which it is earned, regardless of when the income is collected. An item is earned when all events have occurred which fix the right to receive such income and when the amount to be received can be determined with reasonable accuracy.

2.   The amount of income to be recognized is determined by looking at the amount such taxpayer has a right to receive and not the value of the obligation.

3.   An expense is deductible in the year in which all events have occurred which determine the fact of the liability and the amount can be determined with

reasonable accuracy. Furthermore, in most circumstances economic performance must have occurred.

4. The economic performance test is waived and year-end accruals may be deducted if certain conditions are met.

5. Generally, the *all events* and *economic performance tests* will prevent the use of reserves that are frequently used in financial reporting. However, small banks are allowed to use a bad debt reserve. Furthermore, an accrual basis taxpayer in a service business is permitted to not accrue revenue that appears uncollectible based on experience.

D. Hybrid Method -- A hybrid method of accounting involves the use of more than one method. However, the hybrid method may be used only if the taxpayer's income is clearly reflected.

E. Change of Method

1. If a taxpayer desires to change a method of accounting, permission must generally be obtained from the IRS. A change in the *accounting method* encompasses a change of an *overall method* of accounting as well as the treatment of any material item of income or deduction.

2. A change in accounting method is distinguishable from the *correction of an error*. Errors are corrected by a taxpayer filing an amended return.

3. To change from the use of an *erroneous method* (an incorrect rule used consistently year-after-year) to a correct method, permission must be obtained from the IRS.

4. Certain adjustments may be required to items of income and expense to prevent a distortion of taxable income resulting from the change of an accounting method.

The taxpayer has nearly unlimited freedom to *choose* an accounting method on an initial tax return, but it often is quite difficult to get the IRS to approve a *change* from an existing method to another alternative. The tax advisor must be sure to provide full information as to the best long-term tax accounting methods available early in the taxpayer's life-cycle, so as to provide the most effective management of the resulting tax liabilities.

III. Special Accounting Methods

A. Installment Method -- The installment sale provisions, which provide an exception to the general rule of income recognition, allow the taxpayer to spread gain from an installment sale over the collection period. This method of accounting is an important tax planning tool because of tax deferral possibilities.

B. Eligibility and Calculations

1. The installment method applies only to *gains*, and not to losses, from the sale of property where the seller receives at least one payment *after* the year of sale. However, the method may not be used in the following cases.

   a. On gains from property held for the sale in the ordinary course of business.

   b. When depreciation recapture under §§ 1245 or 1250 applies.

   c. On gains from stocks or securities traded on established markets.

2. Nonelective aspect -- Regardless of the taxpayer's method of accounting, as a

general rule, sales *must* be reported by the installment method. A special election is required to report the gain by any other method.

3. The gain reported on each sale is computed by the following formula.

$$\frac{Total\ Gain}{Contract\ Price} \times Payments\ Received = \begin{array}{l}Recognized\ Gain \\ in\ Year\ of\ Payment\end{array}$$

   a. The *total gain* is the selling price reduced by selling expenses and the adjusted basis of the property.
   b. The *contract price* is the amount (excluding interest) the seller will ultimately collect from the buyer. This excludes the seller's liabilities that are assumed by the buyer.
   c. *Payments received* are the collections on the contract price received in the tax year.

4. If the sum of the seller's basis and selling expenses is less than the liabilities assumed by the buyer, the difference must be added to the contract price and to the payments (treated as *deemed payments*) received in the year of sale.

5. Gain attributable to *depreciation recapture* is recognized in the year of the sale, and the remaining gain may be recognized using the installment method.

6. Other items considered to be payments received in the year of sale include the following.
   a. Purchaser's evidence of indebtedness payable on demand and certain other readily tradable obligations.
   b. Purchaser's evidence of indebtedness secured by cash or its equivalent.

7. If a deferred payment contract for the sale of property with a selling price that is greater than $3,000 does not contain a reasonable interest rate (at least the federal rate), then an interest rate (the federal rate) is imputed. As a general rule, the buyer and seller must account for interest on the accrual basis. Several exceptions exist regarding the rate at which interest is imputed and the method of accounting for interest income and expense.

8. Restrictions and limitations apply to the use of the installment method in the case of related party sales of nondepreciable and depreciable property.

It is possible to structure a property sale so that the sale proceeds are deposited in an escrow account and then disbursed in a later year. The advantage to the seller of this arrangement is not only the security of knowing that the sale has been consummated, but the gain can be deferred for tax purposes using the installment method until the proceeds are made available to the former owner.

C. Disposition of Installment Obligations -- On the disposition of an installment obligation, the taxpayer generally must pay the tax on the portion of gross profit which was previously deferred.

D. Interest on Deferred Taxes -- In some situations, taxpayers are required to pay interest on taxes deferred through the use of the installment method.

E.   Electing Out of the Installment Method

    1.   A taxpayer can *elect not to use* the installment method by reporting on a timely filed return the gain computed by the taxpayer's usual method of accounting (cash or accrual).

    2.   Permission of the IRS is required to revoke an election not to use the installment method.

F.   Long-Term Contracts

    1.   A *long-term contract* is a building, installation, construction, or manufacturing contract that is entered into but not completed within the same tax year. Further, it is long-term *only* if the contract is to manufacture a *unique* item not normally carried in finished goods inventory or if the item normally requires more than 12 calendar months to complete.

    2.   The direct and indirect costs incurred on long-term contracts must be accumulated and allocated to individual contracts. In addition, mixed service costs must be allocated to production.

    3.   The accumulated costs are deducted when the revenue from a contract is recognized. Revenue generally is recognized using one of two methods.

        a.   The completed contract method.

        b.   The percentage of completion method.

    4.   The completed contract method may be used for home construction contracts and certain other real estate construction contracts.

    5.   Under the *completed contract method*, no revenue from the contract is recognized until the contract is completed and accepted by the customer. A taxpayer may not delay completion of a contract for the principal purpose of deferring tax.

    6.   Under the *percentage of completion method*, a portion of the gross contract price is included in income during each period as the contract is completed.

    7.   A *lookback* provision, which is applied in the year a contract is completed, provides that interest is paid to the taxpayer if there was an overpayment of taxes, and interest is payable by the taxpayer if there was an underpayment, because of the application of the percentage of completion method.

    8.   The advantage of the completed contract method over the percentage of completion method is that income is deferred.

TEST FOR SELF-EVALUATION -- CHAPTER 15

True or False

Indicate which of the following statements are true or false by circling the correct answer.

T   F   1.   The tax year for a new corporation begins on the day the corporation begins business.

T   F   2.   The request to change accounting periods is granted automatically by the IRS.

T   F   3.   Taxpayers are not required to annualize taxable income in every situation where a short year occurs.

T   F   4.   A taxpayer who has more than one trade or business may use a different method of accounting for each trade or business.

T   F   5.   For an accrual basis taxpayer, the amount of income recognized is determined by looking at the income such taxpayer has a right to receive and not the value of the obligation.

T   F   6.   Regardless of the taxpayer's method of accounting, as a general rule, eligible sales must be reported by the installment method.

T   F   7.   An accrual basis taxpayer may not deduct an expense until economic performance has occurred even though all events have occurred which determine the fact of a liability.

T   F   8.   The contract price is the selling price less the seller's liabilities that are assumed by the buyer.

T   F   9.   The installment method may be used to report a gain on the sale of depreciable property to a controlled entity.

T   F   10.   Because of the opportunity to defer the recognition of income, the preferred method of reporting long-term contracts is the percentage of completion method.

T   F   11.   A taxpayer may never use a taxable year that exceeds 12 calendar months.

T   F   12.   Generally, S corporations must adopt a calendar year; however, they may elect an otherwise impermissible year under certain conditions.

T   F   13.   The cash method of accounting can be used to measure sales and costs of goods sold even if inventories are material to a taxpayer's business.

T   F   14.   The use of the installment method cannot be used to report gains on property held for sale in the ordinary course of business.

T   F   15.   A personal service corporation generally must use a calendar year; however, a fiscal year can be elected under certain conditions.

Fill-in-the-Blanks

Complete the following statements with the appropriate word(s) or amount(s).

1. A taxpayer may be able to utilize one of the following methods to report revenues earned on long-term contracts: _____ or _____.

2. In an installment sale, the _____ is generally the amount (excluding interest) that will ultimately be collected from the buyer by the seller.

3. If the sum of the seller's basis and selling expenses in an installment sale is less than the liabilities assumed by the buyer, the difference must be _____ to the _____ and to the payment received in the year of the sale.

4. Generally, if a deferred payment contract does not provide a simple interest rate of at least _____, a rate equal to the federal rate is imputed.

5. Subject to exceptions, corporations, partnerships, trusts, and tax shelters may not use the _____ method of accounting.

6. Although exceptions exist, _____, _____, and _____ generally must adopt tax years that conform with their owners.

7. Generally, a taxable year cannot exceed _____ months.

8. A _____ provision requires the recalculation of annual profits reported on a contract accounted for by the percentage of completion method in the year a contract is completed.

9. On the disposition of depreciable property, ordinary income gain attributable to the _____ provisions under §§ 1245 and 1250 is ineligible for installment reporting.

10. The gift of an installment note _____ (will or will not) be treated as a taxable disposition by the donor.

11. In determining the tax year for a partnership, if the principal partners do not all have the same tax year and no majority of partners have the same tax year, the partnership must use a year that results in the _____ of income.

12. A _____ is a corporation whose shareholder-employees provide personal services such as medical, dental, legal, or accounting services.

13. The Code recognizes the following as generally permissible methods of accounting: the _____ method, the _____ method, or a _____ method.

14. The term _____ includes not only the overall method of accounting of the taxpayer but also the accounting treatment of any item.

15. Under the cash method, income is not recognized until the taxpayer actually receives, or _____ receives, cash or its _____.

Multiple Choice

Choose the best answer for each of the following questions.

_____ 1. In general, which of the following is not required to use the calendar year for tax purposes?
a. A partnership.
b. An S corporation.
c. A personal service corporation with annual gross receipts of $7,500,000.
d. An oil and gas tax shelter.
e. All of the above must use the calendar year of reporting for tax purposes, subject to exceptions.

_____ 2. Assume that a contractor has agreed to construct a building for you and the total contract amounts to $200,000. In the first year of construction, $125,000 of costs are incurred. At the time the contract is signed, the contractor estimates that the job will cost a total of $160,000. In the second year, the building is completed for an additional $15,000. If the contractor uses the percentage of completion method, how much income must be recognized in year 1?
a. $0.
b. $25,000.
c. $31,250.
d. $56,250.
e. None of the above.

_____ 3. Refer to the preceding problem. If the contractor qualified to utilize the completed contract method of accounting for costs, the income to be recognized in year 1 would be:
a. $0.
b. $25,000.
c. $32,000.
d. $60,000.
e. $75,000.

_____ 4. James sold the farmland on March 1 of the current year which he had been holding as an investment. He had originally acquired the property in 1986. James's basis on the date of sale is $10,000. The buyer agreed to assume the $15,000 mortgage on the property, and to make a $15,000 cash down payment, and to make annual payments beginning one year after the date of the sale on a 10-year $50,000 installment note which stipulates an appropriate rate of interest. What is the contract price for the above sale?
a. $50,000.
b. $65,000.
c. $70,000.
d. $80,000.
e. None of the above.

_____ 5. Refer to the preceding problem. What amount of gain must be recognized in the year of the sale?
a. $12,187.50.
b. $15,000.00.
c. $16,250.00.

       d. $20,000.00.

       e.   None of the above.

____ 6.   Refer to the preceding problem. What amount must be recognized as income in the year of the first installment payment?

       a. $4,062.50.

       b. $5,000.00.

       c. $10,000.00.

       d. $50,000.00.

       e.   Some other amount.

____ 7.   Certain restrictions apply to personal service corporations. For federal income tax purposes, which of the following statements concerning such entities is not true?

       a.   The corporation provides services through shareholder-employees.

       b.   Substantially all of the activities of the corporation must be the performance of personal services in certain fields.

       c.   A professional accounting or law corporation could be classified as personal service corporation.

       d.   In all cases, a personal service corporation must adopt a calendar year for tax reporting purposes.

____ 8.   In general, which of the following are permissible accounting methods?

       a.   The cash receipts and disbursements method.

       b.   The accrual method.

       c.   The hybrid method.

       d.   Any of the above can be permissible methods.

       e.   None of the above.

____ 9.   Bob sold land held for investment to Ted on March 1, 1995. Bob had acquired the land in 1986 for a cost of $10,000. Ted agreed to assume Bob's $2,000 mortgage on the land, to make a $2,000 down payment, and to make 10 annual payments of $1,000, beginning on March 1, 1996. Assuming no selling expenses were incurred, how much gain must Bob recognize in 1995?

       a. $571.

       b. $667.

       c. $2,000.

       d.   None of the above.

____ 10.   Assume the same facts as in the previous problem except that Bob's basis in the land was only $1,000. How much gain must Bob recognize in 1995?

       a. $2,000.

       b. $2,167.

       c. $3,000.

       d. $4,000.

       e.   None of the above.

____ 11.   White Corporation entered into a $400,000 construction contract that was to take two years to complete. Total costs were estimated to be $350,000. Costs incurred in the first year totaled $210,000. If White Corporation uses the percentage of completion method, how much income must it recognize in year 1 of the project?

       a. $0.

       b. $25,000.

c. $30,000.

d. $50,000.

e.   None of the above.

____ 12.   ABC Partnership is owned equally by Albert, Beth, and Chris. Albert and Beth each close their tax years on January 31 while Chris uses the calendar year to report income.   ABC's tax year must end on what date?

     a.   January 31.

     b.   December 31.

     c.   Determined based on the least aggregate deferral of income.

     d.   None of the above.

____ 13.   Partnerships and S Corporations may elect an otherwise impermissible year under which of the following conditions?

     a.   A business purpose for the year can be demonstrated.

     b.   The entity's year results in a deferral of not more than three months' income, and the entity agrees to make required tax payments.

     c.   The entity retains the same year as was used for the fiscal year ending in 1987, provided the entity agrees to make required tax payments.

     d.   All of the above.

     e.   None of the above.

____ 14.   A personal service corporation can elect a fiscal year if which of the following conditions are met?

     a.   A business purpose for the year can be demonstrated.

     b.   The entity's year results in a deferral of not more than three months' income, the corporation pays the shareholder-employee's salary during the portion of the calendar year after the close of the fiscal year, and the salary for that period is at least proportionate to the shareholder-employee's salary received for such fiscal year.

     c.   The entity retains the same year as was used for the fiscal year ending in 1987, provided that the corporation pays the shareholder-employee's salary during the portion of the calendar year after the close of the fiscal year, and the salary for that period is at least proportionate to the shareholder-employee's salary received for such fiscal year.

     d.   All of the above.

     e.   None of the above.

____ 15.   The accrual basis requirement has three exceptions, which does *not* include which of the following?

     a.   A farming business.

     b.   A defense contractor.

     c.   A qualified personal service corporation.

     d.   An entity that is not a tax shelter whose average annual gross receipts for the most recent three-year period are $5,000,000 or less.

     e.   More than one of the above is an exception.

Code Section Recognition

Several important sections of the Internal Revenue Code are described below. Indicate, by number, the appropriate Code section.

1. _____ The cash method of accounting is prohibited for tax purposes for certain types of taxpayers by this section.

2. _____ This section stipulates that an entity which elects an otherwise impermissible year under certain conditions must make required tax payments.

3. _____ Grants the IRS broad powers to determine whether the taxpayer's accounting method clearly reflects income.

Short Answer

1. Tanya, who is not a dealer, sells land for $10,000 (cash of $2,500 and $7,500 of notes payable to Tanya over the next three years). In addition, assume that an adequate rate of interest will be paid by the buyer. The property's adjusted basis is $8,000 on the date of disposition. Assuming Tanya does not elect out of the installment method, calculate the gain she must recognize over the four year period.

2. Jack, who is not a dealer, sells land for $10,000 (cash of $2,500 and $7,500 of notes payable to Jack over the next three years). In addition, assume that an adequate rate of interest will be paid by the buyer. The property's adjusted basis is $8,000 on the date of disposition and § 1245 depreciation recapture potential is $500. Assuming Jack does not elect out of the installment method, calculate the gain he must recognize over the four year period.

SOLUTIONS TO CHAPTER 15 QUESTIONS

True or False

1. F   The tax year begins on the day the corporation comes into existence.
2. F   The taxpayer must be able to establish a substantial business purpose for the change.
3. T
4. T
5. T
6. T
7. T
8. T
9. F
10. F   Deferral of income recognition is an advantage of the completed contract method.
11. F   If certain requirements are met, a taxpayer may elect to use an annual period that varies from 52 to 53 weeks.
12. T
13. F
14. T
15. T

Fill-in-the-Blanks

1. completed contract method, percentage of completion method
2. contract price
3. added, contract price
4. the federal rate
5. cash receipts and disbursements
6. partnerships, S corporations, and personal service corporations
7. 12
8. lookback
9. depreciation recapture
10. will
11. least aggregate deferral
12. personal service corporation
13. cash receipts and disbursements, accrual, hybrid
14. method of accounting
15. constructively, equivalent

Multiple Choice

1. e
2. c   Revenue [$200,000 X ($125,000/$160,000)] $156,250
        Less: Costs incurred on the contract   -125,000
                                                        $ 31,250
        See Example 33 in the text.
3. a   See discussion preceding Example 31 in the text.
4. c   Selling price $80,000
        Less: Mortgage assumption   -15,000

		Plus: Excess of mortgage over basis	5,000
		Contract price	$70,000

   See Example 23 in the text.

5. d $\dfrac{\$70,000}{\$70,000} \times \$20,000 = \$20,000$

   See Example 23 in the text.

6. b $\dfrac{\$70,000}{\$70,000} \times \$5,000 = \$5,000$

   See Example 23 in the text.

7. d A personal service corporation may adopt a fiscal year if it can persuade the IRS that a good business reason exists for having a non-calendar year.

8. d

9. b $667 = $4,000 (total gain) / $12,000 (contract price) X $2,000 (payments received in the current year). See Example 22 in the text.

10. c $3,000 = $13,000 (total gain) / $13,000 (contract price) X $3,000 (payments received in the current year). See Example 23 in the text.

11. c $30,000 = $210,000 (costs incurred this year) / $350,000 (total expected costs) X $50,000 (total expected income from the project). See Example 33 in the text.

12. a See Example 2 in the text.

13. d

14. d

15. b

Code Section Recognition

1. 448
2. 444
3. 446

Short Answer

1. Amount realized:

Cash		$ 2,500
Notes		7,500
Total amount realized		$10,000
Less: Adjusted basis		8,000
Total gain to be recognized		$ 2,000

  Year 1: $\dfrac{\$2,000 \text{ total gain}}{\$10,000 \text{ (contract price)}} \times \$2,500 = \quad \$625$

  Year 2: $\dfrac{\$2,000 \text{ total gain}}{\$10,000 \text{ (contract price)}} \times \$2,500 = \quad \$625$

  Year 3: $\dfrac{\$2,000 \text{ total gain}}{\$10,000 \text{ (contract price)}} \times \$2,500 = \quad \$625$

Year 4: <u>$2,000 total gain</u>
$10,000 (contract price)   X $2,500 = $625

2.   Amount realized:

Cash	$ 2,500
Notes	<u>7,500</u>
Total amount realized	$10,000
Less: Adjusted basis	<u>8,000</u>
Total gain to be recognized	$ <u>2,000</u>

Year 1: Recapture amount recognized in year of sale $500

<u>$2,000 total gain - $500</u>
$10,000 (contract price)   X $2,500 =   <u>375</u>

Total gain in year 1 $<u>875</u>

Year 2: <u>$2,000 total gain - $500</u>
$10,000 (contract price)   X $2,500 = $<u>375</u>

Year 3: <u>$2,000 total gain - $500</u>
$10,000 (contract price)   X $2,500 = $<u>375</u>

Year 4: <u>$2,000 total gain - $500</u>
$10,000 (contract price)   X $2,500 = $<u>375</u>

Chapter 16
Corporations: Introduction, Operating Rules, and Related Corporations

CHAPTER HIGHLIGHTS

Unlike partnerships and sole proprietorships, a corporation is a taxable entity, separate and distinct from its owners. Although the determination of gross income and many of the deductions are similar to those allowed to individuals, there are many important differences in the tax treatment of corporations. The most important of these is that a corporation is allowed only business-related deductions. Therefore, there is no concept of adjusted gross income for the corporation. Furthermore, most of the deductions from adjusted gross income are eliminated, since many of them are personal, rather than business, expenditures.

I. Taxation of Corporations
   A. The corporate income tax is levied upon a corporate entity, usually as defined by state law. Nonetheless, some non-corporate entities also are subject to the corporate income tax, if they are classified as "associations."
   B. A partnership is taxed as a corporation if it possesses three or more of the following characteristics.
       1. continuity of life;
       2. centralized management;
       3. limited liability; and,
       4. free transferability of ownership.
   C. A trust is taxed as a corporation if it is owned by a group of associates who operate the entity as a business or for a profit motive.
   D. Several states have adopted statutes allowing limited liability companies (LLCs) as a form of doing business. These entities allow limited liability for their owners. In addition, if the LLC has only one more of the corporate characteristics denoted under B. above, the IRS treats the LLC as a tax partnership. If the LLC has more than one of these characteristics, it likely is taxed as a C corporation.

II. The following are similarities between individual and corporate taxable income:
   A. The concepts of gross income, deductions, and exclusions are the same.

However, corporations have fewer exclusions from gross income than do individuals.

B. Both corporations and individuals exclude municipal bond interest from gross income.

C. Deductions include wages, rents, interest, taxes, and cost of goods sold.

D. Gross income includes rents, interest, dividends, sales proceeds, service income, and any recognized gain or loss on property transactions.

E. Both corporations and individuals defer recognized gain or loss on a like-kind exchange.

F. ACRS deductions are allowed, and the corresponding recapture provisions apply to both individuals and corporations. Corporations, however, have more recapture potential under § 1250 than do individuals.

G. Both corporations and individuals are disallowed losses on wash sales of securities and related party transactions.

H. Both individuals and certain corporations have a choice of taxable periods. However, personal service corporations and S corporations are subject to severe restrictions in the use of fiscal years.

I. Capital gains and losses are defined and netted in the same manner for corporations as they are for individuals.

J. Both corporations and individuals are subject to an alternative minimum tax.

III. The following are important differences between the taxation of individuals and corporations:

A. There is no concept of adjusted gross income for corporations. This means that there is no distinction between deductions for and from adjusted gross income for the corporation.

B. There are no standard deduction amounts or personal exemptions for corporations.

C. Corporations cannot use the credit for the elderly, the child care credit, or the earned income credit.

D. There is no exclusion of gain on the sale of a principal residence for corporations.

E. A corporation is not subject to any limitations on casualty loss deductions.

F. Organization expenses of a corporation are deductible if a timely election is made.
   1. The amortization period is sixty months or more, starting when the corporation begins to operate as a trade or business.
   2. The deductible organization expenses must be incurred by the end of the corporation's first taxable year.
   3. Deductible organization expenses include state registration fees, legal and accounting fees, and director and promotional fees.
   4. Expenses associated with obtaining debt, equity, or assets are not deductible as organization expenses.
   5. If the election is not made on a timely basis, organizational expenses cannot be deducted until the corporation ceases to do business or liquidates.

G. Capital gains and losses of a corporation are treated differently than are the capital gains and losses of an individual.
   1. A corporation cannot deduct any portion of net capital losses. Rather, the corporation's net capital losses must be offset against its net capital gains.
   2. Net capital losses can be carried back three years and forward five years. All carryovers are treated as short-term capital losses for a corporation. Carryovers do not lose their identity for non-corporate taxpayers.
   3. The highest tax rate on long-term capital gains of individuals is limited to 28%, as opposed to the 39.6% maximum rate applicable to ordinary income. For corporate taxpayers, capital gains are subject to the normal income tax rates.

H. The limitation on the deduction for charitable contributions also is different for a corporation.
   1. The deduction for charitable contributions is limited to ten percent of taxable income before the dividends-received deduction, charitable contributions, and carrybacks of NOLs and capital losses.
   2. Excess charitable contributions are carried forward for five years. The

current year's contributions must be deducted first, with excess contributions from previous years deducted in chronological order.

3. An accrual-basis corporation may deduct a charitable contribution in the current year, if the contribution is authorized by year-end and paid within 2½ months after the tax year.

I. A corporation receives a dividends-received deduction (DRD) for payments received from other US corporations.

1. This deduction is 100% of the total amount of the dividend received from a corporation that is a member of its controlled group.

2. For dividends received or accrued from a domestic corporation that is not a member of an affiliated group, the DRD percentage depends upon the ownership percentage that the recipient corporation holds in the corporation making the distribution.

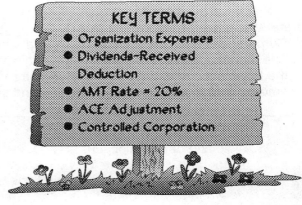

KEY TERMS
- Organization Expenses
- Dividends-Received Deduction
- AMT Rate = 20%
- ACE Adjustment
- Controlled Corporation

     a. If the percentage of ownership is less than 20%, the DRD percentage is 70%.

     b. If the percentage of ownership is 20% or more, the DRD percentage is 80%.

3. There is a limitation on the deduction for dividends received from a corporation that is not a member of a controlled group.

     a. The dividends-received deduction is limited to the DRD percentage of taxable income after charitable contributions, but without regard to any dividends-received deductions claimed; net operating carryovers or carrybacks; and, any capital loss carrybacks to the current year.

     b. The limit on the deduction to the DRD percentage of taxable income does not apply if [Taxable Income - DRD percentage of Dividends Received] creates or enlarges an NOL.

J. Net operating losses are treated differently for corporations than for individuals.

1. A corporation does not have any non-business deductions, so there are no adjustments to taxable income when the NOL is computed.

2. The NOL carryover includes the dividends-received deduction.

3. Corporations carry their NOLs back three years, then forward fifteen years.

K. The passive loss rules apply to individuals, closely held C corporations and personal service corporations.

1. A corporation is closely held if, at any time during the taxable year, more than 50% of the value of the corporation's outstanding stock is directly or indirectly owned by five or fewer individuals.

2. For purposes of the passive loss provisions, a corporation is classified as a personal service corporation if:

     a. the corporation's principal activity is the performance of personal services;

     b. such services are substantially performed by owner-employees; and

     c. more than ten percent of the stock (in value) is held by owner-employees.

3. For individuals and personal service corporations, the passive activity losses

cannot be offset against either active income or portfolio income.
4.   Closely held corporations may offset passive losses against active income, but not against portfolio income.

IV.   Corporate Income Tax
    A.   A corporation must file an income tax return, regardless of whether it has any taxable income.
    B.   The top corporate tax rate is 35%.
    C.   Qualified personal service corporations are subject to a flat 35% income tax rate on all taxable income.

V.   Corporate Alternative Minimum Tax (AMT)
    A.   Corporations also are subject to a 20% *alternative minimum tax (AMT)*.
    B.   The starting point in the computation of *alternative minimum taxable income (AMTI)* is the taxable income of the corporation before any net operating loss deduction. To this amount certain adjustments are added and subtracted and tax preferences are added.

The alternative minimum tax should be seen as a trial balloon that Congress is testing, mainly on equipment-intensive corporations, for adoption someday as the main tax system. The AMT has a broad base, with few deductions, other than for business expenditures, and very few credits to offset against it. As applied to individuals especially, it resembles a consumption tax.

    C.   To the extent that they do not excess 90% of AMTI, net operating losses are a negative adjustment.
    D.   The most common adjustments include:
        1.   A portion of accelerated depreciation on property placed in service after 1986.
        2.   Excess mining exploration and development costs.
        3.   The amount necessary to reflect the use of the completed contract method for contracts entered into after February 28, 1986.
        4.   The *adjusted current earnings (ACE)* adjustment is a means of capturing a measure of economic income within the AMT income base. The ACE adjustment equals 75% of the difference between AMTI (before NOLS or the ACE adjustment) and ACE. ACE is determined by making certain statutorily prescribed adjustments to AMTI and by borrowing certain E&P adjustments. Although ACE incorporates some E&P adjustments, it should not be confused with current E&P. The ACE adjustment can reduce AMTI, but only to the extent of prior positive ACE adjustments.
        5.   The deferred gain on installment sales made by dealers.
    E.   The most common tax preference items include:
        1.   Amortization of certified pollution control facilities.
        2.   The excess of accelerated depreciation over straight-line depreciation on real property placed in service before 1987.
        3.   Tax-exempt interest on private activity bonds.
        4.   Percentage depletion in excess of the property's basis.
        5.   Excess intangible drilling costs.
    F.   The alternative minimum tax is 20% of a corporation's AMTI that exceeds the exemption amount. The exemption amount of $40,000 is reduced by 25 percent of the amount by whic AMTI exceeds $150,000. As a result of the required reduction, no part of the exemption is available to a corporation that has AMTI of $310,000 or more.

G.   A minimum tax credit is available to mitigate the double tax that otherwise would result. The amount that may be carried forward as a credit is equal to the entire amount of the AMT liability.

H.   A corporation with a modified AMTI in excess of $2,000,000 also is subject to an environmental tax. This tax is equal to .12% of the excess of modified AMTI over $2,000,000.

I.   Modified AMTI generally is AMTI computed without regard to any AMT NOL and the environmental tax deduction.

VI.   Controlled Groups

A.   The Code includes the *controlled group* provisions, to discourage taxpayers from dividing Taxable Income amounts among a series of entities, thereby gaining additional tax rate discounts, exemptions, and other limitations.

B.   Members of a controlled group share a number of tax attributes. In each case, one nth of the attribute is available to the group member, where n is the number of corporations in the group. Any other allocation method may be used by the group, however, if all of the members consent to the method. Such consent methods may be changed every year without securing the IRS' permission.

        1.   The 15%, 25%, and 34% marginal income tax brackets.

        2.   The $150,000 or $250,000 accumulated earnings credit. See Chapter 20.

        3.   The $40,000 alternative minimum tax exemption.

        4.   The $2,000,000 environmental superfund tax exemption.

C.   A controlled group exists in two distinct forms.

        1.   The *brother-sister* controlled group exists where five or fewer individuals, trusts, or estates own at least eighty percent of the voting power or stock value of two or more corporations. In addition, the aggregate common ownership of the identified shareholders must exceed fifty percent of the voting power or stock value with respect to all of the corporations.

        2.   The *parent-subsidiary* controlled group exists when one corporation owns at least eighty percent of the voting power or stock value of another corporation.

VII.   Procedural Matters

A.   A corporation reports its tax liability on Form 1120, which is due 2½ months after the end of the tax year. For calendar year corporations, this date is March 15. A corporation must file a return regardless of whether it has either taxable income or tax liability.

B.   Form 1120-A may be used by active, US-based corporations with limited gross receipts (≤ $500,000), Total Income (≤ $500,000), and total assets (≤ $500,000).

C.   Quarterly estimated tax payments are required of the corporation, usually so that at least 100% percent of the year's tax liability is paid prior to the filing of the return.

D.   The corporation reconciles financial accounting income with Taxable Income on Schedule M-1 to the Form 1120. Schedule M-2 reconciles beginning and ending financial Retained Earnings.

TEST FOR SELF-EVALUATION - CHAPTER 16

True or False

Indicate which of the following statements are true or false by circling the correct answer.

T   F   1.   A trust can be subject to the corporate income tax.

T   **F**   2.   A corporation can deduct up to $3,000 in net capital losses in a year.

T   **F**   3.   A corporation can elect to deduct organization expenses over a period of four years or more.

T   **F**   4.   Corporations are permitted to deduct eighty percent of the dividends that are received from nonaffiliated domestic corporations.

T   **F**   5.   Excess corporate charitable contributions may be carried back three years and then carried forward five years.

T   **F**   6.   An accrual-basis corporation only can deduct charitable contributions in the year paid.

T   **F**   7.   A corporation files its annual tax return using Form 1140.   *1120*

T   F   8.   Active US-based corporations with modest income and asset amounts can file the corporate income tax return using a "short form."

T   F   9.   Schedule M-1 of the corporate return is used to reconcile financial net income with taxable income.

T   **F**   10.   A corporation that has AMTI of $200,000 is allowed an AMT exemption of $20,000.

T   F   11.   Closely held corporations may offset passive losses against active income, but not against portfolio income.

T   **F**   12.   An optimal tax strategy would be to split the corporation into separately incorporated divisions, each generating no more than $75,000 of Taxable Income each year.

T   **F**   13.   A personal service corporation with $100,000 of taxable income is subject to a $22,250 tax liability.

Fill-in-the-Blanks

Complete the following sentences with the appropriate word(s) or amount(s).

1.   An environmental tax equal to ___*.12*___ percent is imposed on the excess of _*modified AMTI*_ over _*2,000,000*_

2.   The AMT exemption of ___*40,000*___ is reduced by ___*25*___ percent of the amount by which AMTI exceeds ___*150,000*___.

3.   The maximum amount of the charitable contribution deduction for a corporation is ___*10*___% of

taxable income computed without regard to the __charitable contribution deduction__, __net oper. loss carryback__, __capital loss carryback__, and __dividends received deductions__.

4. The passive loss rules apply to __closely held__ C corporations and __personal service__ corporations.

5. The top corporate tax rate is __35__.

6. Net operating losses of a corporation can be carried back __3__ years and then forward __15__ years.

7. A corporation is allowed a dividends-received deduction of __100__% for dividends from a member of the recipient's controlled group, and either a __70__% or __80__% dividends-received deduction for dividends from any other domestic corporation.

8. The limitation on the dividends-received deduction is the applicable DRD percentage of taxable income, unless the corporation has a __net operating loss__ for the year.

9. A corporation can amortize its organization expenses over a period of __60 mos__ or more.

10. A corporation is subject to a __20__% alternative minimum tax.

11. There are two types of corporate controlled groups: the __brother/sister__ controlled group and the __parent-sub.__ controlled group.

12. Usually, the corporation must pay __100__% of its tax liability for the year by making __quarterly__ estimated payments.

13. On the Form 1120, a corporation reconciles accounting and taxable income amounts on Schedule __M-1__, and beginning and ending retained earnings balances on Schedule __M-2__.

14. The corporation __does not__ (does/does not) apply the concept of Adjusted Gross Income in computing its tax liability.

15. A business can be conducted in the form of a __sole prop.__, __C__ corporation, __S__ corporation, __limited liab.__ company, or __partnership__.

16. Excess __capital losses__ of a corporation are carried back three years and forward five years.

17. A corporation's excess charitable contributions are carried forward __5__ years.

18. A corporation files a tax return by the __15__ day of the __March__ month following the close of the tax year.

19. A corporation must make payments of __estimated__ tax unless its liability is expected to be less than __$500__.

Multiple Choice

Choose the best answer(s) for each of the following questions.

_____ 1. In computing taxable income, corporations and individuals are treated similarly with respect to the following item(s). More than one answer may be correct.
  a. limitation on charitable contributions.
  b. deduction of capital losses.

c.   deferral of recognized gain or loss on like-kind exchanges.

d.   deduction of net operating losses.

____ 2.   X Corporation has taxable income of $300,000. X's federal income tax liability is:

     a. $90,250.

     b. $100,250.

     c. $101,500.

     d. $102,000.

     e.   None of the above.

____ 3.   An accrual-basis corporation can deduct charitable contributions:

     a.   in the year paid only.

     b.   in the current year, if authorized by year-end and paid within 2½ months after the year-end.

     c.   in the year authorized, if paid at any time within the next taxable year.

     d.   only in the year in which they are both authorized and paid.

____ 4.   X Corporation has taxable income of $250,000 and AMTI of $405,000. X's tax liability is:

     a. $73,250.

     b. $80,750.

     c. $81,000.

     d. $85,000.

____ 5.   Depreciation recapture potential in a tax-free transfer of property to a corporation:

     a.   transfers to the corporation.

     b.   remains with the transferor-shareholder.

     c.   is triggered upon transfer of the assets to the corporation.

     d.   is lost forever upon transfer of the assets to the corporation.

____ 6.   In 19X9, a corporation received $10,000 of dividends from an unrelated domestic corporation in which it owned 40% of the stock. Other corporate taxable income was $5,000, and operating expenses were $8,000. The dividends-received deduction is:

     a. $4,900.

     b. $5,600.

     c. $7,000.

     d. $8,000.

     e. $10,000.

____ 7.   Same as 6, except that operating expenses are $6,000 and the recipient corporation owned 20% of the dividend-paying corporation.

     a. $6,300.

     b. $7,000.

     c. $7,200.

     d. $8,000.

     e. $10,000.

____ 8.   Same as 6, except that the recipient corporation owned 15% of the dividend-paying corporation.

     a. $4,900.

     b. $5,600.

     c. $7,000.

     d. $8,000.

     e. $10,000.

_____ 9.   The cash method of accounting is available to which of the following associations?
            More than one answer may be correct.
            a.   regular corporations.
            b.   S corporations.
            c.   corporations with average annual gross receipts of more than $5 million.
            d.   corporations engaged in the trade or business of manufacturing.

_____ 10.   R Corporation had operating income of $200,000, after deducting $12,000 for charitable
            contributions, but not including dividends of $20,000 received from nonaffiliated
            domestic corporations in which R Corporation held more than 20% ownership interest.
            How much is the base amount to which the percentage limitation should be applied in
            computing the maximum allowable deduction for contributions?
            a. $212,000.
            b. $215,000.
            c. $220,000.
            d. $232,000.

_____ 11.   For the year ended December 31, 19X9, Z Corporation had operating income of $9,500. In
            addition, Z had the following capital gains and losses.

                 Net short-term capital gain $1,000
                 Net long-term capital loss   9,000

            How much of the excess of net long-term capital loss over net short-term capital gain
            can Z offset against its 19X9 ordinary income?
            a. $0.
            b. $3,000.
            c. $3,500.
            d. $8,000.

_____ 12.   A Corporation files a consolidated return with its wholly-owned subsidiary, B
            Corporation. During 19X9, B paid a cash dividend of $10,000 to A. How much of this
            dividend is taxable on the 19X9 consolidated return?
            a. $0.
            b. $ 2,000.
            c. $ 3,000.
            d. $10,000.

_____ 13.   ABC Corporation has AMTI of $220,000. In computing ABC Corporation's AMT, what is
            ABC's exemption?
            a. $0.
            b. $17,500.
            c. $22,500.
            d. $40,000.

_____ 14.   X Corporation, a closely held C corporation has $400,000 of passive losses from a
            rental activity, $100,000 of active business income, and $200,000 of portfolio income.
            How much of the passive loss may X offset against its other income?
            a. $0.
            b. $100,000.
            c. $200,000.
            d. $300,000.
            e. $400,000.

_____ 15.   Same as 14., except X is a personal service corporation. How much of its passive loss may X offset against its other income?

a. $0.
b. $100,000.
c. $200,000.
d. $300,000.
e. $400,000.

____ 16.   B Corporation, a calendar year taxpayer, incurred the following items during 19X3. Compute B's charitable contribution deduction for the year.

Operating income	$300,000
Operating expenses	250,000
Dividend received (15% ownership)	70,000
Gift to charity, 9/14/X3	20,000

a. $5,100.
b. $7,100.
c. $12,000.
d. $20,000.

____ 17.   C Corporation, a calendar year taxpayer, incurred the following items during 19X3. Compute C's 19X3 net operating loss.

Operating income	$300,000
Operating expenses	350,000
Dividend received (30% ownership)	100,000

a. $30,000.
b. $50,000.
c. $20,000.
d.   None of the above. Specify_____.

Short Answer

1.   Assume that a corporation is created in 19X7. It contributes $10,000 in 19X7, and $12,000 in 19X8, to a qualifying charitable organization.

(a)   Compute the charitable contribution deduction, if other taxable income before the contribution = $(20,000) in 19X7.

(b)   Compute the charitable contribution deduction, if other taxable income before the contribution = $55,000 in 19X7 (computed after claiming a $5,000 dividends-received deduction and a $10,000 net operating loss deduction) and $130,000 in 19X8.

19X7 deduction =

Carryforward to 19X8 =

$$130,000 \times 10\% = 13,000$$

19X8 deduction =
$$12,000$$
$$1,000$$
$$\overline{13,000}$$

Carryforward to 19X9 = $3,000$

2. A Corporation receives $7,000 Dividend Income. Compute its taxable income if:

   (a) The dividend is from a subsidiary corporation. Other taxable income = $60,000.

   60,000

   (b) The dividend is from an unrelated domestic corporation in which the recipient corporation owns 50% of the paying corporation's stock. Other taxable income = $60,000.

   7,000 ×80% 5600   *60,000 7,000 <56007*

   (c) The dividend is from an unrelated domestic corporation in which the recipient corporation owns 15% of the paying corporation's stock. Other taxable income = $60,000.

   7,000 70% 4900   *60,000 7,000 <4,900>*

   (d) The dividend is from an unrelated domestic corporation in which the recipient corporation owns 50% of the paying corporation's stock. Other taxable income = $(500).

   6500 ×80% 5200 5600   *<500> 7000 <5200>*

   (e) The dividend is from an unrelated domestic corporation in which the recipient corporation owns 15% of the paying corporation's stock. Other taxable income = $(500).

   6500 70% 4550   *<500> 7000 <4550>*

   (f) The dividend is from an unrelated domestic corporation in which the recipient corporation owns 20% of the paying corporation's stock. Other taxable income = $(3,000).

   7,000 80% 5600   *<3000> 7000 <5600>*

3. A Corporation's Taxable Income = $200,000. Compute the federal corporate income tax, if A is NOT a member of any controlled group.

   61,250

680,000

4.   Compute A Corporation's tax liability if taxable income = $2,000,000, alternative minimum
      taxable income = $4,000,000, and modified AMTI = $4,200,000.

800,000

- 2,000,000

2,200,000
× 12%

2 640

800,640

5.   Compute A Corporation's ACE adjustment for each of the indicated years.

	1993	1994	1995	1996
Adjusted Current Earnings	$700,000	$400,000	$800,000	$600,000
Pre-ACE AMT Income	$500,000	$700,000	$700,000	$900,000
	200,000 × 75%	*(300000) × 75%*	*100,000 × 75%*	*(300000) × 75%*
ACE Adjustment	*150,000*	*150,000*	*75,000*	*45,000*

75,000
unused

6.   Z Corporation, a calendar year accrual basis entity, was formed on July 1, 19X3. The following
      items were incurred during 19X3. If Z makes a timely election to amortize qualifying
      organizational expenses, what is its 19X3 deduction?

Expenses of temporary directors	$2,500 ✓
Expenses of printing and selling stock certificates	1,000
Incorporation fee paid to state	500 ✓
Legal fees for drafting corporate charter and by-laws (paid 1/17/X4)	3,000 ✓

6,000 ÷ 5 = 1200 · ½ = 600

SOLUTIONS TO CHAPTER 16 QUESTIONS

True or False

1. T   A trust will be taxed as a corporation if it has more corporate than noncorporate characteristics.
2. F   A corporation's net capital losses must be offset against its net capital gains.
3. F   Organization expenses may be deducted over a period of 60 months or more.
4. F   The DRD percentage varies depending upon ownership percentage.
5. F   Contributions may be carried forward five years, but may not be carried back.
6. F   Such corporations may deduct contributions that are authorized by year end and paid within 2½ months of the next year.
7. F   Form 1120
8. T
9. T
10. F   The AMT exemption is $27,500 [$40,000 - 25%($200,000 - $150,000)].
11. T
12. F
13. F   The tax liability is $35,000 [35% x $100,000]. Personal service corporations are subject to a flat 35% rate of tax.

Fill-in-the-Blanks

1. 0.12, modified AMTI, $2,000,000
2. $40,000, 25, $150,000
3. 10, charitable contribution deduction, net operating loss carryback, capital loss carryback, dividends-received deduction
4. closely held, personal service
5. 35%
6. three, fifteen
7. 100, 70, 80
8. net operating loss
9. sixty months
10. twenty
11. brother/sister, parent/subsidiary
12. 100, quarterly
13. M-1, M-2
14. does not
15. sole proprietorship, C, S, limited liability, partnership
16. capital losses
17. five
18. fifteenth, third
19. estimated, $500

Multiple Choice

1. c
2. b   [(15% x $50,000) + (25% x $25,000) + (34% x $225,000) + 5%($300,000 - $100,000)] See Example 27 in the text.
3. b
4. c   The greater of: (1) 20% x $405,000 = $81,000, or (2) 15%(50,000) + 25%(25,000) + 34%($175,000) + 5%($250,000 - $100,000) = $80,750 See Example 27 in the text.
5. a

6. d   Since a DRD of $8,000 ($10,000 x 80%) creates a NOL, the DRD is not restricted by the taxable income limitation. See Example 24 in the text.

7. c   DRD is subject to the taxable income limitation: 80%($10,000 + $5,000 - $6,000) See Example 24 in the text.

8. a   DRD is subject to the taxable income limitation: 70%($10,000 + $5,000 - $8,000) See Example 24 in the text.

9. b

10. d   ($200,000 + $12,000 + $20,000) See Example 21 in the text.

11. a   Capital losses can only be used to offset capital gains. See Example 11 in the text.

12. a   The dividends received deduction is 100%.

13. c   [$40,000 - 25%($220,000 - $150,000)]

14. b   X may offset the passive loss against the $100,000 active business income, but may not offset the remainder against its portfolio income. See Example 15 in the text.

15. a   For a personal service corporation, passive losses cannot be offset against either active income or portfolio income.

16. c   The ten percent limitation applies to $120,000 [$300,000 - 250,000 + 70,000]. See Example 21 in the text.

17. a $300,000 - 350,000 + 100,000 - (80% x $100,000).   See Example 23 in the text.

Short Answer

1. (a) 19X7 Taxable Income = $(20,000).
         No deduction is allowed.
         19X7 carryforward = $10,000.

    (b) For purposes of the 10% limitation only, 19X7 Taxable Income = $70,000 ($55,000 taxable income + $5,000 DRD + $10,000 NOL deduction) before the contribution.
         19X7 deduction = 10% x $70,000 = $7,000.
         19X7 carryforward = $3,000.

         19X8 deduction limit = 10% x $130,000 = $13,000.
         Use first: 19X8 contribution = $12,000.
         Use second: 19X7 carryforward = $1,000.
         19X7 carryforward to 19X9 = $2,000.

    See Examples 21 and 22 in the text.

2. (a) Taxable Income: $60,000   Other Income
                              + 7,000   Dividend Income
                              - 7,000   100% Deduction
                              $60,000

    (b) Taxable Income: $60,000   Other Income
                              + 7,000   Dividend Income
                              - 5,600   80% Deduction = [80% x $7,000]
                              $61,400

    (c) Taxable Income: $60,000   Other Income
                              + 7,000   Dividend Income
                              - 4,900   70% Deduction = [70% x $7,000]
                              $62,100

    (d) Taxable Income: $ (500)   Other Income
                              + 7,000   Dividend Income

	- 5,200	Limitation on Deduction = [80%	
	$ 1,300	Taxable Income before DRD ($6,500)]	

(e)   Taxable Income: $ (500)   Other Income
                         + 7,000   Dividend Income
                         - 4,550   Limitation on Deduction = [70%
                         $ 1,950   Taxable Income before DRD ($6,500)]

(f)   The usual 80% deduction creates an NOL ($7,000 Dividend Income - $5,600 Dividends-Received Deduction - $3,000 Other Income = $1,600 NOL). So, there is no limitation on the deduction to 80% of Taxable Income.

       Taxable Income: $ (3,000)   Other Income
                          + 7,000   Dividend Income
                          - 5,600   80% Deduction = [80% x $7,000]
                          $ (1,600)

See Example 24 in the text.

3.   15% x $50,000   = $7,500
      25% x $25,000   =   6,250
      34% x $125,000   =   42,500
      5% x $100,000   =   5,000   Extra tax on taxable income > $100,000
                              $61,250

See Example 27 in the text.

4.   *Regular Tax Liability*
           15% x $50,000 $7,500
           25% x $25,000   6,250
           34% x $1,925,000   654,500
           Lesser of: $11,750 or 5% ($2,000,000 - $100,000)   11,750
                                                                    $680,000

      Alternative Minimum Tax
           20% x $4,000,000 $800,000
           Less Regular Tax   (680,000)   120,000

      Environmental Tax
           .12% x ($4,200,000 - $2,000,000)   2,640

      Total Tax Liability $802,640

5.

	1993	1994	1995	1996
Adjusted Current Earnings	$700,000	$400,000	$800,000	$600,000
Pre-ACE AMT Income	$500,000	$700,000	$700,000	$900,000

ACE Adjustment	.75 x ($700,000 - $500,000) = $150,000	.75 x ($400,000 - $700,000) = ($225,000) Limited to prior-year corresponding positive ACE adjustments = $150,000 There is no carryforward of this unused $75,000	.75 x ($800,000 - $700,000) = $75,000	.75 x ($600,000 - $900,000) = ($225,000) Limited to $75,000

6.   All expenses qualify except those related to printing and selling stock. The $2,000 paid in 19X4 is allowed -- the tax year in which the item is incurred dictates the tax treatment.

[$2,500 + 500 + 3,000] / 60 months = $100 deduction per month. For the six months in tax year 19X3, the deduction totals $600.

See Example 25 in the text.

CHAPTER 17
CORPORATIONS: ORGANIZATION AND CAPITAL STRUCTURE

CHAPTER HIGHLIGHTS

*T*he Code allows transfers of property to a corporation to be accomplished tax-free, when the person(s) transferring the property are in control of the corporation immediately after the transfer. This opportunity recognizes that (1) the taxpayer may have non-tax motivations for incorporating, and the tax system should remain neutral in this regard; and, (2) the transferor shareholder may not have any wherewithal to pay the resulting tax on the realized gain. In fact, when the new shareholder *receives* cash or other resources with which to pay the tax, a corresponding amount of the realized gain becomes recognized. The § 351 provisions afford a powerful means by which to defer the tax liability on appreciated business assets, but they also force a deferral of any realized loss on the assets in the hands of the transferor.

I.   Transfers to Controlled Corporations
    A.   Gain or loss is not recognized upon the transfer by one or more persons of property to a corporation, solely in exchange for stock in the corporation, if, immediately after the exchange, such persons are *in control* of the corporation. § 351(a)
        1.   The contribution of services does not qualify as property.
        2.   Persons *in control* must own at least eighty percent of the total combined voting power of all classes of stock entitled to vote, *and* eighty percent of the total number of shares of all other classes of stock of the corporation.
        3.   § 351 is available only to the extent that stock is received by the shareholder; the receipt of causes a portion of any realized gain to be recognized.
    B.   Loss is never recognized in a § 351 transaction. Gain, however, is recognized when cash or *boot*, (i.e., property other than stock) is received by the transferor-shareholder. The gain is limited to the lesser of the amount of cash and the fair market value of property (other than stock) received, or the realized gain. Securities received in a § 351 transaction are treated as *boot*.
    C.   The basis of stock received by a shareholder is the same as the basis of the property transferred, increased by any gain recognized, and decreased by boot received and liabilities assumed by the corporation. Often, this is referred to as a *substituted basis*.

D.   The basis of the property received by the corporation in the transfer is the same as the basis of the property in the hands of the transferor, increased by any gain recognized by the transferor. Often, this is referred to as a *carryover basis*.

E.   A shareholder who contributes both property and services can be used in meeting the 80% control test only if the value of the contributed assets is at least ten percent of the value of the contributed services.

F.   Liabilities assumed by the corporation in a § 351(a) transfer usually do not create recognized gain (§ 357). However, there are two exceptions to this rule.
   1.   If the sum of the liabilities assumed by the corporation exceeds the total of the transferor's adjusted basis in the property transferred, the excess is taxable to the transferor-shareholder.
   2.   If the primary purpose of the assumption of the liabilities is the avoidance of tax, or if there is no bona fide business purpose behind the exchange, the total liabilities assumed are treated as boot.

G.   There is no recapture of ACRS/MACRS deductions in a § 351 transfer, when there is no boot received. Instead, the recapture potential carries over to the corporation.

KEY TERMS
- §351 Tax-Favored Asset Transfer to Controlled Corporation
- Recognized Gain = Boot Received
- Carryover, Substituted Basis
- Thin Capitalization
- §1231 Look-Back Rule
- Depreciation Recapture

H.   § 351 is mandatory. The deferral procedures apply to both realized gains and losses.
   1.   If the taxpayer desires a deduction for a realized loss upon incorporation, one of the § 351 requirements should be violated, or the transfer of the loss assets should be delayed, so as to avoid the postponement of the deduction.
   2.   Similarly, if the contributing taxpayer desires a basis in the stock, or the recipient corporation desires a higher basis in the transferred assets, than is afforded under § 351, some means must be found to avoid the provision altogether.

I.   § 351 also applies to subsequent asset transfers to a corporation. Thus, unless other shareholders are inclined to make a similar contribution, the subsequent contribution of assets to the entity will trigger recognized gain or loss for the less-than-eighty-percent shareholder.

J.   See Exhibit 17-1 for a summary of the basis computations in the context of a § 351 exchange.

II.   Capital Structure of a Corporation
A.   The receipt of money or property in exchange for stock produces neither gain nor loss to the recipient corporation.

B.   Using debt in the capital structure may be advantageous.
   1.   Interest is deductible by the corporation.
   2.   Shareholders are not taxed on the repayment of debt. An investment in stock cannot be withdrawn tax-free when the corporation has Accumulated Earnings and Profits. See Chapter 18 in the text.

C.   Using debt in the capital structure also may be disadvantageous.
   1.   Securities received in a § 351 transaction are treated as boot. Accordingly, the recipient-shareholder is required to recognize gain to the extent of the lesser of boot received or gain realized.
   2.   In certain situations, the IRS will contend that debt is really an equity

interest and will deny the corporation a deduction for interest paid with respect to the debt.   Rather, the payments that are structured as interest will be reclassified as dividends, fully taxable to the recipient to the extent of the payor's Earnings and Profits (see Chapter 18), and non-deductible to the payor corporation.

    a.   This assertion often is made when the ratio of debt to outstanding equity is high, i.e., the corporation is *thinly capitalized*.

    b.   The Treasury has been unsuccessful in drafting Regulations that define thin capitalization and the situations under which interest payments are to be reclassified as dividends.

D.   The Tax Court has held that legal and banking costs incurred by a company in transacting a § 351 exchange are capital expenditures, rather than deductible expenses.

E.   The treatment of contributions to a corporation's capital by non-shareholders reflects the wherewithal to pay concept, as well.

    1.   When an asset other than cash is contributed to a corporation, the entity recognizes no gross income. However, the transferred asset is assigned a zero basis, so that cost recovery and other deductions cannot be claimed with respect to the asset.

    2.   If cash is received by a corporation as a contribution to capital from a non-shareholder, no gross income is recognized.

        a.   However, the basis of any property acquired with the money during a twelve-month period, beginning on the day the contribution was received, is reduced by the amount of the contribution. Thus, only additional investments of after-tax dollars by the corporation create basis in the asset.

        b.   The amount of any cash remaining after the expiration of the twelve-month period is used to reduce the basis of other corporate cost-recovery assets, relative to their relative bases.

            i.   The bases of depreciable assets are reduced first.

            ii.   The bases of amortizable and depletable assets then are reduced, respectively.

            iii.   The bases of all other non-cash assets are reduced last.

III.   **Investor Losses**

A.   Gain or loss on the worthlessness of stock or bonds depends upon whether the securities are capital assets.

    1.   If the stock or bonds were capital assets, a capital loss results on the last day of the tax year in which the assets became totally worthless.

    2.   If the stock or bonds were not capital assets, an ordinary loss is recognized on the day on which the assets became worthless.

B.   Bad debts must be classified as either business or nonbusiness in nature.

    1.   Business bad debts constitute ordinary losses, while nonbusiness bad debts are short-term capital losses.

    2.   Nonbusiness bad debts are deducted only upon total worthlessness.

    3.   All bad debts of a corporation are classified as business bad debts.

C.   Stock issued as § 1244 stock, upon worthlessness or a disposal at a loss, qualifies for ordinary loss treatment.

Knowing that almost nine of every ten new corporations fails within two years, the tax advisor should always counsel the new corporate client to issue stock under §1244. This is a "no-lose" technique, generally adding only one short paragraph to the corporate charter.

1. No more than $1,000,000 of stock can be issued under § 1244 by the corporation.
2. The ordinary loss is limited to $50,000 ($100,000 on a joint return) per tax year. Any excess loss is a capital loss.
3. Only the original holder of the shares can deduct an ordinary loss under § 1244.

Exhibit 17-1
BASIS COMPUTATIONS WHEN § 351 APPLIES

> **Adjusted Basis of Transferred Assets**
>
> **+ Gain Recognized on Exchange**
>
> **- Boot Received**
>
> **- Liabilities Transferred to Corporation**
>
> **BASIS OF STOCK RECEIVED BY SHAREHOLDER**
>
>
> **Adjusted Basis of Transferred Assets**
>
> **+ Gain Recognized on Exchange by Shareholder**
>
> **BASIS OF ASSET TO CORPORATION**

TEST FOR SELF-EVALUATION - CHAPTER 17

True or False

Indicate which of the following statements are true or false by circling the correct answer.

T   (F)   1.   The transfer of assets to a corporation by a controlling shareholder usually is a taxable event.

(T)   F   2.   A corporation generally takes a carryover basis in assets that it receives from a controlling shareholder.

T   (F)   3.   The provisions of § 351 apply when the shareholder receives stock in the entity, or when he or she receives the corporation's debt with a maturity date at least twenty years in the future.

T   (F)   4.   § 351 applies only to contributions that "start up" a new corporation.

(T)   F   5.   When the provisions of § 351 apply, the shareholder's realized gain is recognized to the extent of any boot that he or she receives as part of the exchange.

(T)   F   6.   "Boot" refers to any cash, securities, or property other than stock that is received from the controlled corporation.

T   (F)   7.   Liabilities always are considered boot for purposes of determining recognized gain in a § 351 transfer.

T   (F)   8.   Gain or loss never is recognized in a § 351 transfer.

T   (F)   9.   Depreciation recapture is recognized upon the incorporation of an entity, with respect to assets contributed in-kind by the new shareholders, even when § 351 is in effect.

T   (F)   10. When a corporation receives property from a non-shareholder, it recognizes gross income to the extent of the fair market value of the assets (net of any associated liabilities) on the contribution date.

(T)   F   11. Under the thin capitalization doctrine, the IRS can reclassify proper interest payments as dividends.

T   (F)   12. Legal costs incurred by a company in transacting a § 351 exchange are deductible.

T   (F)   13. When stock becomes worthless, a loss materializes on the day of worthlessness.

(T)   F   14. Nonbusiness bad debts may be deducted only upon total worthlessness.

T   (F)   15. Nonbusiness bad debts constitute long-term capital losses.

T   (F)   16. Any holder of § 1244 stock can qualify for ordinary loss treatment.

Fill-in-the-Blanks

Complete the following sentences with the appropriate word(s) or amount(s).

1. When § 351 applies, the shareholder recognizes gross income to the extent of any boot _received_ .

2. The contribution of a liability to a controlled corporation triggers gain recognition if the debt was not incurred for a _bona   fide   business_ purpose.

3. § 351 gain is triggered upon the receipt by the new shareholder of _any_ corporate debt of the entity.

4. The new shareholder's basis in the stock of a controlled corporation is _increased_ by any gain that he or she recognizes, and it is _decreased_ by the face amount of any debt that he or she transferred to the entity.

5. When a corporation receives non-cash property from a non-shareholder, it assigns a _0_ basis to the asset, and it recognizes _0_ gross income due to the contribution.

6. When a corporation reduces the basis of its existing assets, due to the expiration of the _12_ -month period after receiving cash from a non-shareholder, the bases are reduced according to their relative _basis_ on the date of the contribution.

7. A new shareholder recognizes gross income to the extent of the value of any _services_ that he or she performed as a condition to receiving the stock.

8. Gain or loss is not recognized on the transfer of property to a corporation solely in exchange for _stock_ if the person(s) transferring the property are _in control_ of the corporation immediately after the transfer.

9. When other property or money is received by the transferor in an otherwise tax-free transfer of property to a corporation, gain is recognized to the extent of the lesser of _boot received_ or _realized gain_ .

10. The basis of stock received in a tax-free transfer of property to a controlled corporation is the basis of the property transferred, increased by _gain recognized_ and decreased by _boot rec_ and _liab. assumed_ .

11. The basis of property received by a corporation in a § 351 transfer is the basis of the property prior to transfer _increased_ by gain recognized by the _transferor_ .

12. In a tax-free transfer of property to a controlled corporation, any _depreciation_ recapture potential carries over to the corporation.

Multiple Choice

Choose the best answer(s) for each of the following questions.

USE THE FOLLOWING INFORMATION FOR PROBLEMS 1-3.

Ann, a cash basis taxpayer, incorporates her sole proprietorship. She transfers the following items to New Corp. in exchange for 100% of the corporation's stock.

	Adjusted Basis	Fair Market Value
Cash	$5,000	$5,000
Land	50,000	80,000
Mortgage payable	70,000	70,000
(secured by the land)	∠ 15,000⟩	15 000

1. The gain recognized by Ann is:
    a. $0.
    b. $30,000.
    c. $10,000.
    d. $15,000.
    e. $20,000.

2. The basis of the land to New Corp. is:
    a. $50,000.
    b. $80,000.
    c. $65,000.
    d. $85,000.

3. The basis of the stock to Ann is:
    a. $0.
    b. $55,000.   55,000
    c. $70,000.   15,000
    d. $85,000.   ⟨70 0000⟩

USE THE FOLLOWING INFORMATION FOR PROBLEMS 4-6.

Babs, a cash basis taxpayer, incorporates her sole proprietorship. She transfers the following items to New Corp. in exchange for 100% of the corporation's stock.

	Adjusted Basis	Fair Market Value
Cash	$5,000	$5,000
Land	90,000	80,000
	95,000	85,000

4. The loss recognized by Babs is:
    a. $0.
    b. $5,000.
    c. $10,000.
    d. $15,000.
    e. $20,000.

5. The basis of the land to New Corp. is:
    a. $95,000.
    b. $90,000.
    c. $85,000.
    d. $80,000.

_____ 6.   The basis of the stock to Babs is:
       a. $0.
       b. $5,000.
       c. $80,000.
       d. $85,000.
       e. $90,000.
       (f.) $95,000.

USE THE FOLLOWING INFORMATION FOR PROBLEMS 7-9.

Char, a cash basis taxpayer, incorporates her sole proprietorship. She transfers the following items to New Corp. in exchange for 100% of the corporation's stock (value $185,000), and $40,000 in cash.

	Adjusted Basis	Fair Market Value
Cash	$5,000	$5,000
Land	90,000	190,000
Accounting Services Performed		30,000

_____ 7.   The gain recognized by Char is:
       a. $0.
       b. $30,000.
       c. $40,000.
       (d.) $70,000.
       e. $130,000.

_____ 8.   The basis of the land to New Corp. is:
       a. $0.
       b. $90,000.
       c. $130,000.
       (d.) $160,000.
       e. $190,000.

_____ 9.   The basis of the stock to Char is:
       a. $0.
       b. $95,000.
       (c.) $125,000.
       d. $165,000.
       e. $180,000.
       f. $225,000.

USE THE FOLLOWING INFORMATION FOR PROBLEMS 10-12.

Dot, a cash basis taxpayer, incorporates her sole proprietorship. She transfers the following items to New Corp. in exchange for 100% of the corporation's stock (value $185,000), and $40,000 in cash.

	Adjusted Basis	Fair Market Value
Cash	$5,000	$5,000
Land	200,000	220,000

_____ 10.   The gain recognized by Dot is:
       a. $0.
       (b.) $20,000.
       c. $25,000.

           d. $40,000.

_____   11.   The basis of the land to New Corp. is:
           a. $0.
           b. $200,000.
           c. $205,000.   *200,000*
         (d.) $220,000.   *20,000*
           e. $225,000.

_____   12.   The basis of the stock to Dot is:
           a. $0.
           b. $145,000.
           c. $180,000.   *205,000*
         (d.) $185,000.   *20,000*
           e. $200,000.   *(40,000)*
           f. $225,000.   *185,000*

USE THE FOLLOWING INFORMATION FOR PROBLEMS 13-14.

On January 2, 19X5, Old Corporation received some land and improvements, worth $1,000,000, from a suburb, as an incentive to locate a new plant in that locality.

_____   13.   How much gross income does Old recognize as a result of the receipt of the improved land?
         (a.) $0.
           b. $0 in 19X5, $1 million in 19X6 when the twelve-month period expires.
           c. $1 million in 19X5.
           d. $500,000 in 19X5, under the Economic Development Act (EDA).

_____   14.   What basis does Old take in the improved land?
         (a.) $0.
           b. $0, until 1/2/X6, when basis becomes $1 million.
           c. $1 million.
           d. $500,000, under the terms of the EDA.

_____   15.   Under which doctrine can the IRS reclassify an interest payment as a dividend?
         (a.)   Thin capitalization.
           b.   Form over substance.
           c.   Debt before equity.
           d.   Federal deficit recovery.
           e.   Owner reconciliation.

_____   16.   When § 351 is in effect, how is depreciation recapture treated?
           a.   All recapture potential is forgiven upon incorporation.
           b.   All recapture potential is transferred to the new corporation.
           c.   All recapture potential is assigned to the remaining business assets of the new shareholder.
         (d.)   Any recognized gain is made up of depreciation recapture; unrecognized recapture potential transfers to the new corporation.
           e.   Any depreciation recapture is taxed upon the incorporation, even though § 351 is in effect.

Code Section Recognition

Several important sections of the Internal Revenue Code are described below. Indicate, by number, the appropriate Code section.

1. __7701__ Includes the definition of a corporation.

2. __351__ Allows for the tax-free transfer of property to a controlled corporation.

3. __362__ Determines the corporation's basis in property transferred in a § 351 transaction.

4. __357__ Determines the consequences of contributing liabilities to a controlled corporation, in a tax-free transfer.

5. __358__ Determines the basis of stock or securities received in a tax-free transfer to a controlled corporation.

Short Answer

X Corporation is formed, via the following simultaneous activities.

| Taxpayer | RECEIVED | | | CONTRIBUTED | | Corporation Assumed Taxpayer Liabilities |
	% and Value of Only Class of Common Stock	Cash	One-Year Note, Fair Market Value	Asset to Corporation (Taxpayer's Basis)	Promoter Services (Fair Market Value)	
A	15% $15,000			$ 8,000		
B	15% $15,000			20,000		
C	10% $10,000	$20,000		5,000		
D	10% $10,000		$ 5,000	3,000		
E	10% $10,000	$ 6,000		15,000		
F	10% $10,000			6,000		$4,000
G	10% $10,000			7,000		8,000
H	10% $10,000			-0-	$10,000	
I	10% $10,000			5,000	500	

Complete the schedule below.

Taxpayer	Gain/Loss Realized	Gain/Loss Recognized	Basis of Assets to X	Basis of Stock to Taxpayer
A	7,000	Ø	8,000	8,000
B	(5,000)	Ø	20,000	20,000
C	25,000	20,000	25,000	5,000
D	12,000	5,000	8,000	3,000 - 3,000
E	1,000	1,000	16,000	15,000+1,000 -6,000 10,000
F	8,000	Ø	6,000	2,000
G	11,000	1,000	8,000	Ø
H	10,000	10,000	Ø	10,000
I	5,000	909	5,000	5,909

SOLUTIONS TO CHAPTER 17 QUESTIONS

True or False

1.	F
2.	T
3.	F
4.	F
5.	T
6.	T
7.	F	Liabilities usually do not result in gain recognition, although there are some exceptions to this rule.
8.	F	Gain may be recognized when boot is received by the transferor-shareholder.
9.	F
10.	F
11.	T
12.	F	The Tax Court has held that such costs are capital expenditures, rather than deductible expenses.
13.	F	The loss materializes on the last day of the tax year.
14.	T
15.	F	They are short-term capital losses.
16.	F	Only the original holder of the shares can claim an ordinary loss.

Fill-in-the-Blanks

1. received
2. bona fide business
3. any
4. increased, decreased
5. zero, zero
6. twelve, bases
7. services
8. stock, in control
9. boot received, realized gain
10. gain recognized, boot received, liabilities assumed
11. increased, transferor
12. depreciation

Multiple Choice

1. d ($70,000 Aggregate liabilities - $55,000 Aggregate basis) See Example 15 in the text.
2. c ($50,000 basis of transferor + $15,000 gain recognized by transferor) See Figure 17-2 in the text.
3. a ($55,000 basis of contributed property + $15,000 gain recognized - $70,000 liabilities assumed) See Figure 17-1 in the text.
4. a
5. b
6. f
7. d ($30,000 services + $40,000 boot received) Services meets the 10% test, so §351 applies
8. d ($90,000 basis in land + $70,000 gain recognized)
9. c ($95,000 basis in contributed property + $70,000 ain recognized - $40,000 boot

received)

10.	b	Lesser of boot received ($40,000) or realized gain ($20,000)
11.	d	($200,000 basis in land + $20,000 gain recognized)
12.	d	($205,000 basis in contributed property + $20,000 gain recognized - $40,000 boot received)
13.	a	
14.	a	
15.	a	
16.	d	

Code Section Recognition

1.	7701
2.	351
3.	362
4.	357
5.	358

Short Answer

Taxpayer	Gain/Loss Realized	Gain/Loss Recognized	Basis of Assets to X	Basis of Stock to Taxpayer
A	$ 7,000	$ 0	$ 8,000	$ 8,000
B	(5,000)	0	20,000	20,000
C	25,000	20,000	25,000	5,000
D	12,000	5,000	8,000	3,000
E	1,000	1,000 *	16,000	10,000
F	8,000	0	6,000	2,000
G	11,000	1,000 ◘	8,000	0
H	10,000	10,000 ◉	NONE ■	10,000
I	5,000	909 ●	5,000 ○	5,909

*   Limited to Gain Realized

◘   Liabilities in Excess of Basis

◉   Ordinary Service Income

■   Corporation generally is allowed a compensation deduction.

●   Ordinary Service Income is equal to Stock that was Issued for Services = $10,000 x $500/$5500 = $909

○   The basis of the contributed property is $5,000, and the corporation generally is allowed a compensation deduction of $909.

CHAPTER 18
CORPORATIONS: DISTRIBUTIONS NOT IN COMPLETE LIQUIDATION

CHAPTER HIGHLIGHTS

Generally, corporate distributions are considered dividend income, unless the shareholder can prove otherwise. A distribution is dividend income to the extent of the corporation's Current and Accumulated Earnings and Profits. Certain stock redemptions are treated as an exchange of stock for property and, therefore, result in capital gain. When a corporation distributes appreciated property in redemption of its stock or as a property dividend, the corporation must recognize gain to the extent of the unrealized appreciation.

I.   Taxable Dividends in General
    A.   Shareholders do not recognize taxable income when their corporation generates earnings. (Of course, the corporation pays a corporate income tax.)
    B.   The two most common sources of taxable income to shareholders are:
        1.   Capital gain, when shares of stock in the corporation are sold; and,
        2.   Dividend income, when a distribution is made from the corporation's Earnings and Profits. Such distributions constitute ordinary income.
    C.   The amount of the dividend income for both corporate and noncorporate shareholders is equal to the amount of money distributed plus the fair market value of any other property distributed, minus any corporate liabilities assumed by the shareholder. The shareholder's basis in the property is its FMV.

II.   Sources of Corporate Distributions - see Exhibit 18-1
    A.   First, distributions are from Current E&P.
        1.   This is ordinary income.
        2.   If there is more than one distribution during the year and total distributions are greater than Current E&P, Current E&P is allocated pro rata among the distributions, but Accumulated E&P is applied chronologically until it is exhausted.
    B.   Second, distributions are from Accumulated E&P.
        1.   This is ordinary income.

2.   If Current E&P for the entire year is less than zero, combine it with Accumulated E&P at the date of the distribution to determine whether the distribution is a dividend.

C.   Third, distributions are a return of the shareholder's capital. This produces no taxable income, but it reduces the basis of the shareholder's investment, but not below zero.

D.   Fourth, distributions will result in capital gain (or ordinary income if the stock is not a capital asset), to the extent of the remaining distribution.

E.   All distributions are presumed to be from current E&P, unless the parties can show otherwise.

III.   Computation of Corporate E&P

A.   Earnings and profits is the key to dividend treatment of corporate distributions. A distribution is taxed as a dividend only to the extent that the corporation making the distribution has E&P.

B.   Earnings and profits is not defined directly in the Code. However, it is a concept similar to "Net Receipts Available for Dividend Payments."

C.   Increases to E&P include:

1.   Annual taxable income.

2.   Non-taxable corporate receipts (e.g., tax-exempt interest income, proceeds of key-employee life insurance).

3.   Deduction of excess charitable contributions in succeeding taxable years (note that E&P was reduced in prior year - See D.4. below).

D.   Decreases to E&P include:

1.   Annual corporate deficit;

2.   Annual federal tax liability;

3.   Dividend distributions, which include: cash paid plus the corporation's basis in distributed property, increased by gain recognized on the distribution, net of liabilities assumed.

4.   Non-deductible corporate payments (e.g., premiums on key-employee life insurance, charitable contributions in excess of the ten percent limitation).

5.   Loss on sale between related parties.

6.   A dividend never may reduce E&P below zero; E&P may be reduced below zero only when the corporation generates a loss.

E.   Other items that affect E&P:

1.   The corporation may not reduce E&P for accelerated depreciation or accelerated ACRS/MACRS deductions. The corporation must use a straight-line recovery method for E&P purposes, with useful lives longer than those that apply in the ACRS/MACRS tables;

2.   The corporation increases E&P by the increase in cash surrender value of key-employee life insurance.

3.   A corporation's E&P is increased by the full amount of any deferred installment gain in the year of the sale.

4.   For E&P purposes, a corporation must use the percentage-of-completion method to account for long-term contracts.

5.   Intangible drilling costs and mineral exploration and development costs must be capitalized and amortized over a 60 month and 120 month period, respectively, for E&P purposes.

6.   Only cost depletion can reduce E&P.

F.   The adjusted current earnings (ACE) adjustment is a means of capturing a measure of economic income within the corporate AMT base. ACE incorporates certain E&P adjustments, but should not be confused with current E&P.

IV.   Consequences of a Property Dividend

A.   A corporation recognizes any realized gain (but not loss) when it distributes appreciated property as a dividend to its shareholders.

B. The corporation's E&P is reduced by the lesser of the E&P of the corporation or the new adjusted basis of the distributed property (i.e., basis of the property plus gain recognized by the distributing corporation) less the amount of any liability assumed by the shareholders.

C. E&P is increased by any gain recognized on distributed appreciated property.

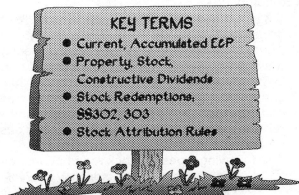

KEY TERMS
● Current, Accumulated E&P
● Property, Stock,
  Constructive Dividends
● Stock Redemptions,
  §§302, 303
● Stock Attribution Rules

D. The shareholder generally recognizes gross income from the dividend equal to the fair market value of the distributed assets. The shareholder's basis in the distributed property is the fair market value of the assets on the distribution date.

V. Constructive Dividends

A. Shareholders may receive dividend income even when no apparent distribution is made.

B. The IRS scrutinizes closely-held corporations (and others) for:
1. Unreasonable compensation paid to shareholder-employees;
2. Bargain sales of corporate assets to a shareholder;
3. Use of corporate assets at little or no cost to the shareholder (e.g., autos and recreation equipment);
4. Payment of shareholder debts by the corporation (e.g., loans, insurance premiums); and,
5. Sham loan or rental agreements between the corporation and the shareholder.

C. Constructive distributions possess the same tax attributes as actual distributions. Accordingly, constructive distributions result in a taxable dividend only to the extent of the distributing corporation's E&P.

VI. Stock Dividends

A. When a corporation distributes additional shares of stock to its current shareholders, generally no taxable income results to the shareholders. In addition, there is no reduction in the corporation's E&P. This result occurs if the shareholders' proportionate interests in the corporation do not change.

B. When a stock dividend is not taxable, a portion of the basis of the stock on which the dividend is distributed must be allocated to the stock dividend. In addition, the holding period of the stock received as a dividend includes the holding period of the formerly held stock.

C. Stock dividends may be taxable if the percent of the shareholder's ownership changes. When the stock dividend is taxable, the corporation treats the distribution the same as other taxable property dividends. The amount of the dividend equals the fair market value of the property received. A taxable stock dividend may arise:
1. Where the distribution is receivable in stock or other property;
2. Where some of the shareholders receive preferred stock and others receive common stock;
3. On distributions on preferred stock;
4. When some of the shareholders receive other property, and some receive additional stock; and,
5. When common stock shareholders receive convertible preferred stock.

D. The rules for determining taxability of stock rights are identical to those for determining taxability of stock dividends.

1.   If stock rights are not taxable and the value of the rights is less than 15% of the value of the formerly-held stock, the basis of the rights is zero unless the shareholder elects to allocate to the rights some of the basis in the formerly-held stock.

VII. Stock Redemptions - Exchange Treatment

A.   § 317 defines a stock redemption as an "*exchange*" of a corporation's stock for property.

B.   Thus, stock redemptions may result in recognition of long-term capital gain or loss to the shareholders. The maximum tax rate on capital gains of individual taxpayers is 28%, compared to the maximum rate of 39.6% on ordinary income. More importantly, a shareholder's recognized gain or loss is measured by the difference between the consideration received and the basis of the stock redeemed (i.e., the shareholder receives a tax-free recovery of his or her basis in the stock), rather than on the full amount of the consideration received.

C.   The following types of stock redemptions result in capital gain or loss treatment:
   1.   Distributions "*not essentially equivalent to a dividend*" [§ 302(b)(1)];
   2.   Distributions that are "*substantially disproportionate*" in terms of shareholder effect [§ 302(b)(2)];
   3.   Distributions in *complete termination* of a shareholder's interest [§ 302(b)(3)]; and,
   4.   Distributions to pay a *shareholder's death taxes* [§ 303].

D.   A corporation recognizes gain, to the extent of the appreciation, upon the distribution of appreciated property to its shareholders in redemption of their stock.

E.   In addition, gain is recognized on the redemption of stock with appreciated property to the extent of recapture under §§ 291(a), 1245, 1250, 1251, and 1252; corporate liabilities assumed by the distributor in excess of the corporation's basis for the asset; and, the excess of the fair market value over the corporation's basis in installment notes receivable that are distributed.

F.   Generally, a distribution is considered to be not essentially equivalent to a dividend [under § 302(b)(1)] when there has been a meaningful reduction of the shareholder's proportionate interest in the redeeming corporation. However, few objective tests exist to determine when a redemption qualifies as not essentially equivalent to a dividend.

G.   A stock redemption is treated as *substantially disproportionate* under § 302(b)(2) if two tests are met:
   1.   The shareholder owns **less than 50%** of the total combined voting power of all classes of the corporation's stock after the redemption; and,
   2.   The shareholder's interest, after the redemption, is **less than 80%** of the ownership interest that he or she held before the redemption.
   3.   For both of these tests, the stock attribution rules of § 318 apply.

H.   For purposes of the "complete termination" test of § 302(b)(3), the *family* stock attribution rules of § 318 are waived if the former shareholder does not have an interest in the corporation, other than as a creditor, for a ten-year period immediately after the redemption. Thus, with minor exceptions, he or she cannot be a shareholder, officer, employee, or director of the corporation over that period. In addition, the former shareholder must agree to notify the IRS of any acquisition of such stock within the ten-year period.

The effect of the stock redemption rules is that the shareholder must give up something of value, namely, control of the corporation, to obtain capital asset treatment on the exchange. This is a costly move by the shareholder in most cases, one in which the tax consequences are secondary to the effect on the dynamics and politics of the organization.

I.   Under § 303, the decedent's executor may redeem, at capital gains rates (i.e., receive *exchange treatment*), an amount of corporate stock equal to the sum of the shareholder decedent's state and federal death tax liabilities and funeral and administration expenses. The value of the stock in the decedent's gross estate must exceed 35% of the decedent's adjusted gross estate to qualify for this exception to the general rule. See Chapter 26.

J.   The stock attribution rules of § 318 treat the shareholder as if he or she also owned the shares that are owned by his or her:

     1.   Spouse, children, parents, and grandchildren;

     2.   Corporation, in which he or she owns at least 50% of the shares; and,

     3.   Partnership, estate, and trust, in any applicable percentage of control.

K.   The distributing corporation's Earnings and Profits are reduced as a result of a stock redemption, in an amount equal to the lesser of:

     1.   The redemption price; or,

     2.   The redeemed stock's ratable share of accumulated earnings and profits, i.e.,

$$E\&P \ \times \ \frac{\text{number of shares redeemed}}{\text{number of shares outstanding}}$$

L.   If §§ 302 and 303 do not apply, then the redemption generates dividend income to the shareholder (to the extent of the corporation's current and accumulated Earnings and Profits) in an amount equal to the cash and fair market value of the property received.

     1.   The shareholder's basis in the stock of the distributing corporation purportedly redeemed is applied, without increase or decrease, to the smaller number of shares retained.

     2.   If no shares are retained, and redemption treatment is denied as a result of the attribution rules, the basis in the stock of the distributing corporation purportedly redeemed flows to the shareholders from which there was attribution (i.e., stock that is *constructively* owned).

Exhibit 18-1
SOURCES OF CORPORATE DISTRIBUTIONS

Current Earnings and Profits*: **TAXABLE**.
Dividend income

Accumulated Earnings and Profits**: **TAXABLE**.
Dividend income

Return of Capital: **NONTAXABLE**; the
shareholder reduces the basis in the stock,
but not below zero

Capital Gain: **TAXABLE**, to the extent of
the amount of the distribution that remains

*If there is more than one distribution during the year AND total
distributions **exceed** Current E&P, allocate Current E&P pro rata among the
distributions, **BUT** apply Accumulated E&P chronologically, until it is

TEST FOR SELF-EVALUATION - CHAPTER 18

True or False

Indicate which of the following statements are true or false by circling the correct answer.

T   F   1.   When there is a deficit in accumulated E&P and a positive balance in current E&P, the two are netted on the date of a distribution in determining the taxability of the distribution to the shareholder.

T   F   2.   The distribution of appreciated property to a shareholder as a dividend results in an increase in E&P that is equal to the difference between the fair market value (FMV) and adjusted basis of the property and a decrease in E&P equal to the lesser of the Corporation's E&P or the FMV of the property.

T   F   3.   A distribution of appreciated property to a shareholder always results in the recognition of gain by the distributing corporation.

T   F   4.   When the IRS determines that a purported loan is actually a constructive dividend, the total amount of the loan will be taxable as dividend income, whether or not there is sufficient E&P to cover the distribution.

T   F   5.   A dividend may reduce E&P below zero.

T   F   6.   To qualify for exchange treatment under § 302(b)(3) (complete termination), the taxpayer must agree to notify the IRS of any acquisition of such stock within a ten-year period.

T   F   7.   A distribution of depreciated property to a shareholder generally results in the recognition of loss by the distributing corporation.

T   F   8.   Under § 303, the decedent's executor may redeem an unlimited amount of stock at capital gains rates.

T   F   9.   A shareholder can never recognize loss on the redemption of his or her stock.

T   F   10.   When there is more than one distribution during the year and total distributions exceed current E&P, current E&P is applied in chronological order beginning with the earliest distribution.

T   F   11.   A stock redemption reduces the corporation's E&P account in an amount not in excess of the ratable share of the corporation's E&P that is attributable to the stock redeemed.

T   F   12.   The alternative to a successful stock redemption is dividend treatment of the distribution under § 301.

Fill-in-the-Blanks

Complete the following statements with the appropriate word(s) or amount(s).

1.   Stock redemptions that qualify for exchange treatment include distributions that are: not essentially equivalent to a dividend; _____ _____; in _____ _____ of a shareholder's interest; and, distributions to pay a shareholder's _____ _____.

2.   Interest income on municipal bonds _____ E&P and federal income taxes paid _____ E&P.

3.   The two sources of taxable income to a shareholder are _____ _____ when stock is sold, and _____ _____ when a corporation distributes Current or Accumulated E&P.

4.   For a shareholder, the amount of a property dividend is the _____ _____ _____ of the asset distributed.

5.   The amount of dividend income that a shareholder must recognize is limited to the corporation's _____ _____ _____.

6.   When current E&P for the entire year is less than the total of all distributions for the year, it is _____ _____ to all distributions occurring during the year.

7.   Accumulated E&P will be applied _____ to the distributions during the year, when no current E&P remains.

8.   E&P represents the corporation's _____ ability to pay a dividend without impairing its _____.

9.   Stock dividends are not taxable if they are _____ _____ distributions of stock.

10.   When a shareholder-employee receives unreasonable compensation, the distributor corporation may be forced to treat a portion of the payment as a _____ _____.

11.   A stock redemption is treated as "substantially disproportionate" if, after the redemption, the shareholder owns less than _____ of the total combined voting power of the corporation's stock and owns less than _____ of the ownership that he or she held before the redemption.

12.   When there is a deficit in accumulated E&P and a positive amount in current E&P, distributions will be regarded as dividends to the extent of _____ E&P.

13.   If stock rights received as a distribution are not taxable and the value of the rights is less than _____ of the value of the old stock, the basis of the rights is _____, unless the shareholder elects otherwise.

14.   A corporation recognizes _____, but not _____, on the distribution of property to its shareholders.

Multiple Choice

Choose the best answer for each of the following questions.

USE THE FOLLOWING INFORMATION FOR QUESTIONS 1-2.

X Corporation distributes a property dividend to its two equal shareholders: Y, an individual, and Z, a corporation. Each receives property with a basis to the corporation of $3,000 and a fair market value of $10,000. The corporation's E&P before the distribution is $8,000.

_____   1.   How much of the distribution is treated as a dividend for Y and Z, respectively?
     a. $3,000, $3,000.
     b. $4,000, $4,000.
     c. $7,000, $7,000.
     d. $10,000, $10,000.

_____   2.   What is the balance of E&P after the distribution?
     a.   ($12,000).
     b. $0.
     c. $2,000.
     d. $8,000.

USE THE FOLLOWING INFORMATION FOR QUESTIONS 3-5.

Z Corporation made three distributions during the year, of $10,000 each, on April 1, May 30, and October 1. Current E&P for the year is $18,000. Accumulated E&P at the beginning of the year was $3,000.

_____   3.   How much of the October 1 distribution was from Current E&P?
     a. $0.
     b. $2,000.
     c. $6,000.
     d. $10,000.

_____   4.   How much of each of the April 1 and May 30 distributions were from Accumulated E&P?
     a. $1,000, $1,000.
     b. $2,000, $0.
     c. $2,000, $2,000.
     d. $3,000, $0.

_____   5.   How much of the April 1, May 30, and October 1 distributions constituted return of capital, if the shareholders' bases in the stock totaled $6,000 before the distributions?

	April 1	May 30	October 1
a.	$ 0	$ 2,000	$ 2,000
b.	$ 0	$ 0	$ 3,000
c.	$ 1,000	$ 4,000	$ 1,000
d.	$ 1,000	$ 4,000	$ 4,000

_____ 6.   X Corporation, a calendar-year taxpayer, had Accumulated E&P of $15,000 on January 1, 19X7. The following transactions took place during the year:

Taxable Income prior to taxable gains from property distributions	$5,000
Tax Liability	2,500
Excess of cost recovery over straight-line	1,000
Premium on Key-Employee life insurance	1,200
Increase in cash surrender value of Key-Employee life insurance	700
Tax-exempt interest	200
Proportionate stock dividend	3,000

What was the balance of X's current and accumulated E&P on December 31, 19X7?
a. $15,200.
b. $17,500.
c. $18,000.
d. $18,200.

USE THE FOLLOWING INFORMATION FOR QUESTIONS 7-8.

H and his wife W each own 50% of Z Corporation. H has all of his stock redeemed for $100,000. H's basis in the stock is $30,000. W's basis in her stock is $35,000. H remains the corporate vice-president after the redemption. Z's current and accumulated E&P totals $80,000.

_____ 7.   What is the tax treatment of the redemption to H?
a. $40,000 dividend income; $20,000 return of capital; $40,000 capital gain.
b. $80,000 capital gain; $20,000 return of capital.
c. $80,000 dividend income, $20,000 return of capital.
d. $100,000 dividend income.

_____ 8.   What is the basis of W's stock after redemption?
a. $0.
b. $35,000.
c. $45,000.
d. $55,000.

USE THE FOLLOWING INFORMATION FOR QUESTIONS 9-10.

Z Corporation had 100 shares of stock outstanding. A, B, and C owned 90, 7, and 3 shares, respectively.

_____ 9.   On December 31, 19X7, Z redeemed 75 of A's shares for $25,000. These shares had a basis of $20,000. Z's Accumulated E&P on 12-31-X7 was $200,000. The amount and nature of income recognized by A is:
a. $0 gain or loss.
b. $5,000, capital gain.
c. $25,000, dividend income.
d. $25,000, capital gain.

_____ 10. Assume instead that Z redeemed six shares of B's stock for $7,000. These shares had a basis of $9,000 to B. What is the amount and nature of income or loss to B?
   a. $0 gain or loss.
   b. $2,000 capital gain.
   c. $7,000 dividend income.
   d. $2,000 capital loss.

USE THE FOLLOWING INFORMATION FOR QUESTIONS 11-15.

P Corporation, which had earnings and profits of $100,000, distributed land to R as a dividend in-kind. P's adjusted basis in this land was $3,000. The land had a fair market value of $12,000 and was subject to a mortgage liability of $5,000, which was assumed by R.

_____ 11. How much was P's recognized gain on the distribution?
   a. $0.
   b. $2,000.
   c. $4,000.
   d. $9,000.

_____ 12. How much of the distribution was taxable to R as a dividend?
   a. $3,000.
   b. $4,000.
   c. $7,000.
   d. $9,000.
   e. $12,000.

_____ 13. R's basis in the land is:
   a. $3,000.
   b. $4,000.
   c. $7,000.
   d. $9,000.
   e. $12,000.

_____ 14. If P's E&P prior to the distribution had been $0, how much of the distribution would be taxable to R as a dividend?
   a. $0.
   b. $3,000.
   c. $7,000.
   d. $9,000.
   e. $12,000.

_____ 15. If P's E&P prior to the distribution had been $100,000, what is the balance of E&P after the distribution?
   a. $88,000.
   b. $93,000.
   c. $97,000.
   d. $102,000.
   e. None of the above.

USE THE FOLLOWING INFORMATION FOR QUESTIONS 16-18.

X Corporation, which has earnings and profits of $9,000, distributed land to C, an individual shareholder. X's basis in the land was $10,000 and, the land had a fair market value of $2,000.

_____ 16. What is the balance of E&P after the distribution?
     a.   ($3,000).
     b.   ($1,000).
     c. $0.
     d. $7,000.

_____ 17. As a result of the distribution, X Corporation recognizes:
     a. $0 gain or loss
     b. $1,000 loss.
     c. $7,000 loss.
     d. $8,000 loss.

_____ 18. How much of the distribution was taxable to C as a dividend?
     a. $0.
     b. $2,000.
     c. $8,000.
     d. $9,000.
     e. $10,000.

_____ 19. X Corporation has 200 shares of stock outstanding. Of these shares, 116 shares are owned by A and the remaining 84 shares are owned by other unrelated individuals. If X redeems 20 shares of A's shares, the redemption will qualify for exchange treatment because it qualifies as:
     a.   not essentially equivalent to a dividend.
     b.   substantially disproportionate.
     c.   complete termination.
     d.   redemption to pay death taxes.
     e.   the redemption does not qualify for exchange treatment.

Code Section Recognition

Several important sections of the Internal Revenue Code are listed below. Give a brief description of the provisions contained in each section.

1. 301 _____

2. 303 _____

3. 302(b)(2) _____

4. 302(b)(3) _____

5. 318 _____

Short Answer

1.   Indicate the effects on Y Corporation's E&P and taxable income for each of the items below.

Question	Item	Effect on Y Corporation's E&P	Gain/Loss Recognized by Y Corporation
a	Current-year Taxable Income = $65,000 *NOTE: This amount includes any gain/loss recognized by Y as a result of property distributions*		
b	Cash dividends paid = $6,000		
c	Federal income tax liability = $11,250		
d	Key-Employee Life Insurance: Premiums Paid = $3,000 Increase in cash surrender value = $1,400 Proceeds received, net of cash surrender value = $75,000		
e	Accelerated depreciation claimed = $8,000 [Straight-line amount = $5,000]		
f	Sale of Depreciable asset for $1,400: Original basis = $15,000 Accumulated MACRS deductions = $12,000 [Accumulated straight-line depreciation would be $8,500]		
g	Distribution of inventory: Fair market value $3,800 LIFO basis $1,000 FIFO basis would be $1,800		
h	Distribution of land: Fair market value $3,800 Basis $1,800		
i	Distribution of land: Fair market value $3,800 Basis $1,800 Subject to liability $1,300		

Question	Item	Effect on Y Corporation's E&P	Gain/Loss Recognized by Y Corporation

j	Distribution of land:
	    Fair market value $2,000
	    Basis $1,800
	    Subject to liability $2,300		

k	Distribution of land:
	    Fair market value $1,800
	    Basis $3,800		

l	Distribution of §1245 asset:
	
	    Fair market value $6,600
	
	    Original basis $7,200
	
	    Accumulated straight-line
	    depreciation $2,800		

2.   X Corporation has 400 shares of common stock outstanding. A and B, individuals, each own 200 shares. Each has a basis in the stock of $25,000. X's E&P = $700,000.

Indicate the tax treatment to A if:

A)   A and B are unrelated. X redeems 100 of A's shares for $20,000.

B)   A and B are sisters. X redeems 100 of A's shares for $20,000.

C)   A and B are spouses. X redeems 100 of A's shares for $20,000.

D)   A and B are spouses. X redeems 200 of A's shares for $40,000. A agrees not to have any financial or operating interest in X for the ten years immediately after the redemption.

E)   A and B are unrelated. X redeems 60 of A's shares for $12,000.

3.   Complete the chart below, indicating the proper tax treatment for each of the following
        independent fact situations. In each case, the shareholder is an individual taxpayer.

Question	Distributed Property	E&P Before Distribution	Amount of Dividend	Effect on E&P
a	Cash, $10,000	$25,000		
b	Cash, $10,000	$8,000		
c	Land, Basis $10,000 Fair market value $13,000	$30,000		
d	Land, Basis $10,000 Fair market value $3,000	$30,000		
e	Land, Basis $3,000 Fair market value $15,000	$0		

SOLUTIONS TO CHAPTER 18 QUESTIONS

True or False

1.   F   Only when there is a deficit in current E&P and a positive balance in accumulated E&P are the two netted on the date of distribution.

2.   T

3.   T

4.   F   In all situations, a distribution is dividend income only to the extent of the corporation's E&P.

5.   F   A dividend cannot reduce E&P below zero.

6.   F   The agreement waives the family attribution rules under § 318. Consequently, if no family members of the redeeming shareholder own stock in the corporation, the agreement need not be made to qualify for exchange treatment under § 302(b)(3).

7.   F   Loss is never recognized.

8.   F   Only the amount of corporate stock equal to the sum of the shareholder decedent's state and federal death tax liabilities and funeral and administration expenses may be redeemed at capital gains rates.

9.   F   A redemption is treated as sale, therefore both gains and losses may be recognized.

10.   F   Current E&P is allocated pro rata among the distributions.

11.   T   See Example 36 in the text.

12.   T

Fill-in-the-Blanks

1.   substantially disproportionate, complete termination, death taxes

2.   increases, decreases

3.   capital gain, dividend income

4.   fair market value

5.   earnings and profits

6.   allocated pro rata

7.   chronologically

8.   economic, capital

9.   pro rata

10.   constructive dividend

11.   50%, 80%

12.   current

13.   fifteen, zero

14.   gain, loss

Multiple Choice

1.   d   The dividend is equal to the fair market value of the property received. Note that the corporation has sufficient E&P. See Examples 11 and 12 in the text.

2.   c   ($8,000 + $7,000 + $7,000 - $20,000) See Examples 17 and 18 in the text.

3.   c   ($18,000 x $10,000/$30,000)

4.   d   Accumulated E&P is applied chronologically.

5.   c   Only $1,000 of the October distribution represents a return of capital ($6,000 basis - $1,000 April 1 return of capital - $4,000 May 30 return of capital = $1,000)

6.   d   ($15,000 + $5,000 - $2,500 + $1,000 - $1,200 + $700 + $200) A proportionate stock dividend is not taxable and, accordingly, E&P is not reduced for such distributions. See Concept Summary 18-1 in the text.

7.   c   Dividend income is limited to the corporation's E&P. H's basis in the shares is reduced by the remaining $20,000 of the distribution.

8.   c   The final $10,000 of H's basis is not "lost"; instead, it is assigned to W.

9.   c   A owns more than 50% of Z corporation after the redemption. See Examples 30 and 31 in the text.

10.   d   Exchange treatment means gains or losses must be recognized. The redemption qualifies as substantially disproportionate. See Examples 30 and 31 in the text.

11.   d   FMV - basis. See Example 15 in the text.

12.   c   ($12,000 - $5,000) See Example 11 in the text.

13.   e   Basis is equal to fair market value. See Example 11 in the text.

14.   c   E&P is increased by the gain recognized on the distribution. Thus, the dividend = $12,000 - $5,000 = $7,000 See Example 16 in the text.

15.   d   [$100,000 + $9,000 gain on distribution - $7,000 ($12,000 new property basis - $5,000 assumed mortgage)] See Example 18 in the text.

16.   c   Distributions can not reduce E&P below zero. See Example 19 in the text.

17.   a   Loss is not recognized on a property distribution. See Example 14 in the text.

18.   b   The dividend is equal to the FMV of the distributed property. See Example 12 in the text.

19.   e   Answer a is incorrect because A continues to have voting control. See Example 27 in the text. Answer b is incorrect because neither the 50% nor the 80% tests are met. Answer c is incorrect because A continues to own stock after the redemption. Answer d is incorrect because A did not die.

Code Section Recognition

1.   Determines the tax treatment of dividends.
2.   Exchange treatment for stock redemptions in a closely-held corporation, to pay death taxes.
3.   Exchange treatment for substantially disproportionate redemptions of corporate stock.
4.   Exchange treatment for redemptions of stock that are complete terminations of the shareholder's corporate interest.
5.   Attribution rules for constructive stock ownership.

Short Answer

1.

Question	Item	Effect on Y Corporation's E&P	Gain/Loss Recognized by Y Corporation
a	Current-year Taxable Income = $65,000 *NOTE: This amount includes any gain/loss recognized by Y as a result of property distributions*	+$65,000	
b	Cash dividends paid = $6,000	-$6,000	
c	Federal income tax liability = $11,250	-$11,250	
d	Key-Employee Life Insurance: 　　Premiums Paid = $3,000 　　Increase in cash surrender value = $1,400 　　Proceeds received, net of cash surrender value = $75,000	-$3,000 +$1,400 +$75,000	
e	Accelerated depreciation claimed = $8,000 [Straight-line amount = $5,000]	+$3,000	
f	Sale of Depreciable asset for $1,400: 　　Original basis = $15,000 　　Accumulated MACRS deductions = $12,000 　　[Accumulated straight-line depreciation would be $8,500]	Taxable Income includes Recognized Loss $1,600 ($1,400 Amount Realized - 3,000 Basis) E&P should show Recognized Loss $5,100 ($1,400 - 6,500 E&P Basis Thus, the necessary adjustment is: -$3,500	
g	Distribution of inventory: 　　Fair market value $3,800 　　LIFO basis $1,000 　　FIFO basis would be $1,800	-$3,800	$2,800 gain recognized
h	Distribution of land: 　　Fair market value $3,800 　　Basis $1,800	-$3,800	$2,000 gain recognized

Question	Item	Effect on Y Corporation's E&P	Gain/Loss Recognized by Y Corporation

i	Distribution of land:
	    Fair market value $3,800
	    Basis $1,800
	    Subject to liability $1,300
		-$2,500	$2,000 gain recognized

j	Distribution of land:
	    Fair market value $2,000
	    Basis $1,800
	    Subject to liability $2,300
		-$0	$500 gain recognized

k	Distribution of land:
	    Fair market value $1,800
	    Basis $3,800
		-$3,800	$0 loss recognized

l	Distribution of §1245 asset: Fair market value $6,600 Original basis $7,200 Accumulated straight-line depreciation $2,800	-$6,600	$2,200 gain recognized

2.   A)   <u>50% test</u>:   After the redemption, A owns 100/300 of the shares = 33%.

         TEST PASSED

         <u>80% test</u>:   After the redemption, A owns 33% of the shares.
                       Before the redemption, A owned 200/400 of the shares = 50%;

                       50% x 80% = <u>40%</u> > 33%

         TEST PASSED

         Thus, A has capital gain = $20,000 - $12,500 (basis) = <u>$7,500.</u>

See Example 30 in the text.

B)   Same as A). Stock attribution rules do NOT apply to siblings. Thus, A has capital gain = <u>$7,500</u>.

C)   Stock attribution rules DO apply to spouses. A is treated as owning 100% of the stock in X before and after the redemption. ***50% and 80% TESTS FAILED.***

         Thus, A has dividend income = $20,000.
         A's basis of $25,000 now applies to the remaining 100 shares.

See Examples 25 and 31 in the text.

D)   Under the stock attribution rules, A is treated as owning 100% of the stock in X before and after the redemption.

But § 302(b)(3) applies -- Complete termination of A's interest in X. Assuming that the ten-year "cooling off" period is met, the family attribution rules are waived.

A is treated as owning 0% of the X stock after the redemption. **50% and 80% TESTS PASSED.**

Thus, A has capital gain = $40,000 - $25,000 = $15,000.

See Examples 31 and 32 in the text.

E)   50% test: After the redemption, A owns 140/340 of the shares = 41%.

TEST PASSED

80% test: After the redemption, A owns 41% of the shares.
                 Before the redemption, A owned 200/400 of the shares = 50%;

                 50% x 80% = 40% < 41%

TEST FAILED

Thus, A has dividend income = $12,000.
A's basis of $25,000 now applies to the remaining 140 shares.

See Examples 30 and 31 in the text.

3.

Question	Distributed Property	E&P Before Distribution	Amount of Dividend	Effect on E&P
a	Cash, $10,000	$25,000	$10,000	-$10,000
b	Cash, $10,000	$8,000	$8,000	-$8,000
c	Land, Basis $10,000 Fair market value $13,000	$30,000	$13,000	+$3,000 gain recognized on distribution -$13,000 FMV of distributed property
d	Land, Basis $10,000 Fair market value $3,000	$30,000	$3,000	-$10,000 [$0 loss recognized on distribution]
e	Land, Basis $3,000 Fair market value $15,000	$0	$12,000	+$12,000 gain recognized on distribution -$12,000 [a dividend cannot reduce E&P below zero]

CHAPTER 19
CORPORATIONS: DISTRIBUTIONS IN COMPLETE LIQUIDATION AND AN OVERVIEW OF CORPORATE REORGANIZATIONS

CHAPTER HIGHLIGHTS

 complete liquidation of a corporation generally is afforded exchange treatment in the same manner as a stock redemption. In this regard, a shareholder recognizes gain or loss equal to the difference between the basis of his or her stock and the liquidation proceeds received. Generally, the gain or loss recognized by the shareholder is a capital gain or loss. The corporation itself also recognizes gain or loss upon the distribution of its non-cash assets in a complete liquidation. However, a parent corporation that meets certain requirements can postpone recognition of gain realized upon the liquidation of a subsidiary.

The Code provides seven different types of tax-free reorganizations. Ordinarily, no gain or loss is recognized by either the acquiring or the acquired corporations who are parties to the reorganization. In addition, no gain or loss typically is recognized to the security holders of the various corporations involved in a tax-free reorganization in the exchange of their stock and securities except when they receive cash or other consideration in addition to stock and securities.

I.   Effect on the Corporation - Complete Liquidation
    A.   Generally, corporations recognize gain or loss when distributing assets *in-kind*, or when selling assets and distributing the proceeds in complete liquidation. In determining the gain or loss on an in-kind distribution, the property is treated as though it is sold to the distributee at fair market value.
    B.   A corporation can deduct the general expenses of a liquidation. Specific liquidation expenses are offset against the selling price of the assets and thereby decrease any recognized gain or increase any recognized loss on the sale.
    C.   For the corporation undergoing liquidation, E&P has no tax effect on the gain or loss to be recognized by the shareholders.

II. Limitation on the Recognition of Losses
    A.   As a general rule, losses on the distribution of property in a complete liquidation are recognized. Exceptions to this rule, however, are provided for distributions to

related parties and certain distributions of built-in loss property.

    1.   No loss can be recognized by a liquidating corporation on any property distributed to a shareholder who, directly or indirectly, owns more than fifty percent of the corporation's stock, unless the loss property is distributed to all shareholders on a pro rata basis **and** the property was not acquired by the liquidating corporation in a § 351 transaction or as a capital contribution within five years before the distribution date.

    2.   No loss can be recognized by a liquidating corporation on distributed property that it acquired shortly before the adoption of the liquidation plan.

        a.   Only the amount of any built-in loss is disallowed.

        b.   The disallowance applies only to assets acquired by the corporation as a contribution to capital (eg § 351).

        c.   Any built-in loss property contributed within two years of the adoption of the liquidation plan is presumed to have a tax avoidance motive and is disallowed, subject to a taxpayer rebuttal.

  B.   § 267 does not apply to any loss of a distributee or of a distributing corporation in the case of a distribution in complete liquidation; however, such losses may be denied under other provisions.

III.   Effect on the Shareholder - Complete Liquidation

  A.   The general rule under Code § 331 requires exchange treatment for the shareholder in a liquidation. In essence, the shareholders are treated as having sold their stock to the corporation being liquidated.

    1.   Gain or loss recognized is equal to the fair market value of the assets received, net of any corporate liabilities assumed [Amount Realized] less the basis of the shareholder's stock in the corporation. Usually, the gain or loss is capital in nature.

Because a liquidation can generate taxable income at both the corporation and shareholder level, it can be an extremely expensive transaction. In the past, liquidations produced tax-free gains at the corporate level, but the 1986 tax act created the double taxation problem that corporate entities now must live with. This consequence alone may drive investors to the S corporation, partnership, or limited liability company form of conducting the business.

    2.   The shareholder's gain on the receipt of installment notes acquired by a liquidating corporation on the sale of its assets may be deferred until the notes are collected. Special rules apply if the installment obligations arise from sales between certain related parties.

    3.   Basis to the shareholder for assets received in the liquidation is equal to the assets' fair market value on the distribution date.

  B.   § 332 provides for the nonrecognition of gain or loss to a parent corporation on a complete liquidation of a subsidiary. If the conditions of § 332 are met, the application of its provisions are mandatory.

    1.   Except for specific grandfathered acquisition provisions, the parent must directly own at least eighty percent of the voting stock and eighty percent of the total value of the subsidiary's stock.

    2.   The subsidiary must distribute all of its property in complete redemption of all of its stock, within the taxable year or within three years from the close of the year in which a plan was adopted and the first distribution made.

3.   The subsidiary must be solvent and the parent must receive at least partial payment for its stock in the subsidiary.

4.   If a series of distributions occurs in the liquidation of a subsidiary, § 332 applies only if the parent owns at least eighty percent of the subsidiary stock on the date the plan is adopted and at all times thereafter.

5.   Under § 334(b)(1), property received by a parent corporation has the same basis as it had in the hands of the subsidiary. The parent's basis in the stock of the liquidated subsidiary disappears. In any case in which gain or loss is recognized by the liquidating corporation with respect to such property, the basis of the property in the hands of the parent is the property's FMV.

6.   Because the parent corporation takes the subsidiary's basis in its assets, the carryover limitations of § 381 apply.

7.   A distribution to a minority shareholder in a § 332 liquidation is treated in the same manner as one made pursuant to a nonliquidating redemption. Accordingly, the subsidiary must recognize gain, but not loss, on distributions to minority shareholders. The minority shareholder is subject to the § 381 carryover limits.

8.   § 337 provides that gain or loss generally is not recognized by the subsidiary upon the transfer of appreciated property to its parent in satisfaction of a debt. However, the parent must recognize a gain or loss.

C.   § 338 allows an acquiring corporation to make an irrevocable election to treat the acquisition of a subsidiary's stock as a purchase of the assets of the acquired corporation. Therefore, the parent corporation can assign a basis to the assets of its subsidiary equal to its cost of the acquired stock. However, several conditions must be satisfied before a corporation can make a § 338 election.

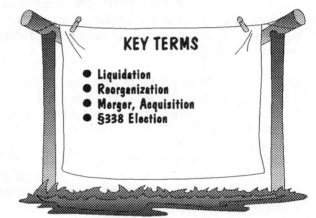

KEY TERMS

- Liquidation
- Reorganization
- Merger, Acquisition
- §338 Election

1.   An irrevocable election must be made by the parent corporation by the fifteenth day of the ninth month following the acquisition month. In certain cases, the IRS may impose the election on the taxpayer.

2.   The parent corporation must acquire eighty percent control of the corporation within twelve months.

3.   The stock acquired in the requisite time period (i.e., twelve months) must be acquired in a taxable transaction (i.e., § 351 and other non-recognition sections will not qualify).

D.   When a § 338 election is made, the following results transpire.

1.   The target corporation (i.e., the purchased subsidiary) is treated as if it had sold its assets to the parent. Generally, the target corporation recognizes gain and loss on the deemed sale.

2.   The subsidiary's assets receive a new stepped-up basis. The stepped-up basis of the subsidiary's assets when a § 338 election is in effect is allocated among the assets by use of the residual method.

3.   The target corporation is treated as a new corporation. Accounting periods and methods may be elected anew.

4.   The tax attributes of the acquired subsidiary are extinguished (i.e., no carryover of NOLs, capital losses, or E&P).

IV.   Corporate Reorganizations

     A.   The Code provides the following seven types of corporate reorganizations that qualify as nontaxable exchanges.

         1.   Type A - a statutory merger or consolidation.

         2.   Type B - the acquisition by a corporation, in exchange solely for all or part of its or its parent's voting stock, of another corporation if, immediately after the acquisition, the acquiring corporation has control of the other corporation.

         3.   Type C - the acquisition by a corporation, in exchange solely for all or part of its or its parent's voting stock, of substantially all of the assets of another corporation. The acquired corporation must distribute to its shareholders the stock, securities and other property it receives in the reorganization and any of its own property.

         4.   Type D - a transfer by a corporation of all or part of its assets to another corporation if, immediately after the transfer, the transferor or one or more of the shareholders, or any combination thereof, is in control of the corporation to which the assets are transferred.

         5.   Type E - a recapitalization.

         6.   Type F - a mere change in identity, form, or place of organization.

         7.   Type G - a transfer by a corporation of all or part of its assets to another corporation in a bankruptcy or receivership proceeding.

     B.   To qualify as a tax-free reorganization, the transaction also must generally satisfy the sound business purpose, continuity of interest, and continuity of business enterprise doctrines.

VI.   Effect on the Corporation - Reorganizations

     A.   Generally, neither the acquiring nor the acquired corporation recognizes gain or loss in a corporate reorganization. However, gain is recognized by the acquired corporation to the extent that it receives cash and other property and does not distribute such property.

     B.   Property that the acquiring corporation receives from the acquired corporation retains the basis it had in the hands of the acquired corporation, increased by the gain, if any, recognized by the acquired corporation on the transfer.

VII.   Effect on the Shareholder - Reorganizations

     A.   Certain corporate reorganizations, governed by §§ 361 and 368, receive tax-free status. These sections override the general result, in which a shareholder recognizes capital gain or loss on the exchange of one security for another.

     B.   Although the "like-kind exchange" provisions specifically do not apply to exchanges of securities, the corporate reorganization provisions generate tax results that are very similar thereto.

     C.   In general, gain or loss realized in a corporate reorganization is not recognized.

         1.   Realized gain is recognized to the extent of cash or other property received by the shareholder. To the extent of the shareholder's ratable earnings and profits, this gain is recognized as dividend income.

         2.   Loss never is recognized by the shareholder.

         3.   With respect to long-term debt, gain is not recognized if securities are surrendered in at least the same principal amount as those received.

     D.   The basis of the securities in the **new** corporation received by the shareholder equals his or her basis in the **old** securities *PLUS* recognized gain and dividend income *MINUS* the amount of cash, and fair market value of other property, received. This procedure defers the unrecognized shareholder gain or loss, but it does not forgive it.

     E.   The basis of other property received is the fair market value of such other property.

TEST FOR SELF-EVALUATION - CHAPTER 19

True or False

Indicate which of the following statements are true or false by circling the correct answer.

T   F   1.   A 100% shareholder can liquidate a corporation (recognizing capital gain) and receive a step-up in basis of the corporate assets that he received, without receiving any dividend income.

T   F   2.   A corporation is required to recognize all gains and losses realized with respect to in-kind liquidating distributions.

T   F   3.   B reorganizations involve the exchange of stock for assets.

T   F   4.   For liquidation loss purposes, the basis of disqualified property that is later sold or distributed to an unrelated party is reduced by the excess of the property's basis on the contribution date over the property's fair market value on such date.

T   F   5.   In a § 332 liquidation, the distributing corporation must recognize gain on a property distribution to minority shareholders.

T   F   6.   To meet the requirements of § 332, the parent corporation generally must directly own 80% of the voting stock or 80% of the value of the outstanding stock.

T   F   7.   A corporation always recognizes gain or loss on the distribution of its assets during the liquidation period.

T   F   8.   For a corporation undergoing a liquidation, E&P has no tax impact on the gain or loss to be recognized by the shareholders.

T   F   9.   A shareholder may recognize gain or loss on the exchange of his or her stock in a tax-free reorganization.

Fill-in-the-Blanks

Complete the following statements with the appropriate word(s) or amount(s).

1.   Liquidating distributions are subject to tax both at the _____ level and at the _____ level.

2.   A corporation may deduct _____ expenses of a liquidation, but it must adjust the gain or loss on the sale of the assets by subtracting _____ liquidation expenses.

3.   C reorganizations involve the acquisition by one corporation, in exchange solely for its _____ _____, of substantially all of the _____ of another corporation.

4.   Under the general rule provided in § 334(a), the basis of property received by an individual shareholder in a complete liquidation is the _____ _____ _____ of the assets.

5.   If depreciated property is acquired by a liquidating corporation in a _____ _____ transaction or as a _____ _____ _____ within _____ years of the adoption of the plan of liquidation, the transaction will be deemed to have occurred for the principal purpose of providing a loss to the corporation.

6.   A subsidiary does not recognize gain or loss on a liquidating distribution to a parent corporation that directly owns _____ _____ _____ of the stock of the subsidiary.

7.   The nonrecognition of gain or loss on liquidating distributions under Code § 332, does not apply to distributions to _____ shareholders.

8.   To qualify for a § 338 election, the stock of the target corporation must have been acquired within _____ months.

9.   In a tax-free reorganization, a _____ is never recognized by a shareholder.

10. With respect to a tax-free reorganization, gain is recognized to the extent of the lesser of _____ _____ or _____ and _____ _____ received.

11. In a tax-free reorganization, the basis of stock and securities received by a shareholder is the same as the bases of _____ _____, decreased by the amount of _____ _____, and increas by the amount of _____ and _____ _____ recognized on the transaction.

Multiple Choice

Choose the best answer for each of the following questions.

USE THE FOLLOWING INFORMATION FOR QUESTIONS 1-2.

X is the sole shareholder of Z Corporation. The basis of the total assets owned by Z is $100,000. The fair market value of these assets is $175,000. X has a basis in her stock of $125,000. The corporation has Accumulated E&P of $50,000. X exchanges all of her shares for all of Z's assets, in a complete liquidation of Z.

_____ 1.   What is the amount and nature of gain recognized by X?
       a. $50,000 dividend income, $125,000 return of capital.
       b. $25,000 capital loss.
       c. $50,000 capital gain.
       d. $50,000 dividend income.

_____ 2.   What is the basis of the assets received by X?
       a. $50,000.
       b. $100,000.
       c. $125,000.
       d. $175,000.

_____ 3.   In a qualified reorganization under § 368, the shareholder's realized gain on the exchange is:
       a.   Not recognized.
       b.   Recognized to the extent of the lesser of the gain realized or the cash and FMV of other property received.
       c.   Recognized in full.
       d.   Recognized to the extent of E&P.

____   4.   In a qualified reorganization under § 368, the shareholder's realized loss on the exchange is:
        a.   Recognized in full.
        b.   Never recognized.
        c.   Partially recognized, to the extent of depreciation recapture.
        d.   Partially recognized, to the extent of liabilities in excess of basis.

____   5.   The basis of securities in the "new" corporation received by a shareholder in a corporate reorganization will be equal to his or her "old" basis, adjusted by which of the following items? More than one answer may be correct.
        a.   Recognized gain and dividend income.
        b.   Cash received.
        c.   Fair market value of other property received.
        d.   Loss recognized.

USE THE FOLLOWING INFORMATION FOR QUESTIONS 6-8.

In 19X9, A Corporation distributes the following assets "in kind," in a complete liquidation of the business.

	Basis to A	Fair Market Value
Land	$20,000	$30,000
Inventory	4,000	14,000
Machinery (original cost $17,000)	10,000	20,000

____   6.   The gain recognized by A on the distribution is:
        a. $ 6,000.
        b. $10,000.
        c. $16,000.
        d. $23,000.
        e. $30,000.

____   7.   The shareholder who receives the machinery will have a basis in these assets of:
        a. $0.
        b. $10,000.
        c. $17,000.
        d. $20,000.
        e.   None of the above.

____   8.   Kurt, the sole shareholder of A has a basis of $30,000 in his A stock. With respect to the liquidating distribution, Kurt recognizes a gain of:
        a. $0.
        b. $30,000.
        c. $31,000.
        d. $34,000.

USE THE FOLLOWING INFORMATION FOR QUESTIONS 9-11.

Pursuant to a tax-free reorganization, X exchanges stock she owns in A Corporation for stock in B Corporation plus $5,000 cash. The stock in A and B have a fair market value of $20,000 and $15,000, respectively.

____   9.   If X's basis in the A stock is $16,000, the gain recognized by X is:

a. $0.
b. $1,000.
c. $4,000.
d. $5,000.
e. $15,000.

____   10.   If X's basis in the A stock is $22,000, the gain or loss recognized by X is:
a. $0.
b. $2,000 gain.
c. $5,000 gain.
d. $2,000 loss.
e. $5,000 loss.

____   11.   Assume the same facts as in Problem 10. X's basis in the B stock is:
a. $0.
b. $15,000.
c. $17,000.
d. $20,000.
e. $22,000.

USE THE FOLLOWING INFORMATION FOR QUESTIONS 12-15.

L Corporation owns 100 percent of the stock of R Corporation. L's basis in the R stock is $200,000. R liquidates and distributes the following assets to L.

	Basis	Fair Market Value
Cash	$100,000	$100,000
Installment Note	25,000	30,000
Inventory	3,000	7,000
Land	50,000	75,000
Totals	$178,000	$212,000

____   12.   R's recognized gain on the liquidation is:
a. $0.
b. $ 5,000.
c. $ 8,000.
d. $34,000.

____   13.   The basis of R's assets to L is:
a. $178,000.
b. $181,000.
c. $183,000.
d. $212,000.

____   14.   Assume that the requirements of § 338 were met and a § 338 election was made. What is the gain recognized by R on the liquidation?
a. $0.
b. $5,000.
c. $8,000.
d. $34,000.

____   15.   Assume the same facts as in problem 14. What is the basis of the assets to L?
a. $178,000.
b. $181,000.

    c. $183,000.
    d. $200,000.
    e. $212,000.

USE THE FOLLOWING INFORMATION FOR QUESTIONS 16-17.

A is the sole shareholder of RT Corporation, and A has a basis in his stock of $20,000. RT Corporation distributes the following assets "in-kind," in a complete liquidation under § 331.

	Basis to RT	Fair Market Value
Cash	$4,000	$4,000
Inventory	6,000	6,000
Land (subject to a mortgage of $15,000)	10,000	12,000

16.   The gain recognized by RT Corporation on the distribution is:
    a. $0.
    b. $2,000.
    c. $3,000.
    d. $5,000.

17.   The gain or loss recognized by A on the distribution is:
    a. $0.
    b. $2,000 gain.
    c. $10,000 loss.
    d. $13,000 loss.

USE THE FOLLOWING INFORMATION FOR QUESTIONS 18-19.

Marty, an individual and sole shareholder of ABC Corporation, has a basis in his ABC stock of $5,000. After adopting a plan of complete liquidation in 19x9, ABC sold all of its assets (adjusted basis of $30,000) to an unrelated party, in exchange for $10,000 cash and installment notes of $40,000. The installment notes are payable over a five-year period, beginning in the following year. Immediately after the sale, ABC distributed the cash and installment notes to Marty.

18.   The gain recognized by Marty in 19x9 is:
    a. $9,000.
    b. $10,000.
    c. $15,400.
    d. $20,000.
    e. $45,000.

19.   The gain recognized by Marty on the collection of each note over the next five years is:
    a. $0 (entire gain was recognized in the year of liquidation).
    b. $6,400.
    c. $7,200.
    d. $8,000.
    e.   It cannot be determined from the information given.

20.   Pursuant to a complete liquidation, XYZ Corporation distributed to its shareholders property with a basis of $350,000 and fair market value of $500,000. The property was subject to a liability in the amount of $600,000. On the distribution, XYZ recognizes a gain of:
    a. $0.

      b. $100,000.
      c. $150,000.
      d. $250,000.

____   21.   In connection with a plan of corporate reorganization adopted in 19X4, R exchanged 100 shares of B Corporation common stock for 300 shares of L Corporation common stock. R had purchased the B stock in 19X1 for $5 per share. Fair market value of the L stock was $9 per share on the date of the exchange. As a result of this exchange, R's long-term capital gain in 19X4 was:
      a. $0.
      b. $1,000.
      c. $1,800.
      d. $2,200.

____   22.   X Corporation acquires all of the stock of Z Corporation for $800,000 and elects to liquidate Z pursuant to an election under §338. If the fair market value of Z's physical assets is $700,000 and Z's basis in the assets is $500, how much of the purchase price must be allocated to goodwill or going concern value?
      a. $0.
      b. $100,000.
      c. $200,000.
      d. $800,000.

Code Section Recognition

Several important sections of the Internal Revenue Code are described below. Indicate, by number, the appropriate code section.

1.   ____   General rule for the treatment of complete liquidation to shareholder.

2.   ____   Allows a parent corporation to treat the acquisition of a subsidiary's stock as a purchase of the subsidiary's assets.

3.   ____   Allows a subsidiary to liquidate into its parent without the recognition of gain or loss.

4.   ____   Allows a parent corporation to liquidate a subsidiary without the recognition of gain or loss.

5.   ____   Provides the general rule for treatment of the corporation in a complete liquidation.

6.   ____   Governs certain tax-free corporate reorganizations.

7.   ____   Governs the determination of the basis of property received as a liquidating distribution.

Short Answer

1.   XYZ distributed the following property in light of its complete liquidation.

Asset	Basis	Fair Market Value
Inventory (FIFO basis)	$70,000	$100,000
Equipment ($40,000 of depreciation has been taken)	20,000	40,000

Securities held as an investment for four months	40,000	60,000
Supplies	0	5,000
Land purchased as an investment in 1960	5,000	90,000

Compute the nature and amount of gain or loss recognized to XYZ.

2.   Terri is the sole shareholder of X Corporation. She holds shares with a basis of $25,000 and long-term debt from X of $18,000.

Y Corporation acquires X in a reorganization, taking all of X's assets (basis $100,000, fair market value $170,000). Y gives Terri shares in Y (fair market value $60,000), long-term debt in Y of $20,000, and $7,000 cash. Y assumes X's debt.

What is Terri's Realized Gain?

What is Terri's Recognized Gain?

What is Terri's basis in the Y Corporation stock?

What is Y's basis in its new assets?

3.   Albert exchanges stock he owns in X Corporation for stock in Y Corporation worth $2,000 and $1,000 in cash. The exchange is pursuant to a tax-free reorganization. Although Albert paid $5,000 for his stock six years ago, it currently has a fair market value of $3,000.

What is Albert's realized gain or loss?

What is Albert's recognized gain or loss?

What is Albert's basis in the Y stock?

SOLUTIONS TO CHAPTER 19 QUESTIONS

True or False

1.	T	Provided that the corporation is not "collapsible" under § 341.
2.	F	The recognition of losses is subject to various limitations.
3.	F	A Type B reorganization involves the exchange of stock for stock.
4.	T	
5.	T	
6.	F	The parent must directly own 80% of the voting stock **and** 80% of the value of the outstanding stock.
7.	F	Gain or loss generally is not recognized in the liquidation of a subsidiary corporation.
8.	T	
9.	F	Loss never is recognized.

Fill-in-the-Blank

1. corporate, shareholder
2. general, specific
3. voting stock, assets
4. fair market value
5. § 351, contributions to capital, two
6. 80% or more
7. minority
8. twelve
9. loss
10. gain realized, cash, other property
11. stock surrendered, boot received, gain, dividend income

Multiple Choice

1.	c	($175,000 - $125,000) See Example 1 in the text.
2.	d	Basis is equal to the fair market value of the assets received.
3.	b	
4.	b	
5.	a,b,c	Loss is never recognized in a qualified reorganization.
6.	e	[($30,000 + $14,000 + $20,000) - ($20,000 + $4,000 + $10,000)].
7.	d	Basis is equal to the fair market value of the machinery.
8.	d	[$64,000 (FMV of assets received) less $30,000 (basis in stock)] See Example 1 in the text.
9.	c	Gain recognized is limited to the lesser of gain realized ($4,000 = $20,000 - $16,000) or boot received ($5,000). See Example 22 in the text.
10.	a	Loss is not recognized in a tax-free reorganization. See Example 23 in the text.
11.	c	$22,000 (basis in stock surrendered) - $5,000 (boot received). See Example 23 in the text.
12.	a	Gain is not recognized in a complete liquidation of a subsidiary.
13.	a	The subsidiary's basis in the assets carries over to the parent. See Example 18 in the text.
14.	d	($212,000 - $178,000). See Example 20 in the text.
15.	d	The basis of R's assets is equal to L's basis in the stock. See Example 20 in the text.
16.	d	FMV of land cannot be computed as less than the mortgage. See Example 3 in the text.
17.	c	Assuming the property is not disqualified property, the loss recognized is $10,000

[$25,000 (FMV of property received) - $15,000 (mortgage) - $20,000 (basis in stock)].

18.   a   ($10,000 cash received less the stock basis allocated to the cash $1,000 [($10,000 / $50,000) X $5,000]) See Example 14 in the text.

19.   c   ($40,000 installment note received less $4,000 stock basis allocated to the installment note = $36,000 gross profit; $36,000 / $40,000 = 90%; 90% X $8,000 annual note collected = $7,200)   See Example 14 in the text.

20.   d   The FMV of the distributed property cannot be less than the amount of the liability. See Example 3 in the text.

21.   a   Gain is not recognized in an exchange of stock in a tax-free reorganization.

22.   b   ($800,000 - $700,000) See Example 21 in the text.

Code Section Recognition

1.   331
2.   338
3.   337
4.   332
5.   336
6.   368
7.   334

Short Answer

1.   XYZ recognizes gain on the distribution of the following property:

Asset	Gain Recognized	Nature of Gain
Inventory	$30,000	Ordinary income
Equipment	20,000	§ 1245 depreciation recapture
Securities	20,000	Short-term capital gain
Supplies	5,000	Ordinary income (tax benefit rule)
Land	85,000	Long-term capital gain
	$160,000	

2.

Amount Realized ($60,000 + $20,000 + $7,000)	$87,000
Adjusted Basis ($25,000 + $18,000)	-43,000
Gain Realized	$44,000
Boot Received	$7,000
Additional Long-term Debt that Terri acquired	2,000
Gain Recognized	$9,000
Basis in X Stock	$25,000
Gain Recognized	+9,000
Boot Received, Excess Long-term Debt	-9,000
Basis in Y Stock	$25,000
Basis of Assets to X = **Basis of Assets to Y**	$100,000

See Example 22 in the text.

3.

Fair market value of Y stock	$2,000
Cash	1,000

Total amount realized	$3,000
Less: Basis in X stock	5,000
Realized loss	$(2,000)
Recognized loss	$ 0

Albert cannot recognize the $2,000 realized loss, because no loss may be recognized in a tax-free reorganization. See § 356(c). Note that gain is not recognized on a boot distribution unless gain is realized on the overall transaction.

Albert's **basis in the Y stock** is $4,000, the same basis as the property exchanged less the cash boot received.

See Example 23 in the text.

CHAPTER 20
CORPORATE ACCUMULATIONS

CHAPTER HIGHLIGHTS

Corporations have a pervasive tax incentive to avoid the payment of dividends to shareholders. Assuming the presence of sufficient Earnings and Profits, dividend payments generate ordinary income to the non-corporate shareholders. On the other hand, an accumulation of corporate earnings causes an increase in the price of the shareholder's stock, producing capital gains upon the sale of the stock. A modest tax benefit results from the conversion of dividend income into long-term capital gain, because long-term capital gains of noncorporate taxpayers are taxed at a maximum rate of 28%, while the maximum tax rate on ordinary income is 39.6%.

The accumulation of earnings in the corporation also defers the second level of tax on the corporation's income, i.e., the income tax at the shareholder level. To discourage the tax-motivated retention of corporate earnings, Congress initiated two penalty taxes - the accumulated earnings tax and the personal holding company tax. Given an adequate degree of dividend payments, corporations can avoid liability under both of these taxes.

I.   Tax on Unreasonable Accumulations
     A.   The penalty tax on unreasonably accumulated earnings is imposed in addition to the regular corporate income tax and the corporate alternative minimum tax. The accumulated earnings tax (AET) is equal to 39.6% of the accumulated taxable income (ATI). The tax is imposed if the Internal Revenue Service can show that a corporation intended to prevent increases in its shareholders' income tax liability by accumulating income, i.e., by not paying dividends. Evidence of such intent includes the presence of:
          1.   Unreasonable compensation, interest, or rental payments to shareholder-employees, -creditors, or -lessors;
          2.   Excessive investment activity, e.g., in marketable securities;
          3.   A history of low dividend payments;
          4.   The use of corporate funds for corporate-shareholder dealings; and,
          5.   Accumulations of funds beyond the corporation's reasonable needs.

B.   Unlike most disagreements with the Service, the burden of proof with respect to the accumulated earnings tax is on the Service. The IRS proposes the liability for the tax, the corporation responds by substantiating the reasonableness of its earnings accumulation, and the Service has the burden to refute the corporation's assertions. When a corporation is found to have unreasonably accumulated earnings, interest is imposed on the underpayment of the accumulated earnings tax from the due date (excluding extensions) of the income tax return for the year the tax was initially imposed.

C.   In computing the AET base, a corporation is allowed an Accumulated Earnings Credit against its Accumulated Taxable Income (See Exhibit 20-1). The amount of the credit is computed as follows.

GREATER of:(i) Base Amount of $250,000 ($150,000 in the case of personal service corporations); OR,
(ii) The "Reasonable Needs" of the business for the year, less the corporation's current net long-term capital gain (net of any tax thereon);
MINUS: The corporation's accumulated earnings and profits at the beginning of the current year.
EQUALS: ACCUMULATED EARNINGS CREDIT

The credit cannot be a negative number. Thus, the accumulated earnings tax falls upon the current year's accumulation of income only, where such accumulations are in excess of a "reasonable" level, i.e., the statutory floor or the requirements of the business. However, a corporation may accumulate capital gains without a penalty tax.

D.   Reasonable needs of a business include:
1.   Expansion of business activities, if accompanied by board of director approval and valid long-range planning activities;
2.   Retirement of debt and replacement of plant and equipment, especially when accompanied by sinking funds;
3.   Acquisition of a business through the purchase of stock or assets;
4.   Self-insurance and realistic business contingencies, especially where projected requirements are documented;
5.   Investments or loans to suppliers or customers, if necessary to maintain the business of the corporation;
6.   IRC §303 redemptions; and,
7.   Working capital. "Reasonable" needs for working capital in a manufacturing setting have been approximated by a court-approved "Bardahl formula." See Exhibit 20-2. Under certain circumstances, a human resource accounting (HRA) approach may be used to determine the working capital needs of a noninventory corporation. See Concept Summary 20-1 in the text for additional items that qualify as reasonable business needs.

E.   Reasonable needs of the business do NOT include:
1.   Loans to shareholders or brother-sister corporations;
2.   Investments unrelated to activities of the business;
3.   Contingencies for general or unrealistic occurrences; and,
4.   Accumulations to retire stock without curtailment of business. See Concept Summary 20-1 in the text for additional items that do not qualify as reasonable business needs.

Exhibit 20-1
COMPUTING ACCUMULATED TAXABLE INCOME

	Current Taxable Income
-	Accrued Federal Income Tax (other than PHC and AET taxes)
-	Charitable Contributions in excess of the ten percent limitation
+	Excess charitable contributions carried over from a preceding taxable year and deducted currently
+	Net Operating Loss and Dividends-Received Deductions
-	Dividends Paid (including the 2½ month "grace period," and consent dividends)
+	Net Capital Loss Carryover
-	Net Long-term Capital Gains, net of tax
-	Current (non-deductible) Net Capital Loss reduced by the lesser of (1) the corporation's nonrecaptured capital gains deduction; or (2) the corporation's accumulated earnings and profits as of the close of the preceding taxable year
-	Accumulated Earnings Credit

ACCUMULATED TAXABLE INCOME

F.   The adjustment for dividends paid includes all "ordinary income" dividends paid to shareholders during the year and any dividends paid within the first 2½ months after the close of the corporation's tax year. It also includes "consent dividends," whereunder the shareholder receives no cash, but agrees to recognize taxable dividend income for the year.

    1.   Consent dividends are useful if the corporation is illiquid, or if the accumulated earnings tax liability is imminent. The dividend increases the shareholder's basis in the corporate stock.

    2.   The dividends-paid adjustment is useful in avoiding the tax, but a careful analysis should be conducted, to assure elimination of the entire liability.

G.   The accumulated earnings tax is not imposed on S corporations, personal holding companies, foreign personal holding companies, tax-exempt organizations and passive investment companies.

Now that the gap between the top corporate and individual tax rates is significant again, one can expect that family corporations will attempt to accumulate sizable amounts of income. Thus, the tax advisor's need to identify and create reasonable business needs increases as the gap between the top tax rates increases.

Exhibit 20-2
"BARDAHL FORMULA" FOR WORKING CAPITAL NEEDS

Cost of Sales PLUS Selling, General, and Administrative Expenses
(other than depreciation and unpaid federal income taxes*)

X $\dfrac{\text{Average Inventory}}{\text{Cost of Sales}} + \dfrac{\text{Average Receivables}}{\text{Net Sales}} - \dfrac{\text{Average Payables**}}{\text{Purchases}}$

*   Various courts have permitted certain taxpayers to include
       depreciation and federal income taxes in the calculation of the
       working capital needs.

**   A number of courts have omitted the reduction for the accounts
       payable cycle.

II.   Personal Holding Company Tax
        A.   The penalty tax on personal holding companies is meant to discourage the
              accumulation of an excessive amount of passive income, e.g., in a situation
              where the company becomes a mere "incorporated checkbook" for investment income,
              and the individual income tax is avoided. As with the accumulated earnings tax,
              the penalty tax on personal holding companies is avoided if sufficient corporate
              dividends are paid. The tax can be analyzed in two stages:
              1.   Determine whether the corporation is a personal holding company.
              2.   If the corporation is a personal holding company, determine its personal
                    holding company income, and the tax liability.
        B.   Certain corporations cannot be qualified as personal holding companies.
              1.   Tax-exempt organizations
              2.   Non-US corporations.
              3.   S corporations.
              4.   Banks and life insurance companies.
        C.   Personal Holding Company status occurs when both of the following tests are met.
              1.   Five or fewer individuals owned more than fifty percent of the value of
                    the corporation's stock at any time during the second half of the
                    corporation's tax year. For purposes of this test, very broad stock
                    ownership attribution rules are applied. A shareholder is treated as
                    "owning" his or her pro rata portion of shares owned by the following.
                    If a corporation has fewer than ten shareholders, this test
                    automatically is satisfied.
                    a.   other corporations, partnerships, estates, and trusts.
                    b.   the shareholder's partners, spouse, ancestors, lineal
                          descendants, and siblings.
                    c.   stock options
                    d.   convertible debt
              2.   Personal Holding Company Income (PHCI) for the year is equal to or
                    greater than sixty percent of Adjusted Ordinary Gross Income (AOGI).

Personal Holding Company Income includes income from dividends, interest, annuities, computer software royalties, and certain personal service contracts, and adjusted income (after attributable expenses) from rents and most royalties. Ordinary Gross Income (OGI) is § 61 Gross Income of the corporation for the year, less gains (only) from capital and § 1231 transactions. Adjusted Ordinary Gross Income is OGI less expenses attributable to rental and royalty income (such as depreciation, interest, property taxes, and rental payments). The adjusted ordinary income computation is illustrated in Exhibit 20-3.

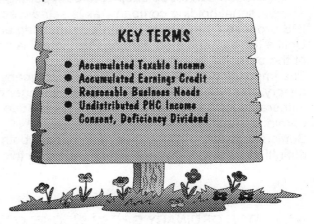

KEY TERMS

- Accumulated Taxable Income
- Accumulated Earnings Credit
- Reasonable Business Needs
- Undistributed PHC Income
- Consent, Deficiency Dividend

    a.   Income from personal service contracts is classified as PHC income only if: (1) some person other than the corporation has the right to designate the individual who is to perform the services, and (2) the person so designated, directly or indirectly, owns at least 25% of the value of the corporation's stock at any time during the taxable year.

    b.   Rental Income can be excluded from Personal Holding Company Income if both of the following tests are met:

        (i)   Adjusted Income from Rents is fifty percent or more of AOGI; and,

        (ii)   Dividends Paid during the year are equal to or greater than the amount by which non-rent Personal Holding Company Income exceeds ten percent of OGI.

        For purposes of the "dividends paid" test for exclusion of adjusted income from rents, consent dividends and dividends paid during the 2 1/2 month grace period (subject to the 20% limitation discussed in D.2. below) are included.

    c.   Similar exclusions are available for adjusted income from mineral, oil, and gas royalties.

D.   The Personal Holding Company tax computation is illustrated in Exhibit 20-4. The tax rate is 39.6% and is levied on Undistributed Personal Holding Company Income. For purposes of computing this tax base, the dividends-paid adjustment includes the following.

    1.   Pro-rata dividends paid during the year, i.e., unreasonable compensation reclassified by the Service as dividends are not included.

    2.   Dividends paid during the 2 1/2 months immediately following the close of the corporation's tax year, to the extent that they do not exceed either

        a.   twenty percent of dividends actually paid during the year; or,

        b.   undistributed PHCI.

    3.   Consent dividends, as defined in I.F. above. These dividends are deemed paid on the last day of the corporate tax year;

    4.   "Deficiency dividends," paid within ninety days of the final assessment

of the tax, e.g., by the Service or by a court decision; and,

5.   A carryover from the two immediately prior tax years of the dividends-paid adjustment that was not used.

6.   Note that this definition of "dividends paid" differs from the one used in computing both the accumulated earnings tax and the exclusion from personal holding company income for adjusted income from rents.

III.   Comparison of AET and PHC Tax

A.   A corporation cannot be subject to both penalty taxes during one tax year.

B.   The personal holding company tax is self-assessed by the corporation, while the IRS proposes the liability for the accumulated earnings tax.

C.   Unlike the accumulated earnings tax, intent is not necessary for the imposition of the personal holding company tax.

D.   The imposition of the personal holding company tax is not affected by the past history of the corporation. In contrast, younger corporations are less vulnerable to the accumulated earnings tax due to the $250,000 accumulated earnings credit.

E.   Sufficient dividend distributions can negate both taxes. However, the definition of *dividends paid* differs under the two taxes.

Exhibit 20-3
ADJUSTED ORDINARY GROSS INCOME COMPUTATION

Gross Income
- Capital Gains
- §1231 Gains

Ordinary Gross Income (OGI)
- Expenses (to the extent of rent income) directly related to gross income from rents i.e., depreciation, property taxes, interest expense and rental expenses
- Expenses (to the extent of royalty income) directly related to gross income from mineral, oil, and gas royalties i.e. depreciation, property and severance taxes, interest expense and rental expenses

Adjusted Ordinary Gross Income (AOGI)

Exhibit 20-4
TAX BASE -- PERSONAL HOLDING COMPANY TAX

     Current Taxable Income
-   Accrued Federal Income Tax (other than PHC and AET taxes)
-   Charitable Contributions in excess of the 10% limitation (although an individual's 20, 30, and 50% limitations apply)
+   Excess charitable contributions carried over from a preceding taxable year and deducted currently
+   Deductions for Dividends Received, and for Net Operating Losses (except such loss incurred in the immediately preceding taxable year)
-   Dividends Paid (including the 2 1/2 month "grace period,"* consent dividends, deficiency dividends, and any dividend carryover)
-   <u>Net Long-term Capital Gains, net of tax</u>

<u>Undistributed Personal Holding Company Income</u>

*   For purposes of the PHC tax only, dividends paid within the 2 1/2 month "grace period" may be deducted only to the extent that they do not exceed either (1) 20% of the total dividends distributed during the tax year (excluding consent dividends), or (2) undistributed PHCI for the tax year.

TEST FOR SELF-EVALUATION - CHAPTER 20

True or False

Indicate which of the following statements are true or false by circling the correct answer.

T   F   1.   The taxpayer's intent to avoid the payment of dividends is considered in the application of the accumulated earnings tax, but not the personal holding company tax.

T   F   2.   A corporation is permitted to accumulate capital gains without incurring either an accumulated earnings tax or a PHC tax.

T   F   3.   Consent dividends and deficiency dividends reduce the corporation's exposure to both the accumulated earnings tax and the personal holding company tax.

T   F   4.   Dividends paid to the corporation's shareholder-officers as unreasonable compensation reduce the exposure to both the accumulated earnings tax and the personal holding company tax.

T   F   5.   The accumulated earnings tax offers a carryover of the unused dividends-paid adjustment.

T   F   6.   If a corporation has ten or more unrelated shareholders, it is impossible for the corporation to be classified as a personal holding company.

T   F   7.   The mere fact that stock of a corporation is widely held does not exempt the corporation from the possible application of either the personal holding company tax or the accumulated earnings tax.

T   F   8.   A corporation may not be required to pay both the personal holding company tax and the accumulation earnings tax in the same tax year.

T   F   9.   Using the peak cycle approach when applying the Bardahl formula decreases the operating cycle percentage which will result in a lower necessary accumulation of working capital.

T   F   10.   The burden of proof with respect to the accumulated earnings tax is on the taxpayer.

T   F   11.   A human resource accounting approach generally is used to determine the working capital needs of a manufacturing corporation.

T   F   12.   For purposes of the PHC tax, the amount included in AOGI as adjusted income from rents cannot be less than zero.

Fill-in-the-Blanks

Complete the following statements with the appropriate word(s) or amount(s).

1.   The _____ dividend procedure is available for the personal holding company tax, but not for the accumulated earnings tax.

2.   To be classified as a PHC, more than _____ percent of the outstanding stock must be held by _____ or fewer individuals at any time during the _____ _____ of the corporation's taxable year and _____ percent or more of the corporation's _____ must be comprised of passive income.

3.   A _____ dividend requires no cash payment. It generates dividend income to the shareholders, and it _____ their bases in the stock.

4.   The "_____" formula quantifies a corporation's reasonable needs for working capital.

5.   For purposes of the accumulated earnings tax, deductions for the following types of dividends are permitted: _____ year; _____ _____ grace period; and, _____ dividends.

6.   The base amount of the accumulated earnings credit is _____ for personal service corporations and _____ for other corporations.

7.   Classification as a PHC requires satisfaction of both the _____ _____ and the _____ _____ tests.

8.   The accumulated earnings tax rate is _____ and the personal holding company tax rate is _____.

9.   The _____ _____ _____ tax is self-assessed by the taxpayer, whereas the Internal Revenue Service bears the burden of proof relative to the _____ _____ tax.

10.   If a corporation has _____ _____ _____ shareholders, the stock ownership test for the personal holding company tax automatically is satisfied.

Multiple Choice

Choose the best answer for each of the following questions.

_____   1.   A corporation has $400,000 of accumulated taxable income. Its accumulated earnings tax is:
        a. $60,000.
        b. $112.000.
        c. $124,000.
        d. $158,480.

_____   2.   A corporation has $450,000 of undistributed personal holding company income. Its personal holding company tax is:
        a. $178,200.
        b. $139,500.
        c. $126,000.
        d. $67,500.

_____ 3.   A calendar-year public accounting firm has Accumulated Earnings and Profits at 1-1-X6 of $170,000. Its 19X6 reasonable business needs total $175,000. The corporation has no 19X6 capital asset transactions. The corporation's 19X6 accumulated earnings credit is:
   a. $0.
   b. $5,000.
   c. $80,000.
   d. $175,000.

_____ 4.   Same as 3., except that 1-1-X6 Accumulated Earnings and Profits are $200,000. The corporation's 19X6 accumulated earnings credit is:
   a.   ($ 25,000).
   b. $0.
   c. $25,000.
   d. $50,000.
   e. $250,000.

_____ 5.   Same as 3., except that the corporation manufactures spare auto parts. Its 19X6 accumulated earnings credit is:
   a. $0.
   b. $65,000.
   c. $80,000.
   d. $170,000.
   e. $250,000.

_____ 6.   With respect to a manufacturing corporation, which of the following is not subtracted from taxable income in determining accumulated taxable income?
   a.   Accrued corporate income tax.
   b.   Charitable contributions in excess of the 10% limit.
   c.   Net long-term capital gains.
   d.   The dividends-received deduction.
   e.   All of the above are subtraction adjustments when determining accumulated taxable income.

USE THE FOLLOWING DATA FOR QUESTIONS 7-10.

Assume that the X Corporation passes the stock ownership test for tax year 19X8.

Income from rental apartments - gross	$700,000
Expenses for rental property	335,000
Interest income - money market fund	120,000
Gross profit, fruits and vegetables ($100,000 sales)	68,000
Corporate Taxable Income - Calendar 19X8	553,000
Dividends paid in cash, January 19X9	10,000

_____ 7.   Compute X's 19X8 Adjusted Ordinary Gross Income.
   a. $485,000.
   b. $553,000.
   c. $585,000.
   d. $920,000.

_____ 8.   Compute X's 19X8 Personal Holding Company Income.
   a. $120,000.
   b. $365,000.
   c. $485,000.

      d. $820,000.

_____ 9. Compute X's 19X8 Personal Holding Company tax.
      a. $0.
      b. $102,194.
      c. $144,532.
      d. $113,144.
      e. $54,747.

_____ 10. X could avoid the personal holding company tax by (more than one answer could be correct):
      a.   Paying $26,000 of dividends during 19X8.
      b.   Eliminating its fruit and vegetable business.
      c.   Increasing its rental income by $31,200.
      d.   Having its shareholders consent to include $31,200 of dividends in their calendar 19X8 tax returns.

QUESTIONS 11 AND 12 ARE BASED ON THE FOLLOWING STATEMENTS WHICH PERTAIN TO EITHER THE ACCUMULATED EARNINGS TAX OR THE PERSONAL HOLDING COMPANY TAX.

      (a)   Imposition of the tax depends on a stock ownership test specified in the statute.
      (b)   Imposition of the tax can be mitigated by sufficient dividend distributions.
      (c)   The tax should be self-assessed by filing a separate schedule along with the regular tax return.

_____ 11. Which of the foregoing statements pertain to the accumulated earnings tax?
      a.   (a) only.
      b.   (b) only.
      c.   (c) only.
      d.   (a), (b), and (c).

_____ 12. Which of the foregoing statements pertain to the personal holding company tax?
      a.   (a) only.
      b.   (b) only.
      c.   (c) only.
      d.   (a), (b), and (c).

_____ 13. In determining accumulated taxable income for the purpose of the accumulated earnings tax, which one of the following is allowed as a deduction?
      a.   Capital loss carryover from prior years.
      b.   Dividends-received deduction.
      c.   Net operating loss deduction.
      d.   Net capital loss for current year.

_____ 14. Which of the following is not a reasonable business need of a corporation: (more than one answer may be correct)
      a.   Avoidance of an unfavorable competitive position.
      b.   Premiums for key employee life insurance policies.
      c.   Debt retirement.
      d.   Loans to shareholders.

_____ 15. Z Corporation is in the business of manufacturing automobiles. Z has no carryovers from prior tax years and has no reasonable business needs that justify accumulations of funds.   Z's financial information for 19X9 is as follows.

Taxable income	$400,000
Tax liability	136,000
Excess charitable contributions	10,000
Short-term capital losses	(20,000)
Dividends received from 50%-owned corporations	200,000
Dividends paid during 19X9	150,000
Accumulated earnings (1/1/X9)	240,000

Z Corporation's accumulated taxable income for 19X9 is
a. $ 74,000.
b. $234,000.
c. $244,000.
d. $254,000.

____ 16.   In determining adjusted income from rents for purposes of the PHC tax, which of the following is not an allowable deduction? (More than one answer may be correct.)
a.   Income taxes.
b.   Interest.
c.   Rent.
d.   Property taxes.
e.   Salaries.

Short Answer

1. What are X Corporation's "reasonable needs" for working capital? X is an accrual-basis, calendar-year manufacturer.

Inventory	12-X5	$2,300,000	12-X6	$2,900,000
Accounts Receivable:	12-X5	$400,000	12-X6	$500,000
Accounts payable:	12-X5	$150,000	12-X6	$450,000

19X6 Net Sales $9,000,000; Cost of Sales $5,200,000; Purchases $4,500,000; General, Selling and Administrative Expenses (other than depreciation and federal income taxes) $300,000.

2. Compute Y Corporation's § 531 liability for 19X8. Y is an accrual-basis, calendar-year architectural firm.

Dividends Paid: 6/1/X8 $30,000; 2/1/X9 $20,000; 6/1/X9 $25,000;
Taxable Income $350,000; Federal Income Tax for 19X8 $119,000.
Dividends Received Deduction $85,000; Net Capital Loss $10,000; E&P, 12/31/X7 $90,000.
"Reasonable Business Needs" for 19X8, $65,000.

3. Is X Corporation a personal holding company for 19X9?

Gross Income = Rents $30,000, Interest $15,000.
Dividends Paid in 19X9 = $12,000.
Expenses Paid for Rental Income = Depreciation $7,000, Property Tax $2,000, Salaries $3,000.

X is owned by individuals A, B, C, D, and trusts E and F. D is the sole beneficiary of E and F.

4. Compute Y Corporation's Personal Holding Company Tax for 19X8. Y is a calendar year taxpayer. Assume that Y already has been classified as a Personal Holding Company.

19X8 Taxable Income $75,000, including $20,000 Dividend Income from an unrelated domestic corporation in which Y owned 35% of the stock.

Federal Income Tax Liability $13,750; Disallowed Charitable Contributions (10% limit) $4,000; Dividends Paid 9/1/X8 $11,000; 3/1/X9 $13,000; 4/1/X9 $9,000.

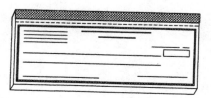

SOLUTIONS TO CHAPTER 20 QUESTIONS

True or False

1.   T
2.   T
3.   F   The deficiency dividend procedure is allowed only for purposes of the PHC tax.
4.   F   For PHC tax purposes, distributions must be pro rata.
5.   F   Only the PHC tax offers a carryover of the unused dividend-paid adjustment.
6.   F   If the shareholders own unequal interests, the corporation may be a PHC.
7.   F   Due to the stock ownership test, a corporation whose stock is widely held generally would not be subject to the personal holding company tax.
8.   T
9.   F   Using the peak cycle approach *increases* the operating cycle percentage which produces a *larger* necessary accumulation of working capital.
10.   F   The burden of proof is on the IRS.
11.   F   A HRA approach may be used to determine the working capital needs of a noninventory corporation.
12.   T

Fill-in-the-Blanks

1.   deficiency
2.   fifty, five, last half, sixty, AOGI
3.   consent, increases
4.   Bardahl
5.   current, 2 1/2 month, consent
6. $150,000, $250,000
7.   stock ownership, gross income
8.   39.6%, 39.6%
9.   personal holding company; accumulated earnings
10.   fewer than ten

Multiple Choice

1.   d   ($400,000 x 39.6%)
2.   a   ($450,000 x 39.6%)
3.   b   (greater of $150,000 credit or $175,000 reasonable business needs) - ($170,000 accumulated E&P at the beginning of the year) See Example 2 in the text.
4.   b   Accumulated E&P exceeds the reasonable business needs ($175,000) and the accumulated earning credit ($150,000). See Example 2 in the text.
5.   c   (greater of $250,000 or $175,000) - $170,000 See Example 2 in the text.
6.   d   The dividends-received deduction is an addition adjustment when computing accumulated taxable income.
7.   b   Gross income is reduced by rental expenses in arriving at AOGI ($700,000 - $335,000 + $120,000 + $68,000) See Example 11 in the text.
8.   c   Rental income is PHCI, since total dividends paid were less than the amount by which the interest income exceeds 10% of OGI. Therefore, PHCI = $700,000 - $335,000 + $120,000. See Example 11 in the text.
9.   c $553,000 - $188,020 federal tax = $364,980 x 39.6% = $144,532. See Example 16 in the text. Deduction for dividend paid is limited to 20% of the dividends paid during the tax year.
10.   a, d   To avoid being a PHC, the corporation must pass the rent test. Therefore,

dividends of $31,200 must be considered paid during 19X8; $31,200 = $120,000 - (10% x $888,000). See Examples 16 and 17 in the text. Dividends paid in January 19X9 may be included in this test only to the extent that they do not exceed 20% of the amount actually paid in 19X9 [$26,000 + (20% x $26,000) = $31,200].

11. b
12. d
13. d
14. d
15. b   [$400,000 - $136,000 - $10,000 - $20,000 + 80%($200,000) - $150,000 - ($250,000 - $240,000) = $234,000] See Example 4 in the text.
16. a, e

Short Answer

1.   Use the Bardahl formula. Reasonable needs for working capital are

[$5,200,000 Cost of Sales + $300,000 General Expenses]

$$x \frac{\text{Average Inventory } \$2,600,000}{\text{Cost of Sales } \$5,200,000} + \frac{\text{Average Receivables} \quad \$ \ 450,000}{\text{Net Sales} \qquad\qquad \$9,000,000}$$

$$- \frac{\text{Average Payables} \quad \$ \ 300,000}{\text{Purchases} \qquad\quad \$4,500,000}$$

$$= \$5,500,000 \ x \ (.5 + .05 - .067) = \$5,500,000 \ x \ .483 = \underline{\$2,656,500}$$

2.   Current Taxable Income $350,000
       Federal Income Tax   -119,000
       Dividends-Received Deduction   +85,000
       Dividends Paid (6/X8 and 2/X9)   -50,000
       Net Capital Loss   -10,000
       Accumulated Earnings Credit (greater of: -60,000
         reasonable needs $65,000 or minimum credit
         $150,000, minus accumulated E&P at beginning
         of the year $90,000)

       Accumulated Taxable Income $196,000

       Accumulated Earnings Tax   39.6% x $196,000 $77,616

       See Example 4 in the text.

3.   **Stock Ownership Test**   Trust ownership is attributed to individual D. Accordingly, under the stock attribution rules, four individuals own X Corporation throughout 19X9.

TEST PASSED

Income Test	Rental Income	$30,000
	Interest Income	+15,000
	Ordinary Gross Income	$45,000 *
	Depreciation - Rentals	-7,000
	Taxes - Rentals	-2,000
	Adjusted Ordinary Gross Income	$36,000 **

Personal Holding Company Income

Include Rentals?

Adjusted Income from Rents ($30,000 - $7,000 - $2,000)	$21,000
50% of AOGI **	$18,000

TEST PASSED

Dividends Paid	$12,000
Non-Rent PHC Income	$15,000
10% of OGI *	-4,500
	$10,500

TEST PASSED

Therefore, rentals are *not* Personal Holding Company Income.

INCOME TEST IS FAILED [PHC Income = Interest $15,000 is less than 60% of AOGI ($36,000 x 60% = $21,600)]

Thus, X Corporation is *not* a personal holding company.

See Example 11 in the text.

4.	Current Taxable Income	$75,000
	Federal Income Tax	-13,750
	Disallowed charitable contribution	-4,000
	Dividends-received deduction	+16,000
	Dividends paid (9/X8 $11,000 + 3/X9 limited to 20% ($11,000) = $2,200)	-13,200
	Undistributed Personal Holding Company Income	$60,050
	Personal Holding Company Tax (39.6%)	$23,780

See Example 16 in the text.

CHAPTER 21
S CORPORATIONS

CHAPTER HIGHLIGHTS

Subchapter S is an elective provision of the Code that allows some "small business corporations" to become non-taxable entities. Income and losses of the corporation pass through directly to its shareholders, who recognize their pro-rata share of the income or loss on their individual returns, in the year with or within which the corporate year ends. Both income and losses pass through to the shareholders on the basis of pro-rata daily ownership. This pass-through of income directly to the shareholders helps to mitigate the effect of double taxation. In addition, shareholders who materially participate in the operations of the business can use the corporate losses to offset any other income that they have.

I.   Subchapter S Provisions
- A.   The Subchapter S provisions of the Code allow certain "small business corporations" to become non-taxable entities.
- B.   S corporations are regular corporations in the legal sense.
- C.   Subchapter S is an elective provision. Failure to make the election, or comply with the requirements once such an election has been made, results in the corporation being taxed as a regular (C) corporation.
- D.   Certain states do not recognize some or all of the Subchapter S provisions. Therefore, in such states, S corporations are subject to state corporate income taxes.
- E.   An S corporation is not subject to the alternative minimum tax, accumulated earnings tax, personal holding company tax or environmental tax. An S corporation, however, may be subject to a corporate-level tax on: built-in gains; excessive passive income; and, state income tax. In addition, upon the conversion from a C corporation to an S corporation, the S corporation must include in income a LIFO recapture amount.
- F.   An S corporation cannot deduct its expenditures in providing fringe benefits to a shareholder-employee owning 2% or more of the corporation's stock.

II. Definition of A Small Business Corporation
     A.   A "small" business corporation must be a domestic corporation.
     B.   The number of shareholders is limited to 35. For this purpose, husband and wife are counted as a single shareholder, regardless of the manner in which they own the stock.
     C.   Shareholders may be individuals, estates, or certain trusts. However, a non-resident alien may not be a shareholder. In addition, another corporation or a partnership may not be a shareholder.
     D.   A qualifying "small" business corporation may have only one class of stock. However, differences in voting rights among shares of common stock are permitted.
     E.   A small business corporation may not be an ineligible corporation, i.e., it may not be a member of an "affiliated group." This rule does not apply if the affiliated corporations are inactive.
     F.   An S corporation can only own up to 79 percent of another corporation.

III. Making the Election
     A.   All shareholders must elect S corporation status, by consenting and filing Form 2553. A husband and wife who both own stock must both consent.
     B.   In community property jurisdictions, both the husband and the wife must sign the consent even though the stock may be owned by only one of the spouses.
     C.   An election must be made before the fifteenth day of the third month of the election year, or at any time in the preceding year, to obtain S status for the current tax year.

IV. Loss of An Election
     A.   When a corporation ceases to meet the definition of a small business corporation, the election will be terminated. The termination is effective as of the date on which the disqualifying event occurs.
     B.   An S election will be terminated at the beginning of the fourth year when the S corporation has Subchapter C accumulated earnings and profits, and passive income exceeds 25% of gross receipts for three consecutive years. Moreover, a penalty tax equal to the highest corporate rate of tax will be imposed on the lesser of the excess net passive income or the corporation's taxable income as computed under Section 1374. This penalty tax applies only if the S corporation has Subchapter C accumulated earnings and profits. The passive income, however, will not trigger an involuntary termination unless it exceeds 25% of gross receipts for three consecutive years.

$$\text{Excess net passive income} = \frac{\text{Passive investment income in excess of 25\% of gross receipts for the year}}{\text{Passive investment income for the year}} \times \text{Net passive investment income for the year}$$

     C.   In addition, a majority of the shareholders may revoke the election voluntarily. The revocation must be filed by the fifteenth day of the third month of the tax year for which the revocation will be effective, or at any time in the preceding year.
     D.   A new shareholder of an S corporation (after the initial election) does not have the power to terminate the election, unless he or she owns more than one-half of the corporation's stock.
     E.   After termination or revocation, a new election typically cannot be made for a period of five years. The IRS may permit an early reelection in either of the following situations:
          1.   There is a more than 50% change in ownership after the first year for which the termination is applicable, or
          2.   The event causing the termination was not reasonably within the control of the S corporation or its majority shareholders.

V.   Taxable Income of an S Corporation
      A.   Generally, the taxable income or loss of an S corporation is determined according to
            the tax rules that are applicable to partnerships.
      B.   Some deductions that usually are
            allowable only to individuals
            are allowed to S corporations.
            However, an S corporation cannot
            claim deductions for the
            standard deduction amount,
            personal exemptions, foreign
            taxes, net operating losses,
            medical and dental expenses,
            alimony paid, personal moving
            expenses, and expenses for the
            care of certain dependents.

KEY TERMS
● Qualifying S Corporation
● Pass-Through Items, Basis of
  Shares
● Accumulated Adjustments
  Account
● Built-In Gains Tax
● Fiscal Year, Fringe Benefits

      C.   Income, losses, deductions, and
            credits that could affect the tax
            liability for any of the
            shareholders are separated from
            the S corporation's ordinary income or loss. Items that flow through separately
            include: short- and long-term capital gains and losses; §1231 gains and losses;
            passive gains, losses and credits under §469; charitable contributions; tax-exempt
            interest; certain portfolio income; investment interest income and expenses; foreign
            tax credits; business credits; and tax preference items.
      D.   The nonseparate income and deduction items are lumped together into an
            undifferentiated amount that constitutes Subchapter S taxable income or loss.
      E.   The separate income, deduction, and credit items are passed through to the
            shareholders, on a pro rata per-share daily ownership basis. However, if a shareholder
            dies or stock is transferred during the taxable year, income, deduction and credits may
            be allocated under the pro rata approach or the shareholders may make a per-books
            election.
      F.   An S corporation is required to make estimated tax payments for its tax liability that
            is attributable to the built-in gains tax and passive investment income tax.
      G.   Generally, all S corporations must adopt a calendar year unless there is a bona fide
            business purpose for a different tax year or a special election under section 444 is
            made to retain a fiscal year.
            1.   If a special election is made to retain a fiscal year, the S corporation must
                  make a special tax deposit with the IRS.
            2.   This deposit is approximately equal to the revenue that the government loses as
                  a result of the S corporation's retention of a fiscal year.

VI.   The Order and Sources of Distributions by an S Corporation without Accumulted Earnings and
      Profits.
      A.   First, distributions are tax-free up to the amount of the shareholder's stock basis.
      B.   Any residual is treated as a gain from the sale or exchange of property.

VII. The Order and Sources of Distributions by an S Corporation with Accumulated Earnings and
      Profits
      A.   First, distributions are tax-free up to the amount in the accumulated adjustments
            account (AAA), limited to the stock basis at the time of the distribution.
            1.   The AAA is a corporate account which represents the cumulative total of
                  undistributed net income items for S corporation taxable years beginning after
                  1982.
            2.   The AAA is adjusted in a similar manner to the shareholder's stock basis except
                  there is no adjustment for tax-exempt income and related expenses or for

Federal taxes attributable to a C corporation tax year. In addition, when the AAA balance is negative, any decreases in stock basis have no impact on the AAA.

B. Second, distributions are tax-free up to the amount of the corporation's previously taxed income (PTI), under prior Subchapter S rules.

C. Third, a distribution in excess of the sum of the AAA and any PTI is treated as a taxable dividend to the extent of Subchapter C accumulated earnings and profits.

D. Fourth, any residual amount is a return of capital to the extent of the shareholder's remaining basis in the S corporation's stock.

E. Fifth, distributions in excess of the shareholder's basis in his or her stock are taxable as capital gains.

F. With the consent of all shareholders, an S corporation may elect to have a distribution treated as made from accumulated earnings and profits, rather than from the AAA.

G. See Exhibit 21-1 to compare this scheme to that for a C corporation.

H. An S corporation recognizes gain when it distributes appreciated property to its shareholders. The character of the gain will depend upon the type of asset distributed. Loss is not recognized on the distribution of depreciated property. However, an S corporation recognizes both gain or loss on liquidating distributions.

VIII. Built-in Gains Tax

A. An S corporation is taxed on **built-in gains** to the extent of the lesser of:
1. The recognized built-in gains for the tax year; or,
2. The amount of taxable income the corporation would have recognized if it were not an S corporation. For purposes of this computation, NOLs and special corporate deductions are not taken into account.

The lesser amount then is reduced by the unexpired C corporation NOL, capital loss or business credit carryforwards. In addition, alternative minimum tax credits carried over from prior C corporation years can be used against the built-in gains tax resulting in post-conversion years.

B. In the case of subchapter S elections made after March 30, 1988, any net recognized built-in gain that is not subject to the built-in gains tax due to the net income limitation is carried forward and is subject to the built-in gains tax to the extent that the corporation subsequently has other taxable income (that is not already subject to the built-in gains tax) for any tax year within the ten-year recognition period.

C. Net unrealized built-in gain is the excess of the FMV of the corporation's assets as of the beginning of its first S corporation taxable year, over the aggregate adjusted basis of its assets at that time.

D. Recognized built-in gain is any gain recognized during the ten-year period beginning with the first day of the taxable year that the corporation becomes an S corporation. All gains recognized during this period are deemed to be built-in gains, unless the S corporation can prove:
1. The asset was not held by the corporation as of the beginning of the first taxable year as an S corporation, or
2. The gain recognized is in excess of the FMV of the asset at the beginning of the corporation's first taxable year as an S corporation, over its adjusted basis at that time.

E. The tax rate is equal to the highest corporate tax rate.

F. The tax does **not** apply to:
1. a corporation that had an S election in effect for the ten previous taxable years;
2. a new corporation (in existence for fewer than eleven years), if the S election was made in the first year of the corporation's operation; or,
3. a corporation that made its S election prior to 1987.

G. Built-in gains, less the built-in gains tax, flow through to the shareholders. The character of the gain is retained as it flows through.

IX.   Net Operating Losses
    A.   NOLs pass through to an S corporation's shareholders.
    B.   A loss is deductible by the shareholders for the year with or within which the corporation's tax year ends.
    C.   NOLs are allocated to the shareholders on a daily basis, in proportion to the percent of stock owned. When a shareholder has acquired stock at different times and for different amounts, a separate-share approach is required.

> Probably the chief attraction of the S election over time is the shareholder's ability to deduct pass-through losses against salary and other income. Any restriction on this ability should be avoided or planned for, to preserve the valuable resulting deductions.

    D.   NOLs reduce the shareholder's basis in the stock.
    E.   A shareholder's deduction for the NOL pass-through is limited to the shareholder's adjusted basis in the stock plus the basis of any loans that he or she has made to the corporation. To the extent that the NOL exceeds this amount, the NOL deduction can be carried over indefinitely to another taxable year. Any loss so carried forward may be deducted only by the same shareholder. Loss carryovers remaining at the end of a one-year S corporation post-termination period are lost forever.
    F.   S corporation shareholders are subject to the §469 passive loss rules. Therefore, shareholders who do not materially participate in operating the business can apply the corporate losses and credits only against income from other passive activities.

X.   Shareholder's Tax Basis in S Corporation Stock
    A.   Initial basis is computed in the same manner as would be the case for the basis in the stock of a regular corporation, e.g., purchase price of the shares.
    B.   The basis of stock in an S corporation is increased further by taxable income, by tax-exempt income, by additional shareholder capital contributions, and by the excess of the deductions for depletion over the basis of the property that is subject to depletion.
    C.   The basis of S corporation stock is reduced by the amount of money and the fair market value of property distributed, by the sum of current and prior years' distributive share of deductible losses, by the shareholder's share of nondeductible expenditures, and by the amount of the shareholder's §611 depletion deduction.
    D.   The shareholder's basis in the stock cannot fall below zero. Excess basis reductions decrease the shareholder's basis in his or her loans to the corporation. When basis is restored (e.g., via additional corporate income or shareholder capital contributions), the basis of the loan is restored before the basis of the stock is increased.
    E.   If a loan is repaid in an amount that exceeds its basis (e.g., because of an NOL pass-through), the excess constitutes a capital gain to the shareholder, provided that the debt is evidenced by an instrument such as a note, bond, or debenture that is a capital asset in the shareholder's hands. If the debt is not evidenced by an instrument, then the character of the gain recognized will be ordinary.

XI.   Advantages of S Corporation Status
    A.   Income of an S corporation is not subject to double taxation, i.e., at both the corporate and the shareholder levels.

B.   Use of the corporate entity allows the owners limited liability.

C.   The corporation can choose desirable tax accounting methods. Thus, the shareholders can control (to a certain degree) the nature and amount of much of their income from an S corporation. However, a corporation that makes an S election is required to use either a calendar year, some other fiscal year for which a business purpose can be established, or make special deposits to retain its current fiscal year.

D.   Unlike a regular corporation, an S corporation may use the cash method of accounting.

E.   Net operating losses, net long-term and short-term capital gains and losses, and other types of income and deductions, and tax credits, flow through to the shareholders.

F.   Income can be shifted to lower-bracket family members, by transferring to them some of the shares in the corporation. However, any family member who renders services or furnishes capital to an S corporation must be paid reasonable compensation, or the IRS may make adjustments to reflect the value of such services or capital.

G.   S corporations are not subject to the environmental tax, alternative minimum tax, accumulated earnings tax or personal holding company tax.

XII.   Disadvantages of S Corporation Status

A.   Corporate income tax rates may be lower than those applicable to high-bracket individuals. Thus, an S corporation may generate unnecessary income tax liability.

B.   It is difficult to elect a fiscal year for an S corporation.

C.   The S corporation may be subject to a corporate-level tax on built-in gains, or excess passive investment income. In addition, the S election is not recognized by the District of Columbia and by a few states; therefore, in those jurisdictions, some or all of the corporation's income may be subject to a state corporate income tax.

D.   C corporations that use the LIFO inventory method are subject to a LIFO recapture tax when they convert to S status.

E.   Many fringe benefits are not available to more-than-2% owner-employees.

F.   Under the passive loss rules, the deductibility of pass-through losses for inactive owners is limited.

G.   Carryovers from subchapter C years are not available to an S corporation for regular tax purposes, but may be available for built-in gains tax purposes.

Exhibit 21-1
SOURCES OF CORPORATE DISTRIBUTIONS

S CORPORATION	C CORPORATION
Accumulated Adjustments Account: Tax-free.	
	Current E&P: Taxable. Cash or other property. Dividend income.
Previously Taxed Income remaining from pre-1983 years: Non-Taxable. Cash only. Nontransferable. S election required for year of distribution.	
Accumulated E&P from prior (and Non-Subchapter S) years: Taxable. Cash or other property. Dividend income. *	Accumulated E&P from prior years: Taxable. Cash or other property. Dividend income.
Return of Capital: Non-Taxable (Reduce Basis).	Return of Capital: Non-Taxable (Reduce Basis).
Capital Gain: Taxable.	Capital Gain: Taxable.

* With the consent of all shareholders, an S corporation may elect to have a distribution treated as made from accumulated earnings and profits rather than from the AAA.

Refer to Chapter 18 for additional explanations concerning distributions from regular corporations.

TEST FOR SELF-EVALUATION - CHAPTER 21

True or False

Indicate which of the following statements are true or false by circling the correct answer.

T **(F)** 1. An S corporation may not deduct expenses of providing certain fringe benefits to any shareholder-employee.

T **(F)** 2. A new shareholder of an S corporation does not have the power to terminate the election by affirmatively refusing to consent to the election, unless he or she owns 50% or more of the voting stock.

T **(F)** 3. A husband and wife are considered to be a single shareholder, for purposes of making an S election on Form 2553.

(T) F 4. Unlike a regular corporation, an S corporation is not subject to the environmental tax.

T **(F)** 5. An S corporation may use a fiscal tax year, provided its shareholders make special deposits with the Federal government.

T **(F)** 6. Any net gains from the recapture of depreciation constitute separately stated income.

T **(F)** 7. When an S corporation's election is involuntarily terminated, the entity is taxed as a regular corporation starting on the day after the date on which the disqualifying event occurred.

T **(F)** 8. After an S election is voluntarily terminated, there usually is a ten-year waiting period before a new election can be made.

(T) F 9. When one S corporation shareholder transfers stock to another shareholder, any AAA on the purchase date is fully available to the purchaser.

T **(F)** 10. The built-in gains tax applies to all corporations that made an S election after 1986.

T **(F)** 11. An S corporation cannot own 80% or more of the stock of another corporation.

(T) F 12. The IRS may permit a corporation to reelect S status prior to the five-year termination waiting period, if there is a more than 50% change in ownership after the first year for which the termination is applicable.

Fill-in-the-Blanks

Complete the following statements with the appropriate word(s) or amount(s).

1.   If an election is made to retain a fiscal year, the S corporation must make a _special_ _tax_ _deposit_ with the IRS.

2.   The S corporation rules _do not_ (do/do not) place a ceiling on the asset value of the entity.

3.   An S corporation election can be made at any time during the preceding taxable year, or by the ___15th___ day of the ___3rd___ month of the election year.

4.   Unexpired C corporation _NOL_, _capital_ _loss_, _business_ _credits_ and alternative minimum tax credit carryforwards can be used against the built-in gains tax.

5.   An S corporation with accumulated earnings and profits from Subchapter C years is subject to the regular corporate income tax to the extent that its _passive_ income exceeds _25_ percent of its gross receipts.

6.   The order of S corporation distributions is: (1) _Acc_ _adj_ _acct_, (2) _previously_ _taxed_ _income_, (3) _Accum_ _earnings_ _and_ _profits_, (4) _return_ _of_ _capital_ and (5) capital gain.

7.   An S election can be terminated in any of the following ways: voluntary _revocation_; cessation of small business _corp_ _status_; or the corporation fails the _passive_ _investment_ limitation.

8.   No more than ___70___ individuals can hold shares in the same S corporation.

9.   S corporation shareholders receive a ratable share of the corporation's income and losses, based upon their _daily_ _stock_ _ownership_.

10.   The deduction for an NOL may not exceed a shareholder's basis in the _stock_, plus the basis of any _loans_ that he or she has made to the corporation.

11.   A shareholder's share of an S corporation's NOL can be _carry_ _over_ to future taxable years, to the extent that it exceeds the basis of the shareholder's stock and the loans made to the corporation.

12.   If a calendar-year S corporation wishes voluntarily to terminate its election retroactive to the beginning of 19X8, shareholders owning _more_ than _50_ percent of the voting stock must notify the IRS to this effect.

13.   A qualified small business corporation must be a _domestic_ corporation and must not be a member of an _affiliated_ _group_ of active corporations.

14.   Any net gains from depreciation recapture constitute _nonseparately_ computed S corporation income.

15.   After an S shareholder's basis in her stock and loans to the corporation have been depleted by the flow-through of corporate NOLs, corporate income will flow through and first restore the basis of her _loans_.

Multiple Choice

Choose the best answer for each of the following questions.

_____ 1.   A qualifying small business corporation:
             a.   May have both common and preferred stock.
             b.   Must be a domestic corporation.
             c.   May have another corporation as a shareholder.
             d.   May not have a trust as a shareholder.
             e.   b and c.

_____ 2.   A business that made an S election upon incorporation in 1993 may be subject to the
             following corporate-level taxes. More than one answer may be correct.
             a.   State corporate income tax.
             b.   Passive investment income tax.
             c.   Federal income tax on built-in gains.
             d.   Capital gains tax.
             e.   a and b.

_____ 3.   An S election may be terminated when:
             a.   Gross receipts exceed five million dollars for the year.
             b.   Any one of the shareholders chooses to revoke the election.
             c.   A new shareholder forgets to make the election on his own.
             d.   A new 75 percent shareholder revokes the election.
             e.   c and d.

_____ 4.   The following items retain their tax character as they flow through to the shareholder
             from an S corporation. More than one answer may be correct.
             a.   Long-term capital gain.
             b.   Short-term capital gain.
             c.   Tax-exempt income.
             d.   §162 expenses.
             e.   §1245 recapture.

_____ 5.   On January 1, 19X9, Don Baker owned 10% of the stock of Electing Corp., which is a
             calendar-year S corporation. On June 14, 19X9, Baker acquired another 10% of Electing
             Corp's stock. For calendar year 19X9, Electing Corp's nonseparately computed income
             is $36,500. What is Baker's share of Electing Corp's income for 19X9?
             a. $3,650.
             b. $5,475.
             c. $5,660.
             d. $7,300.

_____ 6.   The following entity will not qualify as a small business corporation: (More than one
             answer may be correct.)
             a.   A corporation that has 36 shareholders, consisting of eleven married couples
                     and fourteen individuals.
             b.   An active corporation that is a wholly-owned subsidiary.
             c.   A corporation with six individual shareholders and income of over $250
                     million.
             d.   A corporation that has an estate as a shareholder.
             e.   A corporation that owns 100% of an inactive corporation.

_____ 7.   Income of an S corporation is allocated among the shareholders on a pro rata basis,
             according to the:

      a.   Profit and loss ratio.
      b.   Allocation method described in the corporate charter.
      c.   Number of shares owned on the last day of the taxable year.
      d.   Pro-rata number of shares owned, on a daily basis.

____ 8.   X, a calendar year S corporation, distributes $500 to its only shareholder, A, on
December 31, 19X2. A's basis in his stock is $200 on December 31, 19X1. For 19X2, X
Corproation had $800 of nonseparately stated income, $300 of capital losses and $100 of
tax-exempt income. What is A's basis in his stock as of December 31, 19X2?
      a. $0.
      b. $100.
      c. $200.
      d. $300.
      e. $800.

____ 9.   A shareholder's basis in S corporation stock is:
      a.   Unaffected by property distributions.
      b.   Decreased by a distribution from accumulated E&P.
      c.   Originally computed in a manner similar to that used for regular corporations.
      d.   Unaffected by cash dividend distributions.

____ 10.   Deductions for NOLs are limited to: (More than one answer may be correct)
      a.   A shareholder's basis in the stock.
      b. $100,000 per shareholder per year.
      c.   The basis of stock plus any liabilities owed to the corporation.
      d.   The basis of the stock plus the basis of any debt owed by the corporation to the
             shareholder.
      e.   The amount determined under the passive loss rules.

____ 11.   A valid calendar-year S corporation issues a second class of stock on April 1, 19X9.
What is the tax effect of this action?
      a.   The election is lost, effective 1-1-X9.
      b.   The election is lost, effective 4-1-X9.
      c.   The election is lost, effective 4-2-X9.
      d.   The election is lost, effective 1-1-X10.
      e.   There is no effect. The election is not lost.

USE THE FOLLOWING INFORMATION FOR QUESTIONS 12 THROUGH 14.

In 19X2, Cheryl Brown, the sole shareholder of a calendar-year S Corporation, received a loss pass-
through that exceeds her basis in the corporate stock by $10,000. On December 31, 19X2, Brown did not
have any loans outstanding to the corporation. During 19X3, the corporation incurred a $30,000 loss.
On January 1, 19X3, Brown loaned $10,000 to the corporation. On December 31, 19X3, Brown contributed
$25,000 to the capital of the corporation. During 19X4, the corporation generated taxable income of
$12,000.

____ 12.   What is the amount of loss that Cheryl may deduct in 19X3?
      a. $0.
      b. $10,000.
      c. $30,000.
      d. $35,000.
      e. $40,000.

____ 13.   What is the amount of Cheryl's loss carryforward to 19X4?
      a. $0.

    b. $5,000.
    c. $10,000.
    d. $30,000.

_____ 14.   What is Cherl's basis in the S corporation's stock and the loan to the corporation, respectively, at December 31, 19X4?
    a. $0, $0.
    b. $0, $7,000.
    c. $2,000, $10,000.
    d. $3,500, $3,500.
    e. $7,000, $0.

_____ 15.   The basis of shareholder X's stock in her valid calendar-year S corporation is $10,000. Ms. X owns 100 percent of the stock in the corporation, and she has no loans outstanding to the corporation. The corporation's NOL is $12,000. Which statement is true?
    a.   Ms. X claims a $12,000 deduction.
    b.   Ms. X claims a $10,000 deduction. She can carry back the $2,000 excess for three years.
    c.   Ms. X claims a $10,000 deduction. There is no carryback allowed, but she can carryforward the $2,000 excess indefinitely.
    d.   Ms. X claims a $10,000 deduction. There is no carryover of the disallowed loss.

_____ 16.   Which of the following will prevent a corporation from making a valid election to be taxed as an S corporation?
    a.   Having 40 individual shareholders, each of whom is married to one other shareholder.
    b.   Owning 50% of the stock of a domestic corporation.
    c.   Having a partnership as a shareholder.
    d.   Deriving 40% of its gross receipts from passive income services.
    e.   Owning 100 percent of an inactive corporation.

USE THE FOLLOWING INFORMATION FOR PROBLEMS 17 THROUGH 19

New Corp., a calendar year taxpayer, was incorporated in 1985 and elected S corporation status for its taxable year beginning January 1, 1988. On that date, it had net unrealized built-in gains of $1,000,000. In 1993, New Corp. recognized gains of $600,000. If New Corp. had remained a C corporation, it would have had total taxable income in 1993 of $500,000 without taking into account any NOL or special deductions.

_____ 17.   On what amount does New Corp. compute its built-in gains tax?
    a. $500,000.
    b. $600,000.
    c. $1,000,000.
    d.   New Corp. is not subject to the built-in gains tax.

_____ 18.   What is the built-in gains tax that New Corp. must pay?
    a. $0.
    b. $125,000.
    c. $170,000.
    d. $175,000.
    e.   None of the above.   Specify correct amount _____.

_____ 19.   Assume the same facts as above, except that New Corp. recognized the $600,000 gain in 1999. If New Corp. had remained a C corporation, it would have had total taxable income in 1999 of $700,000 without taking into account any NOL or special deductions. On what amount would New Corp. compute its built-in gains tax?

 a. $600,000.
 b. $700,000.
 c. $1,000,000.
 d. New Corp. is not subject to the built-in gains tax.

_____ 20. Which of the following items will not pass through as a separately stated item to an S corporation shareholder?

 a. Capital gains and capital losses.
 b. Tax-exempt bond interest income.
 c. §1245 gains.
 d. §1231 gains and losses.
 e. Tax preference items.

_____ 21. An NOL that exceeds the S corporation shareholder's adjusted basis in his or her stock and loans made to the S corporation may be:

 a. Carried forward for fifteen years.
 b. Carried back three years and forward fifteen years.
 c. Carried forward indefinitely and deducted when and if the basis is restored by any shareholder who owns or purchases the stock.
 d. Carried forward indefinitely and deducted only by the same shareholder when and if the basis is restored.

_____ 22. A C corporation that made an S election this year may be subject to which of the following taxes. More than one answer may be correct.

 a. State corporate income tax.
 b. Built-in gains tax.
 c. Passive investment income tax.
 d. Capital gains tax.
 e. Environmental tax.

_____ 23. On January 31, 19X1, Z Corporation sold all of its stock in its wholly owned subsidiary, X Corporation, to individuals A and B. X is a calendar-year corporation and, A and B filed an S election on March 14, 19X1. The earliest date that X's S election will be effective is:

 a. January 1, 19X1.
 b. February 1, 19X1.
 c. March 14, 19X1.
 d. March 15, 19X1.
 e. January 1, 19X2.

_____ 24. Which of the following is NOT a requirement for a corporation to elect S corporation status? More than one answer may be correct.

 a. Must not have any accumulated earnings and profits.
 b. Must confine stockholders to individuals, estates, and certain qualifying trusts.
 c. Must be a domestic corporation.
 d. Must have only one class of stock.
 e. Must not have a nonresident alien shareholder.

_____ 25. Which of the following rules pertain to S corporations? More than one answer may be correct.

 a. Excess investment interest of the corporation passes through to the shareholders.

   b.   The hobby loss provisions of §183 are applicable.
   c.   An S corporation is not subject to the ten percent of taxable income limitation
            applicable to charitable contributions made by a C corporation.
   d.   Any family member who renders services to an electing corporation must be paid
            a reasonable salary.
   e.   All of the above.

Short Answer

1.   What are the requirements for a corporation to qualify as a "small" business corporation?

2.   Discuss means by which to terminate an S election.

3.   X Corporation has a valid S election in effect. X has no accumulated E&P from Subchapter C
      years. On 1-1-X1, A owns all of the 100 outstanding shares in X. On 10-1-X1, she sells twenty
      shares to B for $30,000. All taxpayers use the calendar year.

            19X1 Salaries: A $75,000;   B $15,000
            19X1 Dividends Paid: $10,000 on 5-1-X1 and $10,000 on 11-1-X1

   A)   X's 19X1 Non-Separately-Stated Income = $200,000
         LTCG = $30,000, on a sale that was completed 2-1-X1   A   95%
         Charitable Contribution = $55,000, made 12-15-X1
         Compute A's and B's 19X1 gross income from X.   B   5%

                        A   B
                     75,000   15,000
                    190,000   10,000
                     18,500   1,500
                     52,250   2,750

   B)   Same as A, but Non-Separately-Stated Income = ($90,000).

                   (45,000)   (5,000)

   C)   Same as A, but X's fiscal year ends on 1-31-X2.

                    75,000   15,000

4.   R is sole shareholder in X Corporation, a valid calendar-year S Corporation. R purchased his shares on 1-1-X1, for $100,000. R loans X $17,000 on 2-1-X1. X loaned R $7,000 on 11-1-X1. 19X1 activities of X include:

Non-Separately-Stated Income	$15,000
Net Long-Term Capital Gain	3,000
Exempt Interest Income	4,000
Dental Expenses of R's mother, paid by X	750
Dividend Paid, 12-31-X1	2,000

A)   What is R's basis in his X shares on 1-1-X2?

[handwritten:]
100,000
15,000
3,000
4,000
(750)

121,250
(2,000)
119,250

B)   Same as A, but 19X1 Non-Separately-Stated Income is ($120,000).

[handwritten:]
100,000   (13,750)   basis 0
(117,000)   loan 3250
4000   gain 2000
(750)
(2000)

C)   Same as A, but 19X1 Non-Separately-Stated Income is ($220,000).

[handwritten:] (113,750)

5.   X Corporation has made a valid S election for 1993. It has Accumulated Earnings and Profits, from Subchapter C years, of $30,000. During 1993, X recognizes:

Sales Receipts	$60,000
Interest Income--AT&T bonds	40,000
Brokerage Fees	5,000

A)   Compute X Corporation's passive income penalty tax.

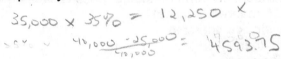

[handwritten:]
35,000 × 35% = 12,250 ✗

35% × 40,000 - 25,000 / 40,000 = 4593.75

B)   Same as A, but X had operating expenses of $85,000 in addition to the brokerage fees.

SOLUTIONS TO CHAPTER 21 QUESTIONS

True or False

1.   F   This rule is applicable only with respect to shareholder-employees owning more than 2% of the S corporation's stock.
2.   F   The shareholder must own more than 50% of the S corporation's stock.
3.   F   Although a husband and wife are considered to be one shareholder for purposes of the number of shareholders requirement, each spouse must consent to the election.
4.   T
5.   F   The corporation, rather than the shareholders, must make the special deposits.
6.   F   Depreciation recapture amounts are included in the corporation's ordinary income (i.e., nonseparately stated income).
7.   F   The entity is taxed as a regular corporation starting on the date on which the disqualifying event occurred.
8.   F   There usually is a five-year waiting period.
9.   T
10.   F   This tax only applies to C corporations that made an S election after 1986.
11.   F   Under certain conditions, an S corporation can establish one or more inactive affiliated corporations.
12.   T

Fill-in-the-Blanks

1.   special tax deposit
2.   do not
3.   fifteenth, third
4.   NOL, capital loss, business credits
5.   passive, 25
6.   accumulated adjustment account, previously taxed income, accumulated earnings and profits, return of capital
7.   revocation, corporation status, passive investment
8.   70 (35 married couples)
9.   daily stock ownership
10.   stock, loans
11.   carried over
12.   more, fifty
13.   domestic, affiliated group
14.   nonseparately
15.   loans

Multiple Choice

1.   b
2.   a   A corporation that has always been an S corporation is not subject to the passive investment income tax, or to the built-in gains tax.
3.   d
4.   a, b, c
5.   c   [$3,650 + 10% ($36,500 x 201/365)]. See Example 15 in the text.
6.   b   An S corporation cannot have a corporate shareholder, and it cannot be a member of an affiliated group of active corporations.
7.   d

8.	d	[$200 + $800 - $300 + $100 - $500 (distribution)]. See Example 18 in the text.
9.	c	
10.	d, e	
11.	b	
12.	d	($10,000 loan to corporation + $25,000 capital contribution) See Example 28 in the text.
13.	b	[$40,000 ($10,000 19X2 loss + $30,000 19X3 loss) - $35,000 loss allowed in 19X3] See Example 28 in the text.
14.	b	$12,000 taxable income less $5,000 loss carryforward from 19X3. The basis in the loan to the corporation is restored before the stock basis.
15.	c	See Example 28 in the text.
16.	c	
17.	a	(Lesser of recognized built-in gains or the amount of taxable income that the corporation would have recognized if it were a C corporation.) See Example 31 in the text.
18.	d	(35% X $500,000)
19.	d	(Built-in gains tax only applies for the ten-year period beginning with the first taxable year as an S corporation.) See Example 31 in the text.
20.	c	
21.	d	(provided also that the deduction finally occurs in a year in which the S election is still effective, or by the end of the one-year post-termination transition period.)
22.	a, b, c	
23.	e	The election is not effective until January 1, 19X2 because the corporation was owned by a regular corporation for part of 19X1, and accordingly, is not eligible to receive S status for 19X1.
24.	a	
25.	e	

Short Answer

1. A qualifying "small" business corporation is a US corporation with 35 or fewer shareholders. For this purpose, a husband and wife are considered to be a single shareholder. The corporation may have only one class of stock outstanding. Only individuals, estates, and certain trusts can be shareholders. Shareholders can not be nonresident aliens and, the corporation cannot be a member of an affiliated group.

2. An S election will be terminated when: the corporation ceases to meet the definition of a small business corporation (e.g., because it has too many shareholders or issues a second class of stock). As of the date of this event, the corporation has a "short" taxable year, for which it is subject to the normal Subchapter C provisions. The S election is effective, however, for the days of the taxable year that occur prior to the event. The owners of a majority of the shares of the corporation voluntarily may revoke the election. An S election will be terminated at the beginning of the 4th year when the S corporation has subchapter C accumulated earnings and profits, and passive income exceeds 25% of gross receipts for 3 consecutive years.

3. Ownership Weights:

    A [100% X 273/365] + [80% X 92/365]   = .95
    B [20% X 92/365]   = .05

		A	*B*
	Salary	$75,000	$15,000
	Dividends	0	0

Non-Separately-Stated Income	190,000	10,000
Long-Term Capital Gain	28,500	1,500
Charitable Contribution	52,250	2,750

See Example 15 in the text.

B)

	A	B
Salary	$75,000	$15,000
Dividends	0	0
Non-Separately-Stated Income	(85,500)	(4,500)
Long-Term Capital Gain	28,500	1,500
Charitable Contribution	52,250	2,750

See Example 15 in the text.

C)

	A	B
Salary	$75,000	$15,000
Dividends	0	0
Non-Separately-Stated Income	0*	0*
Long-Term Capital Gain	0*	0*
Charitable Contribution	0*	0*

*   Pass-Through will appear on A's and B's 19X2 returns. (Note, though, that ownership weights then will change.)

See Example 15 in the text.

4.   A)

Original Basis of Stock	$100,000
Income ($15,000 + $3,000)	+ 18,000
Exempt Income	+ 4,000
Non-Deductible Expenditures	- 750
Subtotal	$121,250
Distribution	- 2,000
Basis of stock, 1-1-X2	$119,250

See Examples 25 and 27 in the text.

B)

Original Basis of Stock	$100,000
Income (-$120,000 + $3,000)	- 117,000
Exempt Income	+ 4,000
Non-Deductible Expenditures	- 750
Subtotal	($ 13,750)

Basis of stock, 1-1-X2 $ 0

Basis of Loan to X, 1-1-X2 ($17,000-$13,750) $3,250

Dividend Paid = Capital Gain $2,000*

*   Assuming that the dividend is not considered to be a repayment of the shareholder's loan.

See Examples 25 and 28 in the text.

C)   Original Basis of Stock $100,000

Income (-$220,000 + $3,000)	- 217,000
Exempt Income	+ 4,000
Non-Deductible Expenditures	- 750
Subtotal	($113,750)

Basis of Stock, 1-1-X2	$ 0
Basis of Loan to X, 1-1-X2 ($17,000 - $113,750)	$ 0
Dividend Paid = Capital Gain	$2,000

Deduction for $220,000 NOL is limited to

Basis Subtotal, before NOL ($100,000 + $3,000 + $4,000 - $750)	$106,250
Basis of Loan to X	+ 17,000
Deduction Limit	$123,250
Loss Carryover by R ($220,000 - 123,250)	$ 96,750

See Examples 25 and 28 in the text.

5.   A) 35% Tax Rate   X $35,000 Net Passive Income ($40,000 - $5,000)

                      X $\dfrac{\$40,000 \text{ Passive Income} - \$25,000 \text{ (1/4 of Gross Receipts)}}{\$40,000 \text{ Passive Income}}$

                      = $4,593.75 Passive Income Penalty Tax

      B) 35% Tax Rate x lesser of:

          (1) $35,000 x $\dfrac{\$40,000 - \$25,000}{\$40,000}$ = $13,125; or,

          (2) $10,000 (Taxable Income; $100,000 - $90,000) = $3,400 Passive Income
                 Penalty Tax. Note: The tax base is limited to taxable income.

See Example 36 in the text.

CHAPTER 22
PARTNERSHIPS

CHAPTER HIGHLIGHTS

 partnership is not a taxable entity. Instead, the income of the partnership flows through to the partners. Income is allocated to the partners according to the partnership agreement. Many items of income and expense retain their character as they flow through to the partners. Generally, if an item of income or expense would affect a partner's income differently if it retained its character, then the character of the item flows through to the partners.

All other items will be netted before they flow through to the partners. A partner's basis in his or her partnership interest is a substituted basis of the property contributed, plus any gain recognized on the transfer, plus his or her share of partnership liabilities contributed by other partners, and minus his or her liabilities that are assumed by other partners. Subject to a few exceptions, there generally is no gain or loss recognized on contributions to the partnership. A partner's basis later is adjusted for liabilities, contributions, withdrawals, profits, and losses.

A partnership takes a carryover basis in the property received. The basis of property received by the partnership is not automatically increased by the gain recognized to the partner as a result of the transfer, unless the partnership would be treated as an investment company if it was incorporated.

I.   Nature of Partnerships
   A.   Partnerships are not separate taxable entities. Rather, the partners carry on
         business as "co-owners," allocating assets and liabilities, profits and losses,
         according to a formal or informal agreement (ie the aggregate concept).
   B.   A partnership, however, is treated as a separate taxable entity for purposes of making
         various tax elections, and for selecting its taxable year, depreciation method, and
         accounting methods (i.e., the entity concept).
   C.   A partnership must actively conduct a trade or business.
   D.   Certain unincorporated organizations may elect not to be treated as partnerships.
         This election generally only applies to joint ventures for the production, extraction,
         or use of property which will not be resold and "investment clubs" that are not engaged
         in a trade or business.

E. A partnership must file an information return (Form 1065) within 3 1/2 months after the end of its taxable year (i.e., April 15th for a calendar-year partnership). Each of the partnership's items is reported on Schedule K.

F. As part of its tax return, the partnership must include a Schedule K-1 for each of its partners. This schedule reports the amount and nature of income that has been allocated to the partner, according to the partnership agreement.

G. *Publicly traded partnerships* (PTPs) are partnerships whose interests are traded on an established securities market or are readily tradeable on a secondary market or the substantial equivalent of a secondary market. Generally, PTPs are treated as corporations.

KEY TERMS
- Entity, Aggregate Concepts
- Special Allocation
- Choice of Tax Year
- Inside, Outside Basis
- Basis of Partnership Interest
- Guaranteed Payment

H. A limited partnership is comprised of one or more general partners and one or more limited partners.

  1. Unless special rules apply, only the general partners are liable to creditors. A limited partner's risk of loss is restricted to his or her equity investment in the partnership.

  2. When a limited partnership uses nonrecourse debt to finance the purchase of property and pledges the property as collateral, usually no partner is personally liable (i.e., the debt is nonrecourse debt).

I. Limited liability companies may receive the benefits of partnership tax treatment and the limited liability afforded corporations under state law.

II. Partner's Share of Income and Expenses

A. The following items retain their character as they pass through to the partners.

  1. Ordinary income from operations, after deducting allowable expenses.
  2. Long- and short-term capital gains/losses, and § 1231 gains/losses.
  3. Charitable contributions.
  4. Tax-exempt interest.
  5. Tax preferences for the alternative minimum tax.
  6. Jobs credit and foreign tax credit.
  7. Expenses that would be itemized deductions or non-business deductions to the partner.
  8. Portfolio income (dividends, interest and royalties) and related expenses.
  9. Non-trade or -business interest expense.
  10. Passive activity items (i.e., income or loss from rental real estate).
  11. Immediately expensed tangible personal property (i.e., § 179 deduction).
  12. Meals and entertainment expenses, subject to the 50% disallowance.
  13. Other items specifically allocated by the partnership agreement.

B. All other income or expense items are netted with ordinary income. A partnership is not entitled to a dividends-received deduction or a NOL deduction. A partnership also cannot deduct payments that it makes for a partner's fringe benefits, since a partner is not considered to be an employee of the partnership.

C. By election, organization costs may be amortized ratably over a period of 60 months or more, starting with the month in which the partnership began business. In contrast, costs of promoting the sale of a partnership interest (*syndication costs*) are not deductible.

D. Partners may allocate specific income, deductions, or credits in any ratio identified in the partnership agreement, if such allocation has economic substance. However, when in-kind property is transferred to a partnership, any realized gain or loss as of the contribution date remains assigned to the contributing partner upon ultimate disposal by the entity in a taxable transaction.

E. The tax year of a partnership generally must be the same as the taxable year of the partners owning more than 50% of profits and capital (i.e., a majority interest).

    1. If the partners owning a majority interest do not have the same taxable year, the partnership tax year must be the same as all of its principal partners (i.e., those owning a 5% or greater interest).

    2. If the principal partners do not have the same tax year, the partnership generally must adopt the taxable year that results in the least aggregate deferral of income.

    3. The partnership generally can adopt any other fiscal year only if permission is received from the IRS.

    4. Under certain circumstances, a partnership may elect to use a tax year other than a required year, provided that the income deferral is three months or less and certain tax deposits are made by the partnership with the Federal government.

F. The partnership tax year will end on the:

    1. Termination of the business;

    2. Death of a partner or termination of his or her entire interest, BUT ONLY for that partner; or,

    3. Sale of a total of 50% or more of the partnership interests within a 12-month period. For purposes of this test, subsequent sales of the same partnership interest within a single twelve-month period are ignored.

III. Forming a Partnership

A. Generally, no gain or loss is recognized by partners or the partnership on contributions that are made to the partnership when the partnership is formed, or contributions made subsequent to the creation of the entity. The following are exceptions to this rule.

    1. If the partnership interest is received solely for services rendered, the FMV of the interest is taxable to the partner as ordinary income;

    2. Liabilities assumed by the partnership that are in excess of the partner's basis in the contributed property create taxable income to the contributor, in an amount equal to such excess;

    3. If the partnership is used to effect a tax-free exchange of assets; and,

    4. The contributing partner is required to recognize gain realized on the transfer of property to a partnership that would be treated as an investment company if the partnership were incorporated.

B. The holding period of a partner's interest acquired by a noncash property contribution includes the holding period of the contributed property. However, the holding period starts on the day the interest is acquired if the contributed property is neither a capital asset nor a § 1231 asset in the hands of the contributing partner.

IV. Partner's Basis in the Partnership Interest

A. Each partner has an *inside basis* and an *outside basis* in partnership assets. **Inside basis** refers to the partner's share of the adjusted basis of the aggregate partnership assets, as determined from the partnership's tax accounts. A partner's **outside basis** represents the actual investment of after-tax dollars that the partner has made in the partnership.

B. The partner's original interest basis equals:

    1. Money contributed,

    2. *Plus* the adjusted basis (to the partner) of other property contributed,

    3. *Plus* gain recognized by the partner under the investment company rule (See III,

A.4).

4. *Plus* the partner's share of partnership liabilities, assumed from other partners on the date of entry.

5. *Minus* the share of the partner's liabilities assumed by the other partners at the date of entry.

C. The following adjustments are made to the partner's original basis.

    1. *Add* additional contributions of assets to the partnership.

    2. *Subtract* withdrawals and distributions of partnership assets.

        a. These payments reduce the partner's basis, but not below zero.

        b. Cash received in excess of the partner's basis will result in income recognition.

    3. *Add* the partner's share of the net income of the partnership.

    4. *Subtract* the partner's share of net partnership losses.

        a. Losses reduce the partner's basis, but basis cannot be reduced below zero. There is an indefinite carryover of such excess losses.

    5. *Add* the partner's share of any tax-exempt income of the partnership.

    6. *Subtract* the partner's share of non-deductible partnership expenses.

    7. *Add* the partner's share of any increases in the partnership liabilities.

    8. *Subtract* the partner's share of any reduction in the partnership liabilities.

V. Basis and Holding Period of Assets to Partnership

A. The basis of the assets to the partnership is a carryover basis from the contributing partner. The basis of property received by the partnership is not automatically increased by the gain recognized to the partner as a result of the transfer, unless the partnership would be treated as an investment company if it was incorporated.

Compare these rules with those of §351. It is much easier for a partner to make a capital contribution subsequent to the formation of a partnership than it is for a shareholder to make such a deferred contribution -- in the latter case, the eighty percent group of owners must act in concert, not an easy feat in the midst of later business dealings.

B. The holding period for an asset contributed to the partnership carries over from the partner to the partnership, i.e., it includes the time held by the partner prior to the transfer.

VI. Non-Liquidating Distributions

A. Generally, there is no gain or loss recognized by the partnership upon a non-liquidating distribution of cash or property to a partner.

    1. Gain is recognized only when money received in a distribution exceeds the basis of the partner's interest immediately preceding the distribution.

    2. Gain recognized relative to a nonliquidating distribution usually is capital in nature. However, ordinary income may be created if the partnership holds any § 751 ("hot") assets.

B. The partner reduces the basis of his or her interest in the partnership, but not below zero, by the adjusted basis of the property to the partnership, or by the amount of cash received. The partnership's basis in the asset carries over to the partner. However, the basis of the property received is limited to the partner's basis in the partnership. Therefore, if the basis of the partnership interest is zero, then the basis of the property distributed is zero.

VII.   Transactions Between a Partner and the Partnership
    A.   Transactions between a partner and a partnership are subject to close scrutiny by the Internal Revenue Service. However, subject to specific conditions, a partner may be treated as a non-partner for certain transactions.
    B.   Losses on a sale between a partner and his or her more than 50% partnership (a "related party") will be disallowed. However, there is a potential offset on a gain that is recognized on a later sale to a third party.
    C.   Gain on a sale between a partner and his or her more than 50% partnership will be ordinary, unless the asset is a capital asset to the purchaser.
    D.   Payments made to partners for services rendered, or for use of the partner's capital determined without regard to partnership income, are called *guaranteed payments*.
        1.   Guaranteed payments are deductible by the partnership, and they are ordinary income to the partner on the last day of the partnership's taxable year, regardless of when they are actually paid.
        2.   Guaranteed payments may produce a loss for the partnership.
        3.   Guaranteed payments are a means by which income may be shifted to certain individuals.
    E.   The nonrecognition treatment accorded to like-kind exchanges does not apply to exchanges between a partnership and a partner directly or indirectly owning more than 50% of the interest in the partnership, or between two partnerships in which the same persons directly or indirectly own more than 50% of the interests.

TEST FOR SELF-EVALUATION - CHAPTER 22

True or False

Indicate which of the following statements are true or false by circling the correct answer.

T   *F*   1.   Partnerships are subject to a flat fifteen percent federal income tax rate.

T   (F)   2.   Each partner can choose a different method of accounting and depreciation computation for purposes of determining his or her taxable income.

(T)   F   3.   If a special election is made, a partnership may choose a tax year that is different than that of all of its principal partners.

(T)   F   4.   *Inside basis* refers to the partner's share of the adjusted basis of the aggregate partnership assets, as determined from the partnership's tax accounts.

(T)   F   5.   The period of time that a partner held the asset prior to the transfer to the partnership is included in the holding period of the asset for the partnership.

(T)   F   6.   A partner may carry over indefinitely any operating losses in excess of his or her basis in the partnership.

T   (F)   7.   Nonliquidating property distributions in excess of a partner's basis result in taxable gain to the partner.

T   (F)   8.   Property distributed to a partner in a non-liquidating distribution always is assigned a carryover basis.

T   (F)   9.   § 1245 gains retain their character as they pass through to the partners.

T   (F)   10.   Losses on sales between a partner and a partnership always are disallowed.

(T)   F   11.   Imposition of the income tax on individual partners and the disallowance of certain deductions and tax credits reflect the influence of the aggregate concept.

Fill-in-the-Blanks

Complete the following statements with the appropriate word(s) or amount(s).

1.   A partnership must file an information return, Form __1065__, within __3 1/2__ months after its year-end.

2.   On a non-liquidating distribution, a partner reduces his or her basis in the partnership by the __cash__ received and the partnership's __adj. basis__ in the property received.

3.   Taxable gain is recognized on a non-liquidating distribution when __cash__ is received in excess of the partner's basis in the partnership.

4.   Losses are disallowed on sales between a partnership and a partner whose direct or __indirect__ interest in the capital or profits of the partnership is more than __50__ percent.

5.   Ordinary income is recognized on a sale between a partner and a partnership, if more than _____50_____ percent of the capital or profits interest is owned directly or indirectly by the same person or persons, unless the property is a capital asset in the hands of the _Purchaser_

6.   A partner's _outside_ basis accounts for the actual investment of after-tax dollars that the partner has made in the partnership.

7.   In a _general_ partnership, creditors are protected by the partner's and the partnership's assets.

8.   The tax year of a partnership generally must be the same as the taxable year of the partners owning a _maj.___int.___.

9.   A limited partnership must have at least ____1____ general partner(s).

10.   Partners may allocate specific income, deductions, or credits in any ratio identified in the partnership agreement provided the allocation has _economic substance_

11.   The _entity_ concept treats partners and partnerships as separate units.

Multiple Choice

Choose the best answer for each of the following questions.

USE THE FOLLOWING INFORMATION FOR QUESTIONS 1-4.

X and Y created the XY Partnership in 19X8. X contributed cash of $10,000 and property with a basis of $5,000 and a fair market value of $90,000 that is subject to a mortgage of $40,000, for a 60% interest. Y contributed $20,000 cash and rendered legal and financial services worth $20,000, for a 40% interest.

_a_ 1.   What is the gain recognized to the XY Partnership as a result of these contributions?
         a. $ 0.
         b. $ 20,000.
         c. $ 45,000.
         d. $100,000.

_c_ 2.   What is the amount of gain or ordinary income recognized by X and Y, respectively?
         a. $0; $0.
         b. $45,000; $20,000.   40,000 x 40% = 16,000   - (10,000 + 5,000)
         c. $ 1,000; $20,000.
         d. $35,000; $20,000.

_a_ 3.   What is the basis of the property (excluding cash) to the partnership?
         a. $5,000.
         b. $50,000.   5,000
         c. $0.
         d. $6,000.

_____ 4.   What is the basis of X and Y's partnership interests, respectively?
         a. $0, $40,000.   20,000
         b. $(1,000), $56,000.   20,000
         c. $60,000, $40,000.   16,000
                                           56,000

     d. $0, $56,000.

_C_   5.   Which of the following items do **not** retain their character as they flow through to the partners? More than one answer may be correct.
     a.   Long-term capital gains.
     b.   Short-term capital gains.
     c.   § 1245 gains.
     d.   Dividend income.

_C_   6.   Z and W owned 90% and 10% of the ZW Partnership, respectively. ZW operated a foundry. Z sold stock in Exxon with a basis of $4,000 to the partnership for $6,000. The amount and character of gain recognized to Z is:
     a. $0.
     b. $2,000 ordinary.
     c. $2,000 capital gain.
     d. $6,000 ordinary.

_b_   7.   Assume the same facts as in 6, except that a machine, a capital asset to Z (instead of stock), was sold to ZW. The partnership intends to use the machine to produce a new product. What is the amount and character of gain recognized to Z?
     a. $0.
     b. $2,000 ordinary.   _not a capital asset to ZW._
     c. $2,000 capital gain.
     d. $6,000 ordinary.

_b_   8.   B and L were equal unrelated partners in the BL Partnership. B sold an old truck to the partnership for $3,000. The truck had been used in B's sole proprietorship prior to the sale. It had a basis of $5,000 to B. What amount and character of loss should B recognize?
     a. $0.
     b. $2,000 § 1231 loss.
     c. $2,000 ordinary.
     d. $5,000 ordinary.

_a_   9.   Assume the same facts as in 8, except that B has a 70% interest in the BL Partnership. What is the amount an character of loss?
     a. $0.
     b. $2,000 § 1231 loss.
     c. $2,000 ordinary.
     d. $5,000 capital.

_a_   10.   Assume the same facts as in 9, except that the BL Partnership sold the truck to an unrelated third-party for $3,525 ten days after purchasing it from B. What is the amount and character of the gain or loss to the partnership?
     a. $0.
     b. $525 § 1231 gain.
     c. $525 ordinary gain.
     d. $1,475 ordinary loss.

_C_   11.   M and N owned 30% and 70% of the MN Partnership, respectively. MN had the following items of income and loss for 19X8:

Sales	$7,000
Cost of sales	2,000
Dividend income	3,000

§ 1231 loss   2,000
§ 1245 gain   1,000

How much will N report as her share of net partnership ordinary income?

a. $1,800.
b. $3,500.
c. $4,200.
d. $4,900.

_C_____ 12.   Ms. X is a calendar year taxpayer who owns a 25% interest in the XYZ Partnership. The partnership's fiscal year ends on June 30. Ms. X received guaranteed payments of $1,000 on October 15, 19X8 and $500 on April 15, 19X9. For the fiscal year ending June 30, 19X9, the partnership income before deducting the guaranteed payments is $80,000. Using only these facts, what is Ms. X's reportable income from the partnership for calendar 19X9?

a. $21,500.
b. $20,375.
c. $21,125.
d. $20,500.
e.   None of the above.

USE THE FOLLOWING INFORMATION FOR QUESTIONS 13-16.

The adjusted basis of Mr. W's partnership interest was $70,000. In a non-liquidating distribution he received $40,000 in cash and land with a fair market value of $38,000 and an adjusted basis to the partnership of $28,000.

_C_____ 13.   What is the amount and nature of the gain to Mr. W resulting from the receipt of the distribution?

a. $8,000 capital gain.
b. $8,000 ordinary income.
c. $0.
d.   None of the above.

_d_____ 14.   What is Mr. W's basis in the partnership and the land respectively, after the distribution?

a. $0, $38,000.
b. $2,000, $38,000.
c. $0, $28,000.
d. $2,000, $28,000.
e. $0, $30,000.

_a_____ 15.   Assume the same facts as given above, except that, instead of receiving $40,000 cash, Mr. W received $74,000 in cash and the land. What is the amount and nature of Mr. W's gain and his basis in the distributed property, respectively?

a. $4,000 capital gain, $0.
b. $0, $28,000.
c. $4,000 capital gain, $28,000.
d. $4,000 ordinary income, $0.

_a_____ 16.   The MC partnership sustained a 19X8 ordinary loss of $84,000. The partnership and its two partners are on a calendar year basis. The partners share profits and losses equally and materially participate in the partnership's business. On December 31, 19X8, C had an adjusted basis of $36,000 for her partnership interest, before considering the 19X8 loss. On her 19X8 individual income tax return, C should deduct a(n):

    a.   Ordinary loss of $36,000.
    b.   Ordinary loss of $42,000.
    c.   Ordinary loss of $36,000 and capital loss of $6,000.
    d.   Capital loss of $42,000.

___C___ 17.   On July 1, 19X8, A received a 10% interest in the T partnership, for past services rendered. T's net assets at July 1, 19X8, had a basis of $140,000 and a fair market value of $200,000. What income should A include in her 19X8 tax return for the partnership interest transferred to her by the other partners?

    a. $0.
    b. $14,000 ordinary income.
    c. $20,000 ordinary income.
    d. $20,000 long-term capital gain.

USE THE FOLLOWING INFORMATION FOR QUESTIONS 18 AND 19

On May 1, 19X1, A was admitted to the B partnership. A's contribution to capital consisted of 500 shares of stock in D Corporation, purchased in 19X0 for $20,000, and which had a fair market value of $100,000 on May 1, 19X1. A's interest in the partnership's capital and profits is 25%. On May 1, 19X1, the fair market value of the partnership's net assets (after A was admitted) was $400,000.

___a___ 18.   What was A's gain on the exchange of the D stock for A's partnership interest?

    a. $0.
    b. $80,000 ordinary income.
    c. $80,000 long-term capital gain.
    d. $80,000 § 1231 gain.

___C___ 19.   On June 1, 19X3, the partnership distributed the 500 shares of D stock to partner K. The fair market value of the stock on the date of distribution was $90,000. What is A's recognized gain on the distribution?

    a. $0.
    b. $17,500.
    c. $70,000.
    d. $80,000.

___a___ 20.   A, B, C, and D formed the ABCD partnership. Each partner owns a 25% interest in ABCD. A and B have taxable years ending June 30 and C and D have taxable years ending Septembe 30. Accordingly, ABCD's taxable year will end on:

    a.   June 30.
    b.   September 30.
    c.   Either June 30 or September 30.
    d.   December 31.

Short Answer

1. ABC Services is owned by individuals A, B, and C. They share profits and losses 40-30-30. A and B have tax years ending June 30th; C uses the calendar year.

    ABC data for the tax year ending 6-30-X8:

Sales	$300,000	§ 1231 Gain, 10-15-X7	$30,000 —
Cost of Sales	120,000	Municipal Bond Interest	10,000 —
Jobs Credit	3,000 ✓	Charitable Contribution	2,000 —

    ABC purchased business equipment, a seven-year MACRS asset, for $80,000 on 11-1-X7. MACRS deductions in excess of the § 179 first-year amount are included in Cost of Sales.

    17,500

    A) C received guaranteed payment of $5,000/month through the year ending 6-30-X8. These were increased to $7,000/month for the year ending 6-30-X9.

        Allocate ABC's income and other items to the three partners for their tax years ending in 19X8.

300,000
(120,000)
(60,000)
120,000

A	B	C
48,000	36,000	36,000
		60,000
12,000	9,000	9,000
4,000	3,000	3,000
1200	900	900
800	600	600
7000	5250	5250

B) C received guaranteed payments of $9,000/month through the year ending 6-30-X8. These were increased to $10,000/month for the year ending 6-30-X9. *108,000*

    B received guaranteed payments of $7,000/month for the year ending 6-30-X8, and $7,500/month for the year ending 6-30-X9. *84,000*

    A received draws from her capital account: $2,500/month. *30,000*

    Allocate ABC's income and other items to the three partners for their tax years ending in 19X8.

300,000
(120,000)
(54,000)
(108,000)
(12,000)

A	B	C
(4800)	(3600)	(3600)
	84,000	108,000
12,000	9000	9,000
4,000	3,000	2,000
1,200	900	900
800	600	600
7,000	5250	5250

2.   Three individuals form the PST partnership on 1-1-X8. The partner's contributions to the partnership are:

P   Cash, $30,000.
S   Organizational Services, fmv $30,000.
T   Store Building, fmv $80,000; basis to T, $27,500
      Mortgage assumed by PST, $50,000.

Each partner receives a ⅓ interest in the new business.

A)   Compute each partner's original basis in the partnership interest.

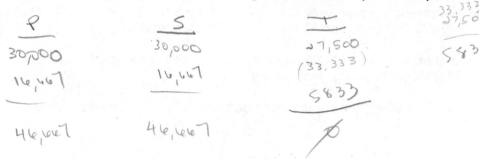

P	S	T	
			33,333
			27,500
30,000	30,000	27,500	
16,667	16,667	(33,333)	5833
		5833	
46,667	46,667	0	

B)   What is the basis of the store to PST?

$27,500

3.   F, an individual, has a 75% interest in the FG Repairs partnership. Both the partners and the
      partnership use the calendar year for tax purposes. F's basis in the partnership interest at
      1-1-X8 is $30,000. FG financial data for 19X8 includes the following.

FG 19X8 ordinary income	$ 20,000
F's Draws in 19X8	30,000
12/31 Cash Distribution to the partners	15,000
12/31 Distribution of Land to F:	
Fair market value	$ 6,000
Basis to FG	5,000
FG Payables, 1-1-X8	$ 27,000
FG Payables, 12-31-X8	20,000
FG Municipal Bond Interest Income	$ 4,000

}(7000)

A)   What is F's basis in the FG partnership before the 12/31 distributions? (Assume that
      the distributions were NOT in liquidation.)

        30,000
        15,000
       ⌊30,000⌋
        ⌊5,050⌋
          3 000   12,750

B)   What is her basis in the land distributed?

        12750
        11 250
        1 500

C)   What is F's basis in the FG partnership after the distribution?

        Ø

D)   What if the cash distributions were $20,000, instead of $15,000?

        12 750
       ⟨15,000⟩   capital
        2 250 gain

E)   What if the cash distributions were $5,000, instead of $15,000?

        12 750
        3 750

        9,000   land basis
        5 000
        4000   basis in
                  partnership

SOLUTIONS TO CHAPTER 22 QUESTIONS

True or False

1.	F	
2.	F	Depreciation methods are selected at the partnership, rather than the partner, level.
3.	T	See § 444.
4.	T	
5.	T	The holding period of contributed property carries over to the partnership.
6.	T	Assuming that the taxpayer remains a partner in the on-going entity.
7.	F	Distributions of assets from a partnership generally are not taxable to the recipient partner.
8.	F	It could have a lower basis if the partner does not have sufficient basis in his or her partnership interest to allocate to the distribution.
9.	F	§ 1245 gains are netted with other income, loss, and deduction items to determine ordinary income from operations.
10.	F	Losses are disallowed only with respect to partners whose direct or indirect interest in the capital or profits of the partnership is more than 50 percent.
11.	T	

Fill-in-the-Blanks

1. 1065, 3 1/2
2. cash, adjusted basis
3. cash
4. indirect, 50
5. 50, purchaser
6. outside
7. general
8. majority interest
9. one
10. economic substance
11. entity

Multiple Choice

1.	a	The partnership does not recognize gain upon the contribution of property.
2.	c	[Gain to X = $16,000 liabilities assumed by Y - ($10,000 cash + $5,000 basis in property contributed)]. Y recognizes $20,000 ordinary income for the interest he received in exchange for providing legal services. See Example 13 in the text.
3.	a	The $1,000 gain on contribution by X does not result in a basis increase, since the partnership would not be an investment company if it were incorporated. See Example 14 in the text.
4.	d	
5.	c	
6.	c	The Exxon stock is a capital asset to the partnership. See Example 43 in the text.
7.	b	The machine is not a capital asset to the partnership. See Example 43 in the text.
8.	b	B does not have a more than 50% interest in the partnership. See Example 42 in the text.
9.	a	Since B owns more than a 50% interest in the partnership, the loss is not recognized. See Example 42 in the text.
10.	a	No gain is recognized, because it does not exceed the loss previously disallowed. See Example 42 in the text.
11.	c	[70% x ($7,000 - $2,000 + $1,000)] See Example 19 in the text.

12. c   [$1,000 + $500 + (25% x $78,500)] See Example 38 in the text.
13. c   The cash distribution is less than the basis in the partnership. See Example 45 in the text.
14. d   Basis = $2,000 ($70,000 - $40,000 - $28,000); basis in land = $28,000 (basis carries over from partnership). See Example 46 in the text.
15. a $74,000 - $70,000 basis in partnership. See Example 47 in the text. W's basis in the partnership after the cash distribution is zero; thus, there is no remaining basis to allocate to the land.
16. a   The deduction for losses is limited to the partner's basis. See Example 31 in the text.
17. c $200,000 x 10%. See Example 13 in the text.
18. a   Generally, no gain is recognized on contributions made to the partnership. See Example 8 in the text.
19. c   A's recognized gain is the lesser of $80,000 (the built-in gain at the time of contribution of the stock) or $70,000 (the gain that would be recognized by the partnership if the stock was sold for its FMV at the time of distribution). See Example 21 in the text.
20. a   Since partners owning a majority interest and the principal partners do not have the same taxable year, the partnership's tax year ends June 30; this year-end results in the least aggregate deferral of income. See Example 18 in the text.

Short Answer

1. A)   Ordinary Income:

Sales		$300,000
Cost of Sales		-120,000
Guaranteed Payments (12 x $5,000)		- 60,000
Total		$120,000

Allocation of tax items for the partners' tax years ending in 19X8

	A	B	C
Ordinary income	$48,000	$36,000	$36,000
Guaranteed Payments	-	-	60,000
§ 1231 Gain	12,000	9,000	9,000
Jobs Credit	1,200	900	900
Charitable Contribution	800	600	600
Municipal Bond Interest (for state tax)	4,000	3,000	3,000
§ 179 Cost Recovery	7,000	5,250	5,250

There is no special treatment for the regular MACRS deductions. The partnership's elections are effective for all of the partners. All income and deduction items flow through on the last day of the partnership's tax year.

See Examples 19 and 36 through 39 in the text.

B)   Ordinary Income:

Sales		$300,000
Cost of Sales		-120,000
Guaranteed Payments(12 x ($7,000 + 9,000)		-192,000
Total		$(12,000)

Allocation of tax items for the partners' tax years ending in 19X8

	A	B	C
Ordinary Income	$(4,800)	$(3,600)	$(3,600)
Guaranteed Payments	-	84,000	108,000

§ 1231 Gain	12,000	9,000	9,000
Jobs Credit	1,200	900	900
Charitable Contribution	800	600	600
Municipal Bond Interest (for state tax)	4,000	3,000	3,000
§ 179 Cost Recovery	7,000	5,250	5,250

Ms. A's draws do not affect partnership income. Guaranteed payments can produce a loss for the partnership.

See Examples 19 and 36 through 39 in the text.

2. A)

	P	S	T
Cash Contributions	$30,000		
Basis of Other Property			$27,500
Gain Recognized on Contribution	-	$30,000*	+ 5,833**
Liabilities Assumed by the partnership from other partners	+16,667	+16,667	-
Partner's Liabilities assumed by the partnership	-	-	-33,333
Original Interest Basis	$46,667	$46,667	$ 0

*Ordinary Income: Compensation for services
**Liabilities assumed by the partnership (2/3 X $50,000) $33,333
       Basis of Property Contributed   -27,500
       Gain Recognized (Liability in Excess of Basis) $5,833

B)   Basis of Store $27,500

Gain recognized does not increase the basis of the store to the partnership, because PST would not be treated as an investment company if it was incorporated. See § 723.

3. A)

Basis, 1-1-X8	$30,000
Distributive Share of Ordinary Income (75%)	+15,000
19X8 Draws	-30,000
Share of Exempt Income (75%)	+ 3,000
Share of Decrease in Liabilities (75%)	- 5,250
Basis before 12-31 Distribution	$12,750

B)

Apply Cash Distribution First (75%)	-11,250
Balance: F's Basis in the Land Received	$1,500

C)   Basis of Partnership to F, 1-1-X9 $ 0

D)   F incurs a capital gain of $2,250, because her share of the cash distributions ($15,000) exceeds her predistribution basis in the partnership interest ($12,750). F's basis in the land and her partnership interest now are zero.

E)   F does not incur a capital gain as a result of the distribution, because her share of the cash distributions ($3,750) does not exceed her predistribution basis in the partnership interest ($12,750). F's basis in the land now is $5,000 (i.e., carryover basis), and her basis in the partnership interest now is $4,000.

CHAPTER 23
EXEMPT ENTITIES

CHAPTER HIGHLIGHTS

Although the primary objective of the Federal tax law is the raising of revenue, economic, social, equity and political considerations play a significant role in the development of tax laws. Social consideration objectives resulted in the enactment of Subchapter F of the Code. Based on the theory that the government is compensated for the loss of revenue by its relief from the financial burden which would otherwise be satisfied by appropriations from public funds and by the benefits resulting from the promotion of the general welfare, certain organizations are provided exemption from Federal income taxation. Depending on the nature and scope of the entity, an organization may be partially or completely exempt from Federal income taxation. In addition, an organization may engage in activities, or fail to act in certain circumstances, that are subject to special taxation.

I. Requirements for Tax-Exempt Status
   A. IRC § 501 provides tax-exempt status for over twenty types of organizations. An organization qualifies for exempt status only if it fits into one of these categories. The most prevalent types of tax-exempt organizations include:
      1. Entities organized and operated exclusively for the following purposes: religious, charitable, scientific, literary, educational, testing for public safety, fostering national or international amateur sports, or prevention of cruelty to children or animals [§ 501(c)(3)].
      2. Civic leagues operated exclusively for the promotion of social welfare, and local associations of employees whose association net earnings are used exclusively for charitable, educational, or recreational purposes [§ 501(c)(4)].
      3. Business leagues, chambers of commerce, real estate boards, boards of trade, and professional football leagues [§ 501(c)(6)].
      4. Fraternal beneficiary societies operating under the lodge system and having a system for the payment of insurance benefits to members and their dependents [§ 501(c)(8)].
      5. Voluntary employees' beneficiary associations having a system for the payment

of insurance benefits to members, their dependents, or their designated
beneficiaries [§ 501(c)(9)].

    6.   Credit unions without stock organized for mutual purposes [§ 501(c)(14)].

B.   Frequently, exempt status requires more than the mere classification in one of the categories of exempt organizations. The definitional requirements of many of the organizations that qualify for tax-exempt status generally include, within the statutory language or by implication, the following factors.

    1.   The organization serves some type of common good.

    2.   The organization is not a for-profit entity.

    3.   The net earnings of the organization do not inure to the benefit of any private shareholder or individual.

    4.   The organization does not exert political influence.

II.   Tax Consequences of Exempt Status

A.   Although an exempt organization generally is exempt from Federal income taxation, engaging in specific transactions or activities will subject the organization to taxation.

    1.   If an exempt organization engages in a prohibited transaction, it will be subject to tax.

    2.   A *feeder* organization is subject to tax.

    3.   A private foundation may be partially subject to tax.

    4.   An exempt organization is subject to tax on its unrelated business taxable income.

B.   If an exempt organization engages in a prohibited transaction, part or all of its income may be subject to Federal income taxation, or the organization may forfeit its exempt status.

    1.   An organization will lose its exempt status if it fails to continue to qualify as a tax-exempt organization.

    2.   Organizations exempt under § 501(c)(3), i.e., religious, charitable, educational, or similar organizations, generally will forfeit their exempt status if the organization attempts to influence legislation (lobbying activities) or participates in political campaigns.

    3.   Qualifying § 501(c)(3) organizations may make an affirmative election that will permit such organizations to participate in lobbying activities on a limited basis without losing their exempt status. When the election is made, a ceiling is placed on lobbying expenditures. Exceeding the ceiling amount can lead to forfeiture of exempt status. Even though the ceiling is not exceeded, a tax may be imposed on some of the lobbying expenditures.

       a.   *Lobbying expenditures* are expenditures made for the purpose of influencing legislation through attempting to affect the opinions of the general public or communicating with any legislator or staff member, or with any government official or staff member who may participate in the formulation of legislation. The statutory ceiling on lobbying expenditures is computed as follows.

150% x Lobbying nontaxable amount = Ceiling amount

The lobbying nontaxable amount is the lesser of $1,000,000 or the amount from a rate schedule in IRC § 4911.

       b.   *Grass roots expenditures* are expenditures made for the purpose of influencing legislation through attempting to affect the opinions of the general public. The statutory ceiling on grass roots expenditures is computed as follows.

150% x Grass roots nontaxable amount = Ceiling amount

The grass roots nontaxable amount is 25 percent of the lobbying nontaxable amount.

4. A § 501(c)(3) organization that elects to make lobbying expenditures on a limited basis is subject to tax on the its *excess lobbying expenditures*.

   a. The tax rate is 25 percent.

   b. Excess lobbying expenditures are the greater of:
       (1) the excess of the lobbying expenditures for the taxable year over the lobbying nontaxable amount; or,
       (2) the excess of the grass roots expenditures for the taxable year over the grass roots nontaxable amount.

5. Under § 503, certain exempt organizations lose their exempt status if they engage in a prohibited transaction.

6. A feeder organization carries on a trade or business for the benefit of an exempt organization and is not exempt from Federal income taxation. The following activities, however, are not subject to the feeder organization rules.

KEY TERMS

- Unrelated Business Taxable Income
- Private Foundation Status
- Lobbying Expenditures
- Unrelated Debt-Financed Income

   a. An activity that generates rental income that would be excluded from the definition of "rent" for purposes of the unrelated business income tax.

   b. Activities that normally would constitute a trade or business, but for which substantially all of the work is performed by volunteers.

   c. Activities that normally would constitute the trade or business of selling merchandise, but for which substantially all the merchandise has been received as contributions or gifts.

III. Tax Consequences of Private Foundation Status

   A. Classification as a private foundation is less beneficial than that as a public charity.

      1. The deduction consequences to the donor may be less favorable than would be the case if the organization were a public charity.

      2. A private foundation may be partially subject to tax.

   B. The Code defines a private foundation by enumerating the § 501(c)(3) exempt organizations that are **not** private foundations. The following § 501(c)(3) organizations are included among those that are defined as being outside of the definition of a private foundation.

      1. Churches; educational institutions; hospitals and medical research organizations; charitable organizations receiving a major portion of their support from the general public or governments; and, governmental units.

      2. Organizations that are broadly supported by the general public (excluding disqualified persons), by governmental units, or by organizations described in 1. above. To satisfy the broadly supported provision, the one-third-support test and the not-more-than-one-third-support test must be met.

         a. Under the **one-third-support test**, the organization *normally* must receive more than one-third of its support each taxable year from: gifts; grants; contributions; membership fees; and gross receipts from admissions, sales of merchandise, performance of services, or the furnishing of facilities, in an activity that is not an unrelated trade or business. However, such gross receipts from any person or governmental agency in excess of the greater of $5,000 or one percent of the organization's support for the taxable year are not counted.

    b.   Under the **not-more-than-one-third-support test**, the amount of support *normally* received from gross investment income and unrelated business income net of the related tax is limited to one-third of the organization's support for the taxable year.

    c.   The term *normally* refers to the tests being satisfied for the four taxable years preceding the current taxable year. Satisfying the test for the current taxable year will result in the subsequent taxable year being treated as satisfying the test.

  3.   Organizations organized and operated exclusively for the benefit of organizations described in 1. and 2.

  4.   Organizations organized and operated exclusively for testing for public safety.

C.   A private foundation may be subject to numerous taxes including: tax based on investment income; tax on self-dealing; tax on failure to distribute income; tax on excess business holdings; tax on investments that jeopardize charitable purposes; and, tax on taxable expenditures. These taxes serve to restrict the permitted activities of private foundations.

IV.   Unrelated Business Income Tax

A.   To be characterized as an activity that generates unrelated business income, the following three factors generally must be present.

  1.   The organization must conduct a trade or business.

  2.   The trade or business must be regularly carried on.

  3.   The trade or business must not be substantially related to the performance of the organization's exempt function.

B.   Even in cases where the three factors are present, the following activities are <u>not</u> classified as an unrelated trade or business.

  1.   Substantially all the work of the trade or business is performed by volunteers.

  2.   The trade or business consists of merchandise sales, and substantially all of the merchandise has been received as gifts or contributions.

  3.   With respect to § 501(c)(3) organizations and state colleges or universities, the trade or business is conducted primarily for the convenience of the organization's members, students, patients, officers, or employees.

  4.   With respect to most employee unions, the trade or business consists of selling to members, at their usual place of employment, work-related clothing and equipment and items normally sold through vending machines, snack bars, or food dispensing facilities.

C.   In determining whether an activity is an unrelated trade or business, special rules apply to the following activities.

  1.   Bingo games.

  2.   The distribution of low-cost articles.

  3.   Rental or exchange of membership lists.

  4.   Qualified public entertainment activities.

  5.   Qualified convention and trade show activities.

  6.   Certain services provided at cost or less by a hospital to small hospitals.

  7.   Certain pole rentals by telephone companies.

D.   Unrelated business income is the income derived from the unrelated trade or business.

E.   In computing unrelated business taxable income, a deduction of $1,000 is permitted.

F.   The formula for the unrelated business income tax is illustrated in Exhibit 23-1.

> In avoiding the UBIT, the "exempt function" rule, the "volunteers" test, the "convenience of" test, and the $1,000 deduction are the most important. In addition, if the business activity is not regularly carried on, eg becuase it occurs only once or twice a year, the tax can be avoided.

V.   Unrelated Debt-Financed Income
    A.   Unrelated debt-financed income increases unrelated business taxable income, and unrelated debt-financed deductions decrease unrelated business taxable income.
    B.   *Debt-financed income* is the gross income generated from debt-financed property.
    C.   *Debt-financed property* is all of the property of the organization held to produce income and on which there is acquisition indebtedness except for the following.
        1.   Property for which at least 85 percent of the use of the property is for the achievement of the exempt purpose of the organization.
        2.   Property whose gross income is otherwise treated as unrelated business income.
        3.   Property whose gross income is derived from certain research and is not otherwise treated as unrelated business income.
        4.   Property used in a trade or business that is treated as not being an unrelated trade or business under one of the statutory exceptions.
        5.   Certain land that is acquired for exempt use within ten years (property acquired for prospective exempt use).
    D.   *Acquisition indebtedness* consists of the following debts with respect to debt-financed property.
        1.   Debt incurred in acquiring or improving the property.
        2.   Debt incurred prior to the acquisition or improvement of the property but which absent such acquisition or improvement, would not have been incurred.
        3.   Debt incurred subsequent to the acquisition or improvement of the property but which would have not been incurred and whose incurrence was reasonably foreseeable at the time of acquisition or improvement.
    E.   The portion of the debt-financed income and deductions that is unrelated debt-financed income and deductions is determined by the following formula.

$$\frac{\text{\textit{Average acquisition indebtedness for the property}}}{\text{\textit{Average adjusted basis of the property}}} = \begin{array}{l}\textit{Debt/basis}\\\textit{percentage}\end{array}$$

        1.   The *average acquisition indebtedness* for a debt-financed property is the average amount of the outstanding debt (ignoring interest) for the taxable year.
        2.   The *average adjusted basis* of the debt-financed property is the average of the property's adjusted basis at the beginning and at the end of the taxable year.
        3.   If debt-financed property is disposed of during the taxable year at a gain, average acquisition indebtedness in the formula is replaced with highest acquisition indebtedness. *Highest acquisition indebtedness* is the largest amount of the property's acquisition indebtedness for the twelve-month period preceding the date of disposition.

Exhibit 23-1
UNRELATED BUSINESS INCOME TAX FORMULA

	Gross unrelated business income
−	Directly connected income
	Net unrelated business income
+	Charitable contributions in excess of 10% of unrelated business taxable income
+	Net unrelated debt-financed income
+	Certain interest, annuity, royalty, and rental income not included in net unrelated business income, received from an organization controlled by the entity (This provision overrides the negative adjustment modification of these items)
−	Income, net of directly related deductions, from dividends, interest, and annuities
−	Net royalty income
−	Net rental income from real property
−	Net rental income from certain personal property
−	Gains and losses from the sale, exchange, or other disposition of property, other than inventory
−	Certain net research income
−	Certain charitable contributions (Note: the total deduction for charitable contributions cannot exceed 10% of unrelated business taxable income)
−	$1,000 statutory deduction
	Unrelated business taxable income
×	Corporate tax rates
	Unrelated Business Income Tax

TEST FOR SELF-EVALUATION - CHAPTER 23

True or False

Indicate which of the following statements are true or false by circling the correct answer.

T   F   1.   In recognition of the equity considerations objective, the Code contains provisions that permit certain organizations to be either partially or completely exempt from Federal income taxation.

T   F   2.   The statutory authority for certain organizations to be exempt from Federal income taxation is provided in Subchapter F of the Code.

T   F   3.   An organization that is classified as a feeder organization is exempt from Federal income taxation.

T   F   4.   Qualifying § 501(c)(3) organizations that make an affirmative election are subject to a 35% tax on excess lobbying expenditures.

T   F   5.   Organizations exempt under § 501(c)(3), i.e., religious, charitable, educational, or similar organizations, will forfeit their exempt status if the organization participates in any lobbying activities.

T   F   6.   Lobbying expenditures are expenditures made for the purpose of influencing legislation through attempting to affect the opinions of the general public or any segment thereof.

T   F   7.   The general objective of the tax on unrelated business income is to tax such income as if the entity were subject to the individual income tax.

T   F   8.   Bingo games generally constitute unrelated trades or businesses.

T   F   9.   In determining unrelated business taxable income, gains and losses from the sale, exchange, or other dispositions of property (other than inventory) are subtracted from net unrelated business income.

T   F   10.   Acquisition indebtedness includes debt incurred in acquiring or improving debt-financed property.

T   F   11.   An organization will be exempt from taxation only if it fits into one of the categories enumerated in the Code.

T   F   12.   Exempt organizations that qualify as private foundations receive more beneficial tax treatment than do those that qualify as public charities.

T   F   13.   If an exempt organization conducts an unrelated trade or business, it may lose its exempt status.

T   F   14.   In computing unrelated business taxable income, a $5,000 statutory deduction generally is available to all exempt organizations.

T   F   15.   A trade or business is not an unrelated trade or business if the persons who perform substantially all the work are volunteers.

T   F   16.   An exempt organization is subject to tax on its unrelated debt-financed income.

T   F   17.   Activities that normally would constitute a trade or business, but for which substantially all of the work is performed by volunteers, are not subject to the feeder organization rules.

Fill-in-the Blanks

Complete the following statements with the appropriate word(s) or amount(s).

1.   In recognition of the _____ considerations objective, Subchapter _____ of the Code provides that certain organizations are exempt from Federal income taxation.

2.   IRC § 501(c)(3) provides exemption from income taxation for entities organized and operated exclusively for the following purposes: _____, _____ scientific, literary, educational, testing for public safety, fostering national or international amateur sports and prevention of cruelty to children or animals.

3.   The underlying rationale for all exempt organizations is that they serve some type of _____ _____.

4.   For failure to distribute all of its income, a tax may be imposed on a nonoperating _____ _____ in the form of an initial tax and an additional tax.

5.   _____ _____ expenditures are those made for the purpose of influencing legislation through attempting to affect the opinions of the general public or any segment thereof.

6.   A _____ organization carries on a trade or business for the benefit of an exempt organization.

7.   In general, _____ _____ _____ is income from activities not related to the exempt purpose of the exempt organization.

8.   A _____ or _____ includes any activity conducted for the production of income through the sale of merchandise or the performance of services.

9.   With respect to debt-financed property, _____ _____ is debt sustained by an exempt organization in association with the acquisition of property.

10.   For an exempt organization to be subject to the tax on unrelated business income, the organization must conduct a _____ or _____ that is not substantially related to the _____ _____ of the organization and is regularly _____ on by the organization.

11.   The election by a § 501(c)(3) organization to be eligible to make lobbying expenditures on a limited basis subjects the exempt organization to tax on _____ _____ _____.

12.   Classification as a private foundation may have an adverse impact on the _____ received by the donee exempt organization and may result in _____ at the organization level.

13.   Unrelated business income is taxed at the same rates as those applicable to _____ taxpayers.

Multiple Choice

Choose the best answer for each of the following questions.

_____ 1. Which of the following statements generally is *not* included in the definitional requirements of many of the organizations that qualify for exemption?
  a.   The organization serves some type of common good.
  b.   The organization is not a for-profit entity.
  c.   The organization does not engage in any unrelated trades or businesses.
  d.   The organization does not exert political influence.
  e.   The net earnings of the organization do not benefit the members of the organization.

_____ 2. A private foundation may be subject to which of the following taxes: (More than one answer may be correct.)
  a.   Tax on failure to distribute income.
  b.   Tax on built-in gains.
  c.   The environmental tax.
  d.   Tax on taxable expenditures.
  e.   Tax on excess distributions.

_____ 3. For an exempt organization to be subject to the tax on unrelated business income, the following factors must be present: (More than one answer may be correct)
  a.   The organization conducts a trade or business that is regularly carried on.
  b.   The trade or business is conducted primarily for the convenience of the organization's members.
  c.   The trade or business is substantially related to the exempt purpose of the organization.
  d.   The organization does not use the funds generated by the trade or business to provide income to help defray the costs of conducting the exempt purpose.
  e.   The trade or business is not substantially related to the exempt purpose of the organization.

_____ 4. Factors to be considered in determining whether a trade or business is regularly carried on include: (More than one answer may be correct.)
  a.   The frequency of the activity.
  b.   The continuity of the activity.
  c.   Whether the activity generates income.
  d.   The manner in which the activity is pursued.
  e.   The number of persons employed in the activity.

_____ 5. In computing unrelated business taxable income, which of the following is not a substraction modification?
  a.   Dividend income.
  b.   Royalty income.
  c.   Gains and losses from the sale, exchange, or other dispositions of property except inventory.
  d.   Unrelated debt-financed income.
  e.   The $1,000 statutory deduction.

_____ 6. X, a qualifying § 501(c)(3) organization, made an election to be eligible to make lobbying expenditures on a limited basis. During the year, X incurs lobbying expenditures of $800,000 and determined its lobbying nontaxable amount to be $600,000. The election results in:
  a.   The loss of X's exempt status.

    b.   Imposition of tax on $800,000 of excess lobbying expenditures.

    c.   A tax liability of $68,000.

    d.   Imposition of tax on $200,000 of excess lobbying expenditures.

    e.   The election neither results in the imposition of tax nor the loss of exempt status.

____ 7.   In determining whether a § 501(c)(3) organization is broadly supported by the general public, governmental units or certain exempt organizations, and thus, is not a private foundation, which of the following tests must be satisfied? (More than one answer may be correct.)

    a.   The one-third-support test.

    b.   The gross income test.

    c.   The normal source of income test.

    d.   The not-more-than-one-third-support test.

    e.   The $5,000 gross receipts test.

____ 8.   During the taxable year, a § 501(c)(3) organization received the following support.

General public for services rendered	$10,000
US governmental unit for services rendered	8,000
State A, for services rendered	15,000
Contributions from disqualified persons	10,000
Gross investment income	12,000

Which of the following statements are accurate? (More than one answer may be correct.)

    a.   The one-third-support test has been met.

    b.   The $5,000 gross receipts test has been satisfied.

    c.   The organization is a private foundation.

    d.   The not-more-than-one-third-support test is satisfied.

    e.   The organization is subject to the unrelated business income tax.

____ 9.   Which of the following activities would constitute an unrelated trade or business for a state university?

    a.   A laundry operated by the university for laundering dormitory linens and students' clothing.

    b.   Operation by the university of parking facilities for faculty and students.

    c.   Operation by the university of banquet facilities that are available to the general public.

    d.   Operation by the university of a bookstore that only sells textbooks.

    e.   None of the above.

____ 10.   An exempt organization may incur an unrelated business income tax on which of the following items of income generated from an unrelated trade or business?

    a.   Dividends.

    b.   Interest.

    c.   Gain from the sale of inventory.

    d.   Royalties.

    e.   None of the above.

____ 11.   Entities organized and operated exclusively for religious, charitable and educational purposes are exempt from Federal income taxation under the following Code Section?

    a.   501(c)(2).

    b.   501(c)(3).

    c.   501(2)(c).

    d.   501(3)(c).

e.   None of the above.

____ 12.   Z, a qualifying religious organization, made an election to be eligible to make lobbying expenditures on a limited basis. Z's excess lobbying expenditures for the current tax year are $100,000. Z's resultant tax liability is?
a. $0.
b. $10,000.
c. $22,250.
d. $25,000.
e. $34,000.

____ 13.   § 501(c)(3) organizations that are not classified as private foundations are called:
a.   Feeder organizations.
b.   Nonprivate foundations.
c.   Private charities.
d.   Public charities.
e.   None of the above.

____ 14.   Assuming that each of the following is held by an exempt organization to produce income and there is acquisition indebtedness on each, which of the following is debt-financed property? (More than one answer may be correct.)
a.   Property used in a trade or business that is treated as not being an unrelated trade or business under one of the statutory exemptions.
b.   Property whose gross income is otherwise treated as unrelated business income.
c.   Property for which at least 75% of the use of the property is for the achievement of the organization's exempt purpose.
d.   Property whose gross income is derived from research for a hospital and is not otherwise treated as unrelated business income.
e.   None of the above.

____ 15.   E, an exempt organization, owns an office building that it leases to Z corporation for $200,000 per year. The acquisition indebtedness at the beginning and end of the tax was $400,000 and $500,000, respectively. The adjusted basis of the building at the beginning and end of the year was $1,000,000 and $800,000, respectively. E's unrelated debt-financed income is:
a. $0.
b. $80,000.
c. $100,000.
d. $135,000.
e. $200,000.

SOLUTIONS TO CHAPTER 23 QUESTIONS

True or False

1.   F   The tax laws providing exemption from income taxation for certain organizations is based on the social consideration objective.
2.   T
3.   F   Feeder organizations are not exempt from federal income taxation.
4.   F   Excess lobbying expenditures are subject to a 25% tax.
5.   F   Qualifying § 501(c)(3) organizations may make an affirmative election that will permit such organizations to participate in lobbying activities on a limited basis without losing their exempt status.
6.   T   Lobbying expenditures are expenditures made for the purpose of influencing legislation through: (1) attempting to affect the opinions of the general public or any segment thereof; or (2) communicating with any legislator or staff member or with any government official or staff member who may participate in the formulation of legislation.
7.   F   The general objective is to tax such income as if the entity were subject to the corporate income tax.
8.   F   Qualified bingo games are not unrelated trades or businesses.
9.   T
10.   T
11.   T
12.   F   For private foundations, deduction tax consequences to the donor may be less favorable than that available for public charities; the classification as a private foundation may result in taxation at the organization level.
13.   T   The unrelated trade or business could result in the loss of exempt status if the magnitude of the trade or business activity is ascertained to be the primary purpose of the organization.
14.   F   The statutory deduction is $1,000.
15.   T
16.   T
17.   T

Fill-in-the-Blanks

1. social, F
2. religious, charitable
3. common good
4. private foundation
5. grass roots
6. feeder
7. unrelated business income
8. trade or business
9. acquisition indebtedness
10. trade, business, exempt purpose, carried
11. excess lobbying expenditures
12. contributions, taxation
13. corporate

Multiple Choice

1.   c   Although the income from an unrelated trade or business is subject to Federal income taxation, exempt organizations are not prohibited from engaging in such activities, as long as such activities are not the primary purpose of the organization.

2.   a, d

3.   a, e

4.   a, b, d

5.   d   In computing unrelated business taxable income, unrelated debt-financed income constitutes an addition modification.

6.   d   ($800,000 lobbying expenditures - $600,000 lobbying nontaxable amount) See Example 1 in the text.

7.   a, d   See Example 2 in the text.

8.   a, d   The one-third support test is met: [$20,000 ($10,000 from general public + $5,000 from U.S. governmental unit + $5,000 from state A) / $55,000 (Total support)] is more than 33.33%. The not-more-than-one-third support test also is met: [$12,000 (investment income) / $55,000 (total support)] is less than 33.33%. See Example 2 in the text.

9.   c

10.   c

11.   b

12.   d   ($100,000 x 25%). See Example 1 in the text.

13.   d

14.   c   To be excluded from the definition of debt-financed property, at least 85% of the property's use must be for the achievement of the organization's exempt purpose.

15.   c   [($400,000 + $500,000) / ($1,000,000 + $800,000) x $200,000] See Example 23 in the text.

Chapter 24
Taxation of International Transactions

CHAPTER HIGHLIGHTS

A ssignment of income, identification of deductions and exclusions, and computation of the foreign tax credit are issues of importance to the US taxpayer doing business abroad, and to the foreign investor looking for tax-advantaged means by which to enter the US market. Generally, governmental bodies wish to ensure that income earned within their jurisdictions does not escape taxation. Conversely, the taxpayer desires to eliminate the possibilities of multiple taxation, and to identify jurisdictions in which the overall tax liability can be optimized. In this chapter, an introduction to the elements of the taxation of international transactions is presented. In addition, problems relative to foreign currency translation and the individual's residency requirements are introduced.

I.   Definitions
    A.   The structure of the federal income tax with respect to international transactions is familiar to us, i.e., computations of taxable income and identification of taxable entities are carried out in a manner that resembles that for fully-US transactions. Several special definitions are employed in this context, however.
    B.   *Incidence of Taxation* -- The federal income tax applies to nonresident aliens and to foreign corporations, to the extent of both US-source income and income that is effectively connected with an active US business.
    C.   *Nonresident Alien* -- An individual who has not secured a "green card," i.e., official immigration status, and who is not a resident of the US.
    D.   *Residency* -- For an individual, residency is determined according to official immigration status, or by satisfying the "substantial presence" test with presence in the US for at least 183 days in the current calendar year or within a three-year period. For estate and gift tax purposes, however, other actions or intentions of the taxpayer may be considered in making the classification.

E.   *US Business* -- A foreign entity operates an active US business if sufficient production, management, distribution, and other business functions are conducted in the US. Securities trading usually is not an active US business, regardless of where the trading is conducted.

F.   *Effectively Connected* -- A taxpayer's activities are effectively connected with a US business if it generates income from assets used by the business, or if the business provided the capital from which the income was generated.

G.   *Foreign Corporation* -- An entity that was not incorporated in the US. The definition may include trusts or partnerships that exhibit sufficient corporate characteristics.

H.   *FIRPTA* -- The Foreign Investment in Real Property Tax Act, enacted in 1980 to assure that foreign taxpayers would not be exempted from paying appropriate income taxes on the sale or exchange of US realty. The Act classifies as effectively connected income any sale of US realty by a nonresident alien or a foreign corporation.

I.   *Controlled Foreign Corporation (CFC)* -- A foreign entity in which more than fifty percent of the value or voting power of the corporation is owned by US shareholders on any day during the entity's taxable year. For this purpose, indirect and constructive ownership is counted, but shareholders owning (directly or otherwise) less than ten percent of the voting power are ignored.

II. The Foreign Tax Credit (FTC)

A.   A credit is allowed against the US tax relative to certain foreign taxes paid, to mitigate the possibility that the taxpayer will be subject to similar taxes in various countries on the same income.

B.   The overall limitation on the foreign tax credit (FTC) relates to the proportion of the taxpayer's overall income that is derived from foreign sources.

$$\text{US Tax before FTC} \quad X \quad \frac{\text{Foreign-Source Taxable Income}}{\text{Worldwide Taxable Income}}$$

C.   The following two other limitations are placed upon the FTC calculation, so that the credit does not exceed actual or implied foreign tax payments. A *direct* credit is allowed dollar-for-dollar for foreign tax payments. An *indirect* credit is allowed for US corporate taxpayers who receive dividends from foreign corporations; the credit relates to foreign taxes that were paid with respect to the dividend distribution, proportionately to the payor's post-1986 undistributed earnings.

$$\textbf{Indirect FTC} \quad = \quad \text{Dividend Paid} \quad X \quad \frac{\text{Foreign Taxes Paid on Post-1986 Earnings}}{\text{Undistributed Post-1986 Earnings}}$$

The dividend income received from the foreign corporation must be *grossed up* by the amount of the deemed-paid taxes (i.e., the amount of the indirect FTC is treated as additional dividend income). The indirect credit is allowed only to a domestic corporation that owns at least ten percent of the payor foreign corporation. The credit can be claimed relative to no more than two tiers of the foreign corporation's subsidiaries.

D.   The foreign tax credit is allowed only with respect to foreign taxes that resemble an income tax, i.e., it is not allowed relative to transfer, excise, or extraction taxes.

E.   The foreign tax credit must be computed with respect to each of several distinct *baskets* of income, and the limitations are applied to each basket separately, so that credits from taxes in high-rate countries cannot be used to augment those for low-rate countries or activities. Accordingly, separate FTCs are computed for each of the following, among others.

1.   Passive income

        2.   Financial services income

        3.   Shipping income

        4.   Foreign-source income from DISCs

        5.   Foreign-source income from the E&P of an FSC

        A look-through rule is applied to identify the constitution of the income underlying a dividend distribution, with respect to controlled foreign corporations.

F.   Any foreign taxes that are used in computing the FTC that are disallowed under the *basket* computations are carried back two years and then forward five years.

G.   The FTC can be used to reduce the taxpayer's alternative minimum tax liability, but only to the extent of ninety percent of the tentative minimum tax.

H.   In lieu of claiming a foreign tax credit, foreign tax payments can be *deducted* by the taxpayer, but one cannot claim both a credit and a deduction for the same tax in the same year. A taxpayer, however, can take a deduction in the same year as a FTC for foreign taxes that are not creditable, e.g., for *soak up* taxes.

I.   With respect to income from operations in US possessions, domestic corporations may elect to receive a credit against US taxes equal to 34% of possession-source taxable income and qualified investment income regardless of whether any tax is paid or due to the possession, i.e., a *tax sparing credit*. No additional credit or deduction is allowed for income taxes actually paid to the possession.

III.   Identifying US-source and Foreign-source Income

A.   One must classify income and expense items as either US- or foreign-source in computing the FTC. In addition, US citizens and resident individuals are allowed an exclusion for foreign earned income. Foreign corporations and individual aliens are subject to tax only on their US-source income.

B.   Interest income is US-source if it is received on debt issued by the US government, a US corporation, or a noncorporate US resident. The interest is foreign-source, however, if the US corporation or resident alien conducts eighty percent of its business out of the US, or if the interest is received on amounts deposited with a foreign branch of a US bank.

C.   Dividend income is classified according to the country in which the payor was incorporated: payments from a US corporation are US-source, and distributions from a foreign corporation are foreign-source. However, a pro rata portion of the dividend of a foreign corporation is US-source if at least 25 percent of its gross income for the last three years was effectively connected with an active US business. Dividends received from FSCs and DISCs can be treated as US-source income.

D.   Income from personal services is classified according to the situs at which the services were performed. Personal service income can be derived wherever capital is not a material income-producing factor, even by a corporation. US service income is treated as foreign-source if the performer is a nonresident alien who earned no more than $3,000, stayed in the US for no more than ninety days during the tax year, and performed the services on behalf of a foreign entity that is not engaged in a US trade or business or a business maintained in a foreign country by a US entity.

E.   Rent and royalty income for tangible property is classified according to the location of the underlying property. Income from intangible assets is assigned to the country in which the patent, copyright, or similar property is used.

    F.   Gain or loss from the sale of real estate is assigned to the country in which the realty is located, i.e., the sale of US real estate produces US-source income. Gain or loss on the sale of personal property is treated as follows.

        1.   Generally, income is assigned to the resident country of the seller, and loss is assigned to the country in which the related (sales or other operating) income had been generated prior to the sale.

        2.   Inventory sales are assigned to the country in which the sale took place.

        3.   Sales of manufactured goods are classified pro rata between the countries of production and sale, based upon independent transfer prices. Lacking such a pricing structure, the income is partitioned on the basis of the underlying sales activities and asset holdings of the seller.

        4.   Gain on the sale of depreciable property is assigned to the country in which the depreciation deductions had been claimed.

        5.   Gain attributable to an office or plant is US-source if the US location is operated by a nonresident alien, and foreign-source if the foreign location is operated by a US resident or corporation.

    G.   Income from transportation and communication is US-source if both sender and receiver are located in the US. Such income is fifty percent US-source if only one node of the activity is located in the US.

    H.   Deductions and losses are directly *allocated* to specific US- or foreign-sources if they relate to identifiable assets or income. Other deductions and losses, including interest charges, then are *apportioned* to US- and foreign-sources, according to some reasonable computational basis, such as relative asset holdings or income generated.

    I.   The IRS is empowered to reassign income, loss, and credit items among related persons, by making IRC § 482 adjustments, to more clearly reflect the taxable income of the members of the group.

    J.   The 20% accuracy-related penalty applies to valuation misstatements where:

        1.   A net § 482 transfer price adjustment exceeds $10 million of taxable income or AMT income;

        2.   The amount paid for goods or services exceeds 200% of the adjusted § 482 price; or,

        3.   The amount received is less than 50% of the § 482 price.

One way around the dangers of a challenge by the IRS to a transfer pricing system is to reach an Advanced Priicing Agreement with the Service before the related tax return is filed. Apple, Toyota, and about twenty other taxpayers currently are working on such agreements with the IRS, although others are scared off by the nature and extent of the (often proprietary) information that must be given to the Service to justify the pricing figures.

IV.   Tax Effects of "Inbound" Transactions

    A.   US tax provisions relative to non-US entities conducting business in this country ("inbound" transactions) include numerous reporting requirements.

    B.   The usual federal income taxes apply to the US-source income of nonresident aliens (NRAs) and foreign corporations, and to the foreign-source income of such entities that is *effectively connected* with an active US business. Non-US corporations usually qualify for the same exemptions from US taxation regarding interest and dividend income as do NRA individuals.

C.   Income is effectively connected with a US trade or business if it is derived from assets used in the trade or business (*asset-use test*), or if the activities of the trade or business were a material factor in the production of the income (*business-activities test*).

D.   A flat thirty percent tax (or in certain cases, a lower treaty rate) is applied to US-source gross income that is not effectively connected with a US business, including portfolio and other fixed, determinable, annual, or periodic (FDAP) income.

E.   NRAs can claim the itemized deductions for casualties and charitable contributions, and they can claim one personal exemption.

F.   The US gross estate of an NRA includes assets located in the US, including any stock or bonds issued by a US corporation or government. However, the US gross estate includes neither the NRA's life insurance proceeds, nor amounts held on deposit by foreign branches of US banks.

         1.   Higher tax rates and a lower unified transfer tax credit apply to an NRA.

         2.   No marital deduction is allowed for assets that pass to a nonresident surviving spouse unless the property passes through a *qualified domestic trust (QDT)*. However, a $100,000 annual gift tax exclusion is allowed on transfers to a noncitizen spouse.

G.   A thirty percent branch profits tax is applied to the "dividend equivalent amount" of a foreign corporation. The tax base, limited to effectively connected and previously untaxed post-1986 E&P, includes the effectively connected income of the entity, *minus* any additional investments made in US assets during the year, or *plus* any decrease in such investments.

H.   Under FIRPTA, all gains and losses from sales of US realty are treated as effectively connected to a US business.

I.   The US has entered into tax treaties with over thirty countries relative to the income tax, and with fewer than twenty countries with respect to the estate and gift tax. The provisions of a treaty commonly override those of the general income tax law. Under such a treaty, definitions and primary taxing rights are established, generally assigning the tax to the resident country of the taxpayer or the country in which permanent assets are constructed, to minimize the opportunity for double taxation.

J.   A $70,000 exclusion against US gross income is allowed with respect to the foreign earned income of a US citizen or resident, to allow for the payment of market or incentive wages in the context of a foreign relocation. The exclusion is allowed if the US individual is physically present in a foreign country for at least 330 full days during twelve consecutive months. The exclusion cannot exceed the excess of foreign earned income over a standard housing cost allowance. A self-employed individual cannot claim the housing cost exclusion, but he or she may be able to deduct foreign housing expenses.

K.   Under Subpart F of this portion of the Code, US shareholders in a controlled foreign corporation (CFC) must include in US gross income a pro rata portion of Subpart F income and increase in earnings that the CFC has invested in US property for the tax year, regardless of whether such earnings have been distributed to them. *Subpart F income* qualifying for this pass-through includes the following.

         1.   Foreign sales, service, shipping, personal holding company, and oil-related income.

         2.   Insurance income.

         3.   Illegal bribes.

       If the first two of these categories does not exceed the lesser of $1 million or five percent of the entity's worldwide gross income, the corporation is treated as having no such income for the year.

L.   The tax years of a CFC and a foreign personal holding company (FPHC) generally must conform to the tax year of its majority US shareholder, i.e., a US shareholder owning more than 50% of the total outstanding stock. A CFC, however, can elect to use a tax year ending one month earlier.

M.   Under previous laws, a taxpayer was allowed to create a Domestic International Sales Corporation (DISC), whose export sales of up to $10 million would not be subject to US income tax until it was repatriated. New DISCs no longer can be created, and existing DISCs must include in US gross income an amount approximating the interest that would be charged on the still-deferred US tax.

N.   About sixteen percent of the export income of a Foreign Sales Corporation (FSC) is exempt from US income tax. A FSC must establish a foreign presence, e.g., by maintaining a foreign office and utilizing foreign management personnel, but this requirement is waived for an entity whose export receipts do not exceed $5 million. A FSC can issue only common stock, and it cannot have more than 25 shareholders.

O.   A taxpayer must include in gross income gain or loss from foreign currency transactions. Such gain or loss arises from changes in exchange rates between the purchase and payment dates of a closed transaction that is denominated in a foreign currency. In determining gain or loss, such transactions are denominated in the functional currency of the taxpayer, and the currency gain or loss is treated separately from the gain or loss on the underlying sale. An implied currency gain or loss is computed when a foreign corporation makes a distribution from earnings and profits: the taxpayers must use the weighted average exchange rate for the post-1986 years in which the distributed earnings were generated.

P.   A corporation's deduction may be deferred for interest expense paid or accrued to a related party that is not fully subject to US income tax on the interest income. This rule is referred to as the *earnings stripping* provision. For this purpose, a related party generally must be affiliated through more than 50% stock ownership.

    1.   If the payor corporation's debt-to-equity ratio exceeds 1.5 to 1, related party interest will be deferred and subject to limitation in the succeeding year to the extent that total interest expense, reduced by taxable interest income, exceeds 50% of the corporation's adjusted taxable income plus the amount by which the 50% income limit has exceeded net interest expense in the prior three years.

    2.   Adjusted taxable income for this purpose is the corporation's taxable income prior to deductions for interest, NOLs, depreciation, amortization, and depletion.

TEST FOR SELF-EVALUATION - CHAPTER 24

True or False

Indicate which of the following statements are true or false by circling the correct answer.

T   F   1.   For taxpayers using the cash method of accounting for tax purposes, an election is available to take the foreign tax credit in the year in which the foreign tax accrues.

T   F   2.   The *indirect* foreign tax credit is available only to non-corporate US taxpayers, with respect to actual or deemed dividends received.

T   F   3.   An indirect foreign tax credit can be claimed for payments received from up to four tiers of subsidiaries by the parent.

T   F   4.   A look-through rule applies in computing the foreign tax credit limitation on a specific type of income, so that payments received from controlled foreign corporations are treated by the US shareholder as though they were earned directly by the recipient.

T   F   5.   Taxes paid that qualify for the foreign tax credit include foreign income, value-added, and oil extraction fees.

T   F   6.   In a single tax year, a taxpayer's return may reflect both a credit and a deduction for foreign tax payments.

T   F   7.   Interest on US Treasury bills always is classified as US-source income.

T   F   8.   Income from personal services is assigned to the country of residence of the performer of the services.

T   F   9.   Income from rental agreements relative to tangible assets is assigned to the country in which the income-producing property is located.

T   F   10.   Gain on the sale of inventory is assigned to the resident country of the seller.

T   F   11.   Interest expenses are assigned to the country that issued the debt.

T   F   12.   An individual without official US immigration status still can qualify as a US resident for income tax purposes.

T   F   13.   A nonresident alien can claim a full unified transfer tax credit against the US estate tax, but he or she cannot claim a marital deduction for assets passing to a nonresident alien surviving spouse.

T   F   14.   The foreign earned income exclusion relates to all amounts received relative to the services that were performed during a given year, regardless of the year in which the taxpayer received them.

T   F   15.   The exclusion for foreign housing costs is not available to a self-employed individual.

T   F   16.   Subpart F income is passed through to US shareholders, whether or not distributed, with respect to controlled foreign corporations.

T   F   17.   A taxpayer can defer US taxation relative to sales made by a DISC until repatriation of the earnings, to a maximum amount of $5,000,000.

T   F   18.   The "foreign presence" requirement is waived for a FSC whose export receipts do not exceed $5,000,000 per year.

T   F   19.   A controlled foreign corporation is a foreign entity in which 80% or more of the value or voting power of the corporation is owned by US shareholders.

T   F   20.   For foreign tax credit purposes, taxes paid in a foreign currency are translated to US dollars at the average exchange rate in effect during the year in which the taxes are paid or accrued.

Fill-in-the-Blanks

Complete the following statements with the appropriate word(s) or amount(s).

1.   The _____ _____ _____ allows a dollar-for-dollar reduction of the US income tax for similar taxes paid to other countries.

2.   To claim the indirect foreign tax credit, the recipient must hold a minimum ownership level of _____ percent in each subsidiary.

3.   To prevent the use of the foreign tax credit derived from specific types of income against the tax liabilities of functionally different types of income, the credit must be applied for each of several "_____s" of income. Excess taxes that are unused under this provision can be carried back _____ and then forward _____ years.

4.   The foreign tax credit can offset no more than _____ percent of the taxpayer's tentative alternative minimum tax.

5.   A dividend paid by a foreign corporation will be classified as US-source if 25% or more of the foreign corporation's gross income for the last _____ years was _____ _____ with an active US business.

6.   Under the provisions of _____, income from the sale of _____ property is assigned to the country in which the assets were located. When personal property is sold, the resulting gain is assigned to the resident country of the _____.

7.   An immigrant can establish US residency for income tax purposes either by obtaining a "_____ _____" or by meeting the _____ _____ test.

8.   A nonresident alien is subject to a flat _____ percent rate of US income tax on his or her gross _____ (FDAP) income. Such individuals also can claim the _____ and _____ _____ itemized deductions, and they can claim one personal exemption.

9.   The tax years of CFCs and FPHCs must conform to that of a more than _____ percent _____ owner

10.   The foreign earned income exclusion is limited to the lesser of $_____ or foreign earned income less the exclusion for qualified _____ costs.

11.　A _____ _____ _____ is one in which more than _____ percent of the outstanding stock is held by US shareholders on any day in the entity's taxable year. In meeting this test, indirect and attributed ownership is counted, but those holding less than _____ percent of the shares are ignored.

12.　In computing a taxpayer's gain or loss from foreign currency transactions, all exchanges are to be denominated in the taxpayer's _____ currency.

13.　A taxpayer can not take a _____ and a _____ for the same foreign income taxes.

14.　Under section 482, the IRS has the power to _____ income among organizations owned or controlled by the same interests.

Multiple Choice

Choose the best answer for each of the following questions.

____　1.　Frank, a US citizen, paid $35,000 in income taxes to Hibernia, the country in which he was assigned to work this year. Hibernia and the US have not enacted any tax treaty to date. Absent any consideration of the foreign taxes paid, assume Frank would owe $38,000 in US income taxes on the Hibernia-source income. Compute Frank's direct foreign tax credit.
　　　a.　$0.
　　　b.　$3,500 (10% limitation).
　　　c.　$35,000.
　　　d.　$210,000.
　　　e.　None of the above.

USE THE FOLLOWING INFORMATION FOR PROBLEMS 2 THROUGH 4

FSub, a foreign corporation, pays a $200,000 dividend to its sole shareholder/parent, DCorp, a domestic corporation, this year. Since 1986, FSub has paid $800,000 in foreign taxes on its $4,000,000 earnings for the period.

____　2.　Compute DCorp's indirect foreign tax credit relative to the FSub dividend.
　　　a.　$0.
　　　b.　$20,000 (10% TRA86 limitation).
　　　c.　$40,000.
　　　d.　$200,000.
　　　e.　None of the above.

____　3.　Derive DCorp's taxable income from the dividend.
　　　a.　$0.
　　　b.　$40,000 (after dividends-received deduction).
　　　c.　$200,000.
　　　d.　$240,000.
　　　e.　None of the above.

____　4.　DCorp's own taxable income for the year totals $10,000,000, and its US tax on this amount, before credits, is $3,400,000. The FSub dividend, and all of DCorp's other foreign transactions which aggregate taxable income of $6,000,000, are included in both of these figures. Derive DCorp's overall limit on the foreign tax credit.
　　　a.　$0 (DCorp has more than one foreign subsidiary).

    b. $340,000 (10% FIRPTA limitation).
    c. $2,040,000.
    d. $3,400,000.
    e.   None of the above.

_____ 5.   Which of the following is *not* an income basket to be used in computing the foreign tax credit limitation?
    a.   Personal services income.
    b.   Financial services income.
    c.   Foreign-source income received from a DISC.
    d.   Shipping income.
    e.   All of the above are treated as income baskets.

_____ 6.   Compute DCorp's foreign tax credit with respect to dividends received this year from its two foreign subsidiaries. DCorp's worldwide taxable income amounts to $10,000,000, and its US tax liability on that amount, before the foreign tax credit, is $3,100,000.

Payor	Type of Income	Dividend	Related Foreign Tax
Attina	Shipping	$400,000	$55,000
Bulovah	Banking	400,000	162,500
Totals		$800,000	$217,500

    a. $55,000.
    b. $124,000.
    c. $162,500.
    d. $217,500.
    e.   None of the above.

_____ 7.   Compute DCorp's US-source income relative to dividends received from its three foreign subsidiaries.

Payor	Dividend	Percent of Last Three Years' Income	
		Active Foreign	Effectively Connected to US
Arriva	$1,000	10	90
Balbona	$1,000	80	20
Cheetah	$1,000	0	100

    a. $1,400.
    b. $1,600.
    c. $1,900.
    d. $2,000.
    e. $2,500.

_____ 8.   Milway Airlines operates a flight from Raleigh to Paris. On Flight 101 to Raleigh, Milway carries forty US passengers and sixty French passengers, and it earns $110,000. Compute Milway's US-source income from the flight.
    a. $0.
    b. $44,000.
    c. $55,000 (50-50 presumption).
    d. $66,000.
    e. $110,000.

_____ 9.   Compute the US-source taxable income derived by the Boucher Realty Corporation for the year. General overhead expenses amounted to $75,000.

Activity	Income/Net Gain	Direct Expenses
German rentals	$200,000	$ 40,000
Sales of German buildings	$200,000	$ 15,000
US rentals	$200,000	$ 65,000
Totals	$600,000	$120,000

    a. $60,000.
    b. $110,000.
    c. $135,000.
    d. $200,000.
    e.   None of the above.

_____ 10.   This year, FCorp began to sell its equipment in the US through DSub, a 100%-owned subsidiary. DSub's net investment in US assets increased $200,000 during the year, and its current US taxable income would have been $750,000. Compute the tax base for the branch profits tax on FCorp for the year.
    a. $0 (three-year exemption).
    b. $550,000.
    c. $750,000.
    d. $950,000.
    e.   None of the above.

_____ 11.   Continue with the facts of problem 10. What is the applicable rate for FCorp's branch profits tax?
    a.   10%
    b.   34%
    c.   35%
    d.   50%
    e.   None of the above.

_____ 12.   Which of the following does *not* constitute Subpart F income?
    a.   Illegal bribes.
    b.   Foreign base company interest income.
    c.   Foreign base company sales and service income.
    d.   Insurance income.
    e.   All of the above are included in Subpart F income.

_____ 13.   Select the *correct* statement.
    a.   "Interest charge DISCs" still exist under the tax law.
    b.   DISCs were repealed by TRA86.
    c.   The same taxpayer cannot operate both a FSC and a DISC.
    d.   The US' major trading partners encouraged expansion of the DISC provisions in TRA86.
    e.   All of the above statements are correct.

_____ 14.   FSub, a foreign corporation, sells a computer on 12-1-X1 to DCorp, a US corporation. DCorp paid the full purchase price on 12-15-X1. FSub's functional currency is the Kronos (*K*). The sale is made for 100,000*K*. Both entities use the calendar year. Determine the amount of DCorp's 19X1 currency gain on the purchase.

Date	Exchange Rate
1-1-X1	1*K* : $1
12-1-X1	1.1*K* : $1
12-15-X1	1.3*K* : $1

12-31-X1	$1.4K : \$1$
1-15-X2	$1.5K : \$1$

    a. $0.
    b. $13,986.
    c. $19,480.
    d. $20,000.
    e. $23,077.

_____ 15.   Continue with the facts of problem 14, except that the parties set the payment date as 1-15-X2. Determine the amount of DCorp's 19X1 currency gain on the purchase.
    a. $0.
    b. $13,986 .
    c. $19,480.
    d. $24,242.
    e.   None of the above.

_____ 16.   Sam, a US resident was present in a foreign country for all of 19X0. During 19X0, Sam earned $90,000 from the performance of personal services. On 1/1/X1 Sam returned to the US and remained there. Of the 19X0 foreign earned income, Sam received $60,000 in 19X0 and $30,000 in 19X1. For 19X1, how much of the foreign earned income exclusion ca Sam claim?
    a. $0.
    b. $10,000.
    c. $30,000.
    d. $60,000.
    e. $70,000.

_____ 17.   Continue with the facts of problem 16, except that Sam did not receive the $30,000 until 19X2. For 19X2, what is Sam's foreign earned income exclusion?
    a. $0.
    b. $10,000.
    c. $30,000.
    d. $60,000.
    e. $70,000.

_____ 18.   Xenia, an alien, was present in the US for 40 days in 1992, 120 days in 1993, and 133 days in 1994. Which of the following statements are correct?
    a.   Xenia may elect to be treated as a resident for part of 1992.
    b.   Xenia is a US resident for 1992 and 1993.
    c.   Xenia is a US resident for 1994.
    d.   Xenia is not considered to be a US resident in 1992, 1993 or 1994.
    e.   Xenia is a US resident for 1992, 1993 and 1994.

SOLUTIONS TO CHAPTER 24 QUESTIONS

True or False

1.	T	
2.	F	It is available only to corporate taxpayers who have received such dividends during the year.
3.	F	The credit is available only for a three-tier arrangement (parent and two levels of subsidiaries).
4.	T	
5.	F	If the levy conveys a specific benefit to the taxpayer, like a natural resource extraction fee, it does not qualify for the credit.
6.	T	This is allowed if, for instance, the taxpayer is subject to tax in more than one foreign country, or to more than one type of tax in the same country, but not with respect to the same tax in the same country.
7.	F	Counter-examples include such income earned on amounts deposited in a foreign branch of a US bank.
8.	F	It is assigned to the country in which the services are performed.
9.	T	
10.	F	It is assigned to the country in which the sale took place.
11.	F	It is assigned to the countries on the basis of the taxpayer's asset bases.
12.	T	The taxpayer could base his or her US residency on the substantial presence test.
13.	F	The unified credit available at death is $13,000.
14.	F	The exclusion is lost for amounts received more than one tax year after that in which the services are performed.
15.	T	A deduction for such amounts may be available, however.
16.	T	
17.	F	The correct amount is $10,000,000.
18.	T	
19.	F	A CFC is a foreign entity in which more than 50% of the value or voting power of the corporation is owned by US shareholders, on any day during the entity's tax year.
20.	F	For FTC purposes, taxes paid in a foreign currency are translated into US dollars at the exchange rate in effect when the taxes are actually paid.

Fill-in-the-Blanks

1. foreign tax credit
2. ten
3. basket, two, five
4. ninety
5. three, effectively connected
6. FIRPTA, real, seller
7. green card, substantial presence
8. thirty, portfolio, casualty, charitable contribution
9. 50, US
10. 70,000, housing
11. controlled foreign corporation, fifty, ten
12. functional
13. credit, deduction
14. reallocate

Multiple Choice

1.   c   Frank bears the legal incidence for the tax in both countries. See Example 2 in the text.

2.   c $200,000 X ($800,000 / $4,000,000) See Example 3 in the text.

3.   d   Gross up taxable income by the amount of the credit. See Example 3 in the text.

4.   c $3,400,000 X ($6,000,000 / $10,000,000) See Example 4 in the text.

5.   a

6.   e   Limit under the basket concept = $179,000, rather than $217,500
          Shipping limit = Lesser of $55,000 or [$400,000 X ($3,100,000 / $10,000,000)] = $55,000
          Banking limit = Lesser of $162,500 or [$400,000 X ($3,100,000 / $10,000,000)] = $124,000.

7.   c $900 + $0 (fails 25% test) + $1,000 See Example 10 in the text.

8.   c   Transportation income is assigned fifty-fifty to the originating and destination countries.

9.   b $200,000 - $65,000 - [$75,000 X ($200,000 / $600,000)]

10.   b   Decrease the tax base for increases in US investments.

11.   e   The tax is applied at a 30% rate.

12.   b

13.   a

14.   b   Gain is computed only with respect to the period between the purchase and payment dates.

100,000K / 1.1K	$90,909	
100,000K / 1.3K	-76,923	
Currency Gain	$13,986	

          See Example 30 in the text.

15.   a   The transaction is not closed in 19X9. See Example 31 in the text.

16.   b   ($70,000 statutory limit minus the $60,000 excluded for 19X0) See Example 30 in the text.

17.   a   No exclusion is allowed for 19X2 because the $30,000 was received after the close of the taxable year following the taxable year in which the services were performed. See Example 20 in the text.

18.   d   Xenia does not satisfy the substantial presence test in 1992, 1993 or 1994; her physical presence for the three-year period ending in 1994 consisted of 180 days [(40 days X 1/6) + (120 days X 1/3) + (133 days X 1)]. See Example 14 in the text.

CHAPTER 25
TAX ADMINISTRATION AND PRACTICE

CHAPTER HIGHLIGHTS

A
lthough the tax system in the United States is based upon the concept of self-assessment, many returns are audited each year, to ensure taxpayer compliance. Audits may take the form of a mere letter from the IRS, or they may be full-scale undertakings conducted at the taxpayer's place of business. After an audit, an agent will attempt to reach an agreement with the taxpayer concerning the amount of the additional assessment, if any. Where an agreement cannot be reached, the taxpayer is given an opportunity to argue before the appeals division of the IRS. When an agreement cannot be reached at the appeals level, the taxpayer's only choice is to take the case to court. In addition to knowing the procedures for negotiating a settlement in cases of dispute, tax practitioners must become aware of the requirements imposed upon them, and of penalties for failure to comply with the requirements. In recent years, Congress has been encouraging the IRS to more strictly enforce the Code's penalty provisions.

I. IRS Procedure - Individual Rulings
   A. Individual Rulings are issued by the National Office of the IRS.
   B. They represent the current position of the IRS on the tax consequences of a particular transaction with a given set of facts.
   C. Individual Rulings frequently are declared obsolete or superseded.
       1. Revocation usually is not retroactive.
       2. The IRS may revoke any Ruling if, upon subsequent audit, the agent finds a material misstatement of fact.
   D. The IRS issues rulings on uncompleted, actual transactions or on transactions that have been completed prior to the filing of the tax return.
   E. The IRS will not rule on all issues.
       1. It will not rule on a question of fact only.
       2. It will not rule on a hypothetical issue.

F.   Although a ruling may be relied upon only by the taxpayer who requested and received it, the ruling may provide substantial authority for a position that is taken in a tax return, and thus, eliminate the imposition of a penalty for the substantial understatement of a taxpayer's income tax.

G.   The IRS ruling policy is an attempt to promote a uniform application of the tax laws.

H.   Generally, the taxpayer must pay a user fee when requesting a ruling from the IRS.

II.   IRS Procedures - Other Issuances

    A.   Revenue Procedures are published statements of current internal practices and policies of the IRS.

    B.   Determination letters are issued by the District Director for completed transactions, when the issues are covered by judicial or statutory authority, Regulations, or Rulings.

    C.   Technical Advice Memoranda are issued by the National Office of the IRS upon a request from an IRS Agent, Appellate Conferee, or District Director.

III.   The Audit Process

    A.   Selection of returns for audit is done in the following ways:

        1.   The IRS uses computerized formulas to select the returns that are most likely to have errors and render positive tax liabilities after review.

        2.   Certain groups of taxpayers are more likely to be audited, e.g., individuals with gross incomes greater than $50,000, self-employed individuals, and cash-oriented businesses.

        3.   A return may be audited if a corresponding information return does not match the information on the tax return, if an individual's itemized deductions or other deductions are excessive, or if a past audit led to the assessment of a substantial deficiency.

    B.   A *correspondence audit* occurs when an obvious error is made on a return, e.g., where the taxpayer has made a math error, or where he or she has failed to use a statutory limitation.

        1.   A letter of explanation and a bill for the additional taxes will be sent to a taxpayer.

        2.   Taxpayers usually are able to handle such errors through direct correspondence, without a visit to an IRS office.

    C.   An *office audit* is used for individuals with few or no items of business income.

        1.   The audit is conducted by a representative of the District Director's Office.

        2.   The individual usually is asked to substantiate a deduction, credit, or item of income.

    D.   A *field audit* most often is used for business returns.

        1.   Such an audit is conducted by an IRS agent at the office or home of the taxpayer.

        2.   A field audit usually is more extensive, covering many more items than would an office audit.

        3.   Upon the showing of reasonable cause, a taxpayer can have an office audit changed to a field audit.

    E.   Taxpayers' Rights.

        1.   Prior to, or at the initial interview, the IRS must provide the taxpayer with an explanation of the audit process that is the subject of the interview and describe the taxpayer's rights under that process.

        2.   Upon advance request, a taxpayer may make an audio recording of any in-person interview with an IRS officer or employee concerning the determination and collection of any tax.

    F.   A taxpayer may attempt to settle with an agent after the audit.

        1.   The agent must adhere strictly to IRS policy. He or she cannot attempt to settle an unresolved issue based upon a perceived probability of winning in

      court.
   2. Questions of fact usually can be solved at the agent level.
   3. Following an audit, the IRS may either accept the return as filed or recommend certain adjustments. The agent's findings are summarized in a *Revenue Agent's Report* (RAR).
   4. If an agreement is reached, Form 870 is signed by the taxpayer.
     a. The signing of this form stops the running of interest on the additional assessment thirty days after the form is filed.
     b. The taxpayer is barred from appealing to a higher level of the IRS or taking the issue to Tax Court after filing Form 870.
     c. However, a taxpayer may pay the tax and file a claim for refund in the Claims Court or a Federal District Court.

IV. The Taxpayer Appeal Process
  A. When an agreement cannot be reached at the agent level, the taxpayer receives a copy of the RAR and a letter stating that he or she has 30 days to request an administrative appeal.
   1. If an appeal is not made, a statutory notice of deficiency, i.e., 90-day letter, will be issued to the taxpayer.
   2. A request for appeal must be accompanied by a written protest. However, if the proposed deficiency does not exceed $10,000 or if the deficiency resulted from a correspondence or office audit, a formal letter of protest is not required.
  B. The Appeals Division of the IRS may settle disputes based on a perceived probability of winning in court (i.e. hazards of litigation).

KEY TERMS
- Correspondence, Field, Office Audit
- 30, 90-Day Letters
- Accuracy-Related Penalty
- Statute of Limitations
- Practice Before the IRS
- Ethics of Tax Practice

  C. The Appeals Division usually will not raise new issues on appeal. However, if the disputed tax is substantial, and the issue has a significant administrative impact, the Appeals Division will raise a new issue.
  D. Both the Appeals Division and the taxpayer have the right to request technical advice from the National Office of the IRS.
  E. If the taxpayer cannot reach an agreement with the Appeals Division, the Service then will issue a statutory letter of deficiency. After receiving the deficiency letter, the taxpayer has 90 days to file a suit in the Tax Court.
  F. If an agreement is reached at the appeals level, the taxpayer must file Form 870AD, which is a binding agreement for both the IRS and the taxpayer absent fraud, malfeasance, concealment, or misrepresentation of material fact.
  G. The Code provides specific authority for the IRS to negotiate a compromise where there is doubt as to the taxpayer's ability to pay the tax. Form 656 (Offer in Compromise) must be filed with the District Director or IRS Service Center.
   1. When there is doubt as to the amount of tax liability involved, a closing agreement may be appropriate.
   2. The IRS has statutory authority to enter into a written agreement allowing payment of taxes on an installment basis if such agreement will facilitate collection.

V. Interest
  A. During negotiations, interest accrues with respect to overpayments, deficiencies, and

unpaid taxes.

B.   The taxpayer may stop the running of interest by signing Form 870 and paying the tax.

C.   Interest begins to accrue from the unextended due date for filing the tax return and continues to accrue until 30 days after the filing of the Form 870.

D.   Interest on overpayments is not allowed on refunds returned within 45 days from the date the return was filed or due, whichever is later.

E.   Interest rates are adjusted on a quarterly basis as of January 1, April 1, July 1, and October 1 of each year.

F.   Interest that accrues is compounded daily.

G.   The interest rate charged on underpayments is one percentage point higher than the interest rate charged on overpayments.

H.   For C corporations that have an underpayment of tax that exceeds $100,000 for any single taxable period, the interest rate charged on the underpayment is increased by two percentage points.

I.   Interest paid by an individual taxpayer to the IRS is characterized as personal interest. No portion of personal interest is deductible.

VI.   Penalties

A.   Penalties are imposed to ensure that the self-assessment features of the tax system function efficiently. They are an addition to the tax liability and are not deductible by the taxpayer.

B.   A penalty of 5 percent per month of the tax due is imposed on a taxpayer who *fails to timely file* a tax return. The total penalty is limited to 25 percent of the tax due. If the failure to file is fraudulent, the penalty is increased to 15 percent per month, up to a maximum of 75 percent of the tax due.

C.   A penalty of 1/2 percent per month of the tax due is assessed, when the taxpayer *fails to pay the tax* due on the return in a timely manner. The penalty is increased to one percent of the underpaid tax per month after the IRS notifies the taxpayer of the underpayment. The maximum penalty that may be imposed is 25 percent of the outstanding tax.

D.   For purposes of both the failure to file and failure to pay penalties, the term "tax due" refers to the net balance due, rather than the total tax shown on the return.

E.   When both the failure to file and the failure to pay penalties are incurred, the failure to file penalty is reduced by the failure to pay penalty, provided that a return was filed. However, if a return never was filed, both penalties will apply without reduction.

F.   A valid extension of time to file a tax return will eliminate the failure to file penalty, but it will not eliminate the failure to pay penalty.

G.   The negligence, substantial understatement and valuation penalties have been consolidated into a single *accuracy-related* penalty. The accuracy-related penalty is imposed at the rate of 20 percent on the portion of any underpayment attributable to

1.   negligence;

2.   substantial understatement of income tax;

3.   substantial valuation overstatement;

4.   substantial estate or gift tax valuation understatement; or

5.   substantial overstatement of pension liabilities.

The accuracy-related penalty, however, will not be imposed where reasonable cause is shown for the underpayment and the taxpayer acted in good faith.

Many tax practitioners today believe that the elaborate penalty system put into effect during the 1980s has made them operate as agents of the IRS, rather than as taxpayer advocates. The voluntary compliance aspect of the tax system sometimes is difficult to see when discussing matters of collection and enforcement of the revenue laws.

H.   A 75 percent penalty on the amount of underpayment is imposed on any underpayment resulting from fraud. The fraud penalty only applies to the part of an underpayment that actually is attributable to fraud, i.e., not the entire underpayment. In addition to the civil fraud penalties, the Code contains various criminal sanctions.

I.   A penalty is imposed for the failure to make adequate and timely estimated tax payments. The penalty is based on the amount and duration of the underpayment and the interest rate that currently is established by the Code.

J.   Failure to make deposits of taxes, and overstatement of deposits, result in the following penalties.

       1.   Up to 15 percent of the underdeposited amount, depending on when the underpayment is corrected and whether the taxpayer received a delinquency notice;

       2.   25 percent of the overstated deposits;

       3.   Various criminal penalties; and,

       4.   100 percent of the overstatement or underdeposit, if the employer's actions are willful.

K.   There is a $500 penalty on individuals who file incomplete returns or returns that are obviously incorrect. The tax law also imposes a civil penalty of $500 when a taxpayer claims withholding allowances based on false information.

L.   The IRS has the authority to waive the underpayment penalty if the underpayment is due to casualty, disaster, or other unusual circumstance.

VII.   Administrative Powers of the IRS

A.   The IRS can issue summons to responsible parties to appear before the IRS and to produce the books and records that are necessary for determining the correct amount of tax due.

B.   The IRS may assess a deficiency, and demand payment of the tax, when the taxpayer has failed to file a return.

C.   No assessment or effort to collect the tax may be made until 90 days after the issuance of a statutory notice of deficiency (i.e., a 90-day letter).

D.   Following the assessment of tax, a taxpayer usually is given 10 days to pay the tax before collection efforts are begun.

E.   The IRS may negotiate a compromise in the deficiency when there is doubt as to the amount of the liability or the taxpayer's ability to pay.

F.   A Closing Agreement is binding on the government and the taxpayer, except upon a subsequent showing of fraud, malfeasance or misrepresentation of a material fact.

VIII.   The Statute of Limitations

A.   The statute of limitations defines the period of time during which one party may pursue an action against the other.

B.   Any tax imposed must be assessed within three years of the filing of the tax return, or the due date of the tax return, whichever is later.

       1.   If no return is filed or a fraudulent return is filed, the assessment can be made at any time, i.e., the statute of limitations never begins to run.

       2.   Where the taxpayer understates gross receipts by 25% or more, the statute of

limitations is extended to six years. There is no comparable rule for an overstatement of deductions.

    3.   The statute of limitations also can be extended by mutual consent of the District Director and the taxpayer.

  C.   A claim for refund must be filed within three years of the date the return was filed, or within two years from the payment of the tax if this was later. However, a seven-year period of limitations applies to refund claims relating to bad debts and worthless securities.

IX.   The Tax Practitioner

  A.   Practice before the IRS generally is limited to CPAs, attorneys, and other persons enrolled to practice before the IRS.

  B.   Exceptions to the above include the following:
      1.   A taxpayer always can represent himself or herself;
      2.   Regular full-time employees may represent their employer;
      3.   Corporations may be represented by a bona fide officer;
      4.   Partnerships may be represented by any partner;
      5.   A taxpayer may be represented at the agent level by whomever prepared the tax return; and,
      6.   A person may represent a member of his or her immediate family if no compensation is received for such services.

  C.   The following requirements are imposed upon those governed to practice before the IRS:
      1.   An obligation to make the client aware of any error or omission made on the return;
      2.   A duty to submit records or information lawfully requested by the Service or the taxpayer;
      3.   An obligation to exercise due diligence in preparing the return;
      4.   A restriction against causing unreasonable delay in the disposal of a disputed issue;
      5.   A restriction against charging "an unconscionable fee;" and,
      6.   A restriction against representing clients with conflicting interests.

  D.   Anyone, regardless of his or her educational background, can prepare a return, subject to the following requirements:
      1.   A person holding himself out as a "tax expert" will be liable for penalties upon filing negligent returns.
      2.   All paid preparers must sign the client's return as preparer.
      3.   Penalties for the filing of a fraudulent return are applied to every preparer who was aware of the misstated facts.
      4.   There are penalties for disclosing tax information to unauthorized parties.
      5.   Non-attorneys must be careful to avoid the unauthorized practice of law.
      6.   A tax preparer may be subject to numerous other penalties.

X.   Ethical Considerations: "Statements On Responsibilities In Tax Practice" -- Issued by the AICPA

  A.   A CPA must sign every return prepared by him or her, whether or not it was prepared for a fee.

  B.   A CPA need not sign a return that he or she merely has reviewed for errors.

  C.   A CPA should sign a return only if he or she has made an appropriate effort to find an answer for all questionable items.

  D.   A CPA may prepare returns using estimates that are derived in a generally acceptable manner.

  E.   A CPA may sign a return containing a departure from the treatment of an item determined in a prior administrative proceeding.

  F.   A CPA should advise a client promptly upon the discovery of an error.

  G.   When a CPA is representing a client in an administrative proceeding with respect to a return in which there is a material error known to the CPA, the CPA should request the taxpayer's permission to disclose the error to the IRS. If the client refuses, the CPA should consider withdrawing from the engagement.

H.   A CPA may rely on the information furnished to him or her by the client, i.e., without a detailed audit of the summarized data. However, a CPA should make reasonable inquires if the information appears to be incorrect, incomplete, or inconsistent.

I.   A CPA may take a position contrary to the Treasury Department or IRS interpretation. However, in order to do so the CPA must have a good faith belief that the position has a realistic possibility of being sustained administratively or judicially on its merits if challenged.

J.   In providing tax advice to a client, the CPA must use judgement to ensure that the advice reflects professional competence and appropriately serves the client's needs.

TEST FOR SELF-EVALUATION - CHAPTER 25

True or False

Indicate which of the following statements are true or false by circling the correct answer.

T   F   1.   The IRS will issue an individual ruling on any issue requested by the taxpayer.

T   F   2.   A letter ruling may be relied upon only by the taxpayer who requested and received it.

T   F   3.   Letters of Determination are issued for completed transactions only.

T   F   4.   With respect to noncorporate taxpayers, the rate of interest that the IRS charges on an underpayment is one percentage point less than the rate of interest that it pays on an overpayment.

T   F   5.   Persons other than CPAs, attorneys, and enrolled agents are not allowed to practice before the IRS.

T   F   6.   When a taxpayer overstates deductions by more than 25% of the gross income stated on the return, the statute of limitations is increased to six years.

T   F   7.   If the IRS believes the assessment or collection of a deficiency is in jeopardy, it may assess the deficiency and demand immediate payment.

T   F   8.   The statute of limitations for an assessment of taxes never can extend beyond three years from the filing of a return.

T   F   9.   The statute of limitations for a claim for refund resulting from a bad debt deduction is six years.

T   F   10.   Both the Appeals Division and the taxpayer have the right to request technical advice from the National Office of the IRS.

T   F   11.   According to the AICPA, a CPA may prepare a tax return using estimates received from a taxpayer.

T   F   12.   The IRS requires all persons who prepare tax returns for a fee to sign as preparer of the return.

Fill-in-the-Blanks

Complete the following statements with the appropriate word(s) or amount(s).

1.   CPAs must conduct their tax practices following the AICPA's _____ _____ _____ _____ _____ _____.

2.   A _____ audit usually is handled through the mail, without requiring an office visit by the taxpayer.

3.   A _____ audit generally is used for corporate returns, or for returns of individuals engaged in business or professional activities.

4.   In most cases involving proposed deficiencies of $10,000 or more, a request for an appeal from an agent's decision must be accomplished by a written _____.

5.   After signing a Form 870 and paying the tax, the taxpayer may file a suit for refund in the _____ Court or the _____ Court, but not in the _____ Court.

6.   A tax preparer who is not a _____, _____ or _____ _____ may represent a taxpayer the agent level.

7.   The Code provides specific authority for the IRS to negotiate a compromise if there is doubt either in determining the _____ of the actual liability or in the taxpayer's _____ _____ _____.

8.   A claim for refund must be filed within _____ years of the date the return was filed, or _____ years from the payment of the tax, whichever is later.

9.   Willful failure to make deposits of withholding tax can result in a penalty equal to _____% of the amount not deposited.

10.   Interest on overpayment of taxes will not accrue when a refund is made within _____ days from the date the return was filed or due, whichever is later.

11.   _____ _____, which was issued by the Treasury Department, prescribes the rules governing practice before the IRS.

12.   A _____ _____ _____ defines the period of time during which one party may pursue against another party a cause of action or other suit allowed under the governing law.

Multiple Choice

Choose the best answer for each of the following questions.

_____ 1.   When is a request for technical advice appropriate? (More than one answer may be correct.)
   a.   The issue in dispute is not treated by law or precedent and/or published rulings or regulations.
   b.   There is reason to believe that the tax law is not being administered consistently by the IRS.
   c.   The taxpayer does not know how the tax law affects his or her transaction.
   d.   The question involves a hypothetical situation for which the IRS has declined to issue a private ruling.

_____ 2.   Individual Rulings will be issued on which of the following? More than one answer may be correct.
   a.   Hypothetical transactions.
   b.   Questions of fact.
   c.   Proposed transactions.
   d.   Completed transactions for which a return has not been filed.

_____ 3.   Which of the following is issued by the District Director, as an opinion on the classification of a completed transaction?
   a.   Individual Ruling.
   b.   Determination Letter.
   c.   Technical Advice Memorandum.

        d.   Revenue Ruling.

_____ 4.   Which of the following methods are used to select tax returns for audit? More than one
      answer may be correct.
      a.   Computer-generated formula.
      b.   Tip from informant.
      c.   Amount of gross income.
      d.   Type of income, e.g. cash-oriented business, not wages

_____ 5.   Which type of audit is used most often for individuals who have chiefly wage income, in
      order to substantiate items of income or deduction?
      a.   Field.
      b.   Office.
      c.   Home.
      d.   Correspondence.

_____ 6.   An agent may do which of the following when attempting to negotiate a settlement after
      an audit? More than one answer may be correct. He or she may:
      a.   Attempt to settle an unresolved issue, based on the hazards of litigation.
      b.   Settle a question of fact.
      c.   Request technical advice from the National Office.
      d.   Reach an agreement that will be accepted unconditionally by the District
            Director.

_____ 7.   When signing a Form 870, the following result(s) occur. More than one answer may be
      correct.
      a.   The taxpayer still may appeal to a higher level of the IRS.
      b.   The interest on the assessment stops accruing immediately.
      c.   The agreement is binding on both the taxpayer and the IRS.
      d.   The tax must be paid, but a suit for refund can be filed in the District Court
            or the Claims Court.

_____ 8.   When an agreement cannot be reached with an agent, a letter is transmitted, stating
      that the taxpayer has 30 days to:
      a.   File a suit in Tax Court.
      b.   Request an administrative appeal.
      c.   Pay the tax.
      d.   Find additional facts to support his or her position.

_____ 9.   A statutory notice of deficiency gives the taxpayer 90 days to:
      a.   Pay the tax.
      b.   Request an appeal.
      c.   File a suit in Tax Court.
      d.   File a protest.

_____ 10.   Which of the following requirements of the AICPA applies to CPAs in tax practice? More
      than one answer may be correct.
      a.   A CPA may not prepare a return using estimates.
      b.   A CPA need not sign a return if he or she did not receive a fee for preparing it.
      c.   A CPA must sign a return that he or she merely has reviewed.
      d.   A CPA need not disclose a position taken that is contrary to a Treasury
            Interpretation.

_____ 11.   With respect to noncorporate taxpayers, if the interest rate on an overpayment of tax
      is 10 percent, the rate of interest on an underpayment of tax is:
      a.   9 percent.

   b.   10 percent.
   c.   10.5 percent.
   d.   11 percent.

_____ 12. Same as 11., except that the taxpayer is a C corporation that has underpaid its 19X1 taxes by $200,000. The rate of interest on the underpayment of tax is:
   a.   10 percent.
   b.   11 percent.
   c.   12 percent.
   d.   13 percent.
   e.   14 percent.

_____ 13. X underpaid $5,000 of her prior-year income taxes; $4,000 of the underpayment was attributable to negligence. X's negligence penalty is:
   a. $0.
   b. $200.
   c. $400.
   d. $800.
   e.   None of the above.

_____ 14. Which of the following old-law penalties are part of the accuracy-related penalty? More than one answer may be correct.
   a.   Failure to file penalty.
   b.   Negligence penalty.
   c.   Tax return preparer penalties.
   d.   Penalty for substantial understatement of tax liability.
   e.   Fraud penalty.

_____ 15. Which of the following statements concerning the failure to file a return penalty is not correct? More than one answer may be appropriate.
   a.   If the failure to file is fraudulent, the penalty is 20% per month, for a maximum of 5 months.
   b.   If the failure to file is not fraudulent, the maximum penalty is 25%.
   c.   The penalty is imposed on the balance due, rather than the total tax, shown on the return.
   d.   A valid extension of time to file a return will eliminate the failure to file penalty.
   e.   When both the failure to file and the failure to pay penalties are incurred, the failure to file penalty is reduced by the failure to pay penalty provided a return was filed.

Short Answer

1. Generally, only CPAs, Attorneys, and Enrolled Agents are allowed to practice before the IRS. List exceptions to this rule.

2. List some of the liabilities and penalties imposed upon tax preparers.

3.   Discuss the circumstances in which a CPA should sign a client's tax return as preparer.

4.   Distinguish among individual rulings, Revenue Rulings, and Determination Letters.

5.   What are the situations in which a closing agreement will be issued?

SOLUTIONS TO CHAPTER 25 QUESTIONS

True or False

1.   F   In certain circumstances, such as cases that essentially involve a question of fact, the IRS will not issue a ruling.
2.   T
3.   T
4.   F   The rate of interest that is paid on an overpayment is one percentage point less than the rate charged on an underpayment.
5.   F   Persons other than CPAs, attorneys and enrolled agents are allowed to practice before the IRS in limited situations.
6.   F   Where a taxpayer understates gross receipts by 25% or more, the statute of limitations is extended to six years; however, there is no comparable rule for an overstatement of deductions.
7.   T
8.   F   The statute of limitations extends beyond three years in numerous situations including when a fraudulent return, or no return, is filed.
9.   F   The statute of limitations with respect to bad debt deductions is seven years.
10.   T
11.   T   A CPA may do so if it is impractical to obtain exact data.
12.   T

Fill-in-the-Blanks

1.   Statements of Responsibility in Tax Practice
2.   correspondence
3.   field
4.   protest
5.   Claims, District, Tax
6.   CPA, attorney, enrolled agent
7.   amount, ability to pay
8.   3, 2
9.   100%
10.   45
11.   Circular 230
12.   statute of limitation

Multiple Choice

1.   a, b
2.   c, d
3.   b
4.   a, b, c, d
5.   b
6.   b, c
7.   d
8.   b
9.   c
10.   d
11.   d   (10% + 1%)
12.   d   (10% + 1% + 2%)

13.   d   The accuracy-related penalty is $800 ($4,000 x 20%).
14.   b,d
15.   a   When the failure to file is fraudulent, the penalty is 15% per month, up to a maximum of
                75%.

Short Answer

1.   a)   A taxpayer always can represent him- or herself.
      b)   Regular full-time employees may represent an employer.
      c)   Corporations may be represented by a bona fide officer.
      d)   A partnership may be represented by any partner.
      e)   Any tax preparer may represent a client at the agent level, but only CPAs, Attorneys,
             and Enrolled Agents may go beyond this level.
      f)   An individual may represent a member of his or her immediate family if no compensation
             is received for such services.
      g)   Trusts, receiverships, guardianships, or estates may be represented by their trustees,
             receivers, guardians, or administrators or executors.

2.   a)   A person holding him- or herself out as a tax practitioner will be liable for
             negligence when filing returns.
      b)   There are extensive penalties for filing fraudulent returns. These are applied to
             return preparers who are aware of the misstated facts.
      c)   There are penalties for disclosing tax information to unauthorized persons.
      d)   Non-attorneys must be careful to avoid the unauthorized practice of law.
      e)   There also are penalties imposed upon a paid return preparer, for negligence or
             intentional disregard for the Treasury's rules or regulations; for the willful
             understatement of a tax liability; for the failure to sign a return or retain a list of
             persons for whom returns were prepared; for the failure to furnish a client with a copy
             of a return; or, for signing or negotiating the refund check of a client.

3.   A CPA is required to sign any tax return that he or she has prepared, whether or not he or she
      received any compensation. A CPA is not required to sign a return that he or she merely
      reviewed. However, if, through the review, information obtained is equivalent to the
      knowledge obtained from preparing a return, a CPA may sign the return.

4.   Individual rulings are issued by the National Office and represent a written statement of the
      position of the Service concerning the tax consequences of actions that are contemplated by a
      specific taxpayer. Revenue Rulings are official pronouncements of the IRS and are designed to
      provide interpretation of the tax law to the general public. Determination Letters are issued
      by the District Director as an opinion on the classification of a completed transaction.

5.   Revenue Procedure 68-16 has enumerated four situations in which closing agreements are issued.
      a)   An executor or administrator requires a determination of the tax liability either to
             facilitate the distribution of estate assets or to relieve himself or herself of
             fiduciary responsibility.
      b)   A liquidating corporation needs a determination of tax liability to proceed with the
             process of dissolution.
      c)   A taxpayer wishes to close returns on an annual basis.
      d)   Creditors demand evidence of tax liability.

CHAPTER 26
THE FEDERAL GIFT AND ESTATE TAXES

CHAPTER HIGHLIGHTS

The federal estate tax and gift tax compose a unified tax on transfers of property from one taxpayer to another. Although the Code may give one the impression that there are two separate taxes in operation, the transfer tax system actually entails *one tax*, levied on transfers that occur both during the taxpayer's lifetime ("inter vivos" transfers) and at or after his or her death. The unified tax is cumulative in effect, and it uses a progressive rate structure.

The federal gift tax complements the federal estate tax. It is part of the unified transfer tax system that was put into place by the Tax Reform Act of 1976. Because the federal gift tax is imposed upon the taxpayer's right to transfer property for less than full and adequate consideration, it acts as a *backstop* to the estate tax, preserving the integrity of the transfer tax system as a whole.

I. Formula for the Federal Gift Tax - See Exhibit 26-1
    A. The objective of the federal gift tax formula is to compute a tax on the current year's taxable gifts.
    B. However, since the transfer tax system applies a unified, cumulative, progressive transfer tax, all prior taxable gifts must enter into the calculation. As is the case with the estate tax formula, the current year's taxable transfers are *put onto stilts*, possibly raising them into a higher gift tax bracket.
    C. There are several important distinctions between the gift and estate tax formulas. For gift tax purposes, all prior taxable gifts are added into the transfer tax base, whereas, in the estate tax formula, only post-1976 taxable gifts are added back. This is the case even though the Tax Reform Act of 1976 changed radically the concept of the taxable gift.
    D. Another important distinction between the gift and estate tax formulas is the credit allowed for taxes attributable to prior taxable gifts.
        1. For estate tax purposes, actual gift tax paid on post-1976 gifts, net of the unified credit allowed in the year of the gift, constitutes the reduction.

2. For gift tax purposes, however, the reduction is a hypothetical number, i.e., the gift tax that would have been payable, using the unified transfer tax rate schedule that is effective for the current year and before applying the unified transfer tax credit, on all prior years' taxable gifts.

3. Given that the composition of the tax base differs between the gift and estate taxes, the difference between the two reductions is proper. This difference recognizes that the gift tax base may include taxable gifts made prior to the introduction of the unified transfer tax rate schedule in 1976. To correspond the amount of the *stilts* with the tax thereon, the use of this hypothetical number is necessary.

E. Application of the unified transfer tax credit also differs between the two transfer tax formulas.

    1. For estate tax purposes, the entire credit that is appropriate for the year of death is applied.

    2. For gift tax purposes, only that portion of the current year's credit that has not been exhausted by prior taxable gifts can be applied.

    3. This distinction is necessary because of the use of the hypothetical gift tax reduction, explained above.

II. Definition of a Gift

A. To be considered a gift, the transfer must be made for less than *full and adequate consideration*, where the donor retains no right to reclaim or repossess the property. However, there is no requirement that the transfer be made out of love or affection, or with any donative intent.

    1. Transfers to political organizations are exempt from the gift tax.

    2. In addition, very few business transactions are gifts. The Regulations presume that such transfers are at arm's length, i.e., for full consideration. No judgments are made as to the propriety of such business acumen.

    3. The federal gift tax does not apply to tuition payments made to an educational organization on another's behalf. Nor does it apply to amounts paid for medical care on another's behalf.

The gift-tax definition of a gift is much narrower than the income-tax definition, such as that of Duberstein. For identifying a gift-tax gift, one simply compares the value of assets received with the value of those given up. If that difference is positive, one is a donee.

B. One does not make a gift when he or she names another as the beneficiary of a life insurance policy. The gift of such a policy requires the transfer of all of the *incidents of ownership* for the policy. *Incidents of ownership* include the power to change beneficiaries, to revoke an assignment, to pledge the policy for a loan, or to surrender or cancel the policy.

C. When property is purchased by more than one party as equal co-owners, but equal consideration is not given, a gift may result. Exceptions to this rule include:

    1. A gift via unequal contributions to a joint bank account. In this situation, a gift occurs only in the year, and to the extent, that a co-owner withdraws more from the account than he or she contributed; and

    2. The same rule applies to co-ownership of US Savings Bonds.

D. In general, the settlement of marital rights in a divorce proceeding is subject to the gift tax. However, if a final decree of divorce is obtained within **two years after, or one year before**, the exercise of a written agreement between spouses, in settlement of such marital rights, the transfer is exempt from gift tax (IRC § 2516). Similarly, *child support* payments are exempt from gift tax.

III. Deductions and Exclusions

    A. Transfers to charitable organizations qualify for the gift tax charitable deduction. No dollar or percentage limitations exist with respect to the gift tax charitable deduction.

    B. For gifts after 1981, a marital deduction, similar to that for the estate tax, is available for the gift tax.

        1. There is no dollar or percentage limitation on the amount of the gift tax marital deduction if the donee spouse is a U.S. citizen.

        2. The deduction also is available for a transfer of community property.

        3. To qualify for the deduction, the property generally must be of a nature such that it will be included in the donee's gross estate, i.e., unless it is consumed during the survivor's lifetime.

        4. The first $100,000 of gifts per year to a spouse who is not a U.S. citizen is excluded from the gift tax. However, to the extent that gifts are made in excess of this amount, no marital deduction is permitted.

    C. An annual exclusion of $10,000 per donee is available to reduce the amount of the current year's taxable gift (IRC § 2503). To qualify for the annual exclusion, the donee must receive a "present interest" in the property transferred, i.e., he or she immediately must receive possession or enjoyment of the property.

        1. With respect to property transferred to a trust, an annual exclusion is available for each beneficiary of the trust.

        2. Under IRC § 2503(c), the donor may create a trust for the benefit of a minor, even though the minor cannot obtain use or enjoyment of the trust property until he or she attains age 21, and still qualify the gift for the annual exclusion. However, certain stringent conditions must be met before this exception will apply.

    D. **Taxable gifts** constitute the amount of gifts given during the year reduced by the annual exclusions and the marital and charitable deductions.

IV. Transfer Tax and the Unified Transfer Tax Credit

    A. The **unified credit** is $192,800. The **exemption equivalent** of the credit is $600,000.

    B. The benefits of the graduated estate and gift tax rates and of the unified credit are eliminated by increasing the tax by the lesser of $552,000 or 5% of the taxable transfers in excess of $10,000,000.

    C. The unified transfer tax credit allowed for gift tax purposes is the same as the credit available to offset the federal estate tax, except for gifts made during the first six months of 1977.

    D. The unified transfer tax credit is reduced, for both gift and estate tax purposes, by 20 percent of the old-law specific exemption used on gifts between September 9 and December 31 of 1976.

V. Gift-Splitting

    A. Spouses can elect to treat gifts of either of their separate property to third parties as having come equally from both of them. This gift-splitting election allows for the optimal use of the spouses' unified credits and annual exclusions (IRC § 2513).

    B. The gift-splitting election applies to all gifts made by the spouses in the taxable year of the election.

    C. To split gifts, the spouses must be legally married to each other at the time of the gift, and both must be citizens or residents of the U.S. on the date of the gift.

VI. Formula for the Federal Estate Tax - See Exhibit 26-2

    A. Note that the objective of the formula is to compute a tax on the **Taxable Estate**, i.e., the transfer of assets by the decedent at or after his death.

B.   However, to compute this tax using the unified, cumulative, progressive transfer tax system, taxable gifts made after 1976 must enter the calculation. In effect, the Taxable Estate is *put onto stilts*, by adding the post-1976 taxable gifts, so that the Taxable Estate may be put into higher brackets in the progressive transfer tax rate structure than otherwise might be the case.

C.   For purposes of this formula, "Taxable Gifts" has a precise technical definition. See III. D of this outline.

D.   If the decedent paid a gift tax on his lifetime gifts, such taxes are used to reduce the transfer tax payable at death. In effect, this reduction brings the Taxable Estate back off the *stilts* that are used to compute the tax.

VII.   Elements of the Gross Estate

A.   Property owned outright by the decedent is included in his or her **gross estate**. There are few exceptions to this definition.

      1.   Generally, all personal- and business-use, tangible and intangible property is included, wherever it is situated (IRC § 2033).

      2.   This property is valued at its fair market value at the date of the decedent's death (or on the alternative valuation date if applicable). Exceptions to this rule exist, however, for certain farm and business property, and to alleviate potential hardships that may occur when a large estate tax is due from an illiquid estate (IRC §§ 2031, 2032, 2032A).

B.   The gross estate includes proceeds from life insurance policies on the decedent's life, if the policy (1) is payable to, or for the benefit of, the estate; or, (2) was under the control of the decedent before his death, e.g., as to the designation of beneficiaries or the ability to cancel the policy (IRC § 2042). This provision includes whole life and term insurance, group life policies, and travel and accident insurance, including those policies provided by an employer.

KEY TERMS
- Transfer Tax
- Exemption Equivalent
- Marital, Charitable Deductions
- Annual Gift Tax Exclusion
- Incidents of Ownership
- QTIP, IRD, GSTT

C.   Policies owned by the decedent, payable upon the death of some other party, are included in the decedent's gross estate, but under § 2033, i.e., not under § 2042. The amount includible in the gross estate is the replacement value of the policy on the other person's life.

D.   Property owned jointly by the decedent and another party may enter the gross estate (IRC § 2040).

      1.   One-half of the value of property owned jointly by spouses is included automatically in the gross estate of the first spouse to die, regardless of whether the spouses contributed equally to the original purchase of the asset.

      2.   Property held in a joint tenancy with someone other than the decedent's spouse is included fully in the decedent's gross estate.

      3.   To the extent, however, that the executor can prove that the co-owner(s) contributed to the original purchase price of the asset, a pro rata exclusion from the gross estate is allowed, equal to

$$\frac{\text{Surviving Co-owner's Contributions}}{\text{Total Contributions}} \quad x \quad \text{FMV of Asset}$$

4.   Community property, and property held as a tenancy in common, are included in the gross estate, according to the decedent's proportionate ownership rights.

5.   Dower and curtesy interests are included in the gross estate of the first spouse to die (IRC § 2034).

E.   If the decedent made a gift of some property during his or her lifetime, but the gift was in some measure *incomplete*, the property is included in the gross estate. Such property is valued in the gross estate at the date of death, and not the date of the original gift! For transfer tax purposes, a gift is *incomplete* if:

1.   the donor-decedent continued to use the property or receive income from the property after the *gift*, or he or she could designate who could use the property or receive the income (IRC § 2036); or,

2.   the donor-decedent had the right to cancel the *gift* or to change its terms (IRC § 2038).

F.   If the decedent owns an annuity contract that has a survivorship provision, an amount equal to the cost of a comparable annuity purchased at the decedent's death, times the percentage of the purchase price of the original annuity that the decedent provided must be included in the gross estate. If the decedent's employer provided the annuity under a qualified or non-qualified plan, the employer's contribution to the purchase price is attributed to the decedent.

G.   An adjustment is made to the gross estate with respect to taxable gifts made by the decedent **within three years** of his death. The gross estate includes:

1.   Gift taxes paid on gifts made within three years of death; and,

2.   The face value of life insurance policies on the decedent, if the decedent made gifts of such policies within three years of his or her death.

This adjustment is in addition to that for certain *incomplete* gifts (See E., above) (IRC § 2035). Of course, the estate still claims a credit for the gift taxes paid, even if the taxes are included in the gross estate.

VIII.   Death Tax Deductions

A.   The expenses of administering the estate, including executor's commissions, legal and accounting fees, and certain selling expenses, are allowed as a deduction from the gross estate.

B.   Other deductions include certain funeral expenses for the decedent; accrued property, gift, and income taxes; casualty or theft losses that occur during the administration of the estate; and, other debts, mortgages, and liabilities of the decedent, for which there was personal liability (IRC §§ 2053, 2054). If the decedent held non-recourse financing on any property, the asset should be included in the gross estate "net" of the related liability.

C.   A deduction is allowed for charitable bequests directed by the will, or initiated before death (IRC § 2055). The bequest must be mandatory in amount, but a third party can have the power to select the specific charitable beneficiary.

D.   If the surviving spouse is a U.S. citizen, transfers to the decedent's spouse qualify for the marital deduction.

1.   There is no dollar limitation on the amount of property transferred for which a marital deduction can be claimed (IRC § 2056).

2.   The property can pass to the surviving spouse as heir of the will, co-owner of jointly-held property, or beneficiary of a trust or life insurance policy.

3.   When the property is subject to a mortgage or other encumbrance, it passes net of the corresponding liability. However, if the executor is required under the terms of the decedent's will or under local law to discharge the mortgage or

other encumbrance out of other assets of the estate or to reimburse the surviving spouse, the payment or reimbursement constitutes an additional interest passing to the surviving spouse.

4. Generally, however, to claim a marital deduction the property must be of a nature such that it will be included in the survivor's gross estate, if it is not consumed during the survivor's lifetime.

5. A *terminable interest* does not qualify for the marital deduction. A marital deduction, however, is allowed for transfers of qualified terminable interest property **(QTIP)**.

6. In general, the marital deduction is not allowed for transfers to a spouse that is not a U.S. citizen unless the property transferred satisfies the normal requirements for the martial deduction and passes to a qualified domestic trust **(QDT)**.

IX. Death Tax Credits

A. The unified transfer tax credit is applied against the tax on total taxable transfers (IRC § 2010).

1. The entire amount of the credit is applied, regardless of whether some or all of the credit was used relative to lifetime gift activity of the decedent.

2. The credit, however, effectively is used only once, since the tax to which it was applied is included in the estate tax formula. Recall that the tax on total transfers includes the taxes computed with respect to those gifts (i.e., the "stilts" concept). With respect to U.S. citizens and residents, the unified credit is $192,800.

B. To mitigate the possibly harsh effects of multiple death taxation, a credit is allowed for state death taxes paid. The amount of the credit is the lesser of the taxes actually paid to the appropriate state(s), or an amount from a rate schedule in the Code (IRC § 2011).

C. Credits also are allowed for foreign death taxes paid, and for federal death taxes paid on property acquired by the decedent shortly before his or her own death (IRC §§ 2013, 2014).

X. Generation Skipping Transfer Tax

A. The generation skipping transfer tax **(GSTT)** is imposed in situations in which a younger generation is bypassed in favor of a later generation. The tax applies both to the lifetime transfers and to transfers by death.

B. This tax is imposed at the highest transfer tax rate - **55%**.

C. In determining the transfers subject to the generation skipping tax, each grantor is entitled to a $1 million exemption.

Exhibit 26-1
TRANSFER TAX FORMULA--TRANSFERS BY GIFT

TOTAL GIFTS   to which the gift tax might apply

- GIFT TAX DEDUCTIONS   (charitable and marital deductions)

- ANNUAL EXCLUSIONS

TAXABLE GIFTS MADE THIS YEAR

+ TAXABLE GIFTS MADE IN ALL PRIOR YEARS

TOTAL TAXABLE GIFTS

TAX ON TOTAL TAXABLE GIFTS   (Consult Rate Schedule)

- TAX PAYABLE ON PRIOR GIFTS *

- UNUSED UNIFIED TRANSFER TAX CREDIT

GIFT TAX PAYABLE THIS YEAR

*   Computed without regard to the unified transfer tax credit at the rates currently in effect, regardless of the actual rate existing at the time of the gift.

Exhibit 26-2
TRANSFER TAX FORMULA--TRANSFER AT DEATH

GROSS ESTATE

- **DEDUCTIONS**   **(expenses, indebtedness, taxes, losses, charitable bequests, and marital deduction)**

TAXABLE ESTATE

+ **TAXABLE GIFTS**   **made after 1976**

   TAXABLE TRANSFERS   **Consult Rate Schedule**

TENTATIVE TRANSFER TAX

- **ACTUAL GIFT TAXES PAID**   **on post-1976 gifts**

- **CREDITS**   **(unified credit, state death tax credit, credit for tax on prior transfers and foreign death tax credit)**

   TRANSFER TAX AT DEATH   **on Taxable Estate**

TEST FOR SELF-EVALUATION - CHAPTER 26

True or False

Indicate which of the following statements are true or false by circling the correct answer.

T   F   1.   The annual federal gift tax exclusion is $10,000 per donor.

T   F   2.   To be exempt from federal gift tax, a property settlement transfer must be included in the divorce decree.

T   F   3.   A gift is a transfer of property that is made out of love or admiration for the donee. A mere transfer of property for less than adequate consideration is not sufficient to constitute a gift.

T   F   4.   For gift tax purposes, the unexhausted unified transfer tax credit is the unified transfer tax credit for the applicable year, less all prior gift taxes paid.

T   F   5.   For gift tax purposes, only the post-1976 taxable gifts are added into the transfer tax base.

T   F   6.   A donor's taxable gifts are equal to the value of the gifts given during the year reduced by the marital and charitable deductions.

T   F   7.   If the decedent's retirement annuity has no survivorship feature, it will be excluded from the gross estate.

T   F   8.   The effect of a disclaimer is to pass the property to someone else.

T   F   9.   All property owned by the decedent as a joint tenant with one other party who is not his or her spouse is included in the gross estate of the first co-owner to die, to the extent of 50 percent of the fair market value of the property.

T   F   10.   The federal gift tax is reduced only by the unexhausted portion of the unified transfer tax credit.

T   F   11.   The generation skipping transfer tax applies only to lifetime transfers.

T   F   12.   To elect gift-splitting, the spouses must be legally married to each other at the end of the tax year.

Fill-in-the-Blanks

Complete the following statements with the appropriate word(s) or amount(s).

1.   Except for gifts of _____ interests, a donor is allowed an annual exclusion of $_____ per donee.

2.   For federal gift tax purposes, a gift is defined as a _____ _____ _____ for less than _____ and _____ _____.

3.   The highest transfer tax rate is _____.

4.　　Gift-splitting allows for a more optimal use of both the _____ _____ _____ _____ and the _____ _____ of the electing spouses.

5.　　A _____ interest is an unrestricted right to the immediate use, possession, or enjoyment of property or the income therefrom.

6.　　Proceeds of a life insurance policy on the decedent will be included in his or her gross estate if he or she possessed _____ _____ _____ over the policy.

7.　　To mitigate the possibly harsh effects of multiple transfer taxation, tax credits are allowed for _____ _____, _____ _____, and _____ _____ taxes paid.

8.　　Regardless of the type of property involved, any federal gift tax paid on a taxable gift made by the decedent within _____ _____ of his or her death must be included in his gross estate.

9.　　The federal death tax applies to every _____ or _____ of the United States, and to property situated in the United States that is owned by others.

10.　　For estate tax purposes, the transfer tax base includes both the _____ _____ and any taxable gifts made by the decedent after 19__.

11.　　The unified credit is _____ and the exemption equivalent of the credit is _____.

12.　　A _____ is a refusal by a person to accept property designated to pass to that person.

Multiple Choice

____　1.　The donor takes out a life insurance policy on her own life and names Donee to be the beneficiary of the policy. The face amount of the policy is $600,000. Annual premiums total $14,000. The donor pays these premiums for five years. She is still living. What is the total amount of taxable gifts by Donor with respect to the policy over the five years?
　　　　a.　　$0.
　　　　b.　　$20,000.
　　　　c.　　$70,000.
　　　　d.　　$600,000.
　　　　e.　　$670,000.

____　2.　Same as 1., except that Donee took out, and continues to own, the policy. Donor pays the premiums.
　　　　a.　　$0.
　　　　b.　　$20,000.
　　　　c.　　$70,000.
　　　　d.　　$600,000.
　　　　e.　　$700,000.

____　3.　Same as 1., except that the donor dies after making the fifth payment, and Donee receives the face value of the policy.
　　　　a.　　$0.
　　　　b.　　$20,000.
　　　　c.　　$70,000.
　　　　d.　　$600,000.
　　　　e.　　$670,000.

_____ 4.   The donor puts $100,000 into a joint savings account in 19X7. Donee, the only other (equal) co-owner of the account, puts $20,000 into the account. What is the amount of the donor's 19X7 taxable gift to Donee?
   a. $0.
   b. $30,000.
   c. $40,000.
   d. $100,000.

_____ 5.   Same as 4., and Donee withdraws $35,000 from the account in 19X8. Compute the donor's 19X8 taxable gift to Donee.
   a. $0.
   b. $5,000.
   c. $15,000.
   d. $35,000.

_____ 6.   Maria died in September 19X7. At the time of her death, she had the following interests in property:

Property	FMV at Death
Cash invested in a CD that matures January 19X8.	$115,000
Face amount of life insurance policy on Maria's life purchased by her and given to her brother Tony in 19X6.	175,000
Apartment house owned jointly with Tony. Maria paid 70% of the original cost and Tony paid the remaining 30%. Tony can prove that he made the 30% contribution to purchase the property.	300,000
Clothes, jewelry, and furniture.	90,000

Maria gave Tony $25,000 in cash in August, 19X7. No gift tax was due, because of the annual exclusion and the unified credit.

What is Maria's gross estate?
   a. $415,000.
   b. $440,000.
   c. $500,000.
   d. $590,000.
   e. $680,000.

_____ 7.   Same as 6., except that Tony is Maria's husband. Maria's gross estate is:
   a. $205,000.
   b. $340,000.
   c. $415,000.
   d. $530,000.
   e. $590,000.

_____ 8.   Neal died in December 19X7, when he had the following interests in property:

Property	FMV at Death
Face amount of group life insurance policy paid for by employer. Neal had the right to change beneficiaries.	$60,000
Life interest in a trust established by Neal's father; Neal had a special power of appointment.	140,000
Residence owned by Neal and his wife as joint tenants. His wife paid for the home entirely.	220,000

Neal gave his son IBM stock in 19X6, when it was worth

$510,000. Neal and his wife did not elect gift-splitting.
A $59,500 gift tax was paid.

600,000

What is Neal's gross estate?
a. $170,000.
b. $229,500.
c. $369,500.
d. $670,000.
e. $770,000.

_____ 9. Same as 8, the amount of Neal's taxable transfers is:
a. $0.
b. $ 60,000.
c. $560,000.
d. $570,000.
e. $619,500.

_____ 10. The decedent owned land with her brother, as equal joint tenants. The land cost $100,000 in 19X1, and the decedent's brother can prove that he paid $40,000 of this amount. The decedent paid the balance. At her death in 19X7, the land has a fair market value of $400,000. With respect to the land, decedent's gross estate must include:
a. $100,000.
b. $200,000.
c. $240,000.
d. $400,000.

_____ 11. Same as 10., but the co-owners hold the property as equal tenants in common.
a. $100,000.
b. $200,000.
c. $240,000.
d. $400.000.

_____ 12. Same as 10., but the decedent's co-owner is her husband.
a. $100,000.
b. $200,000.
c. $240,000.
d. $400.000.

_____ 13. Same as 10., but the decedent's brother has lost the records that prove his $40,000 contribution.
a. $200,000.
b. $240,000.
c. $280,000.
d. $400,000.

_____ 14. The decedent's will allows the executor to "donate from my estate to Green Bay University, a qualifying charity, an amount not less than $100,000." The executor pays $210,000 to the university. With respect to this 19X7 death, the allowable federal estate tax charitable contribution deduction is:
a. $0.
b. $100,000.
c. $105,000 (50% limitation).
d. $210,000.

_____ 15.   The decedent's wife, pursuant to the will and other proper documents, receives $200,000 life insurance proceeds in which the decedent held the incidents of ownership; real estate worth $315,000; and, the decedent's share of joint tenancy property. The total fair market value of the jointly owned property is $100,000. The decedent's gross estate equals $1,000,000. No other deductions are allowed. The marital deduction that is allowable for this 19X7 death is:
a. $365,000.
b. $500,000 (50% limitation).
c. $565,000.
d. $615,000.
e. $619,500.

_____ 16.   The decedent gave to his sister in 19X7 a painting worth $70,000. As his unified transfer tax credit had been exhausted, he paid a $22,200 federal gift tax. When the decedent died in 19X9, the painting was worth $50,000. With respect to the painting, the decedent's gross estate must include:
a. $0.
b. $22,200.
c. $50,000.
d. $70,000.

_____ 17.   In problem 16., what is the maximum amount of unified transfer tax credit that can be applied on the decedent's estate tax return?
a. $0.
b. $37,000.
c. $192,800.
d. $600,000.

_____ 18.   In 19X1, Mary made an incomplete gift of her home, which was valued at $400,000, to her son. When Mary died in 19X5, the home was valued at $700,000. With respect to the home, Mary's gross estate must include:
a. $0.
b. $300,000.
c. $400,000.
d. $700,000.

_____ 19.   In 19X2, Art paid $50,000 of Jim's medical bills and gave him a car valued at $8,000. Jim is Art's brother. What is the amount of Art's 19X2 taxable gifts?
a. $0.
b. $8,000.
c. $48,000.
d. $58,000.

Short Answer

1.   Review the estate and gift tax formulas, noting their similarities and differences.

2.   Discuss property that would make good and bad candidates for lifetime gifts.

3.   Donor gave Donee $500,000 in 19x3. Compute her 19x3 federal gift tax.

4.   Donor gave Donee $400,000 in 19x3 and had given Donee $220,000 in 1979. Compute her 19x3 federal gift tax.

5.   Same as 4., except that Donor gave Donee $600,000 in 19x3 and Donor had given Donee $215,000 1975. Compute her 19x3 federal gift tax.

6.   Discuss tax planning considerations concerning the estate tax marital deduction.

7.   Discuss the federal estate tax treatment of gifts made within three years of the decedent's death.

8.   The decedent's gross estate was valued at $1,100,000. Allowable federal estate tax deductions totalled $150,000. The decedent died on 9-10-x5. The decedent had given $560,000 cash to her brother, on 11-10-x1. The gift tax that she paid on this transfer was $18,500. The decedent made no other lifetime gifts. Compute her federal death tax payable. Ignore state death taxes.

9.   Compute how much should be included in the decedent's gross estate for each item below. Each case is independent.

      a.   The decedent was a minister. At death, she owned the following.

	Basis	Fair Market Value
Auto, artwork, furniture	$20,000	$12,000
Clothes, kitchenware	1,800	450
Bibles, religious materials	1,000	965

      b.   At the date of his death, decedent held $20,000 of promissory notes issued by him to his daughter. In his will, decedent forgives these notes, relieving his daughter of any obligation to make payments thereon.

      c.   The decedent's employer provided her with a $50,000 group-term life insurance policy on her life. The decedent paid none of the premiums; her surviving husband received the policy proceeds.

      d.   The decedent owned a life insurance policy on her own life. The policy proceeds were $35,000. The decedent gave the policy to her beneficiary-husband five years before her death.

      e.   The decedent owned a life insurance policy, proceeds $35,000 on the life of her husband. The cost of a comparable policy was $8,100.

      f.   The decedent died intestate. The applicable state statute guarantees that her husband will receive a one-third interest from the $450,000 gross estate, as a curtesy interest.

      g.   The decedent's collection included a painting worth $75,000. It was purchased by the decedent's wife from her separate funds after their marriage. The spouses lived in California, a community property state.

    h.   The decedent owned a painting worth $75,000. It was purchased by the decedent and his wife as joint tenants. The decedent contributed $6,000 of the original $10,000 purchase price.

    i.   The decedent owned a painting worth $75,000. It was purchased by the decedent and his sister as joint tenants.

    j.   The decedent transferred an asset worth $10,000 to a trust. He retained an income interest in the trust for eight years after the transfer; the trust corpus was to go to the decedent's grandchild thereafter. The asset was worth $30,000 when the decedent died, five years after the transfer.

10.   The decedent died in 19x5, with a taxable estate of $600,000. She had made taxable gifts in 1978 totalling $136,000, and she paid the federal gift tax of $600 at that time.

The decedent's estate included assets transferred by bequest from C. C's estate had paid a federal death tax of $3,900 on the property with respect to the 19x1 death. This amount was less than the tax that was attributable to the asset in the decedent's estate.

State inheritance taxes payable upon the decedent's death were $7,650. Federal transfer tax before credits on the decedent's taxable estate was $243,120. Compute the remaining federal estate tax liability for the decedent.

11.   Donor gave Donee a taxable gift of $12,000,000; Donor had not made any taxable gifts in prior years. Compute Donor's federal gift tax.

12.   Catherine Greene died on February 2, 19x5. Compute her transfer tax payable.
    a.   Catherine's personal belongings were valued at $400,000.
    b.   She transferred all of the incidents of ownership in a $350,000 life insurance policy on her life to her brother on 1-1-x3; no gift taxes were paid on this transfer.
    c.   Executor fees were $15,000.
    d.   Catherine was a 50% joint tenant with her sister Joyce in a plot of land that they

purchased in 1963 for $100,000. At the date of her death, the land was worth $400,000. Joyce claims she provided $50,000 of the purchase price, but she can prove that she provided only $10,000.

e.   Catherine bequested $25,000 for pre-school education. The executor was empowered to choose between two donees, the United Way and the Metropolitan Museum of Art.

f.   Catherine's husband was given $150,000 cash from Catherine's estate. He was not entitled to any other property from his wife's estate.

g.   Catherine had made taxable gifts of $15,000 to her grandson on 2-1-x0 and $25,000 to him on 3-1-x1. Neither gift resulted in a tax liability payable, but $900 of the unified credit was exhausted on the first gift and $1,500 was exhausted on the second gift.

h.   State inheritance taxes paid by the estate were $30,000.

SOLUTIONS TO CHAPTER 26 QUESTIONS

True or False

1. F $10,000 per donee.
2. F   Property settlements can escape gift tax if the divorce occurs within a prescribed period of time; the settlement, however, is not required to be included in the divorce decree.
3. F   This is the definition of a gift for income tax, but not transfer tax purposes.
4. F   It is less all prior gift taxes "deemed" paid.
5. F   All prior gifts are added back.
6. F   The value of the gifts also must be reduced by the annual exclusions to arrive at the amount of taxable gifts.
7. T   At the date of death, the annuity terminates.
8. T
9. F   100% is included, unless a contribution by the other party can be proven.
10. T
11. F   The GSTT applies both to lifetime transfers and transfers by death.
12. F   The spouses must be legally married to each other at the time of the gift.

Fill-in-the-Blanks

1. future, $10,000
2. transfer of property, full, adequate consideration
3. 55%
4. unified transfer tax credits, annual exclusions
5. present
6. incidents of ownership
7. federal gift, state death, foreign death
8. three years
9. citizen, resident
10. taxable estate, 1976
11. $192,800, $600,000
12. disclaimer

Multiple Choice

1. a   Naming another as a beneficiary of a life insurance policy does not constitute a gift.
2. b   5 x ($14,000 - $10,000 annual exclusion), assuming that the policy was not taken out before 1982. See Example 47 in the text.
3. a   The life insurance proceeds constitute a testamentary transfer.
4. a   A gift occurs only in the year, and to the extent, that a co-owner withdraws more from the account than he or she contributed.
5. b   ($35,000 - $20,000 contribution - $10,000 annual exclusion)
6. d   [$115,000 + $175,000 (the life insurance was transferred within three years of death) + $210,000 (70% x $300,000) + $90,000]
7. d   [$115,000 + $175,000 + (50% x $300,000) + $90,000]
8. b   [$60,000 + (50% x $220,000) + $59,500]
9. e   ($229,500 - $110,000 marital deduction + $500,000 post-1976 taxable gifts)
10. c   (60% x $400,000). See Example 38 in the text.
11. b   (50% x $400,000). See Example 37 in the text.
12. b   (50% x $400,000). See Example 40 in the text.

13. d The entire value must be included in the decedent's gross estate. See Example 38 in the text.

14. a The amount of the charitable contribution must be specified in the decedent's will.

15. c [$200,000 + $315,000 + (50% x $100,000)]. See Example 49 in the text.

16. b Gift taxes paid on gifts made within three years of death must be included in the gross estate. See Example 30 in the text.

17. c For estate tax purposes, the entire credit that is appropriate for the year of death is applied.

18. d Since the gift in 19X1 was incomplete, the FMV at the date of death must be included in the gross estate.

19. a ($8,000 - annual exclusion) Note that the payment of Jim's medical bills is not subject to the gift tax.

Short Answer

1. Differences -   Selection of prior taxable gifts, and the tax thereon
          Treatment of unified credit
  Similarities -   Rate schedule
          Amount of unified credit, since 7-1-77
          Charitable and marital deductions
          Cumulative application

  See Exhibits 26-1 and 26-2.

2. Good candidate - Non-income producing (except to a low-bracket donee)
          Depreciable, with a high fair market value, but a low adjusted basis
          Group-term life insurance
  Bad candidate -   Low basis, high fair market value
          Installment notes
          High-income producing (except to a low-bracket donee)

Solution to Problem	3.	4.	5.
Total Gifts	$500,000	$400,000	$ 600,000
Annual exclusion	- 10,000	- 10,000	- 10,000
Taxable gifts	$490,000	$390,000	$ 590,000
Prior Taxable gifts	+ 0	+217,000[1]	+ 429,000[2]
Total Taxable gifts	$490,000	$607,000	$1,019,000
Tax on Total Taxable gifts	$152,400	$195,390	$ 353,590
Hypothetical Tax on Prior gifts[3]	- 0	- 60,240[4]	- 131,660[5]
Unused Unified Credit[6]	-192,800	-154,800[7]	- 154,800[8]
Gift Tax Payable	$ 0	$ 0	$ 67,130

[1]$220,000 - $3,000 annual gift tax exclusion for years prior to 1982.

[2]$217,000 + $215,000 - $3,000 annual exclusion.

[3]Gift tax "deemed" paid without regard to the unified credit.

[4]Tax on $217,000.

[5]Tax on $429,000.

[6]Allowable credit = $192,800.

[7]Tax on the 1979 gift: $60,240 - $38,000 (1979 unified credit) = $22,240 actually paid.
   Unified credit remaining: $192,800 - $38,000 used in 1979 = $154,800.

[8]The actual gift tax paid on the 1975 gift is irrelevant. It used the old rate schedules, and

did not exhaust the unified transfer tax credit. The 1979 unified credit was used as indicated in Note 7.

See Example 21 in the text.

6.   When both spouses are US citizens, the payment of an immediate federal estate tax is unnecessary, due to the unlimited marital deduction. However, the unified credit of the first spouse to die should not be wasted.

The present value of the federal death tax, if it is deferred by a large marital deduction, may be very small. However, the value of the asset may grow, due to inflation or appreciation, in the hands of the survivor.

State death taxes may not allow an unlimited martial deduction.

A terminable interest does not qualify for the marital deduction. With the proper election, a marital deduction is allowed for transfers of qualified terminable interest property (QTIP).

7.   § 2035 implements a gift tax "gross-up," i.e., the federal gift taxes paid on gifts made within three years of death are included in the decedent's gross estate.

Life insurance proceeds from policies on the decedent's life that were transferred by the decedent within three years of death are included in the gross estate. Property interests transferred by gift within three years of death that would have been included in the gross estate by virtue of the application of §§ 2036 (transfers with a retained life estate), 2037 (transfers taking effect at death), and 2038 (revocable transfers) also are included in the decedent's gross estate.

"Incomplete" gifts, are included in the decedent's gross estate. Other taxable gifts made by the decedent within three years of her death are merely "adjusted taxable gifts."

8.
Gross estate	$1,100,000	(already includes the $18,500 gift tax)
Deductions	- 150,000	
Taxable Estate	$ 950,000	
Adjusted Taxable Gifts	+ 550,000	(net of $10,000 annual exclusion)
Taxable Transfers	$1,500,000	
Tentative Transfer Tax	$ 555,800	
Gift Tax Paid	- 18,500	
Unified Credit	- 192,800	
Transfer Tax at Death	$ 344,500	

9.
a.	$13,415	Fair market value.
b.	$20,000	Fair market value.
c.	$50,000	The decedent held the incidents of ownership for the policy.
d.	$0	The decedent's spouse owned the policy.
e.	$8,100	IRC § 2033.
f.	$450,000	The gross estate includes the curtesy interest. See Example 29 in the text.
g.	$37,500	Community property. See Example 40 in the text.
h.	$37,500	IRC § 2040. See Example 40 in the text.

i.	$75,000	Unless the decedent's sister can prove her own contribution to the original purchase price. See Example 38 in the text.
j.	$30,000	IRC § 2036 (retained life estate).

10.

Taxable Estate	$ 600,000
Adjusted Taxable Gifts	+ 136,000
Taxable Transfers	$ 736,000

Tentative Transfer Tax	$ 243,120	
Gift Taxes Paid	- 600	
Unified Credit	- 192,800	
Credit for Prior Transfers 80% ($3,900)	- 3,120	Fourth year prior to decedent's death
Credit for State Death Tax	- 7,650	Lesser of table amount (on $540,000) or actual amount paid
Estate Tax Payable	$ 38,950	

See Exhibit 26-2 and Example 60 in the text.

11.

Total Gifts	$ 12,010,000
Annual Exclusion	(10,000)
Taxable Gifts	$ 12,000,000
Prior Taxable Gifts	0
Total Taxable Gifts	$ 12,000,000

Tentative Tax on Total Taxable Gifts		
Regular Tax	$ 6,240,800	
Additional Tax (5% x $2,000,000)	100,000	$ 6,340,800
Less: Unused Unified Credit		(192,800)
Gift Tax Liability		$ 6,148,000

See Example 21 in the text.

12.

Personal belongings	$400,000
Life insurance (transferred within three years of death)	350,000
Land (90% x $400,000)	360,000
Gross Estate	$1,110,000

Executor Fees	(15,000)
Charitable Contribution	(25,000)
Marital Deduction	(150,000)
Taxable Estate	$ 920,000

Adjusted taxable gifts made after 1976	40,000
Taxable Transfers	$ 960,000

Tentative tax on total transfers	$ 330,200
Less:	
Unified Credit	(192,800)
State Death Tax Credit (lesser of $28,720 or $30,000)	(28,720)
Estate Tax Due	$ 108,680

See Exhibit 26-2.

CHAPTER 27
INCOME TAXATION OF TRUSTS AND ESTATES

CHAPTER HIGHLIGHTS

rusts and estates are distinct taxable entities, separate from their beneficiaries, trustees, and grantors. Both of these entities can be useful for estate and gift tax planning purposes. In this chapter, we examine the income tax consequences of creating and operating trusts and estates, as they are presented in Subchapter J of the Code.

I.   Definitions
   A.   An estate is a temporary entity, used to collect, preserve, and distribute the assets of the decedent, and satisfy his or her outstanding liabilities. Parties involved include the decedent, his or her beneficiaries, and the executor or administrator of the estate. The term of the estate will be monitored closely by the Internal Revenue Service. The estate is ignored for tax purposes if the Service believes that the existence of the entity has been prolonged unduly. The assets of the probate estate are not identical to the decedent's assets that are subject to the federal estate tax. For instance, some assets included in the gross estate are disposed of outside of the probate estate, e.g., life insurance proceeds and jointly-owned property.
   B.   A trust is an entity that protects, conserves, and distributes the assets contributed to it by the grantor, according to the terms of the trust instrument, and satisfies attendant liabilities. Parties involved include the grantor, the beneficiaries of the trust, and the trustee. Beneficiaries of a trust fall into two categories: those holding an income interest, who are entitled to receive the trust's accounting income during the term of the trust, and those holding a remainder interest, who will receive the trust principal upon termination of the trust. The term of the trust is dictated by the trust agreement. It could be for a fixed number of years, i.e., a term certain, or it could be measured by the lifetime of one or more individuals.
        The assets of the trust are only those whose titles are transferred by the grantor to the trustee, and any income earned subsequently on the trust principal (or "corpus").

1. The Code defines a simple trust as one that:
   a. Is required to distribute its annual accounting income;
   b. Makes no distributions of corpus during the year; and,
   c. Has no charitable organizations as beneficiaries.
2. A complex trust is defined as any trust other than a simple trust. For any given trust, the classification as a simple or complex trust may change from year to year.

II. Nature of Trust and Estate Taxation
   A. Generally, the entity acts as a conduit of the taxable income that it receives. Thus, to the extent that such income is distributed or deemed distributed by the entity, it is taxable to the beneficiary. Taxable income retained by the entity is taxable to the entity itself. Taxable income of the entity is reported on Form 1041, which is due 3 1/2 months after the end of the entity's taxable year. The executor must file a return if the estate has gross income of at least $600 for the year. The trustee must file a Form 1041 if the trust either receives gross income of at least $600 for the year or has any taxable income.
   B. In any given year, the alternative minimum tax (AMT) may apply to a trust or estate. However, few of these entities generally will incur the tax, unless they are engaged in the active conduct of certain types of businesses.

KEY TERMS

- Income, Remainder Interest
- Distribution Deduction
- Distributable Net Income
- First, Second-Tier Distributions
- Entity Accounting Income

   1. In general, derivation of alternative minimum taxable income (AMTI) for a trust or estate follows the rules that apply to individual taxpayers.
   2. The entity is allowed a $22,500 annual exemption amount which phases out at a rate of one-fourth of the amount by which AMTI exceeds $75,000.
   C. The entity may elect any tax accounting method that is allowed by the Code for individual taxpayers. An estate may elect to use a fiscal year for tax purposes. However, all trusts, except certain charitable trusts and tax-exempt trusts, must adopt a calendar taxable year.
   D. An estate is allowed a $600 annual personal exemption. Trusts that are required to distribute their accounting income currently receive a $300 exemption. All other trusts are limited to a $100 annual exemption.

III. Taxable Income Computation - See Exhibit 27-1
   A. The entity's accounting (or "state law") income is determined by the trust instrument or will. Where such document is silent, state laws determine whether an item is to be allocated to the income or remainder beneficiary. For a simple trust, trust accounting income is the amount that is paid or deemed paid to the income beneficiary. As determined below, some or all of this amount is taxable to the recipient. Generally, depreciation expense, capital gains and losses, casualty gains and losses, and one-half of administration expenses are allocated to corpus. Other income items, operating expenses, and the remaining one-half of administration expenses generally are allocated to income. The grantor or decedent can alter these conventions in the trust agreement or will.
   B. Computation Guidelines

1. Gross income of the entity, as defined in IRC § 61, is the starting point for determining the taxable income of the entity. For the most part, this amount is computed as it would be for an individual. For instance, municipal bond interest is exempt from gross income, and the deduction for an entity's net capital losses is limited to $3,000 per year. The gross income of the entity also includes income in respect of a decedent (IRD).

2. The tax basis for property controlled by the entity is computed as it would be for an individual. Property acquired by the trust or estate from a decedent generally takes a basis equal to the property's fair market value at the date of the decedent's death. Other property acquired by a trust receives a carryover basis from the grantor, as adjusted by § 1015 for federal gift taxes paid, and increased by any gain (or decreased by loss) recognized by the grantor upon the transfer.

3. Generally, no gain or loss is recognized by the entity upon distribution of assets to a beneficiary under the will or trust agreement. However, there are several exceptions to this general rule.

    a. When property that has appreciated or declined in value in the hands of the entity is distributed in lieu of a specific dollar or asset bequest, gain or loss is recognized to the entity.

    b. If the fiduciary elects, the trust or estate may recognize any realized gain or loss on a property distribution that is not a specific gift, bequest, or charitable contribution, as if the property had been sold to the beneficiary for its fair market value on the date of distribution.

4. To the extent that they have been included in gross income, charitable contributions are deductible by the entity without any dollar or percentage limitation. The contribution must be paid in the year that the deduction is claimed, or in the immediately following year. In addition, the contribution must be authorized by the will or trust agreement.

5. Losses on wash sales or between related parties are disallowed.

6. To the extent that an expenditure is allocable to tax-exempt income, a deduction is disallowed. Typically, a pro-rata allocation is made, using the income elements of entity accounting income. This limitation most often is applied to administration expenses and charitable contributions.

7. Trusts and estates are allowed cost recovery deductions. However, such deductions are allocated pro rata to recipients of entity accounting income. Thus, a simple trust, for example, receives no such deduction.

8. IRC § 642(g) prohibits the deduction of certain expenditures, e.g., administration expenses, on both the estate tax return and the estate's income tax return. Nonetheless, the executor is permitted to allocate such deductions in an optimal manner. The prohibition against double deductions does not apply to expenses in respect of a decedent.

9. A deduction is allowed to the entity for most distributions made to beneficiaries.

10. A trust or estate is allowed a deduction for casualty or theft losses not covered by insurance or other arrangement.

11. Net operating losses of the entity are subject to carryover provisions, i.e., carry back three years and carry forward fifteen years. In the year of the termination of the trust or estate, unused net operating and capital loss carryforwards are "distributed" to the income beneficiaries.

C. The distribution deduction is limited to the lesser of distributable net income (DNI) of the entity (less any net tax-exempt income that is included in distributable net income), or the amount actually distributed to the beneficiaries during the year. Distributable net income equals entity taxable income before the distribution deduction, with the following adjustments:

1. Add back the entity's personal exemption.
2. Add tax-exempt income, net of disallowed deductions attributable to such income.
3. Remove capital transactions of the entity; i.e., subtract net long-term capital gains or add back the net capital loss allocated to corpus.

D. Beneficiaries are taxed on the entity accounting income that they receive, or in the case of a simple trust, the accounting income that they are deemed to have received. However, such taxable income is limited to distributable net income allocable to the beneficiaries.

E. Under the throwback rule, a beneficiary's tax on a distribution of income accumulated by a trust in a prior year will approximate the increase in the beneficiary's tax for such a prior year that would have resulted had the income been distributed in the year that it was earned by the trust. The tax, as computed, is levied for the distribution year.

F. The character of the income received by the beneficiaries (e.g., ordinary income, net long-term capital gain, dividend income, exempt income) retains the proportions found within distributable net income.

G. Where the entity has more than one beneficiary, a further proration is required. The amount and character of distributable net income taxable to the beneficiary is based upon the percentage of entity accounting income received.

H. Allocations of distributable net income by estates and complex trusts are determined under a special rule. DNI is allocated first to "first-tier" beneficiaries, i.e., those that are required by the document. To the extent that the DNI of the entity has not been exhausted by the first-tier distributions, it is allocated to "second-tier" beneficiaries. For this purpose, first-tier distributions are those of current entity accounting income required to be distributed by the trust document. All other proper payments are second-tier distributions. The character of the distributions as first- or second-tier is determined by the trust document.

Typically, the trust document should place lower-income and -wealth beneficiaries, such as the very young, the elderly, and those with mental or physical handicaps, on the first tier, as they are more likely to need the cash from the distribution, and they are likely subject to a lower marginal tax rate. This approach also increases the chances that upper-income and -wealth beneficiaries, now on the second tier, will receive non-taxable distributions of corpus.

Exhibit 27-1
TAXABLE INCOME OF TRUSTS, ESTATES, AND BENEFICIARIES

1.   Determine Entity Accounting Income

2.   Determine Entity Taxable Income Before the Distribution Deduction

3.   Compute Distributable Net Income and the Distribution Deduction

4.   Compute Entity Taxable Income
(Step 2 less the deduction determined in Step 3)

5.   Allocate Distributable Net Income, and its Character, to the Beneficiaries. Use the Tier system, if necessary.

TEST FOR SELF-EVALUATION - CHAPTER 27

True or False

Indicate which of the following statements are true or false by circling the correct answer.

T   F   1.   Distributable net income does not include net tax-exempt interest.

T   F   2.   The distribution deduction is limited to the distributable net income (DNI) of the entity (less any net tax-exempt income that is included in distributable net income), or the amount distributed during the year.

T   F   3.   Depreciation deductions are allocated to trust beneficiaries on their ratable portion of DNI received.

T   F   4.   If the fiduciary elects, a trust or estate may recognize gain or loss on an in-kind property distribution that is not a specified gift, bequest, or charitable contribution.

T   F   5.   The first step in determining the taxable income of a trust or estate is to compute the entity's distribution deduction.

T   F   6.   A beneficiary must include in his or her taxable income the amount of accounting income actually received during the year.

T   F   7.   Trusts and estates are required to use a calendar tax year.

T   F   8.   If the trustee can determine, within guidelines included in the trust document, the timing of income or corpus distributions, the trust is referred to as a reversionary trust.

T   F   9.   The personal exemption allowed for all complex trusts is $100.

T   F   10.   Estates and complex trusts are not subject to a limitation on the extent of their deductible charitable contributions for a given year.

T   F   11.   The assets of the estate are identical to the decedent's assets that are subject to the federal estate tax.

Fill-in-the-Blanks

Complete the following statements with the appropriate word(s) or amount(s).

1.   The parties to an estate include the _____, his or her beneficiaries, and the _____.

2.   The parties to a trust include the _____, his or her beneficiaries, and the _____.

3.   Trusts and estates are treated as _____ taxable _____, but they are taxed using a modified _____ concept.

4.   A trust consists of its _____ (or principal), and its accumulated or distributed _____.

5.   A(n) _____ will be ignored for tax purposes, if the IRS believes that the existence of the

entity has been prolonged unduly.

6.   The annual personal exemption for a trust that is required to distribute its current accounting income is $_____. Other trusts receive a $_____ annual exemption.

7.   Beneficiaries of trusts and estates can hold an _____ interest or a _____ interest.

8.   Where a will or trust instrument is silent, _____ _____ determine(s) whether an item is to be allocated to corpus or the income beneficiary.

9.   DNI equals entity taxable income before the _____ _____, plus the entity's personal exemption, plus net _____ income, and less _____ _____ of the entity.

10. _____ _____ _____ is the maximum amount taxable to the beneficiaries from estate or trust distributions.

11. If the grantor of a trust retains the remainder interest, such interest is known as a _____ _____.

12. A trust must be classified as either a _____ trust or a _____ trust.

Multiple Choice

Choose the best answer for each of the following questions.

____ 1.   The income taxation of fiduciary entities is governed largely by which subchapter of the Internal Revenue Code?
a.   C.
b.   J.
c.   K.
d.   S.

____ 2.   During 19X2, the R trust received taxable income of $20,000 and $10,000 of tax-exempt interest. The trustee paid fiduciary fees of $6,000 and a charitable contribution, as authorized by the trust agreement, of $9,000. For 19X2, the R trust is allowed a charitable contribution deduction of:
a. $0.
b. $3,000.
c. $6,000.
d. $9,000.

____ 3.   Same as 2., except that the trust document requires that the charitable contribution be paid from taxable income. The R trust is allowed a charitable contribution deduction of:
a. $0.
b. $3,000.
c. $6,000.
d. $9,000.

USE THE FOLLOWING INFORMATION FOR PROBLEMS 4 THROUGH 8

A simple trust has one income beneficiary. Its 19X2 accounting income is $9,000, including $6,000 taxable interest, $4,000 exempt interest, and $1,000 administration expense. No other trust activities occurred during the year.

____ 4.   The beneficiary received from the trust:
      a. $6,000.
      b. $8,700.
      c. $9,000.
      d. $10,000.

____ 5.   The deduction allowable to the trust for administration expense is:
      a. $0.
      b. $400.
      c. $600.
      d. $1,000.

____ 6.   Distributable net income is:
      a. $6,000.
      b. $7,100.
      c. $9,000.
      d. $10,000.

____ 7.   The trust's deduction for distributions to beneficiaries is:
      a. $5,100.
      b. $5,400.
      c. $5,600.
      d. $7,100.
      e. $9,000.

____ 8.   Taxable income of the trust is:
      a.   ($300).
      b. $0.
      c. $1,000.
      d. $5,000.

USE THE FOLLOWING INFORMATION FOR PROBLEMS 9 THROUGH 16

An estate distributes an asset to its sole income beneficiary. The distribution was not a specific bequest. The basis of the asset to the estate is $1,000, and the asset's fair market value is $5,000. Distributable net income of the estate is $9,500. No other distributions are made, nor was an election made by the fiduciary with respect to this distribution.

____ 9.   The estate's distribution deduction, and the beneficiary's taxable income, from the distribution is:
      a. $1,000.
      b. $4,000.
      c. $5,000.
      d. $9,500.

____ 10.   The basis of the asset to the beneficiary after the distribution is:
      a. $1,000.
      b. $4,000.
      c. $5,000.

       d. $9,500.

_____ 11.   Gain recognized to the estate due to the distribution is:
       a. $0.
       b. $1,600 (after the 60% net long-term capital gain deduction).
       c. $4,000.
       d. $5,000.

_____ 12.   An executor elected to recognize gain or loss on the distribution of an asset as if the property had been sold to the beneficiary. The estate's distribution deduction, and the beneficiary's taxable income, from the distribution is:
       a. $1,000.
       b. $4,000.
       c. $5,000.
       d. $9,500.

_____ 13.   If the distribution was made in lieu of a specific bequest of $9,000 cash, the gain recognized to the estate due to the distribution, if the executor did not elect to recognize gain or loss on the distribution is:
       a. $0.
       b. $1,600 (after the 60% net long-term capital gain deduction).
       c. $4,000.
       d. $5,000.

_____ 14.   How much income must the beneficiary recognize only as a result of the distribution in problem 13?
       a. $0.
       b. $4,000.
       c. $5,000.
       d. $9,500.

_____ 15.   If the fair market value of the property is $500, rather than $5,000, the estate's distribution deduction, and the beneficiary's taxable income, from the distribution is:
       a. $ 500.
       b. $1,000.
       c. $4,000.
       d. $5,000.
       e. $9,500.

_____ 16.   If the fair market value of the property was $5,000, but the distributable net income was only $400, the estate's distribution deduction, and the beneficiary's taxable income, from the distribution is:
       a. $ 400.
       b. $ 500.
       c. $1,000.
       d. $4,000.
       e. $5,000.

_____ 17.   Under the terms of the RT Trust, the trustee has complete discretion as to the timing of the distributions from RT's current accounting income. The depreciation deduction allowable to RT in the current year is $120,000 and the trust agreement allocates all depreciation expense to corpus. In the current year, the trustee distributes 25% of trust accounting income to A and 45% of the trust accounting income to B. The trust may claim a depreciation deduction of:

        a. $0.
        b. $30,000.
        c. $36,000.
        d. $54,000.
        e. $120,000.

18.   IRC § 642 identifies which of the following as the annual maximum amount to be included as gross income by all of the income beneficiaries of the trust or estate?
        a.   Fiduciary (accounting) income
        b.   Entity taxable income
        c.   Adjusted gross income, before the standard deduction
        d.   Distributable net income
        e.   20% of the entity's gross income

19.   The Edgerton Estate generated Distributable Net Income this year of $100,000, one-half of which was tax-exempt interest, and the balance of which was long-term capital gain. Kyle Edgerton, the sole income beneficiary of the Estate, received a distribution of the entire $150,000 fiduciary income of the entity. How is this distribution accounted for by Kyle?
        a. $150,000 ordinary income
        b. $75,000 long-term capital gain, $75,000 exempt interest
        c. $100,000 ordinary income
        d. $66,667 long-term capital gain, $33,333 exempt interest
        e. $50,000 long-term capital gain, $50,000 exempt interest

20.   The Eagleton Trust generated Distributable Net Income this year of $100,000, one-third of which was portfolio income, and the balance of which was exempt interest. Under the terms of the trust, Clara Eagleton is to receive an annual income distribution of $40,000. At the discretion of the trustee, additional income distributions can be made to Clara, or to Clark Eagleton III. This year, the trustee's distributions to Clara totalled $70,000. Clark received $30,000. How much of the trust's distributable net income is assigned to Clara?
        a. $100,000, under the "majority of income" rule
        b. $70,000
        c. $50,000
        d. $30,000
        e. $0

21.   The Eagleton Trust generated Distributable Net Income this year of $100,000, one-third of which was portfolio income, and the balance of which was exempt interest. Under the terms of the trust, Clara Eagleton is to receive an annual income distribution of $40,000. At the discretion of the trustee, additional income distributions can be made to Clara, or to Clark Eagleton III. This year, the trustee's distributions to Clara totalled $70,000. Clark received $60,000. How much of the trust's distributable net income is assigned to Clark?
        a. $100,000, under the "generation-skip" rule
        b. $60,000
        c. $46,154
        d. $40,000
        e. $0

22.   The trustee of the Epsilon Trust distributed an asset to Telly, a qualifying income beneficiary. The asset's basis to the trust was $10,000, and its fair market value on the distribution date was $30,000. Which of the following statements is true?
        a.   Lacking any election by the trustee, Telly's basis in the asset is $10,000

b. Lacking any election by the trustee, Telly's basis in the asset is stepped up to $30,000

c. Lacking any election by the trustee, the trust recognizes $20,000 gross income on the distribution

d. Assuming that the trustee made an election under IRC § 643(e), the trust is allowed a $10,000 distribution deduction for this transaction

e. Assuming that the trustee made an election under IRC § 643(e), Telly recognizes $20,000 gross income on the distribution

_____ 23. Three weeks after Tina died, her brother Tony properly received Tina's last paycheck from her employer. The gross amount of the check was $2,000, and a $150 deduction for state income taxes was subtracted in computing the net amount of the payment. Which of the following statements is true?

a. Tony deducts the $150 on his income tax return for the year; no other deduction is allowed for the taxes

b. Tina's executor deducts the $150 on Tina's last income tax return

c. The $150 is deductible only on the income tax return of Tina's estate

d. The $150 is deductible only in computing Tina's Taxable Estate

e. The $150 is deductible both on Tony's income tax return and on Tina's estate tax return.

Short Answer

1. The Bellow Trust has the following activities during 19X2.

Dividend Income	$100,000
Tax-Exempt Interest Income	15,000
Recognized Long-Term Capital Gain, allocated by the agreement to income beneficiaries	25,000
Fiduciary's Fees	10,000
Contribution to Mt. Olive Church, Paid on 8-30-X3 from 19X2 trust accounting income, as authorized by the trust agreement.	20,000
Deduction for Discretionary Beneficiary Distributions (assumed)	98,214

The trustee could, at her discretion, distribute any amount of the B Trust income or corpus during the term of the trust. Compute Bellow's taxable income.

2.   The Cello Trust, a simple trust, receives the following items.

Taxable Income	$ 30,000
Tax-Exempt Interest	10,000
Long-Term Capital Gain - allocated to corpus	5,000
Fees - allocated to income	4,000

   a)   Compute Cello's accounting income.

   b)   Compute Cello's taxable income before the distribution deduction.

   c)   Calculate Cello's distributable net income and the distribution deduction.

   d)   Complete the computation of Cello's taxable income.

3.   The DayGlo trust has net rental income of $40,000. The trust agreement allocates to corpus:

Net Long-Term Capital Gain	$10,000
Administration Fees	3,000

   a)   Compute the trust's accounting income, required under the agreement to be distributed completely every year.

   b)   Compute the trust's distributable net income.

   c)   Compute the trust's taxable income.

   d)   Compute the taxable amount received by the trust beneficiaries. None of the beneficiaries are charitable organizations.

4. a) The Elbow Trust has distributable net income of $20,000. The trust agreement requires the full distribution of current accounting income. Capital gains are allocated to the income beneficiaries.

The trust recognizes:

Ordinary Income	$30,000
Tax-Exempt Income	4,000
Long-Term Capital Gain	2,000
Trust Accounting Income	$36,000

Compute the nature and amount of the taxable distributions to equal beneficiaries Ankle and Boot.

b) The Fallow Trust has Distributable Net Income of $18,000. The trust agreement allows additional payments from income and corpus.

Trust Accounting Income is $30,000. A is guaranteed a payment of $20,000 per year from the trust. During the year, the trust makes payments of $30,000 to A, and $10,000 to B.

Compute the nature and amount of the taxable distributions to beneficiaries Alfalfa and Beanz.

c) Assume that Fallow is subject to the same trust agreement as in problem b) above.

Distributable Net Income is $28,000 and trust accounting income is $30,000. The trust makes payments of $20,000 each to Alfalfa and Beanz.

Compute the nature and amount of the taxable distributions to Alfalfa and Beanz.

SOLUTIONS TO CHAPTER 27 QUESTIONS

True or False

1. F   DNI includes tax-exempt interest, reduced for allocable deductible expenses.
2. T
3. F   Depreciation is allocated based on the distributions of trust accounting income.
4. T
5. F   The first step in determining taxable income is to compute the accounting income of the entity.
6. F   A beneficiary is taxed only on the amount of DNI that is allocated to him or her.
7. F   Estates and certain charitable trusts may elect to use a fiscal year.
8. F   The trust is referred to as a sprinkling trust.
9. F   A trust that is required to distribute all of its income currently is allowed an exemption of $300. All other trusts are allowed a $100 exemption each.
10. T
11. F   Some assets included in the gross estate are disposed of outside of the probate estate.

Fill-in-the-Blanks

1. decedent, executor/executrix
2. grantor, trustee
3. separate, entities, conduit
4. corpus, income
5. estate
6. 300, 100
7. income, remainder
8. state laws
9. distribution deduction, tax-exempt, capital transactions
10. distributable net income
11. reversionary interest
12. simple, complex

Multiple Choice

1. b
2. c   [$9,000 - 10/30($9,000)]. See Example 17 in the text.
3. d   See Example 18 in the text.
4. c   For a simple trust, trust accounting income is the amount that is paid or deemed paid to the income beneficiary. See Examples 4, 5, and 6 in the text.
5. c   [$1,000 - 4/10($1,000)]
6. c $5,100 (taxable income before distribution deduction) + $300 personal exemption) + $3,600 (net tax-exempt interest). See Example 20 in the text.
7. b $9,000 (DNI) - $3,600 (tax-exempt component). See Example 20 in the text.
8. a $5,100 (taxable income before distribution deduction) - $5,400 (distribution deduction). See Example 20 in the text.
9. a   These amounts are equal to the basis of the assets to the estate. See Examples 7 and 8 in the text.
10. a   The basis of the assets carries over to the beneficiary. See Examples 7 and 8 in the text.
11. a   Unless the estate makes an election, no gain or loss is recognized on the distribution of the asset. See Examples 7 and 8 in the text.

12.   c   Because the election was made, the distribution deduction and taxable income are equal to the FMV of the asset. See Examples 9 and 10 in the text.

13.   c   See Examples 9 and 10 in the text.

14.   a   See Example 9 in the text.

15.   a   See Example 10 in the text.

16.   a   The distribution deduction and the beneficiary's taxable income is limited to DNI. See Example 8 in the text.

17.   c   Since 30% of accounting income was accumulated by the trust, RT may claim a $36,000 depreciation deduction ($120,000 X 30%). See Example 15 in the text.

18.   d

19.   e

20.   b

21.   d   Clara receives $40,000 DNI on the first tier. There is now $60,000 DNI remaining, which is allocated pro rata to the second tier beneficiaries. Clark receives $40,000 DNI ($60,000/$90,000 x $60,000)

22.   a

23.   e

Short Answer

1.

Gross Taxable Income Dividends		$100,000
NLTCG		+ 25,000
		$125,000

Deductions: Distributions (given)	$98,214	
Fees (125/140 x $10,000)	8,929	
Charitable Contribution		
(125/140 x $20,000)	17,857	
Exemption	100	-125,100
Taxable Income		$ (100)

See Example 20 in the text.

2.   a)

Taxable Interest	$ 30,000
Exempt Interest	10,000
Fees	(4,000)

Trust Accounting Income (Simple Trust: This amount must be distributed)	$ 36,000

See Examples 4 through 6 in the text.

b)

Taxable Interest	$ 30,000
Long-Term Capital Gain of Corpus	5,000
Exemption	(300)
Fees (30/40 x $4,000)	(3,000)
TI before Distribution Deduction	$ 31,700

c)   TI before Distribution Deduction $ 31,700

Exemption   +   300
NLTCG of corpus   - 5,000
Exempt interest $ 10,000
Disallowed Expenses (10/40 x $4,000)   - 1,000   + 9,000

Distributable Net Income $ 36,000

Distribution Deduction ($36,000 - $9,000 Net Exempt
    Income) $ 27,000

d)   TI before Distribution Deduction $ 31,700
    Distribution Deduction   - 27,000
    Trust Taxable Income $ 4,700

See Example 20 in the text.

3.   a)   Trust Accounting Income $ 40,000

    b)   Net Rental Income $ 40,000
    Long-Term Capital Gain of Corpus   10,000
    Fees   (3,000)
    Exemption   (300)

    TI before Distribution Deduction $ 46,700

    TI before Distribution Deduction $ 46,700
    Exemption   +   300
    NLTCG of Corpus   -10,000

    Distributable Net Income = Distribution Deduction $ 37,000

    c)   TI before Distribution Deduction $ 46,700
    Distribution Deduction   - 37,000

    Trust Taxable Income $ 9,700

    d) Received by beneficiaries (Trust Accounting Income) $ 40,000

        Taxable [Limit: DNI] $ 37,000
        Non-Taxable [PLUG]   3,000

See Example 20 in the text.

4. a) All distributions to Ankle and Boot are first-tier distributions. The beneficiaries' total taxable income is limited to DNI. The character of the amount received is determined by the composition of DNI.

Allocation	Ankle	Boot
Ordinary Income (30/36 x 1/2 each x $20,000 DNI)	$ 8,333	$8,333
Tax-Exempt (4/36 x 1/2 x DNI)	1,111	1,111
Long-Term Capital Gain (2/36 x 1/2 x DNI)	556	556
Non-Taxable (PLUG)	8,000	8,000
Total Distribution (1/2 of accounting income)	$18,000	$18,000

See Example 29 in the text.

b) First-tier Distribution to Alfalfa, $20,000.
Second-tier Distribution to Alfalfa, $10,000; to Beanz, $10,000.

The beneficiaries' taxable income still is limited to DNI of $18,000. DNI is exhausted by required first-tier distribution.

Allocation		Alfalfa	Beanz
First-tier	- Taxable	$18,000	
	- Non-Taxable	2,000	
Second-tier	- Non-Taxable	$10,000	$10,000

See Examples 25 through 27 in the text.

c) The first-tier distribution to Alfalfa is still $20,000. However, DNI is not exhausted by this distribution. Nevertheless, the beneficiaries' taxable income still is limited to DNI of $28,000.

First-tier Distribution to Alfalfa, $20,000.
Second-tier Distribution to Alfalfa, $0; to Beanz, $20,000.

Allocation		Alfalfa	Beanz
First-tier	- Taxable	$20,000	
Second-tier	- Taxable		$ 8,000
	- Non-Taxable		12,000

See Examples 25 through 27 in the text.

CHAPTER 28
WORKING WITH THE TAX LAW

CHAPTER HIGHLIGHTS

here are three primary sources of federal tax law: statutory, administrative, and judicial. Each of these sources contributes significantly to the development and evolution of tax law. Therefore, each of these influences must be considered and understood when working with the tax law. Numerous resources are available to assist an individual when studying the tax law or when a tax problem is being investigated. If a thorough research effort is to be performed, it is important that the researcher consider all aspects of the law's development and status, from its origin up to the very day that the research is being conducted.

I.   Tax Sources -- The three sources of federal tax law are *statutory*, *administrative* and *judicial*.

     A.   Statutory Sources of the Tax Law

        1.   The statutory provisions comprising the tax law are contained in the *Internal Revenue Code of 1986*, which was redesignated as such by the Tax Reform Act of 1986. The present codification of the tax law amends, deletes, or adds provisions to the prior law, the *Internal Revenue Code of 1954*.

        2.   The 1954 Code was preceded by the *Internal Revenue Code of 1939* which was the initial attempt to codify all of the tax law provisions in a logical sequence in a separate part of the federal statutes.

        3.   The legislative process generally originates in the *House Ways and Means Committee*. Tax bills are also considered by the *Senate Finance Committee*. However, in order for legislation to become law, differences between the House and Senate versions must be resolved, the final version must be approved by Congress, and finally, the President must sign the legislation.

        4.   The Code is arranged by subtitles, chapters, subchapters, parts, sections, subsections, paragraphs and subparagraphs.

        5.   Tax treaties with foreign countries have been established with the intent of assisting tax enforcement and mitigating double taxation. Neither a tax law nor a tax treaty automatically takes precedence.

B.   Administrative Sources of the Tax Law -- The source of administrative pronouncements is either the US Treasury Department or one of its instrumentalities (e.g., the IRS or a District Director of the IRS). These pronouncements come in the form of *Treasury Department Regulations, Revenue Rulings, Revenue Procedures*, and other administrative pronouncements. These different sources possess varying degrees of authority.

C.   Judicial Sources of the Tax Law

    1.   If no satisfactory remedy to a dispute is achieved administratively within the IRS, a taxpayer may take the dispute to one of *four* federal courts. These four trial courts (courts of original jurisdiction) are: *a Federal District Court*, the *Court of Federal Claims*, the *US Tax Court*, and the *Small Cases Division of the US Tax Court*.

    2.   Some of the differences between the four trial courts follow.

KEY TERMS
- Sources of the Tax Law
  - Statutory
  - Administrative
  - Judicial
- Tax Research
- Tax Planning (Avoidance)
- Tax Evasion

        a.   There is only one Court of Federal Claims and one Tax Court, but there are many Federal District Courts.

        b.   The number of judges who would hear a taxpayer's case could vary, depending on the court involved.

        c.   The Court of Federal Claims meets most often in Washington, D.C., whereas the other courts will hear cases at specified times and places throughout the country.

        d.   The Court of Federal Claims has jurisdiction in judgement upon any claim against the United States that is based on the Constitution, any Act of Congress, or any regulation of an executive department.

        e.   The Tax Court hears only tax cases; whereas, the Court of Federal Claims and the District Courts hear nontax litigation as well as tax litigation.

        f.   Some courts have developed reputations for being more or less flexible in certain types of cases. For example, the Court of Federal Claims appears to be a more favorable forum for issues having an equitable or pro-business orientation as opposed to purely technical issues.

        g.   The District Court is the only court in which a taxpayer can obtain a jury trial.

        h.   A taxpayer may go to the Tax Court without first paying the disputed tax deficiency; whereas, with the Court of Federal Claims and the District Courts, the taxpayer must first pay the tax deficiency and then sue for a refund.

        i.   Appeals from the Tax Court and the District Court are taken to the Court of Appeals. However, appeals from the Court of Federal Claims are taken to the Court of Appeals for the Federal Circuit.

    3.   There are 13 circuits in the Court of Appeals, including the Washington, D.C. Circuit and the Federal Circuit. Each circuit, except for the

District of Columbia Circuit and the Federal Circuit, has several states within its jurisdiction.

4. The Supreme Court will not hear an appeal from a lower court automatically, but instead, it will hear only those cases that it feels are of particular importance (e.g., to resolve a conflict between the Court of Appeals). If the Supreme Court accepts jurisdiction, it will grant a *Writ of Certiorari*.

5. The Tax Court (formerly the Board of Tax Appeals) issues two types of decisions: *regular* and *memorandum* decisions. The regular decisions are published by the government in a series designated *Tax Court of the United States Reports*. The memorandum decisions are published by Commerce Clearing House in *CCH Tax Court Memorandum Decisions* and by Research Institute of America (RIA) in *RIA T.C. Memorandum Decisions*.

6. Tax cases heard before the other courts are also printed by Commerce Clearing House (*US Tax Cases* or *USTC*) and by Research Institute of America (*American Federal Tax Reports* or *AFTR* series).

7. West Publishing Company publishes all District Court decisions (tax and nontax) in their *Federal Supplement Series*. They publish decisions from the Court of Federal Claims and the Court of Appeals in their reporters-- designated *Federal Second Series* and *Federal Third Series*. West's *Supreme Court Reporter* contains all of the Supreme Court decisions.

8. The US Government Printing Office also publishes the Supreme Court decisions in the *United States Supreme Court Reports*.

II. Working With the Tax Law -- Tax Research
  A. Tax research involves the following procedures.
    1. Identifying and refining the problem.
    2. Locating the appropriate tax law sources.
    3. Assessing the validity of the tax law sources.
    4. Arriving at the solution or alternative solutions with due consideration given to nontax factors.
    5. Effectively communicating the solution(s) to the taxpayer or the taxpayer's representative.
    6. Following up on the solution(s) where appropriate in light of new developments.
  B. In locating the appropriate tax law sources, a tax researcher should use one or more of the major tax services as well as reviewing tax periodicals for articles relating to a particular problem.
  C. After the sources of tax law have been located, they must be assessed based on the facts and circumstances at hand.
  D. The researcher should communicate the results of the tax research after the problem has been adequately examined. This communication is often accomplished by a memo which should tell the taxpayer the following.
    1. What was researched.
    2. The results of the research.
    3. The justification for the recommendation made.

Tax research is increasingly being conducted, not with stacks of case books and legal pads, but with CD-ROM and modem resources, as the publishers of primary and secondary source materials convert their output to electronic form. Researchers can, by using electronic tax research materials, make certain that the most current law sources are available to them, and optimize the use of existing computer equipment, including laser printers, communication devices, and high-speed processing chips.

III.   Working With the Tax Law -- Tax Planning
   A.   A primary purpose of tax planning is to minimize a taxpayer's total tax liability. However, nontax considerations should be taken into account as well as tax considerations when a taxpayer considers alternative business activities and goals.
   B.   A distinction exists between legal tax planning -- *tax avoidance*, and illegal tax planning -- *tax evasion*.

TEST FOR SELF-EVALUATION -- CHAPTER 28

True or False

Indicate which of the following statements are true or false by circling the correct answer.

T   F   1.   The codification of tax law that is used today is known as the *Internal Revenue Code of 1986*.

T   F   2.   The Joint Conference Committee is called on to resolve differences between the House Ways and Means Committee version and the full House version of tax legislation.

T   F   3.   Revenue Rulings are issued by the Ways and Means Committee.

T   F   4.   A distinction exists between temporary regulations and proposed regulations.

T   F   5.   Appeals may be made directly from the Court of Federal Claims to the Supreme Court.

T   F   6.   In tax cases, the taxpayer has a choice between one of only three trial courts: the US District Court, the US Tax Court, and the Court of Federal Claims.

T   F   7.   No appeal is available for cases heard in the Small Cases Division of the US Tax Court.

T   F   8.   A jury trial is available in both a District Court and in the Court of Federal Claims.

T   F   9.   Tax evasion and tax avoidance are two terms that mean essentially the same thing.

T   F   10.   Tax research is a process that begins with identifying and refining the problem.

T   F   11.   Income tax Regulations are issued by the IRS.

T   F   12.   Final Regulations are issued as Treasury Decisions.

T   F   13.   Revenue Rulings carry the same legal force and effect of Regulations.

T   F   14.   For the Court of Federal Claims or a District Court to have jurisdiction, the taxpayer must pay the tax deficiency assessed by the IRS and sue for a refund.

T   F   15.   Tax Court Memorandum decisions are not published by the US Government.

Fill-in-the-Blanks

Complete the following statements with the appropriate word(s) or amount(s).

1.   Federal tax legislation generally originates in the _____ where it is first considered by the _____ Committee.

2.   The _____ is the committee in the Senate that considers tax legislation.

3.   _____, which may be legislative, interpretive, or procedural by nature, are issued by the US Treasury Department under authority granted by Congress.

4.   _____ are issued by the IRS and are interpretive in nature, but do not carry the same legal force as regulations.

5.   The Internal Revenue Bulletins are reorganized and published semi-annually in bound volumes called _____.

6.   Appeals from the US Tax Court or the US District Courts are taken to the _____.

7.   The _____ hears only tax cases, while the _____ and the _____ hear nontax litigation as well as tax litigation.

8.   For the _____ or _____ to have jurisdiction, the taxpayer must first pay any tax deficiency assessed by the IRS and then sue for a refund.

9.   The _____ and _____ must abide by the precedents set by the Court of Appeals of jurisdiction.

10.   Before 1943, the US Tax Court was called the _____.

11.   A tax dispute may be heard before the Small Cases Division of the US Tax Court if the amount involved does not exceed _____.

12.   When the Senate version of a tax bill differs from that passed by the House, the _____ is called on to resolve these differences.

13.   Proposed, final, and temporary Regulations are published in the _____.

14.   An _____ by the IRS indicates that it agrees with a decision reached by the Tax Court.

15.   The role of appellate courts is limited to a review of the record of trial compiled by the _____.

Multiple Choice

Choose the best answer for each of the following questions.

____   1.   Which of the following is not an available major tax service?
        a.   *Standard Federal Tax Reporter* (Commerce Clearing House).
        b.   *United States Tax Reporter* (Research Institute of America).
        c.   *Federal Tax Coordinator 2d* (Research Institute of America).
        d.   *Tax Management Portfolios* (Bureau of National Affairs).

e.   All of the above are major tax services.

_____   2.   The Internal Revenue Code is not organized by which of the following categories?
a.   Subtitles.
b.   Paragraph.
c.   Section.
d.   Listing.
e.   Chapter.

_____   3.   Which of the following is not an administrative source of the federal tax law?
a.   Treasury Department Regulations.
b.   Board of Tax Appeals rulings.
c.   Revenue Rulings.
d.   Revenue Procedures.
e.   Treasury Decisions.

_____   4.   Which of the following is not printed in the Internal Revenue Bulletin?
a.   Code Sections.
b.   Revenue Rulings.
c.   Revenue Procedures.
d.   Announcements.
e.   Treasury Decisions.

_____   5.   Which of the following is not a court of original jurisdiction?
a.   US Tax Court.
b.   Small Cases Division of the US Tax Court.
c.   US District Court.
d.   Court of Federal Claims.
e.   All of the above are courts of original jurisdiction.

_____   6.   Which of the following courts normally meets only in Washington, D.C.?
a.   Court of Federal Claims.
b.   US Tax Court.
c.   US District Court.
d.   US Court of Appeals.
e.   Both a and b.

_____   7.   Which courts hear only tax litigation?
a.   Court of Federal Claims.
b.   US Tax Court.
c.   US Court of Tax Appeals.
d.   US Court of Appeals.
e.   Both b and c.

_____   8.   Appeal to the Supreme Court is made by:
a.   A *Writ of Certiorari*.
b.   Having a conflict in the districts.
c.   Having a conflict between two or more US Courts of Appeal.
d.   Having the Commissioner of the IRS petition the Chief Justice of the Supreme Court.
e.   None of the above.

_____   9.   The following citation is associated with which of the volumes listed below:
Walter H. Johnson, 34 TCM 1056.
a.   *C.C.H. Tax Court Memorandum*.

b.   *RIA T.C. Memorandum Decisions.*
c.   *Tax Court of the United States Reports.*
d.   *BNA Daily Tax Reporter.*
e.   None of the above.

10.   The court cases heard in the US District Court, the Court of Federal Claims, and the US Court of Appeals are reported by:
a.   Commerce Clearing House.
b.   Research Institute of America.
c.   West Publishing Company.
d.   a and b.
e.   a, b, and c.

11.   If the prefix 1 precedes a Regulation, that designation indicates that it is what type of Regulation?
a.   Income tax.
b.   Gift tax.
c.   Estate tax.
d.   Employment tax.
e.   None of the above.

12.   Appeals from the Court of Federal Claims are heard by what court?
a.   US District Court
b.   US Tax Court.
c.   US Court of Tax Appeals.
d.   US Court of Appeals (Federal Circuit).
e.   None of the above.

13.   The result of an appeal could be any of a number of possibilities, which could not include which of the following?
a.   Affirm.
b.   Reverse.
c.   Remand.
d.   Any of the above could be a possibility.
e.   None of the above.

14.   Which of the following is *not* a computer-based tax research system?
a.   ALLTAX.
b.   TAXRIA.
c.   WESTLAW.
d.   LEXIS.
e.   ACCESS.
f.   All of the above are computer-based tax research systems.

15.   If a taxpayer loses a case taken to the Small Cases Division of the US Tax Court, an appeal could be heard by which court?
a.   US Tax Court.
b.   US Court of Appeals.
c.   Court of Federal Claims.
d.   Supreme Court.
e.   None of the above.

SOLUTIONS TO CHAPTER 28 QUESTIONS

True or False

1. T
2. F   The committee is used to resolve differences between the House version and Senate version of a tax bill.
3. F   Revenue Rulings are official pronouncements of the National Office of the IRS.
4. T
5. F   Appeals from the Court of Federal Claims are made to the Court of Appeals for the Federal Circuit.
6. F   Four trial courts are available, including the Small Cases Division of the US Tax Court.
7. T
8. F   A jury trial is available only in the District Court.
9. F   Tax avoidance is legal and tax evasion is illegal.
10. T
11. F   Regulations are issued by the US Treasury Department.
12. T
13. F
14. T
15. T

Fill-in-the-Blanks

1. House of Representatives, Ways and Means
2. Senate Finance Committee
3. Treasury Department Regulations
4. Revenue Rulings
5. Cumulative Bulletins
6. US Court of Appeals (i.e., of a regional circuit and not the Federal Circuit)
7. US Tax Court, US District Courts, Court of Federal Claims
8. Court of Federal Claims, US District Courts
9. US District Courts, US Tax Court
10. Board of Tax Appeals
11. $10,000
12. Joint Conference Committee
13. Federal Register
14. acquiescence
15. trial courts

Multiple Choice

1. e
2. d
3. b
4. a
5. e
6. a
7. b
8. a
9. a
10. e

11.   a
12.   d
13.   d
14.   a
15.   e   No appeal is available for cases heard in the Small Cases Division of the US Tax
                 Court.